D0490381

Writing for Business

BUSINESS ENGLISH AND COMMUNICATION

Marie M. Stewart is chairman of the Business Department at Stonington High School, Stonington, Connecticut. Doctor Stewart has written many magazine articles on business education and is coauthor of five business English textbooks. Doctor Stewart's wide teaching experience includes elementary school, high school, business school, USAF clerk-typist school, and university graduate school. She has also had considerable experience in business both as an office worker and as a communications consultant. Dr. Stewart is in demand as a speaker on communication to such groups as business teachers, secretaries, and office managers.

E. Lillian Hutchinson, for many years head of the Editing and Styling Department of the Gregg Publishing Division of McGraw-Hill Book Company, has readied hundreds of manuscripts and trained editorial personnel for the exacting work of editing texts on business subjects. She is coauthor of the various editions of this book; of *Words,* Fourth Edition; and of *Reference Manual for Stenographers and Typists,* Third Edition. She also writes for *Today's Secretary* and answers queries on business English for the magazine. Miss Hutchinson's contributions to business education have been recognized by her inclusion in *Who's Who of American Women.*

Frank W. Lanham is assistant professor of business education at the University of Michigan. His diversified teaching experience includes high school, college, technical institute, and university. In addition to research and writing, Doctor Lanham's activities include serving as director or speaker in communication and business education workshops and as consultant in business curriculum and school evaluation studies and in cooperative work-study programs. He is a member of the Joint Publication Commission of Eastern and National Business Teachers Associations.

Kenneth Zimmer is professor of business education and director of the School of Business of the Richmond Professional Institute of the College of William and Mary. Doctor Zimmer has had high school, college, and university teaching experience, as well as business experience. He is an officer of the Richmond Chapter of the National Office Management Association. In addition to his teaching and administrative duties, Doctor Zimmer has conducted special training programs for many business organizations and has spoken before various business and professional groups.

BUSINESS ENGLISH AND COMMUNI-CATION

Second Edition

Marie M. Stewart, Ph.D.

E. Lillian Hutchinson

Frank W. Lanham, Ph.D.

Kenneth Zimmer, Ed.D.

Gregg Publishing Division
McGraw-Hill Book Company, Inc.

New York   Chicago   Corte Madera, Calif.
Dallas   Toronto   London

Business English and Communication, Second Edition

Copyright © 1961 by McGraw-Hill Book Company, Inc.
Copyright 1953 by McGraw-Hill Book Company, Inc.
All rights reserved. This book, or parts thereof, may
not be reproduced in any form without permission of
the publishers.

2 3 4 5 6 7 8 9 QB–61 9 8 7 6 5 4 3 2 1

61309

Library of Congress Catalog Card No. 60–12779

Published by Gregg Publishing Division
McGraw-Hill Book Company, Inc.
Printed in the United States of America

Preface

Thousands upon thousands of successful business employees received their training in business English from the various predecessors of this book. For nearly fifty years, **Business English and Communication** in its several editions has served as the solid foundation upon which success in business has been built.

The "Who" and "Why" of This Book. Business English and Communication is intended for the student who expects to enter the world of business—the retailer, the stenographer, the secretary, the accountant, the correspondent, the general office worker, the manager. In fulfilling this purpose, **Business English and Communication** proudly clings to the belief that *effective* business English is *correct* business English. The standards of business are high, and no amount of rationalizing can justify the "sugar-coating" of English usage on the theory that what seems "natural" is correct. The business employee is judged by the way he speaks, by the way he spells, by the way he writes, by the way he punctuates—in short, by the way he handles his language. Often he demonstrates his fitness for a good position or for a promotion by the way he communicates. The standards of **Business English and Communication** are the standards of business, for nothing less than a thorough mastery of the tools of communication will, in the opinion of the authors, suffice. The cry from businessmen for employees proficient in communication grows louder and louder as communication grows more and more important.

Features of This Edition

Total Communication. In **Business English and Communication** five major phases of communication are emphasized:

1. Vocabulary, pronunciation, and spelling
2. Basic grammar and punctuation
3. Business letter writing, report writing, memorandums, telegrams, news releases, minutes of meetings, and various other written business communications

v

4. Speaking, listening, and reading

5. Human relations as influenced by communication

Business English and Communication is not merely a grammar–letter-writing text. It emphasizes *total communication*—speaking, writing, listening, and reading. The typical office worker spends about 45 per cent of his communicating time in listening and a large percentage in speaking—in conversation, on the telephone, before an audience, and so on. These communication skills, long neglected in business English textbooks, have, in this book, been given the recognition they deserve.

Complete Revision. *Business English and Communication* is a complete and modern revision. While it retains the authoritativeness of its immediate predecessor, *Business English and Letter Writing* by Hagar, Stewart, and Hutchinson, it features an especially well-integrated teaching plan that makes it easy to teach and easy to learn. Topics not previously covered include listening, conversing, meeting the public, using the telephone, communications in human relations, communicating in groups, and various new forms of business writing—news releases, minutes of meetings, and social-business letters. A new unit, "The Secretary's Responsibility for Correspondence," will have special appeal for teachers whose students are headed for secretarial and supervisory positions. Many topics have been expanded; notably vocabulary, letter writing, and other types of business writing. *Business English and Communication* is refreshingly new, modern—practicable!

Functional Grammar. Grammar and punctuation—the heart of the true business English text—are given an especially functional and interesting treatment. The dull, hard-to-understand classic rules (and exceptions) of grammar have given way to fresh, easy-to-grasp principles. Often these principles are implemented by a device called "Quick Trick"—a dramatic way to fix a rule in mind. This is "no-nonsense" grammar. For too long, students have been forced to memorize complicated grammar rules that had their origin in the mists of antiquity and have little connection with today's writing. Here, only the rules that the students will *use* are presented.

Practical Letter Writing. In *Business English and Communication,* the letter-writing emphasis is on the letters that young graduates may be expected to write. Most books give little space to routine or everyday letters; yet these are the letters most often written by the newly graduated. *All* types of business letters are covered in this book—sales, collection, adjustment, credit, and so on; and heavy emphasis is placed on inquiry letters, letters that answer inquiries, simple information letters, and the previously mentioned secretarial letters.

Generous Learning Activities. An outstanding feature of *Business English and Communication* is the abundance of practical exercises, especially in the grammar and punctuation sections, where mastery can be assured only by continuous and meaningful practice. An engaging type of exercise in the grammar and punctuation sections is the "Error Hunt," in which the student imagines that he is proofreading someone else's work and tries to find all the errors (a not infrequent activity in the business office!). Exercises for the other units are comparably generous and practical. The pattern of end-of-unit activities provides for a continuing emphasis on all aspects of communication: Learning Exercises, Vocabulary and Spelling Refreshers, and Communication in Action. In each unit, at least one of the activities is designed to challenge the brighter student, thus furnishing concrete help to the teacher whose classes are heterogeneously grouped.

Supporting Materials. Accompanying the text is a workbook containing enrichment exercises not included in the textbook, as well as certain forms required for textbook activities; a set of objective tests, including an inventory test; and a teacher's manual and key, which, in addition to a complete key to the exercises, contains important instructional aids for the teacher.

Marie M. Stewart
E. Lillian Hutchinson
Frank W. Lanham
Kenneth Zimmer

Contents

5   Review of Punctuation, Abbreviations, and Figures   212

6 Writing for Business 310

7 Speaking for Business 509

xi

BUSINESS
ENGLISH
AND
COMMUNICATION

1

THE ART OF COMMUNI-CATING IN BUSINESS

UNIT 1

Communication in Everyday Life

Let's Take an Imaginary Trip

Assume that you have planned for months to visit Washington, D. C. This is your first flight. Many people help you: the travel agent who makes your reservations; the driver of the limousine you board at the airline office in the city; the helpful skycaps at the air terminal; and the young customer service agent, Mr. George Sanderson, who checks your ticket reservation and baggage. These and others whom you don't see help you prepare for your departure. Each performs a service that contributes to your pleasure and excitement. Each uses communication skills to do his job.

With all the confusion and noise of the busy terminal, you wonder whether you will hear your flight called. But there it is! "Flight 625 is now loading at Gate 21."

Miss Linda Rogers, your stewardess, welcomes you aboard as she checks the names on the passenger list. The pilot and the copilot closet themselves in the mechanical brain at the front to receive final instructions from the tower. Your plane taxis to the runway. There is a pause. Miss Rogers casually looks to see that you have fastened your safety belt. The whirl of the motors causes the ship to quake in anticipation. Your pulse quickens. Then, with a surge of power you are lifted into the clouds and over the horizon to Washington.

You have taken all for granted: the thoughtful courtesies, the pleasant directions, the effortless explanations delivered with poise and confidence by the airline people. You probably don't think of such casual contacts as communication, but they are. They are business communication at work. They show basic communication skills applied to business tasks.

Basic Skills of Business Communication

Early in her preparation as an airline hostess, Linda learned that basic skills in communication were her most important tools for meeting and satisfying the needs of her passengers. The four basic communication skills used by Linda and the other airline people were: (1) writing, (2) reading, (3) speaking, and (4) listening.

Writing. In order to sell you a flight on Linda's plane, the airline made use of the writing skill of its employees. Written travel folders and advertisements helped to awaken your desire to travel. Time schedules, rate schedules, reservation lists, tickets, and baggage checks—all were necessary to make the trip a reality. Think, too, of the many written documents you did not see, such as flight plans; weather reports; orders for food, gasoline, oil, and repairs; work schedules for airline employees; and accounting papers to record your fare and to pay for merchandise, salaries, and services purchased by the airline. In these and hundreds of other documents, the writing skills of business people were used to satisfy your needs and the needs of others like you who travel by air.

Reading. Linda and George soon learned the importance of a basic skill in reading in order to do their jobs well. Even before they were hired, reading was the most important single tool they used to prepare for their careers. As employees, they know that every paper has to be read carefully and every bit of information and every direction accurately absorbed and followed.

Imagine what could have happened to you if any of the written documents connected with your flight had been misread or misunderstood. Suppose the control tower and the pilot had interpreted the weather report as reading "fog" instead of "fair." Suppose George Sanderson had attempted to collect $63.95 for your ticket instead of the correct fare of $36.59. Yes, accurate reading is a most important basic communication skill. Through careful reading and interpretation, business people are able to meet and satisfy the needs of their customers.

Speaking. The basic skill of speaking was also used by Linda and George to help you enjoy your flight. You were pleased by the friendly greetings, the interest shown in you and in your comfort, and the thoughtful attention to your needs as each airline employee spoke to you. Even the skycap promoted friendly relations for his company as he chatted with you about your baggage. Through conversation, both in person and on the telephone, business people satisfy the needs of customers.

Listening. It may surprise you to find listening included as a basic business communication skill, for its importance has rarely been emphasized. Yet, listening is often the most important communication skill. Imagine for a moment a different scene at the airport. Suppose one of the flight stewardesses had been in the cafeteria for a cup of coffee prior to her flight. Just as she was served, the loud speaker blared, "Flight 412 will load at Gate 16 in five minutes." She heard the loud speaker, but she wasn't listening. Not until the repeat announcement five minutes later did she realize that it was *her* flight being called. Imagine her wild dash to the plane! Imagine the embarrassment of knowing that she had delayed the other members of her crew and her passengers because she had not listened! Skill in listening is basic, too, if a business employee is to help meet the needs and wants of customers.

Standards of Business Communication

The young adult who has not entered business is likely to take his communication skills for granted, even though they may be poor. In everyday living a person has a limited circle of family and friends who accept him as he is, who usually overlook or tolerate poor written and oral communication skills. Yet, when this person enters business, he must be prepared to meet the high standards of communication expected by employers. His communication must be simple and clear, accurate and concise, and, at the same time, of a quality that develops good human relations.

Simplicity and Clarity. Business communication must be simple and clear; and usually the simplest way of expressing an idea is the clearest. For instance, consider the following sentence taken from a letter of application: "I beg to inform you that I saw your most generous job offer for a stenographer in the recent issue of the local newspaper and in reference to which I wish you to consider my application for a job in your firm." Obviously, this long and involved sentence does not meet the business standard for simplicity and clarity. This applicant doesn't have a chance of being considered for the job. On the other hand, a simple statement like "I should like to apply for the stenographic vacancy in your firm" does meet the standard; and, because of its simplicity, it is also a clear statement. This applicant is more likely to get the job.

Accuracy and Conciseness. Business communication must be accurate and concise. In business, time is money; and communication time is money, too. Whenever an error is made because of an inaccurate communication, time is wasted in correcting it. Suppose a salesclerk were understood to have said $17 instead of the correct

$70 as the price of an item. If you were the customer, think of all the explaining the clerk would have to do when you received your bill for $70 instead of the $17 you thought you owed. Not only would time and money be lost, but probably a good customer, too!

Good Human Relations. Business communication must contribute to good human relations—both with customers and among people working together in a business. Whether the communication is by letter or in person, through a newspaper advertisement or over the telephone, the purpose of all business communication is to influence people favorably toward the business and toward its product. If, because of poor human relations, customers don't buy from your company, neither you nor anyone else will long be employed. Good human relations, on the other hand, can help you turn potential customers into active customers and friends.

Within a business, too, harmonious working relations must be maintained. Employees must work together in order to get the job done. But no one likes to be around or to work with a disagreeable, discourteous, or tactless person. Such a person hinders the smooth flow of work. Business cannot tolerate him as his friends might. To be successful in business, a person must show courtesy, tact and consideration, and a genuine respect and liking for his co-workers. These are the ingredients of good human relations that business expects all employees to possess.

Learning Exercises

1 Write a short statement (50 words or fewer) on the topic, "Why I Chose Business as a Career." Your instructor will ask some of you to read your statements aloud in class. What communication skills were put into action by the speaker? by the audience? Discuss.

2 List specific communication skills that would be used in each of the following situations:

    a A radio or television program
    b Purchase of food or clothing at a shopping center
    c An athletic contest
    d A dinner with family or friends
    e A library assignment in preparation for a report

3 List specific ways in which improvement in each of the basic communication skills can help you enlarge your circle of friends.

4 What business position would you most like to obtain? Make a list of the ways in which high quality in the four basic communication skills will help you obtain and advance in your chosen job.

Communication in Action: *The Talkative Visitor*

As receptionist, you have seldom been as busy as when Mr. Jonas arrives to keep an appointment with the manager, Mr. Perkins. Mr. Perkins will not be able to see Mr. Jonas for about ten minutes because his previous appointment has not ended. Mr. Jonas is in a talkative mood—and you are extremely busy on an urgent report you are typing. Suggest courteous ways in which you can handle Mr. Jonas and still not lose too much time.

UNIT   2

Oral Communication in Business

May I Help You?

Do you remember the conversation with George Sanderson when he checked your reservation at the airline ticket counter? Recall this incident for a moment. Actually, it wasn't so much what George said as *how* he said it that impressed you so favorably toward him and toward his company.

George was helping another customer change a flight reservation as you walked to the ticket counter. When he finished, you heard him bid her good-by with: "Have a pleasant flight." From the way he said it, you felt that he meant it. Then he approached you. Did he say, "Hello" or "May I help you"? You may not remember exactly; but there was something about his total manner, his poise, his pleasant smile and greeting that said, "I'm glad you came. You're at the right place and I'm here to help you." You handed him your ticket. He telephoned the reservations office that you were there for Flight 625. He weighed and tagged your baggage;

he stamped your ticket and stapled the claim check to your ticket booklet; he gave some simple directions about boarding your flight and about reconfirming your return reservation in Washington. He listened and answered two or three questions. Then he closed the conversation with: "It's a perfect day for flying. Have a good time in Washington."

This conversation is a good example of effective oral communication in business. Thousands of similar oral communications take place daily in business all over the country.

Kinds of Oral Communication in Business

To observe oral communication in business, assume that you are going on a conducted tour through the offices of the Ajax Company, manufacturers of home appliances. You have already telephoned to make the appointment. As your trip is described, list the different kinds of oral communication you observe. You'll be surprised at the number and variety of oral communications used in business.

You Visit the Ajax Company. Miss Alice Lang, receptionist, greets your group when you arrive. By telephone, she notifies Mr. James of your arrival. Mr. James is a public relations employee who will be your guide. As you wait for him in the reception room, you note that Alice, in addition to discharging her receptionist duties, operates the PBX (private branch telephone exchange) for all incoming and outgoing calls. Primarily, then, her duties require oral communication.

Mr. James briefly describes the trip you are to take through the offices. You will visit the president's executive suite, the personnel department, the stenographic pool, and the purchasing department.

At the beginning of the tour, you are taken to the employees' cafeteria for refreshments. You observe employees coming and going on their coffee break. They spend a few minutes in the cafeteria chatting and relaxing as they sip coffee, milk, or tea. In one corner of the room, Mr. James points out five supervisors, each with a coffee cup before him and all in serious conversation. Mr. James's comment is: "A great deal of work is accomplished in the cafeteria over a cup of coffee."

The company's president greets you in his outer office. He has excused himself for a moment from a meeting with eight other executives, who are seated around a conference table in his inner office. Research and design, product engineering, processing, scheduling, tool design, maintenance, quality control, purchasing, and sales departments are represented. These executives are discussing proposed changes in next year's model of one of Ajax's products. They are pooling their knowledge, experience, and keenness of mind in planning and scheduling the company's production for the following year.

In the personnel department, several offices are occupied by job applicants who are talking with personnel interviewers. In a conference room, a group of supervisors is watching a film called "Developing Employee Morale." Elsewhere, a group of new employees is listening to a lecture about employee job benefits and company employment policies. Someone in the recreation department is on the telephone, arranging an employee bowling league. In still another interview office, an employee is discussing the possibility of a transfer to a different department.

In the stenographic pool, two girls are proofreading masters of minutes to be duplicated for the Board of Directors' meeting—one reads from the rough draft while the other checks. Several stenographers are listening and transcribing from dictation belts. The pool supervisor mentions that many executives in the company have on their desks telephonelike instruments that are connected with the dictation recording machines in the central stenographic pool. She adds, however, that a number of stenographers are out on assignment taking dictation directly from company officers.

Bedlam seems to reign in the purchasing department. Clerks are placing telephone calls for their employers. Men are talking on the telephone to far-off places to check on materials purchased but not received. Salesmen from other firms are discussing their products with purchasing agents. Everyone seems to be talking or listening as he performs his share of the purchasing duties.

Thus, you observe many different kinds of oral communication in the offices of Ajax Company. So it is in all business. Each kind of oral communication—from the semisocial chatting in the cafeteria to the formal lecture on company policy in the personnel department—serves a business function. And each employee must possess a quality of oral communication that enables him to get the job done both when he does the talking and when others talk to him.

Quality Factors in Oral Communication

Return for a moment to your oral encounter with George Sanderson. What factors made this exchange so satisfactory? What factors determine the quality of any oral communication—(1) when you talk or (2) when others talk to you?

When You Talk. Appearance, facial expression, and voice—each contributed to George's success when he talked with you. Each is important, too, when you talk. Why? The following discussion will give you the answers.

Appearance. The business person who presents a meticulous, well-groomed appearance is more likely to feel self-confident when he talks with others. In the mind of the listener, also, a person with a pleasing look about him creates a favorable impression that makes you want to listen. George's well-scrubbed, neatly groomed appearance added to his feeling of poise and confidence. But suppose that George had approached you in a pair of dirty coveralls, with the remnants of grime and grease under his fingernails. You would have felt repelled and George would have felt embarrassed because of his untidiness. The pleasing appearance he did present gave you both a feeling of confidence in each other.

Facial Expression. A person's face reflects his inward feelings. Imagine your impression of George if he had approached you with a pained facial expression, as though he had a headache. You would have felt that he was anticipating a painful experience with you, wouldn't you? Instead, George's face showed enthusiasm and interest. By his facial expression he indicated that he enjoyed serving you.

A Pleasing Voice. A pleasing voice is vibrant and alive. Although George had served more than a hundred people before you, the eagerness in his voice told you that *you* were important to him. By his voice, he showed interest in you as a customer. He was thoughtful, too; for his voice was loud and clear. Each word was enunciated carefully to be easily understood. He varied his tone, pitch, inflection, and speed to add vitality to his voice. Indeed, the fullness and richness with which he spoke made his words sound almost musical.

These, then, are the quality factors of oral communication used by George when he talked: appearance, facial expression, and a pleasing voice. George also showed a high quality of oral communication in the way he listened to what you had to say.

When Others Talk. How often have you listened to a speaker, hearing every word but not knowing what was said? If you are guilty of this practice, as most people are, you need to develop your listening ability—for good listening is a most important factor in oral communication.

The average person can improve the quality of his listening ability fourfold. To do it, you need to know some of the characteristics of a good listener. Then you can put them into practice as you listen to others talk.

A Good Listener. The good listener *is a courteous person.* He is attentive and sympathetic toward the speaker, and he concentrates on what is being said. Have you ever tried to talk with someone who was too preoccupied to know what you were saying? Such a person is a poor listener and a discourteous individual. The courteous person shows by his attentiveness that he is eager to hear you.

The good listener *relates what he hears* to what he already knows. If the thought of the speaker is new or his vocabulary different, the good listener mentally changes what is said into his own words in order to grasp the meaning. And if he is still not sure, he questions the speaker about what he does not understand.

The good listener also *attempts to organize, classify, and evaluate* what he hears. He reviews in his mind the major points made by a speaker. He follows the reasoning in the evidence presented and takes into consideration any inconsistencies as he weighs the value of what he hears. Have you ever talked with a person who seemed to anticipate what you were going to say? Such a person was not a mind reader. He had probably organized, classified, and evaluated what you said as you spoke and so had a good clue to what you would say next.

Finally, because the good listener concentrates his complete attention on what is being said; because he relates what he hears to what he knows; and because he organizes, classifies, and evaluates, he *responds* to what he hears. He shows by words and actions that he understands and appreciates what is said. The ability to respond and contribute to oral communication is, then, the test of all good listening.

Learning Exercises

1 Reread the description of your visit to the offices of Ajax Company, listing on the left side of a paper each example of oral communication that you observed. In a second column, list the job classification of the person engaged in each type of oral communication. In a third column, make a note of any special tools or materials used by the employee.

2 Rewrite the scene of your checking-in at the airline ticket counter (page 7). This time George Sanderson is preoccupied. He has a hundred and one other things to do and shows his impatience in serving you. Be ready to enact the conversation in class (with you as George Sanderson). In what ways does George's preoccupation affect the quality of his talking? of his listening? Discuss.

3 Give directions for finding some obscure place with which your classmates are familiar. Do not tell them what the place is. If your directions are clear, they will recognize where you are directing them.

4 Be prepared to describe orally an experience in which you were unfavorably impressed by a salesclerk. What errors in speaking or listening caused your negative reaction?

Communication in Action: *Conflicting Instructions*

An older employee in your department has been watching you as you make out a sales summary report. "The way you are doing that report is wrong," she says. You're quite certain that you are doing the job the way your supervisor told you to do it. What should you say or do?

UNIT 3

Written Communication in Business

The Need for Writing in Business

Oral communication cannot satisfy all communication needs, either in business or in your everyday life. Writing is also required; often it is the only means of communication possible. When you must "talk" to a person who is not available at the moment, for instance, you can use a letter or a memorandum to reach him. Through letters and memorandums, you can "talk" to people all over the world, and each can "hear" the same message at his convenience. Whenever in business it is necessary to remember what has been said, writing provides the medium of memory needed. Most contracts for sales and purchases and many other important agreements are put in writing to provide proof and a permanent record of terms or conditions agreed upon. Writing helps people think and speak more clearly; for writing permits a

[handwritten margin notes: "Three different kinds of writing", "letter within the company", "report in detailed information"]

person to organize, summarize, and solve problems. Indeed, business needs so many different kinds of writing that employers consider writing skills of first importance in hiring a business worker.

Reading and Writing in a Job

In a visit to any business office, such as yours to the Ajax Company, you would observe a multitude of written communication. Thousands upon thousands of letters, interoffice memorandums, and reports are stored in long rows of files. On each desk, file baskets are stacked with current papers. Catalogues, reference books, magazines, and similar written materials line bookshelves accessible to most workers. Near each desk, wastepaper baskets, often overflowing before the end of the day, collect discarded writing. Business people write, write, write! And business people read. You could, therefore, conclude that reading and writing are among the most important duties performed by business workers. And you would be right!

As a business worker, you'll soon recognize how much your success depends upon reading and writing. During an ordinary business day, for example, your supervisor could ask you to perform any of the following tasks, each requiring a written communication or some reading.

"Take a letter, please, to . . ."

"Confirm my telephone conversation to . . ."

"May I have the file of . . ."

"I like the idea, but PIW (put it in writing)."

"Let me examine the sales recap (or summary)."

"Check our absenteeism with that of other companies."

Each of these tasks is typical of the written communication expected of a business employee. You can think of similar examples. And you could add to the list considerably as you performed the reading and writing required in a job. Some of these types of written communication are so frequently used and so important in every business job as to deserve an early, though brief, introduction. They are:

1. The business letter
2. The interoffice memorandum
3. The report
4. Telegrams, minutes, and news releases

The Business Letter. In business the letter is used more extensively than any other type of written communication. Letters are written to buy and sell goods, to welcome new customers, to ask for information, to answer inquiries, to request or to make adjustments, to collect overdue accounts, and to build a friendly attitude toward a business and its products. Letters are also written to get jobs. Just about everyone in business writes these kinds of letters. In fact, just about everyone writes some of these letters in his everyday living, too. Extremely valuable to you, then, are the knowledge and practice you need to develop your letter-writing skills. The ability to write a good letter has boosted the chances of thousands like you for advancement in both business and social affairs. You'll receive specific knowledge and practice in writing all types of business letters in Units 38 to 54.

The Interoffice Memorandum. The interoffice memorandum, as illustrated on page 485, is a type of business letter, with one big difference: a memorandum is written by a person in the company to communicate with someone else in the same company. Because a memorandum is circulated within the company, it is likely to be less formal than most letters that are mailed to people outside the company. A vacation schedule may be released; notice of a meeting may be sent to certain executives; plans for expansion of the company may be revealed to all employees—these messages for people within the company would be written in the form of memorandums. Before you enter business, you should know how to prepare interoffice memorandums—an important kind of written communication. In Unit 55, you will receive the instruction you need.

The Report. Business depends on the many reports written about the different activities carried on in the various departments of a company. A report is usually more detailed and follows a more rigidly prescribed form than other kinds of written communication. Reports are often prepared to summarize business activities. For example, each department head may be asked to write a report—monthly, quarterly, or annually—that describes the important accomplishments within each major function of the business. These reports, like the balance sheet and other financial statements prepared by the accounting department, tell management what has happened. Many other study reports are used to help solve company problems. The advertising department, for example, may be requested to study and report on proposed changes in the advertising budget. The sales department, through a report, may study and recommend redistributing sales territories and sales quotas. Engineering design may report on research in the proposed use of plastics, instead of metal, in a particular product. Accounting presents reports on the differences between expected production costs and actual costs. The credit department reports on delinquent accounts and the proposed action to be taken in each instance. As you can see, the business report is an important document. You will learn to write business reports in Unit 56.

Telegrams, Minutes, and News Releases. Telegrams, minutes of meetings, and news releases represent a wide variety of miscellaneous business writing that you will need to know how to prepare. Though not used so frequently as other forms of writing, they are important in the conduct of a successful business. And every business employee must know how to compose them.

A *telegram or cablegram* is a type of letter used when speed is important. The telegram is the fastest of all written communication. Because the cost of sending telegrams is high, you need to learn how to write them to convey your message in as few words as possible.

Minutes of meetings are a special form of report used to record important proceedings. In larger firms, much of the internal business is conducted through small groups and committees. The actions of these groups are recorded in minutes. These minutes serve as a memory, or record, of the meeting. To know how to write concise and clear minutes of meetings is important to all who enter business.

Courtesy Security Steel Equipment Corporation

In business, you will be called upon to use the four basic communication skills—writing, reading, speaking, and listening. Make sure that your skills will meet the high standards of business.

Newspaper releases about a phase of a business operation are an important form of public relations. Whenever a newsworthy event occurs, the company announces it through the columns of local newspapers. Such an event may be the opening of a new branch office, the promotion of an executive, the development and marketing of a new product, or an expanded or different type of service offered by the company. Whatever the event, newspaper editors prefer and are more likely to publish news items prepared in news release form. Each of the miscellaneous forms of business writings—telegrams, minutes, and news releases—is considered in detail in Unit 57.

Learning Through Reading and Writing

Much of what you now know, you learned by reading and writing. Primarily through these skills, you will also learn while on the job. And the person with the best reading and writing skills will learn and advance most in business. This person—you, we hope—because he knows more, and because he can learn more through good communication skills, will be the outstanding candidate for promotion.

To obtain your initial job and be ready for promotion, you must use every opportunity to develop your skills of reading and writing to their highest pitch. And that is exactly what your study of business communication will enable you to do. The units on vocabulary and on developing vocabulary power (Units 4 to 10) will increase your word skills so that you may understand and use reading and writing to best advantage. Through the review of grammar and punctuation (Units 13 to 37), you will also sharpen your reading and writing tools. While the knowledge needed to develop reading and writing skills is given you in these units, the practice is up to you. If you use the learning exercises in the textbook and in the workbook to build your knowledge, you will have the reading and writing skills necessary to obtain and to advance in a business job.

Learning Exercises

1 How good are your reading and writing skills for business? Write a paragraph that describes your present level of skill in reading and writing. Write a second paragraph that states specifically what you will do to make these skills even better. Read and discuss your paragraph in class.

2 Make two lists of different kinds of written communications: (1) those you have received during the past month, and (2) those you have sent in the same period.

3 Describe in a sentence the function served by each of the following types of written communications. Do some serve more than one function? Discuss.

a A marriage license
b Minutes of a club meeting
c A birthday greeting card
d A catalogue from a mail order house
e A newspaper advertisement
f A textbook on written communication
g An outline for a speech
h Class notes and reading notes
i A file drawer of letters
j A study report on letter-writing practices in your office

4 "If speaking is so much easier than writing, why don't businessmen always use the telephone instead of writing letters?" a student once asked. List the reasons that make this suggestion impractical.

Communication in Action: *Being Blamed for Mistakes of Others*

You and another stenographer take dictation and write letters for the same executive. When you take some letters to him that you have just typed, he is checking others—not typed by you—and calls your attention to several mistakes. What will you say or do?

2
WORDS
AT
WORK

UNIT 4

How Vocabulary Affects Communication

The preceding units have proved that the very existence and progress of business depend on efficient communication—in speaking, in listening, in reading, and in writing. To be able to communicate efficiently, in turn, depends on the possession of a good vocabulary.

What Is a Good Vocabulary?

A person's vocabulary—the stock of words at his command, to understand as well as to use—may be described as "good" when it is sufficient for understanding exactly what is meant by what the person hears or reads and for saying or writing what he himself really intends to say or to write. Weakness in any of these respects results in embarrassment and mistakes. A few examples will show how lack of a good vocabulary is a handicap.

A clerk-typist was asked to type a certain report in triplicate. Not knowing what "triplicate" meant, he prepared an original copy and one carbon copy. He thought he had completed the work. Instead, he had to type another copy, resulting in loss of time and the impatience of his department head. *The possessor of a good vocabulary understands the meaning of the words most frequently used in business and in daily life.*

Candidates applying for jobs in a certain office were asked to write what their previous experience had been. One applicant wrote simply, "Along clerical lines." Another wrote: "Typing letters and reports, using adding machine, opening and distributing mail, checking inventories." Which applicant made the more favorable impression? The one who gave more explicit information, of course. *The possessor of a good vocabulary uses precise, not vague or general, words.*

Mr. Leroy told an employee to leave a memo on Mr. Kent's desk saying that he (Mr. Leroy) had gone out to

Newton to inspect the two sites that had been suggested for their new factory building. Mr. Kent found this memo: "Mr. Leroy has gone out to inspect sights for the new factory." Would either Mr. Leroy or Mr. Kent feel that the girl who wrote that memo would be good secretarial material should a position become vacant? *The possessor of a good vocabulary is familiar with those words that are pronounced exactly alike but are spelled differently and have different meanings.* This knowledge, of course, is called for in written communication.

Gertrude wondered why people smiled one day when she referred to "the notorious scientist, Albert Einstein." They knew, of course, that she meant "noted"; but her embarrassing blunder was not soon forgotten. *The possessor of a good vocabulary does not confuse words that look or sound* SOMEWHAT *alike.*

A thank-you note read: "Thank you for your generous donation to the Fresh Air Fund. This year especially, such donations are greatly appreciated." The substitution of "gift" for the second "donation" would have added variety to the wording. *The possessor of a good vocabulary achieves variety in his communications by the use of synonyms* (words that have the same or very nearly the same meaning as another word).

Mary commented that one of her friends was "not a believing type." Margaret agreed, "Yes, she *is* inclined to be skeptical." Instead of preceding "believing" with "not" in order to express a meaning opposite to believing, Margaret chose a word that, in itself, meant just the opposite—"skeptical." Such words are known as *antonyms.* *The possessor of a good vocabulary adds variety to his communications by using antonyms.*

Jack told a friend he was going to stop at the photo shop to leave some "filums" to be developed. A mispronunciation like this instantly reveals slovenly speech habits. *The possessor of a good vocabulary does not mispronounce words in spoken communication.*

A stenographer's transcript contained the phrase "seperate accomodations." As the dictator was very particular about his correspondence, she had to retype the entire letter in order to insert the correct "separate accommodations." *The possessor of a good vocabulary spells words correctly in written communications.*

A Good Vocabulary in Social Life

Most of the anecdotes just narrated pertain to office experiences in which a good vocabulary is essential. However, your ability to use words effectively is just as much an asset in school and social situations. If you can say or write just what you mean, so that others will not misunderstand you, your ability will be recognized. As a member

Unit 5, is devoted to methods of using it. Another very important help is a thesaurus, which is described in Unit 6.

Our Changing Vocabulary

Just as the language of every person changes and increases, the English language changes, too. It is said that about 5,000 words a year are being added to our dictionaries. These additions are especially numerous in times of great national and international activity and during times of scientific advances. Some of the additions are entirely new words, like *motel;* others are new meanings added to words already in the dictionary, like *guinea pig.* (Because that little animal was used so frequently for experimental work in the medical laboratory, the word has come to denote any subject of experimental work.)

Here are a few examples of new words or old words with added meanings:

From world affairs, social, political, and economic—*police state, curtain* (as *iron curtain, bamboo curtain*), *liquidate, brainwashing.*

From our changing social life—*desegregation, supermarket.*

From our expanding building and highway development—*prefabricate, cloverleaf.*

From the advertising and publicity business—*feature, know-how,* the various combinations with *-conscious,* as *clothes-conscious, color-conscious.*

From the television, radio, and motion picture industry—*kinescope, montage, commercial* (as a noun).

From popular music—*swing, calypso, downbeat.*

From developments in medicine and psychology—*tranquilizers, allergy, antibiotic, escapism.*

Moreover, some words that were once disdainfully called "business jargon" have come to be accepted as "real" words, like *mortician* and *beautician.*

Also, certain abbreviations have come to be accepted as words—as *auto, bus, taxi, pro, gym.* These clipped forms, however, are more suitable in spoken or informal English than in formal writing. It should be noted that, unlike real abbreviations, these shortened words are not followed by a period.

And it may surprise you to learn that some of our commonly used words were originally considered slang. For example, *mob, sham,* and *lynch,* once not accepted as "good" words, are now acceptable.

Changes in the meanings of words are nothing new in the development of our language. The English language has always been shifting. Who would think that *silly* once meant "good" or "happy," that *fond* meant "foolish," and that *curious* meant "careful"? *Broad-*

of a club, league, or any other association, for example, it is
than likely that you will have many occasions for expressing opi
or making suggestions during meetings. The boy or girl who
word a recommendation clearly or summarize the feelings of a g
precisely will, in all probability, be elevated to a position of le
ship in the club. As secretary, he would have the responsibili
keeping the minutes of meetings and conducting club corres
ence. Such activities are excellent preparation for business.

There are many other personal-life situations in which you
find the possession of a good vocabulary of inestimable value.
occasions as the buying or the selling of goods, the adjustme
complaints, the sending of telegrams, the use of the telephon
expression of congratulations and of sympathy—all these and
more offer opportunities to use a vocabulary effectively.

How to Improve Your Vocabulary

How do you begin to acquire a good vocabulary? First and
most, by becoming word-conscious. The opportunities for cultiv
word-consciousness are all about you.

1. As you listen to the radio or watch TV, be on the alert for
that are new to you. Also listen for words used in a way that
familiar to you. For example, a literary critic in reviewing
novel referred to the author's "pedestrian style of writing." T
"pedestrian" meant a walker. Reference to a dictionary showed
as an adjective, the word also means prosaic, dull.

The broadcasts and telecasts of news commentators are ca
prepared and offer excellent examples of well-chosen words.
most commentators have had speech training, and their pron
tion is usually correct.

2. Observe the speech of your teachers or of the executiv
department heads in your office. More than likely, these person
arrived at their superior positions because of their ability
words correctly.

3. When you overhear conversations on the street, in buses
trains, concentrate on any errors you hear and mentally substi
correct forms. You need not cultivate the unpleasant and rud
of deliberately listening in on other people's conversations; b
"loud mouths" make their remarks audible to everyone, ther
opportunity to profit from any mistakes they may make.

4. Form the habit of reading the car cards in buses an
searching for words new to you.

5. Naturally, magazines, bulletins, advertisements, new
books—all offer a gold mine for building your vocabula
greatest help of all, the dictionary, is so important that a wh

cast originally meant "to sow seed." Now we more often use the word as a radio term.

In addition, the way in which words were used in sentences differed from the way in which they are used at present. For example, in olden days if *you* referred to one person, a singular verb was used. Those who today are tempted to say "You was" would have felt right at home!

Naturally, many words have been dropped because they do not apply to our modern way of life. When gentlemen ceased to wear high boots, they no longer required *bootjacks* to help remove that style of footwear. Hence this word is seldom used except in museum catalogues. Similarly, under our democratic way of life it is no longer fitting for the writer of a business letter to sign himself as "Your obedient servant." It was in days of long ago when people were divided into two classes, masters and servants, and when a letter written to an absent master by the servant in charge of the master's estate was therefore appropriately signed as a servant.

Words like *erstwhile, quoth,* in common use a hundred years ago, just do not fit our direct, rapid-fire speech and writing.

How Does One Decide What Changes Are Acceptable?

Of course you wish your vocabulary, both spoken and written, to be up to date as well as acceptable. How are you to judge whether words are acceptable or not? Here's one caution and one recommendation.

Caution: Be wary of slang, for several reasons. Many persons do not understand slang. Therefore you run the danger of failing to make yourself really understood. Your conversation and writing can be fresh, modern without resorting to slang. How many of you, for example, use the *twenty-three* or *skidoo* that was so popular a generation ago? Yes, the word that is on everyone's tongue today is hopelessly out of date tomorrow. The greatest danger of using slang, however, is that the constant repetition of stock expressions to cover any and all situations impoverishes your vocabulary and weakens the exactness of your thinking.

The Recommendation: Observe the type of vocabulary that appears in our well-edited magazines and newspapers. Such periodicals have high standards. They accept and use words only after they have been sanctioned by the use of the best writers. You will be amply repaid if you form the habit of writing in a special section of your notebook any unfamiliar words that you encounter, with their definitions. Review these words occasionally, checking to see how many have become part of your vocabulary.

You will soon find that this concentration on words is a game—real fun. Unlike most games, it also pays big dividends, for one of the surest ways of winning advancement is by building a good vocabulary. A person who can use words effectively develops self-confidence and an outstanding personality. The words you use interpret *you* to the world.

Learning Exercises

1 **"Terrific" Means What?** Jane had formed the habit of characterizing anything of which she approved or about which she was enthusiastic as "terrific." Choose more meaningful words to describe each of the following nouns.

a a friend's new hat	**f** the new dramatic coach
b an apple pie	**g** the new English teacher
c a motion picture	**h** her department supervisor
d a ball game	**i** the school band's new uniforms
e a new novel	**j** dinner at a new restaurant

2 **New Words.** The terms listed here are either new words or old words with new or added meanings. Refer to an up-to-date dictionary, like the Merriam-Webster *New Collegiate Dictionary*, Sixth Edition, for the definitions. Then for each word write a sentence that will convey these meanings.

a omnibus	**f** ad-lib
b topflight	**g** gremlin
c streamlined	**h** featherbedding
d candid camera	**i** stereophonic
e emcee	**j** angle (in writing)

3 **Sound-Alikes.** In each of the following sentences, choose from the words within parentheses the word that correctly expresses the meaning.

a My, but this (current, currant) jelly is good!

b Yes, I (ought, aught) to open a savings account.

c They searched the attic but found no one (their, there).

d Two large ocean liners docked at adjoining (piers, peers) this morning.

e As I don't pretend to be a (profit, prophet), I can't forecast the results.

f At the end of the first (scene, seen) all the characters had been introduced.

g We were (shone, shown) many courtesies in our tour through the plant.

h No one (aloud, allowed) through these gates!

i Because of the high humidity, the pipes in our (seller, cellar) are dripping.

j Stainless (steal, steel) is increasingly popular for tableware.

4 **Sound- or Look-Almost-Alikes.** In each of the following sentences, choose from the words within parentheses the word that correctly expresses the meaning.

a I have my mother's (receipt, recipe) for Christmas cookies.

b The (trail, trial) through the woods was clearly marked.

c He first (attend, attained) prominence during the campaign for governor.

d The first (addition, edition) of the novel has already been exhausted.

e She is still (mourning, morning) the loss of her mink stole.

f He was (prosecuted, persecuted) relentlessly by his political enemies.

g I have just signed a (petition, partition) that we return to standard time.

h He was unpleasantly (official, officious) in carrying out his duties.

i There's no logic behind that (inane, insane) remark.

j The rate of infant (morality, mortality) has been steadily declining.

5 **Which Is Right?** Here are ten frequently used words. Which are misspelled? Respell them correctly.

a atheletic   **f** controversy
b parallel   **g** nickle
c priviledge   **h** occurrence
d recipient   **i** Febuary
e accidently   **j** congradulations

6 **A Synonym Hunt.** For each of the following words, think of another word of similar meaning. The hints enclosed in parentheses may help you.

a Commence (a 5-letter word starting with *b*)
b Procure (a 6-letter word starting with *o*)
c Casual (a 7-letter word starting with *off*)
d Colossal (a 4-letter word starting with *h*)
e Approximately (a 5-letter word starting with *a*)
f Nevertheless (a 3-letter word starting with *y*)
g Courteous (a 6-letter word starting with *p*)
h Humorous (a 5-letter word starting with *f*)
i Scatter (a 6-letter word starting with *sp*)
j Frank (a 7-letter word starting with *s*)

7 **What's the Opposite?** For each of the italicized words choose from the words that follow it the one most nearly opposite in meaning.

a *Lenient:* abundant, scarce, weak, strict
b *Remote:* fictitious, close, real, unnecessary
c *Superior:* defective, minor, inferior, worthless
d *Ignorance:* knowledge, ability, truthfulness, familiarity
e *Approximately:* almost, exactly, gracefully, incorrectly

Communication in Action: *Giving Credit to Others*

Your supervisor says to you, "That was an excellent job you did in putting the vacation schedule together." But, in fact, you didn't prepare the schedule; the job was done by one of your co-workers, Floyd Moore. Reply to the supervisor.

UNIT 5

Steps in Vocabulary Improvement — the Dictionary

Why the Dictionary Is a "Must"

By this time you fully realize that, in order to achieve the goal of improving your vocabulary, you need the backing of authority, some source that "knows all the answers." This source is a *reliable, up-to-date* dictionary.

Between the covers of a reliable, up-to-date dictionary you will find information that will help on a multitude of vocabulary problems. In fact, the dictionary is one of the most comprehensive reference books that have ever been compiled—but, you must know *how* to use your dictionary if you are to obtain the help you seek.

Notice the term *"your* dictionary." Of course your classroom is equipped with a dictionary, and doubtless your school library has an unabridged (large) dictionary; but you should have your own desk copy so that you can look up information just when you need it. The purchase of your own copy will be one of the most rewarding purchases you will ever make.

Looking Up Spelling

One of the most frequent uses of the dictionary is to verify spellings of which you are uncertain. Here are a few tips to help you in your search.

1. Be sure that you *really see* the letters in their correct order. When you have looked up a word and have turned away from your dictionary, be sure, for example, that you saw *nickel,* not *nickle;* or *Britain,* not *Britian.*

2. Be sure that you have not mentally inserted letters that are not in your word; for example, it is *harass,* not *harrass; commitment,* not *committment; inoculate,* not *innoculate.* On the other hand, be on guard against failing to see some letter; for example, it is *parallel,* not *paralel; safety,* not *safty; occurrence,* not *occurence.*

3. Be sure that you have not found some other word that is spelled somewhat like the one you seek. Observance of definitions will help you here. Suppose that in your reading you encounter the sentence, "The *incidence* of smallpox in this country is low." You're not just sure what *incidence* means. You refer, too hastily, to the dictionary and find *incident,* the plural of which, of course, would be *incidents.* You read the definition, however, and find the meaning "an accidental happening," a meaning that does not fit the sentence. By again checking the spelling, you note the correct sequence of letters, i-n-c-i-d-e-n-c-e. The meaning of this word, "range of occurrence," fits your sentence.

4. If you find two spellings given for a word—as *traveler, traveller*—this means that, while both forms are considered correct, the first is preferable. Make it a rule, therefore, to choose the first.

5. Note carefully how compound words are shown—whether they appear as one solid word, like *armchair;* as two separate words, as *postal card;* or as a hyphenated word, as *half-mast.* Not all dictionaries use the same method of indicating hyphens. Some indicate a

real hyphen by a heavy hyphen; others indicate it by a double hyphen. The introductory pages of your dictionary will give you this information.

6. Notice whether an accent mark appears with any letter in your word. These accents are a necessary part of certain words of foreign origin, such as *à la carte, café, naïve, première, façade, tête-à-tête.* In many such words, if the accent mark were omitted, the word would mean something entirely different. For example, a *résumé* is a summary, while *resume* is a verb meaning "to begin again"; a *visé* is an official indorsement on a passport, while a *vise* is a clamp used to hold objects securely.

The key to avoiding these pitfalls in verifying spelling is concentration. Keep your attention centered on each letter of each word you look up.

Looking Up Pronunciation

There is also a technique in verifying the pronunciation of a word.

1. Notice, first, how the word is divided into syllables. This division has a great bearing on pronunciation. For example, if *hy-poc-ri-sy* were divided *hypo-crisy*, how different the pronunciation would be! Also, the syllabication of a word may determine what part of speech it is. *Rec-ord* is a noun; *re-cord,* a verb. Any student who aims to become a stenographer or eventually an editor must become syllable-conscious, for the correct point of division of words at the ends of lines of printing and writing depends on syllabication.

2. The ways in which the letters in a word are sounded are indicated, usually in parentheses, immediately following the word. A phonetic alphabet is used, in which the vowels and some consonants are marked with small marks called "diacritical marks." Each dictionary carries a key to these marks, with applications to everyday words, so that you may be sure you understand the sound indicated.

This phonetic, respelled form of the word is also accented and syllabified. The accent marks indicate stressed syllables only. They are *not* part of the printed or written form of the actual word, like the accents described in point 6 above. The stress marks appear *after* the last letter of the syllable to be accented. The accent mark called *acute* that is part of certain foreign words appears *over* the vowel to be accented. Look up *blasé,* for example. Notice that the acute accent appears *over* the *é* and the stress mark *after* the syllable *sé;* thus *bla-sé'.* Some dictionaries insert the accent, or stress marks, in the full word as well as in the respelled form.

Any word of more than one syllable has an accent mark, and many words contain two accent marks, a stronger primary accent and a

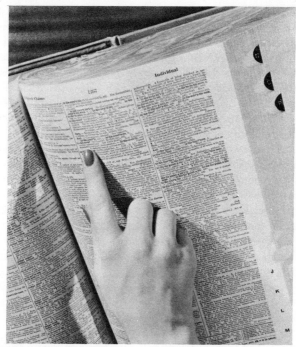

Webster's New International Dictionary, Second Edition, copyright, 1934, 1939, 1945, 1950, 1953, by G. & C. Merriam Co. Illustration reduced in size by permission of the publishers.

The unabridged dictionary is the most comprehensive reference book available. Form the habit of consulting it daily.

secondary accent; for example, *tes'ti-mo'ni-al.* In many words, the position of the accent determines the meaning of the word; for example, an *ob'ject* is an aim; to *ob-ject'* is to protest.

3. Some words may be pronounced in more than one way. For example, vowels may be given different sounds. *Aunt* may be pronounced *änt* (the *a* having the same sound as in *arm*) or *ȧnt* (the *a* having the same sound as in *grass*). Also different syllables may be stressed; for example, *acclimate* may be pronounced *ă-klī'mĭt* or *ăk'lĭ-māt.* Make it a rule to choose the first form, just as you do in choosing the preferred spelling when two forms are allowable.

Looking Up the Meaning of Words

The third essential technique in dictionary use concerns efficient methods of looking up the meanings of words.

1. Become familiar with the order in which the definitions are arranged in your particular dictionary by consulting the introductory

section. Dictionaries differ in this detail. Most of them list definitions according to the historical development of the word. Therefore, many obsolete (marked *Obs.*) and archaic (*Arch.*) meanings appear before later and present-day meanings. In other dictionaries, the obsolete and archaic meanings appear after the current ones. In all dictionaries, specific labels—such as *Law, Med.* (Medicine), and so on—precede the definitions that apply to these fields, and these definitions are placed after all the others. These labels will help you decide on the suitability of the word for your purpose.

2. Some words have only one definition; others, like *run,* may have a score or more, each numbered. Therefore, do not stop when you have read one or two definitions. Read several and you will discover many precise meanings of the word heretofore unknown to you.

3. Read any illustrative sentences or phrases containing the word and examine any pictorial illustration accompanying it. These sentences and illustrations often clarify the meaning greatly.

4. If the definition contains a word that you do not know, look up that word also.

5. If there is a *See* or a *Cf.* (meaning "compare") notation after the definition, look up the word referred to. You will find valuable supplementary information.

6. Notice the synonyms (*Syn.*) and antonyms (*Ant.*) if any are given. The following unit will have more to say on these words.

Other Information to Help You

Although the dictionary is most often consulted to verify spelling and pronunciation and to look up the meanings of words, it also offers an abundance of other information that you should learn to consult. It is possible here only to suggest the types of data that an ambitious student will wish to utilize.

1. Information on grammar. All such entries will be more meaningful to you after you have completed Units 13–26.

2. Commonly used foreign words and phrases.

3. Names of prominent persons and of important places. (If the latter appear in a separate list, the list is called a *gazetteer.*)

4. Correct abbreviations.

5. The capitalization of proper names and proper adjectives.

6. Usually in appendixes: common Christian names of men and women, words that rhyme, tables of weights and measures, special signs and symbols, forms of address, preparation of copy for the press, proofreading symbols, lists of colleges and universities in the United States and Canada, and so on.

Learning Exercises

1 **How Speedy Are You?** Do you really know the exact order of the letters of the alphabet?

a In your dictionary, locate the following words, taking each one in the sequence in which it is shown. Note the exact time when you start your search; also the exact time when you finish. How many minutes did it take you?

intelligence	inference	conversation
contribution	phenomenal	persistence
alternate	interrogate	advantageous
residuary	subsidiary	environment
executor	equitable	realty

b Now type these words in alphabetic order.

2 **Look at Them Twice.** Among the following words are several typical and common malformations (**Hint:** Look up the meaning of that word!) caused, usually, by lack of attention to the letter-by-letter spelling of the word. A few of the words, however, are shown correctly. Respell those that are wrong.

a ninty
b ocassionaly
c occurence
d nineth
e existence
f Philipines
g vegitable
h rhythm
i prarie
j similiar

3 **Syllables Plus Accents.** Here are ten words that you are likely to encounter almost any day. If you are a typist, you must know their breakdown into syllables in order to be able to select the points at which to divide at line ends. Accents also have a bearing on choosing the best division points. Therefore, without consulting your dictionary, indicate the syllable divisions and the accenting of the words. Then check your choice by the dictionary.

a fortunate
b injurious
c optimistic
d incomparable
e through
f misrepresentation
g aggressive
h extraordinary
i Cincinnati
j identity

4 **Which Spelling Is Preferred?** Without consulting your dictionary, indicate which of the two spellings shown for the following words you consider preferable. Then check your selections by the dictionary.

a acknowledgment, acknowledgement
b instalment, installment
c quartet, quartette
d anaemic, anemic
e flier, flyer
f traveller, traveler
g catalog, catalogue
h canceling, cancelling
i advisor, adviser
j benefited, benefitted

5 **How Do You Pronounce Them?** Respell the following words by sound (phonetically) according to what you consider the correct pronunciations. Afterwards check your forms with the dictionary.

a apparatus
b apricot
c applicable
d financier
e inquiry
f juvenile
g irate
h height
i avenue
j percolate

6 **Foreign Expressions You Meet.** Ten frequently used foreign expressions are listed in column A. Match these against the correct meanings in column B.

A	B
a carte blanche 6	1 For each person
b bon voyage 8	2 A social blunder
c faux pas 2	3 Common spirit of a group
d esprit de corps 3	4 Social knowledge
e à la mode 9	5 Solid ground
f per capita 1	6 Unlimited authority
g ex cathedra 10	7 Luxurious
h terra firma 5	8 A good journey
i de luxe 7	9 After the fashion
j savoir-faire 4	10 With authority
a la cart	11 One by one
	12 Unexcelled
	13 To the manner born

Check your selections against the dictionary.
Copy in your notebook the phonetic spelling of each expression.

Communication in Action: *Preparing a Job Summary*

You are leaving your job as secretary to accept a better one nearer your home. Your replacement, a recent graduate, works with you during your last week to "learn the ropes." You decide that a brief, typewritten summary of the procedures in your office would be helpful. Outline what this summary might contain. Why would such a guide be helpful to a new worker?

UNIT   6

Steps in Vocabulary Improvement — Achieving Variety

Why Aim for Variety?

Do you realize that you may be using many standard words over and over again to express a variety of situations, events, or emotions? You could, for example, describe your boss, last evening's TV program, the weather, your new coat—almost anything you approve of or are enthusiastic about—as *nice* (or anything you don't like as *not nice*). You probably intend one of these meanings for *nice:*

> Your boss: *considerate, even-tempered, pleasant, agreeable, patient, appreciative*
> Last evening's TV program: *amusing, well acted, exciting, dramatic, thrilling, true to life, informative*
> The weather: *pleasant, fair, exhilarating, stimulating*
> Your new coat: *becoming, practical, comfortable, stylish*

How much more interesting, informative, and vivid your descriptions would have been had you chosen the really descriptive term rather than the vague, outworn *nice.*

Some of the Worst Offenders

Other overused, cover-all words are:

good	awful	big	say	know	come
lovely	fine	little	think	fix	go

Now don't form the erroneous impression that these words are entirely taboo. They are essential for many occasions, but they are abused by overuse. To prove this, in each of the following sentences substitute for the italicized words the words in parentheses.

> **The stenographer made a *bad* mistake in her transcript.** (inexcusable)

> **The Armed Forces are always seeking *fine* young men.** (promising, alert, spirited)

> **We both had a *lovely* time at the party.** (delightful, enjoyable)

> **Dad has an *awful* cold.** (heavy)

> **"Mary has lost her purse!" *said* Jane.** (exclaimed, shouted)

> **The old man *went* slowly down the road.** (limped, shuffled, hobbled, crept)

You surely cannot deny that the substitution of the parenthetical words would give both accurate and more interesting and vivid pictures in these sentences.

Consider, also, the difference that the improved sentences would make to a listener. He would understand precisely what the speaker had in mind instead of having to infer or even guess the meaning.

Then there are those hackneyed phrases that were originally apt and mildly amusing but that have long since lost all element of surprise or sincerity. Some of these expressions are worn-out figures of speech like *cold as ice, the staff of life, green with envy.* Surely, *chilled, bread,* and *envious* are more direct and meaningful. Other timeworn expressions are proverbs or threadbare quotations, like "Truth is stranger than fiction," "He who hesitates is lost," "Variety is the spice of life," and so on. You can express yourself so that the meaning is entirely apparent without using such trite sentences.

The Key to the Situation

Why do people keep on using these weak, outworn words and expressions? One short word gives the answer—laziness. The users just do not have sufficient interest to take the time and trouble to select more accurate words and expressions. They follow the line of least resistance and utter the same old words over and over and over again.

There is no doubt that you, by the time you have reached this course, have encountered in your reading many of the words that you need in order to add variety to your speech and writing. Unquestionably, also, you have heard a great many of these words from your teachers, your principal, and speakers on the radio and TV. All you need to do is to start using the substitutions. How do you start?

Learn to Use Synonyms

What, exactly, is a synonym? A *synonym* is a word that has the same or nearly the same meaning as another word—*glad* and *happy*, for example. Most synonyms, however, are not *completely* synonymous; that is, though they have the same *basic* meaning, each synonym has a slightly different shade of meaning. For example, look up the word *get* in your dictionary. You will find the following listed as synonyms: *obtain, procure, secure, acquire, gain, win, earn*. Notice that each of these words, although it has the fundamental idea of *get*, has its own shade of meaning. For example, you would *obtain*, not *win*, a position; you would *win*, not *acquire*, a prize. Because the English language was derived from so many other languages— Latin, Greek, French, German, Anglo-Saxon, and others—it is exceedingly rich in synonyms; therefore, it is possible to express fine shades of meaning by choosing the synonym that expresses that meaning.

Your prime source of help in learning to differentiate the meanings of synonyms is your dictionary. Form the habit of noticing whether synonyms (also antonyms) are listed at the end of the entry under any word that you may look up. If they are, read the differentiations and try to frame sentences or phrases using the synonyms. For example, suppose you have looked up *occurrence* (perhaps in order to check on the number of *c*'s and *r*'s in the word). Having obtained that information, stop to notice the list of synonyms: *event, incident, episode, circumstance*. From the differentiations given, you can "concoct" these phrases and sentences: "The final *event* that led up to World War II was . . . ," "We have completely forgotten the unpleasant *incident*," "The *episode* of launching the first world satellite," "Missing my bus was the first *circumstance* in a long series of delays."

If you follow this plan of applying the different words conscientiously, you will be surprised by your growing awareness of distinctions in meanings that you had never thought of before.

The Thesaurus. Many students, as well as writers and editors, overlook the help to be obtained from that most useful reference book on words, the thesaurus. Roget's is the classic work.

A thesaurus is a collection of words and phrases arranged according to *ideas*. Its object is the exact opposite of the object of a dictionary. A dictionary gives the meaning of the *word* that one has in mind. A thesaurus enables one to find the word by which to express an *idea* one has in mind. In other words, a thesaurus goes one step farther than a dictionary. In using the dictionary or a book of synonyms, one must have at least one word in mind; in using a thesaurus, one can start with a general idea!

Suppose, for example, you wish to write some comments on new fall clothing styles. You wish to emphasize their smartness. Using the thesaurus, you find *smart* in the index, with the following variations of the idea: *pain, grief, active, clever, cunning, to feel, witty, neat, fashionable.* Each of these items is followed by the number of the section where the words expressing that variation can be located. Of course, *fashionable* conveys the shade of meaning you seek. When you turn to the section number given, you find a listing like this:

852. Fashion

(*Nouns*). Ton, tonishness, style, *bon ton,* mode, vogue.

Manners, breeding, politeness, gentility, decorum, *bienséance, savoir-vivre,* punctilio, form, formality, etiquette, custom, demeanour, air, port, carriage, presence.

The world, the fashionable world, the *beau monde,* high life, society, town, court, gentility, civilisation, civilised life, *see* Nobility (875).

(*Phrase*). The height of fashion.

(*Verb*). To be fashionable.

(*Adjectives*). Fashionable, in fashion, in vogue, *à la mode,* modish, tony, tonish, stylish, smart, courtly, *recherché,* genteel, *comme il faut,* well-bred, well-mannered, polished, gentlemanlike, ladylike, well-spoken, civil, presentable, refined, thoroughbred, *dégagé,* jaunty, swell, swagger, unembarrassed.

(*Phrase*). Having a run.

(*Adverbs*). Fashionably, in fashion, etc.

Where else could you have found *style, mode, vogue, the height of fashion, à la mode, modish, jaunty,* etc., all in one list?

Learn to Use Antonyms

There are two types of antonyms. In one type, a prefix meaning *not* has been added to the word for which the antonym is desired. For example:

By adding	to	the result is
in	active	inactive
im	mature	immature
ig	noble	ignoble
il	literate	illiterate
ir	responsible	irresponsible
ab	normal	abnormal
dis	satisfied	dissatisfied
non	sense	nonsense
un	natural	unnatural

The three prefixes *in, non,* and *un* are widely used to "manufacture" almost any word of opposite meaning that may be desired, but the person who has a wide enough vocabulary to choose an entirely different word as the antonym is a master of words. Such a person, wishing to characterize a certain statement as "not correct," would be able to describe it as *erroneous* instead of just prefixing an *in* to *correct.*

Learning Exercises

1 **Coloring Your Speech.** Substitute for the colorless words, printed in italics, specific or emphatic words that will make the following sentences more graphic.

  a He *walked* slowly down Main Street.
  b I *said* that I would meet George at ten o'clock.
  c I consider that a *good* plan.
  d That store has a *poor* policy in dealing with its customers.
  e The results *show* what can be done if one tries.
  f He is building a *small home* near the lake.
  g The *route* home led through the woods.
  h I *saw* my first robin this morning.
  i He *ate* his supper in five minutes.
  j She bought some *beautiful* vases in France.

2 **Match-mates.** Match each word in column A with a word or phrase in column B that has the same meaning.

A	B
a remuneration	**1** Infer
b undue	**2** Congratulations
c accelerate	**3** Pathetic
d cryptic	**4** Wealthy
e felicitations	**5** Speed up
f deplete	**6** Excessive
g apathy	**7** Fascinating
h category	**8** Classification
i opulent	**9** Indifference
j surmise	**10** Exhaust
	11 Mysterious
	12 Self-evident
	13 Pay
	14 Poverty-stricken

6783

3 **Wanted — the Opposites.** Substitute words of opposite meaning for the words italicized below.

 a Jane *answers* entirely too many questions.
 b Her physician told the patient to *descend* the stairs slowly.
 c The forged check proved the prisoner's *innocence*.
 d Between the hills nestled an *artificial* lake.
 e His *definite* recommendations left us confused.
 f The high wind *collected* leaves all over the lawn.
 g Her suggestion was much too *conservative*.
 h We have an *inadequate* supply of everything we need.
 i Miss Drew is very *strict;* otherwise I should not have passed the exam.
 j Because of the *scarcity* of talent, the play was a hit.

4 **Replacing "Awful."** Substitute a more precise adjective for the overworked *awful* in these expressions.

a an awful cold	**f** awful manners
b an awful hurry	**g** an awful meal
c an awful storm	**h** an awful-looking room
d an awful hat	**i** an awful pain
e an awful mistake	**j** an awful boss

5 **Choose the Positive.** Convert the following negative statements into positive forms.

 a That is no small task.
 b This is not a bad idea.
 c The building will be started at no distant date.
 d She is no ordinary typist.
 e He is nobody's fool.
 f The crate must contain no fewer than 5 dozen eggs.
 g I wish a shade no darker than this sample.
 h She is no novice.
 i Her popularity is due in no small measure to her sunny disposition.
 j I was not a little surprised at the results.

6 **One Out of Four Is Wrong.** In these six groups of four words each, three words in each group have similar meanings, but one is not related. Which word is the intruder?

a showy, gaudy, delicate, pretentious
b discouraged, depressed, dejected, elated
c enlarge, contract, expand, amplify
d evening, dusk, dawn, twilight
e hesitant, brave, dauntless, intrepid
f erudition, scholarship, learning, sensibility

7 Consult the thesaurus for additional substitutions that might be selected in place of any four of the italicized words in Exercise 1.

Communication in Action: *Vocabulary Game*

It is better to know big words than to use them. Consider this gem: "Simians indigenous to Zamboanga are destitute of caudal appendages." This means that monkeys in Zamboanga have no tails! The game of changing popular sayings into difficult words, such as in the example, is fun and will add to your recognition of words. Use a dictionary to find difficult synonyms for words in three popular sayings. Try them out on your class. Discuss the desirability of having a larger vocabulary than you use in speaking or writing.

UNIT 7

Steps in Vocabulary Improvement — Pronunciation

How Important Is Correct Pronunciation?

Did you ever stop to think that everyone talks more than he writes? This is just as true in business life as in home and social life. Indeed, many positions in a business office may require little written communication but a great deal of spoken communication. The telephone operator, the messenger, the receptionist, the salesclerk— all write less frequently than they talk. *But* much of their talking is with the public, with customers or prospective customers, or with employees in higher positions. It is most important, therefore, that words be distinctly and correctly pronounced, to save both you and your employer from embarrassment. Also, if a listener must ask a speaker to repeat, time is wasted.

A girl applying for a position may be carefully groomed and may give the outward appearance of being a promising employee. She would not be guilty of chewing gum or cleaning her nails during an interview. But, if she tells the employment manager that she saw the position for which she is applying advertised in a "noospaper," that she can begin working on "Febuary 1," and that she really would like to work for this "Kumpni," how long will the illusion of superiority last? It has probably already vanished.

Why We Pronounce as We Do

We all learned to talk by imitating the speech of those around us: first of members of the family; then of neighbors and friends; later of schoolmates, teachers, co-workers, and others with whom we have come in contact. Some of the pronunciations imitated may have been incorrect.

Those who come from homes where most words are correctly sounded do have a head start over those from homes where, through carelessness or lack of training, incorrect pronunciation is common. In our land of opportunity, however, everyone has a good chance to achieve the best that is offered, if he will but try. The acquiring of correct pronunciation habits is no exception, especially if we pattern ours after those who know: teachers, ministers, the educated persons in the community, and superior radio and television speakers.

Persons from homes of foreign-language backgrounds have their special speech difficulties: Germans and French with *th*, Scandinavians with *j*, Scotsmen and Irish with trilled *r*'s. The British, who speak the same language that we do, have certain idiosyncrasies of pronunciation; for example, clipping syllables, thus shortening *secretary* to "secretry." Other persons have trouble with final *ng*, giving it a "guh" sound, like "longuh" for *long*.

What Makes a Certain Pronunciation Correct?

Who decides whether or not a certain pronunciation is correct? Doubtless your answer is, "The dictionary." This answer is only partially correct.

Even though the dictionary is the book to which we go to determine correct pronunciation, this does not mean that dictionary editors have arbitrarily chosen certain pronunciations as correct. Instead, they first recorded the pronunciations that are used by the largest number of the best educated and most cultured speakers in the country. Then, they selected the most frequently used of these pronunciations. However, the best educated and most cultured people in the Midwest may pronounce a certain word very differently from the way that a cultured Southerner, New Englander, New Yorker, or even persons from points within these general localities would pronounce it. For example, a cultured Southerner is likely to say "pa" for *pie* or "moah" for *more,* while a New Englander might say "pahk" for *park* or "idear" for *idea,* and so on.

So accustomed have residents in the various areas become to these speech patterns that they have always heard, that they do not even detect any difference between these forms and the forms that are given in the dictionary. Then, often, when they do grasp the differences, they are not willing to adopt the standard pronunciation, not wishing to be considered "different." The solution seems to be to observe how the best educated persons in a community, who are presumed to have been "exposed" to correct pronunciations, speak and then to adopt their standards. New achievements in science are making the world smaller every day; therefore, the necessity for eliminating colloquial differences in our speech is increasing.

Sometimes two or more pronunciations for a word are given in the dictionary. In such cases, the first is considered preferable, although the others given are acceptable. In this textbook the Merriam-Webster *New Collegiate Dictionary,* Sixth Edition, is the standard for both pronunciation and spelling. Therefore, only the first of two or more pronunciations of a word is considered.

As you learned in Unit 5, pronunciations are indicated by a phonetic alphabet and by accent marks. Each dictionary has its own method of indicating the sounds of letters. Refer to the front pages of your dictionary for a key to the markings.

Mispronunciations Most Frequently Encountered

Irrespective of home or regional environment, however, certain types of mispronunciations are widely prevalent. In order to make it easier for you to overcome tendencies to mispronounce words in these various classes, they are grouped for study as follows:

Omission of Letters or Syllables. Some of our most useful and common words are sadly mistreated when letters or even whole syllables are dropped.

Lost Consonants. The consonants most often dropped are *t, d,* and *g* when the letters are in combination with some other consonant. Thus, *fact* becomes "fac"; *yield* becomes "yiel"; and *going* becomes "goin." The *w* sound, too, frequently is carelessly pronounced; for example, "wat" for *what*. Practice the following phrases aloud until you are sure you do not slight the underlined consonant sounds.

recognized candidate	February second
tourist list	three hundred thirty-three
factual arrangement	through thick and thin
current account	lingering and longing
collect payment	being a linguist
competent party	test of strength
demand payment	assistant management
trust fund	seemingly strict
next payment	bonded debt outstanding
kept a strict accounting	judgment for the tenant
arranging pictures	attempted bankrupt
earned discount	outstanding print
consigning the prints	whistle while thinking
width and length	why white wheels

Lost Vowels. As with consonants, when two vowels occur together in a word, the sound of one tends to be slighted. Thus, *li-on* becomes an indistinct "lin." Too, a single vowel used as a syllable is frequently overlooked and not sounded in words. A careless person will say "captal," completely ignoring the single-vowel syllable *i*. Pronounce the word correctly—"cap-*i*-tal." Be sure you see each of the vowel sounds; and be sure you do not lose any of them when you practice the following phrases.

metropolitan area	especially positive
federal cabinet	terrible sophomore
ridiculous accident	indirect but definite
municipal regulation	generally separate
cruel lion	variable regulation
excellent family	family history
accurate and regular	usually interesting
alphabetical list of liabilities	popular battery
eleven manufacturers	separate poem
variable capital	original company
temporarily separated	indirectly responsible
ivory tower	positive verification
veteran general	particularly quiet

Lost Syllables. It is only a step for a person who drops consonant and vowel sounds to drop syllables from words, too. Such a person "c'lects the rent" instead of "col-lects." It is as though he wished to make a contraction out of every word he speaks. Now that you know how to sound all necessary consonants and vowels, you will find the phrases below easy to practice as you pronounce all the syllables of all words.

accidentally hurt (*not* acci-dently)

little people (*not* lil)

laboratory technician (*not* lab-atory)

just *obligation* (*not* obgation)

five-year *guarantee* (*not* garn-tee)

detailed *itinerary* (*not* itinree)

generally acceptable (*not* gen-rally)

occasionally wrong (*not* occa-sionly)

Addition of Letters or Syllables. Just as serious a diction fault as dropping sounds is the frequent mistake of adding extra sounds.

As you say aloud the following italicized words, watch to see if you ordinarily add extra incorrect sounds to them.

a fine *athlete* (*not* athalete)

the *height* of fashion (*not* heighth)

across the street (*not* acrost)

broken *umbrella* (*not* umber-ella)

one roll of *film* (*not* filum)

drowned duck (*not* drownded)

grievous fault (*not* grievious)

rhythm for dancing (*not* rhythum)

pop *singer* (*not* sing-ger)

fourth *finger* (*not* fing-ger)

disastrous results (*not* disas-terous)

entrance examination (*not* en-terance)

a *hindrance* to progress (*not* hinderance)

a *mischievous* child (*not* mis-chevious)

a good *preventive* (*not* pre-ventative)

a *burglar* alarm (*not* burgular)

The remedy for these types of pronunciation errors is attention to spelling. If you spell these words correctly, you will pronounce them correctly. Vice versa, if you misspell them, you will mispronounce them. Many spelling errors are caused by mispronunciation.

Silent Letters. As we shall see when we study spelling in the following unit, among the chief stumbling blocks to correct spelling are the silent letters that occur in many of our most frequently used words. Because we do not hear these letters, they do not constitute a serious threat to correct pronunciation except in a few important words in which letters that should be silent are often sounded. As you read the following words aloud, make a special effort *not* to sound the letters that are printed in italics.

al*m*ond	post*h*umous	sal*v*e	ve*h*ement
of*t*en	sal*m*on	s*w*ord	ve*h*icle
indi*c*t	mor*t*gage	cor*p*s	

Troubles with Vowels. Many words are mispronounced because certain vowels are incorrectly sounded.

The Sound of Long "u." You recall the would-be employee mentioned at the start of this unit who referred to a "noospaper." This incorrect use of the o͞o sound instead of the long *u* sound that is heard in *human* is, unfortunately, a common error. It makes a decidedly unpleasant impression on hearers who are speech-conscious.

Read the following words aloud, concentrating on using the long *u* sound.

annuity	neurotic	due
new	revenue	duke
New York	institution	duty
numerous	substitution	culinary
neuritis	latitude	tube
neuralgia	multitude	

Troubles with "a." In another group of words, the sound of long *a*, the sound in *hate*, is incorrectly replaced by the short sound of *a*, the sound heard in *hat*.

The following words are typical. Again, read the list aloud.

āviator	grātis	rādiator
blātant	implācable	stātus
dāta	ignorāmus	tenācious
flāgrant	lātent	ultimātum
gāla	pātronage	verbātim

Vice versa, in the following words, the short *a* should be used instead of the long *a*.

Ărab	măltreat	păgeant
deprăvity	păgination	Spokăne

Troubles with "i." In some frequently used words, the sound of long *i*, as heard in *wide*, is incorrectly replaced by the short sound heard in *hit*.

alumnī	grīmy	stīpend	vīa

On the other hand, in these words, the short *i* should be used rather than the long *i*.

finance	Ĭtalian	respīte
financial	ĭtalics	

Substituting One Vowel for Another. In another type of mispronunciation, an entirely different vowel is substituted for the correct one. In the following words, the letters that are often thus replaced are underscored. Read the list aloud, clearly enunciating the underlined letters. This type of mispronunciation also is often closely linked with misspelling.

accurate	just	preparation
description	mathematics	privilege
despair	optimistic	restaurant
divide	particular	sacrilegious
escalator	percolator	separate
existence	permanent	

Incorrect Accent. Many ludicrous errors are caused by placing the stress, or accent, on the wrong syllable of a word.

1. In the following words, the accent should be on the *first* syllable.

*des*picable	*for*midable	*thea*ter
*dic*tionary	*hos*pitable	*pref*erable
*ex*plicable	*il*lustrate	*lam*entable

Now try reading these phrases aloud.

*ad*mirable work	an *ap*plicable case
*am*icable arrangement	a *com*parable example
an *in*teresting experiment	an *in*famous crime

2. In these words, accent should be on the *second* syllable.

ac*cli*mate	re*mon*strate	in*qui*ry
as*pir*ant	ob*lig*atory	om*nip*otent
in*ex*plicable	pre*ced*ence	in*cog*nito

Also read these phrases aloud to help fix in your mind other words accented on the second syllable.

an in*dis*putable fact	a note of con*dol*ence
an ir*rev*ocable decision	a de*mon*strative child
a su*per*fluous supply	an ex*tra*ordinary (tror) occurrence

3. In these words, accent should be on the *final* syllable.

al*ly*	di*rect*	fi*nance*
bou*quet* (ka)	dis*charge*	re*search*
de*tail*	ex*pert* (adj.)	po*lice*

Also read these phrases aloud to help fix in your mind other words accented on the final syllable.

an a*dult* point of view	a rou*tine* checkup
the chauf*feur* for the president	the pre*tense* of poverty

Just Plain Tricky. Many words often mispronounced cannot be classified under any of the groupings just listed. There is only one way of mastering the correct pronunciations of these offenders. Concentrate on each one, first looking it up in your dictionary and then repeating it many times. Here are representative words of this type.

absorb	deaf	once
absurd	denunciate	partner
apron	err	peremptory
associate	gist	perhaps
association	homogeneous	perspire
attorney	hundred	perspiration
bona fide	library	possess
clothes	luxurious	prerogative
censure	luxury	quay
codicil	martial	reservoir
column	medieval	soot
congratulations	mercantile	strength
coupon	Nebraska	suppose
		tremendous

Some Tips to Help You

These miscellaneous suggestions will help you in your battle with mispronunciations.

1. Be especially careful in pronouncing personal names. People resent having their names mispronounced just as they resent having them misspelled. If a girl wants to be called "Jo-an'" rather than "Jōn" or "Jo'an," follow her preference.

2. Likewise, be especially careful in pronouncing geographic names. In many, the spelling is no guide to the pronunciation. If you are the least uncertain, check the gazetteer in your dictionary. Just to prove this statement, here are a few geographic names that bear watching. You may be surprised when you verify their pronunciations.

Abilene	Edinburgh	Norfolk
Bethlehem	Haverhill	Southampton
Cannes	Illinois	Valparaiso
Cherbourg	Lima	Versailles

3. Be especially careful with foreign words and phrases. Some very amusing (and embarrassing) mistakes can be made by pronouncing them, especially French words, as they are spelled. The dictionary gives the closest approximation possible to the English sounds.

4. Guard against running words together, making such sounds as "wotcha doon?" (what are you doing?), "shoulda" (should have), "willyuh?" (will you?), or "jeet?" (did you eat?). Nothing more quickly brands a person as illiterate as do these slovenly substitutions for expressions.

5. When you learn a new word, learn its correct pronunciation at once. In other words, when you look up the spelling and meaning of a word, notice also its pronunciation and practice it.

6. When you speak to a group of people, speak more slowly than you ordinarily do and enunciate carefully.

The person who faithfully carries out the suggestions outlined in this unit will surely acquire an enviable reputation for correct speech.

Learning Exercises

1 **Letters You Don't Hear.** How many words can you think of that contain the following silent letters?

    a Words beginning with silent *p*
    b Words beginning with silent *k*
    c Words beginning with silent *w*
    d Words containing a silent *s*
    e Words containing a silent *l*

2 **Making a Choice.** Which of the four words that follow each of these questions answers the question correctly?

    a Which of these words is accented on the *first* syllable: exquisite, acclimate, detail, abdomen?
    b Which of these words is accented on the *second* syllable: refutable, secretive, mischievous, eczema?
    c Which of these words is accented on the *final* syllable: irate, combat (noun), pretense, paraffin?
    d Which of these words should be pronounced as two syllables only: film, caramel, athlete, every?
    e Does the syllable *new* in *newspaper* sound most like: a cat's mew, a cow's moo, a day's tour, an author's book?

3 **Count the Syllables.** How many syllables has each of these words?

a accidentally	**d** umbrella	**g** drowned
b remembrance	**e** elm	**h** idea
c grievous	**f** hindrance	**i** learned (adj.)

4 **How Is "u" Sounded?** In which of the following words is the *u* pronounced as in *human?*

a recuperate	**d** upheaval	**g** Tuesday
b institute	**e** student	**h** column
c utterance	**f** illustrate	**i** gratitude

5 The Accent Changes the Meaning. Each of the following words means one thing when accented on the first syllable and something else when accented on the final syllable. Write definitions for the words in each pair and indicate what part of speech each word is.

a desert   d produce   g contest
b extract   e digest   h object
c minute   f absent   i rebel

6 The Sound of "i"

a In which of the following words should the *i* be sounded as in *ice:* admirable, finance, grimy, reptile?

b In which of the following words should the *i* not be sounded as in *ice:* via, alumni, respite, stipend?

c In which of the following words is the *a* sounded as in *make:* Spokane, tenacious, task, depravity?

d In which of the following words is the *a* sounded as in *cat:* apricot, status, verbatim, depravity?

7 Add or Subtract. The following words appear spelled as they are often mispronounced because a letter or a syllable has been either added or dropped. Respell all words correctly.

a accelrate   d labratory   g probly
b Febuary   e strenth   h sufferage
c filum   f sophmore   i acrosst

Communication in Action: *Small-Group Discussion Technique*

The small-group discussion technique is often used to solve problems. It is based on the idea that two heads are better than one. Here is the way it works: (1) Divide your class into small groups of four, five, or six. (2) Make sure everyone in each group is acquainted. (3) Elect a chairman. (4) Agree quickly on a recorder who will take notes and report the major points of the discussion later to the entire class. (5) Make sure that everyone understands the problem you are to discuss. (6) Be sure that everyone enters into the discussion. Here is the problem: What are some ways to encourage students to make more effective use of their time in studying? When you are through, evaluate the process.

Section 2   Spelling and Word Usage

UNIT   8

Spelling and Vocabulary

Attitude Toward Spelling

Undoubtedly you approach this and the following unit with dread. You may have what is known as a "mind set" against spelling. You are sure that you are not a "born speller," and there's little use in trying to become a good speller. But remember this: spelling ability is valued so highly by employers that the person who possesses this skill is better equipped for a successful business career than one who lacks the skill.

A misspelling may even be expensive. Not so long ago it was found that *attendance* had been misspelled *ence* in the New York State Education Law. The State Education Department requested that the mistake be corrected. It was necessary for the Legislature to pass a bill in order to make this change. Cost of the processing: $1,000. A pretty costly error.

Granted that there seems to be no rhyme nor reason for the way in which many words are spelled—still, informed persons expect to see words in a standard form that is recognized as correct. There is no alternative but to master that form. The purpose of these units is to help you to do just that.

What Causes Us to Misspell?

Misspelling may be due to several causes. Strangely enough, many of these reasons are physical in origin. The hand, the ear, the mouth, the eye, each or all, may have failed to co-operate as fully as they might have done in your task of learning to spell correctly.

The Hand Affects Spelling

Poor handwriting has been blamed for many things, and it really does have an effect on spelling. If your style of writing is "sloppy," the resulting inaccuracies in forming letters may lead to actual misspelling. Suppose you fail to close your *a*'s, so that an *a* may be mistaken for a *u*, or suppose your *e*'s and *i*'s look nearly alike—especially if you are careless about including your dots—or suppose there's little difference in the lengths of your *t*'s and *l*'s and that you fail to cross your *t*'s. Not too important, you may think; but you are building up a real handicap for yourself. Your eye is not being trained to detect wrong letters at a glance.

Misspelling Caused by Mispronunciation

Unit 7 pointed out that mispronunciation often causes misspelling. Therefore your ear and your tongue, as well as your hand, may lead you astray.

Here are a few suggestions to guide you in overcoming the most common mispronunciations that may be causing you to misspell.

1. Give attention to the vowels in unaccented syllables, saying the vowels aloud distinctly (as in *sepArate, everYbody, histOry*). Some "tricks" have been devised for overcoming this type of trouble, such as, "There's *a rat* in *separate*." "Poor gra*mmar* will *mar* your progress," or "Stationery means pap*er*" (to distinguish the word from *stationary*, meaning "fixed").

Another device for overcoming this type of difficulty is to think of a word derived from or related to the one that is puzzling you. The sound of the vowel in the derivative is often clear and will give you the key to the correct vowel in the parent word.

In the following list the troublesome vowel in the first word of each pair is italicized. In the derived or related word (the second word), the entire syllable in which that vowel occurs is in italics.

compare	com*par*able	medicine	me*dic*inal
compete	com*pet*ition	prepare	prep*ar*ation
despair	*desp*eration	ridicule	ri*dic*ulous

2. Pronounce all the consonants between syllables accurately (as in *goverNment, quaNtity, suRprise*).

3. When you form an adverb from an adjective ending in *al*, like *usual*, or in *ic*, like *frantic*, be sure that you pronounce the *ally* ending (as in *general, generally; incidental, incidentally; tragic, tragically*).

Yes, you must train your ear and your mouth, as well as your hand, to help you acquire correct spelling habits.

Visualizing Words

Now we come to that most important sensory organ, the eye. You must cultivate the ability to "see" the correct form of a word in your mind. You may have noticed that some persons test the spelling of a word by writing it—to judge whether or not it *looks* right.

Part of the failure to see a word correctly results from our habits of rapid reading. In reading, we do not look at each letter in a word but get a mental picture of the whole word or even a whole phrase. In spelling, on the other hand, we must know *all* the letters that should appear in a word and the *order* in which they should appear. Therefore, it is most important to *take time* to learn to spell—time to look at a word in detail and to consult a dictionary when in doubt.

Silent Letters

A vast number of words in the English language contain letters that are not pronounced. These silent letters are "hangovers" from the foreign-language words from which our present-day words were derived. *Debt,* for example, was derived from the Latin *debitum,* meaning "owed." Our present-day word still carries that *b,* although it is not pronounced.

Some of our most frequently used words contain silent letters, as the following representative list indicates. (The silent letters are italicized.)

clim*b*	*g*naw	al*m*s	*p*neumonia
com*b*	ali*g*n	hal*f*	*p*sychology
bom*b*	sig*n*	tal*k*	mor*t*gage
dou*b*t	autum*n*	fol*k*	cat*c*h
s*c*ene	*g*host	wal*k*	lis*t*en
mus*c*le	*g*nat	solem*n*	*g*uard
We*d*nesday	*k*now	condem*n*	*g*uess
han*d*kerchief	*k*nee	receip*t*	*w*rite
e at the end of	*k*nife	*p*salm	s*w*ord
life, tube, etc.	*k*nack	*p*neumatic	ans*w*er

Do all these words look natural to you? Good! This means that your mind has accepted the silent letters as part of the words. What you have done with these common words you can do with unfamiliar ones that you may come upon. We repeat: take time to *see* all the letters in any new word and time to look up the word.

Different Spellings of Related Words

Another type of spelling difficulty is caused by confusion over words that are seemingly related in meaning but spelled slightly differently, as *four* and *forty, nine* and *ninth, speak* and *speech, comparison* and *comparative, disaster* and *disastrous, maintain* and *maintenance* (but *mountain* and *mountainous*). Your mind's eye, as well as your physical eye, must be trained to *see* the correct forms.

Words That Sound Alike

A somewhat different type of word trouble results because many groups of words are pronounced *exactly alike* but are spelled differently, as *principal* and *principle, loan* and *lone.*

Then there are other groups of words that are either pronounced *somewhat alike* or are spelled *somewhat alike*, as *respectfully* and *respectively, later* and *latter, formerly* and *formally.* These words are constantly confused. Imagine the surprise of a dictator at finding that his reference to a person as being "the soul of honesty" has become "the sole of honesty" in the transcript! Unit 10 is devoted to many of the most frequently confused words of this type. Your workbook contains others.

Different Sequences of Letters

The English language abounds in groups of words in which the same letters appear in one order in one word but in a different order in another word seemingly resembling the first in spelling, as *gauge* and *guard, diary* and *dairy, quiet* and *quite.* In most of these cases visual memory is the key to mastering the correct spellings. The following special groups of words of this type deserve your concentrated attention.

The "ie" and "ei" Words. We will begin with the classic *ie* or *ei* problem. It is safe to claim that there is not a person alive who has not been unsure of the sequence of these two letters in many words.

No better or simpler aid to mastering the varying spellings has been devised than the rhyme with which you are familiar:

> Put *i* before *e*,
> Except after *c*,
> Or when sounded like *a*,
> As in *neighbor* and *weigh*.

Take the first line, "Put *i* before *e*." This brief admonition means that the succession *ie* occurs more frequently than the other order. In this *ie* sequence the sound is very often long *ē*. Here are some of the words to which this line refers.

achieve	fierce	piece	shriek
belief	friend	pier	siege
believe	grief	pierce	sieve
brief	grieve	priest	thief
cashier	hygiene	relief	variety
chief	mischief	relieve	view
field	niece	shield	wield
			yield

Now take the second line of the jingle, "Except after *c*." In these words the opposite sequence—*ei*—occurs.

conc*ei*t   dec*ei*ve   rec*ei*ve
c*ei*ling   perc*ei*ve   rec*ei*pt

Now take the third and fourth lines, "Or when sounded like *a*, as in *neighbor* and *weigh*." Here are common words in which the sequence is sounded like long *a*.

*ei*ght   h*ei*r   r*ei*n   sl*ei*gh   w*ei*ght
fr*ei*ght r*ei*gn   sk*ei*n   th*ei*r

When you have mastered these three rules, concentrate on the following *exceptions* that you will have numerous occasions to use.

counterf*ei*t   l*ei*sure   surf*ei*t   defic*ie*nt
*ei*ther   n*ei*ther   w*ei*rd   effic*ie*nt
for*ei*gn   s*ei*ze   financ*ie*r profic*ie*nt
forf*ei*t   sover*ei*gn anc*ie*nt   suffic*ie*nt
h*ei*ght

In all these *ei, ie* words, penmanship is especially important as a means of overcoming confusions.

The "ain" or "ian (iar)" Words. The following brief list of frequently occurring words that are often confused in spelling should be memorized so well that you will write the correct sequences of letters automatically.

ain		**ian** (or **iar** °)		
Britain	certain	median	civilian	politician
captain	mountain	guardian	familiar	physician
chieftain	villain	brilliant	peculiar	

° Do not be misled and apply the same sequence to *similar*, however.

Similar Word Beginnings

Several groups of words have similar prefixes, and sometimes the addition of one of these prefixes to a word introduces a spelling problem.

A prefix is a syllable placed before a word or a root word in order to make another word of different meaning. For example, *bi*, which means "two," in *bicycle* and *bimonthly; re*, which means "again," in *redecorate* and *reorganize;* or *circum*, which means "around," in *circumference* and *circumstance*.

Ante and Anti. You've often heard someone say disgustedly of a person who opposed some action, "Of course, he's *anti* everything!"

You know that that person has the reputation of being against almost anything. So you should have no difficulty in remembering the meaning of the prefix *anti*. You can then easily remember that the *e*-ending prefix *ante* means "before." These words illustrate these meanings:

antedate	anteroom	antitrust
antecedent	antifreeze	antidote

Dis and Des. In your endeavor to distinguish between the word beginnings *dis* and *des*, you must realize that *dis* is a complete prefix either imparting a negative meaning or the sense of "away from," as in *disown* and *disqualify*. Sometimes the basic word to which the *dis* is joined starts with *s*. The result is two *s*'s. Study these sets of *dis*-beginning words:

disable	disbelieve	dissatisfy	dissimilar
disagree	discard	dissect	dissolve
disapprove	discharge	disservice	dissuade

In words that begin with *des*, on the other hand, only the *de* is the prefix. The *s* is the first letter of the base word. *De* means "down, away from," as in *debase*, *depose*. Here are some common words starting with *des* (*de* + *s*):

describe	despair	descend	destroy

The "in" and "en" Beginnings. Both *in* and *en* as prefixes mean "in, into." To understand the reasons for the choice of one over another would necessitate knowing several ancient languages from which the words were derived. You can choose the correct spellings by a much simpler method—by memory work.

en

enable	encumber	engross	enrage
enact	endear	enhance	enrich
encounter	endeavor	enjoy	enroll
encourage	endow	enlarge	ensue
encroach	engage	enlighten	entreat

in

inclose °	inflict	inland	insure °
include	inform	inquire °	instruct
incur	infringe	inroads	intrude
indorse °	inhale	insert	intrust °
induce	inject		

Note: The words starred may also be spelled with *en*. If you encounter these spellings, do not consider them incorrect.

You learned in Unit 6 that the prefix *in* can also be used to form a word opposite in meaning to another word. (See page 36.)

For, Fore, or Four. It will be well worth your time to memorize the principal words that start with *for, fore,* and *four.*

> **For:** forbear, forward, forget, forbid, forgo (to give up)
> **Fore:** foreclosure, foreman, foregoing (preceding), forecast
> **Four:** fourteen, foursome, fourth

Learning Exercises

1 **Spell Them.** The following words are spelled phonetically as they are often mispronounced. Spell each correctly.

a genuwine	**e** anartik	**h** genrilly
b lenth	**f** athaletic	**i** Febuary
c hoseree	**g** akumpnement	**j** histry
d tremenjus		

2 **Letters You Don't Hear.** The following brief definitions indicate frequently used words that contain silent letters. Spell the words. To help you, the number of letters in each word are given.

a A body of land surrounded by water   (6 letters)
b To strike or rap   (5 letters)
c Unruffled; still   (4 letters)
d The opposite of day   (5 letters)
e The branch of medicine that deals with mental disorders (10 letters)
f The opposite of right   (5 letters)
g A lien on property by which the property is made security for a loan   (8 letters)
h A song of praise   (4 letters)
i A twenty-fourth part of a day   (4 letters)
j A visitor   (5 letters)

3 **Same Letters in Different Order.** Here are ten pairs of definitions. The two words defined in each pair contain exactly the same letters, but in different order. What are the words?

a A white metal. A sharp, thin fragment.
b A pillar. To check; hold back.
c Haphazard. Relating to a cause.
d A heavy metal. To distribute; apportion.
e Stockings. Long-handled tools for weeding.
f Disabled in leg or foot. Opposite of female.

g A courageous deed. Destiny.

h Pertaining to army life. Pertaining to marriage.

i A slice of meat or of fish. A pointed stick driven into the ground.

j A spiritual being. The area formed when two straight lines meet.

4 **Is It "ei" or "ie"?** Should *ei* or *ie* appear in the following blank spaces to complete the correct spellings of these words?

a gr__ve   e bel__ve   h c__ling
b f__rce   f rev__w   i s__ge
c rec__pt   g w__ght   j s__ze
d n__ther

5 **Is It des- or dis-?** Do the following words start with *des* or *dis?*

a ____cribe   e ____pondent   h ____cend
b ____astrous   f ____ease   i ____pise
c ____appoint   g ____solve   j ____prove
d ____troy

6 **Is It for, fore, or four?** Should *for*, *fore*, or *four* appear in the blank spaces in the following words?

a ____close   f be____
b ____bear (to refrain) g ____ward
c ____man   h there____ (hence)
d ____teen   i ____some
e ____gone   j ____getful

7 **Choose the Correct Vowel.** Should an *a*, an *e*, or an *o* appear in the blank space in each of the following words?

a scen__ry   e mem__ry   h invent__ry
b flatt__ry   f machin__ry i satisfact__ry
c liter__ry   g volunt__ry j arbitr__ry
d advis__ry

Communication in Action: *Untangling Pompous Prose*

You are asked to revise and simplify a report that contains the following sentences. See if you can rewrite the paragraph in everyday language.

"Subsequent to March 1 Miss Garvin terminated her employment with this organization after a considerable number of years of continuous and exemplary service. Apropos to her departure Miss Garvin stated that she had procured an infinitely superior connection in an executive capacity. We must employ perseverance in endeavoring to obtain a suitable replacement of comparable caliber."

UNIT 9

Spelling and Vocabulary *(Continued)*

This unit deals with the spelling problems that arise when one wishes to add such endings as *ing, ed, ness, full, tion, ize, able,* and so on to a word.

Rules and Exceptions

At the outset you should know that it will be necessary for you to read and understand *some* rules that will help you with these problems; also, that some of the rules have important exceptions. The rules and the exceptions (these exceptions apply particularly to the material in the first part of this unit) have been made as simple as possible. Once you understand the rules and the reasons for the exceptions, you should be able to apply the information automatically. In other words, you should not have to stop and repeat the rule to yourself. Your mind's eye will have been trained to recognize the correct form for the type of situation encountered. This is visual memory.

The last part of the unit presents almost no rules. Mastery of the material presented there depends almost entirely on memory work.

When a Word Ends with Silent "e"

A vast number of our most commonly used words end with silent *e* (as *care, hope, please*). You will, therefore, have many occasions on which you will wish to add suffixes to these words in order to make derived words. These "manufactured words" may be adjectives, like *careful;* nouns, like *pleasure;* adverbs, like *wholly;* or the past tenses or present participles of regular verbs, as *hoped* and *hoping.* (You will learn more about these verb forms in Unit 14.)

You have noticed that sometimes the silent *e* appears in the derived word, as in *achievement,* but that sometimes it does not, as in *achieving.* Why?

Rule 1. When the added suffix begins with a *vowel,* in most cases the silent *e* is dropped.

> **use:** using, usable, usage
> **desire:** desiring, desirable, desirous

Exceptions to Rule 1. You will be less annoyed over the necessity of learning exceptions to spelling rules if you remember that there is usually an excellent reason for the exception. The chief reasons are: (*a*) to avoid the mispronunciation that might result if the regular rule were applied, or (*b*) to avoid confusion between the word being formed and some other word.

a. Consider a word ending with a soft-*c* sound, such as *peace.* If Rule 1 were followed and the *e* dropped before a suffix beginning with *a* (as *able*), some such ludicrous pronunciation as "peekable" would result. Likewise, in adding a suffix beginning with *o* (as *ous*) to a word with a soft-*g* sound, as *courage,* if the *e* were dropped the resulting "couragous" would be pronounced with a hard-*g* sound.

		But:
notice	noticing	noticeable
service	servicing	serviceable
pronounce	pronouncing	pronounceable
change	changing	changeable
advantage		advantageous
encourage	encouraging	
outrage		outrageous

b. In another group of words, the silent *e* is retained when *ing* is added, to prevent confusion with another similarly spelled word:

> **sing** (to produce music vocally): singing
> **singe** (to scorch): singeing
>
> **die** (to cease to live): dying
> **dye** (to color): dyeing

or to keep the root word apparent, as:

hoe: hoeing	**decree:** decreeing	**mile:** mileage
shoe: shoeing	**agree:** agreeing	**acre:** acreage
eye: eyeing	**see:** seeing	

Rule 2. When an added suffix begins with a consonant, in most cases the silent *e* is retained.

use: useful, useless   **tire:** tireless, tiresome
like: likely, likeness   **apprentice:** apprenticeship

Exception to Rule 2. Many of our most commonly used words, however, are exceptions to Rule 2. Memorize the following words and make them part of your spelling vocabulary.

acknowledge: acknowledgment   **due:** duly
judge: judgment   **true:** truly
argue: argument   **awe:** awful
abridge: abridgment   **whole:** wholly
nine: ninth   **wise:** wisdom

Doubling the Final Consonant

The rules that determine whether or not you will double the final consonant of a word when adding a suffix are really not so difficult as they are often represented to be. Consider the nature of that final consonant. It may be: (1) a single consonant, as in *run;* (2) a doubled consonant, as in *enroll;* or (3) two different consonants, as in *perform.* Most of the trouble arises with type 1, the single consonant. So suppose we dispose of the two simpler types—2 and 3—first.

Words Ending in a Double Consonant. When adding *any* suffix to a word that ends in a doubled consonant, just keep both these consonants.

dull: dullness, dulling
skill: skilled, skillful
install: installing, installment
embarrass: embarrassing, embarrassment

In a few cases where a tripled final consonant would result, however, drop one of the three identical letters.

dull: dully   **full:** fully

Words Ending in Two Different Consonants. When a word ends in more than one consonant, the final consonant is *not* doubled when a suffix beginning with a vowel is added.

perform: performance   **confirm:** confirming

Words Ending in One Consonant. Now for some rules that, if remembered, will make spelling easier for you.

The first thing to remember is that the following instructions apply only to changes made when suffixes that begin with *vowels* (*ing, ed, able, ance,* and so on) are added. No problems arise when the terminations begin with consonants (*ment, ness, ful,* and so on).

If you wish to add *ing* (or any vowel-beginning ending) to a word that ends in one consonant, consider:

1 Whether the word consists of *one* syllable only, in which the final consonant is preceded by *one* vowel, as *ship, plan, drop* (but not *need, brief,* which have two vowels).

2 Or whether, if the word consists of *more than one* syllable, the accent is on the last syllable, as in *occur, regret, begin* (but not *benefit* nor *open,* where the accent is on the first syllable).

If your word meets these two requirements, the last consonant is doubled.

ship: shipping, shipped, shipper, shippable
plan: planning, planned, planner
drop: dropping, dropped
occur: occurring, occurred, occurrence
regret: regretting, regretted, regrettable
begin: beginning, beginner

If your word does *not* meet requirements 1 and 2, the final consonant is *not* doubled.

brief: briefer, briefest, briefing, briefed
need: needed, needing, needy
benefit: benefited, benefiting
open: opening, opened, opener

A special rule applies to the addition of a suffix to a word that ends in the hard sound of *c,* as *picnic.* To preserve that hard sound, a *k* is added to the word before adding the suffix.

picnic: picnicking   **panic:** panicky   **frolic:** frolicksome

Now reread requirement 2. Notice the condition, "if the accent is on the *last* syllable." The accent *is* on the last syllable in *occur, regret,* and *begin;* also in *defer* and *confer.* But what happens to the accent in *defer* and *confer* when *ence* is added? The accent shifts to the first syllable of the new words, *def'erence, con'ference.* Hence the final consonant is not doubled.

 Suggestion: At this point stop and restudy this rule on doubling the final consonant. Remember that it is your ability to apply it automatically that will count.

Final "y"

Many of our common words end in *y: happy, beauty, money.* When deciding how to spell words formed by adding suffixes to these words, it is necessary to consider (1) whether the final *y* is preceded by a consonant or a vowel, and (2) whether the suffix begins with a consonant or a vowel.

1. If the *y* is preceded by a consonant, the *y* becomes *i* when any suffix except one that begins with *i* is added.

lonely: loneliness	**fly:** flying
mercy: merciful	**copy:** copying
defy: defiance	**modify:** modifying
history: historical	(*but* modifies)
satisfactory: satisfactorily	**accompany:** accompanying
comply: compliance	
pity: pitiful	

Exceptions:

shy: shyness	**lady:** ladylike
spry: spryly	**baby:** babyhood

2. On the other hand, if the *y* is preceded by a vowel, the *y* is usually retained before *all* suffixes.

obey: obeyed	**delay:** delayed
annoy: annoyance	**betray:** betrayal
gay: gayest	**array:** arrayed

Exceptions:

say: said	**day:** daily
lay: laid	**pay:** paid

The rules for forming the plurals of *y*-ending nouns are given in Unit 16.

"Never Trust" Endings

The remainder of this unit deals with several groups of word endings that sound alike but are spelled differently. When a word in any one of these groups is met, a "red light" should flash—a danger signal that warns that, unless you *know* that you know the right spelling of the word, you should consult your dictionary. If you do this conscientiously, you will gradually accumulate a stock of words that you can be sure of spelling correctly.

Never Trust a "seed" Ending. Let's master first the comparatively brief list of words that end with the sound of "seed."

Only one word ends in *sede: supersede.*

Only three words end in *ceed: exceed, proceed, succeed.* But—and this is important—words derived from these three words are spelled with only one *e,* as *excess, procedure, success.*

All other words of this group are spelled in *cede: precede, secede, accede, concede, intercede, recede,* and *cede* itself.

Never Trust a "shun" Ending. When you hear a word ending in the sound of "shun," remember that the spelling could be *tion, sion, cion, cian, tian, sian,* or *xion.* Words with these endings are very common; therefore, it will pay you to memorize the following illustrations.

tion

collection	distribution	illustration
completion	exhibition	opposition
communication	function	recognition
connection	invitation	repetition
distinction	location	

sion

aversion	conversion	expression
compulsion	discussion	persuasion
conclusion	expansion	provision

cion: coercion, suspicion
cian: electrician, optician, musician, physician
tian: Christian
sian: artesian
xion: complexion

Never Trust an "ize" Ending. The endings *ize, ise,* and *yze* are all pronounced "īz." *Ize*-ending words are the more numerous, however. The most frequent words in the three groups are:

ize

apologize	economize	standardize
authorize	humanize	summarize
characterize	memorize	systematize
criticize	realize	visualize

ise

advise	despise	revise
advertise	devise	supervise
arise	enterprise	surprise
comprise	exercise	surmise
compromise	merchandise	

yze

analyze   paralyze

As you can see, you will find almost daily use for many of these words; hence the necessity of making their correct spelling automatic.

Never Trust an "uhble" Ending. The adjective endings *able* and *ible* both signify "able to, capable of, fit, or worthy to be." The *able* form is the commoner of the two; but a great many of our everyday adjectives end in *ible*. (In a few cases dictionaries allow both spellings. Whenever two spellings are allowable, choose the preferred one.)

able

admirable	excusable	practicable
applicable	hospitable	perishable
capable	imaginable	suitable
changeable	incurable	teachable
comfortable	indispensable	tolerable
comparable	inevitable	unbearable
desirable	justifiable	unbelievable
disagreeable	laughable	unmistakable
durable	lovable	usable

Also, whenever you have occasion to invent an adjective with the meaning of "able," the *able* spelling should be used, as *get-at-able*.

ible

accessible	edible	invisible
admissible	feasible	legible
audible	forcible	perceptible
combustible	horrible	permissible
comprehensible	impossible	plausible
contemptible	incredible	responsible
corruptible	indelible	suggestible
discernible	indefensible	susceptible
divisible	intelligible	tangible
		terrible

Never Trust an "ance (ant)," "ence (ent)," or "ense" Ending. The noun endings *ance* or *ence*, with their corresponding adjective endings *ant* or *ent*, cause many confusions in spelling. There are also a few important nouns that end in *ense*. Here's your memory work.

ance (nouns)

assistance	perseverance	resistance
attendance	preponderance	significance
extravagance	reluctance	tolerance
intolerance	repentance	vigilance

ant (adjectives)

assistant *	perseverant	resistant
attendant *	preponderant	significant
extravagant	reluctant	tolerant
intolerant	repentant	vigilant

ence (nouns)

antecedence	existence	obedience
competence	independence	persistence
confidence	innocence	prevalence
eminence	insistence	prominence
		reverence

ent (adjectives)

antecedent *	existent	obedient
competent	independent	persistent
confident	innocent	prevalent
eminent	insistent	prominent
		reverent

ense: defense, dispense, expense, offense, pretense, suspense

* Also nouns.

Never Trust an "ar," "er," or "or" Ending. The noun endings *ar*, *er*, and *or* all indicate "one who, that which." It is not strange that it is difficult sometimes to remember which ending belongs with a certain word. This list is worth studying.

ar: beggar, liar, scholar, vicar

er

condenser	eraser	officer
consumer	manufacturer	subscriber
employer	messenger	thinker

or

administrator	conductor	proprietor
ancestor	debtor	visitor
benefactor	distributor	

Never Trust an "ary," "ery" Ending. Several important words end in *ery*; others in *ary*.

ary: notary, actuary, dictionary, secretary, dignitary
ery: millinery, stationery, cemetery, confectionery, monastery

Never Trust an "ous," "ious," or "eous" Ending. Adjectives ending in *ous*, which signifies "full of, having"—as in *nervous*—are very common. Often, however, an *e* or an *i* precedes the *ous* ending. Uncertainty as to the correct letter will be avoided by remembering this list of commonly used adjectives.

ious		eous
avaricious	gracious	courteous
cautious	judicious	hideous
copious	religious	instantaneous
conscious	spacious	gorgeous
conscientious	suspicious	miscellaneous
curious	tedious	simultaneous
delicious	various	
dubious	vicious	

Other "Never Trust" Endings. In addition to the commonly confused word endings just studied, there are other groups. You may find it helpful to prepare your own personal list of words falling into these groups:

1. Endings pronounced "shunt," spelled sometimes *cient* (as *ancient*) and sometimes *tient* (*patient*)

2. Endings pronounced "an" (a long *a* sound), sometimes spelled *ain* (as *brain, chain, gain, pain*) and sometimes *ane* (as *cane, crane, plane*)

3. Endings pronounced "shul," sometimes spelled *cial* (as *special*) and sometimes *tial* (as *partial*)

4. Endings pronounced "us," sometimes spelled *us* for the noun forms (as *fungus*) but *ous* for the adjective form (*fungous*)

5. Words that end in *el* (as *label, model, nickel*) or in *le* (as *whistle, giggle*)

6. Words that end in *ledge* (as *knowledge*) or in *lege* (as *college, allege, privilege*)

Learning Exercises

1 Add a Syllable. How are the following words spelled when the syllables indicated are added?

a stop + ing
b occur + ence
c cancel + ed
d credit + or
e bag + age
f perform + ance
g drug + ist
h brief + est
i control + able
j install + ment

2 **Take Your Pick.** Which words in the following ten lines are misspelled? Respell them.

 a requirement, truely, changeless, feild
 b managment, enterprize, suitable, recording
 c meaning, acheive, regretable, curious
 d becomeing, amplifier, payed, resistence
 e approximately, excelence, analize, patience
 f arguement, beged, terrible, complexion
 g receipt, solicitted, embarrassment, ancester
 h merryly, agreeing, ladilike, superceed
 i envyous, location, forgivness, daily
 j changeable, label, fully, interruptting

3 **"Shun" These Words.** Add the termination pronounced "shun" to each of the following words.

 a deprecia＿＿＿   **d** colli＿＿   **g** comple＿＿＿
 b dimen＿＿   **e** expul＿＿   **h** deduc＿＿
 c resigna＿＿   **f** techni＿＿   **i** occas＿＿

4 **That "ize" Ending.** Choose *ize, ise,* or *yze* for the endings of the following words.

 a item＿＿   **d** monopol＿＿   **g** util＿＿
 b ar＿＿   **e** franch＿＿   **h** emphas＿＿
 c civil＿＿   **f** disgu＿＿   **i** anal＿＿

5 **How Is "uhble" Spelled?** How are the following words spelled when the "uhble"-sounding suffix is added?

 a receive＿＿   **d** accept＿＿   **g** advise＿＿
 b convert＿＿   **e** reverse＿＿   **h** sense＿＿
 c sale＿＿   **f** value＿＿   **i** move＿＿

6 **Going to "seed."** Which of the following words ending with the sound of "seed" are misspelled?

 a precede   **f** receed
 b superceed   **g** exceed
 c intercede   **h** cede (to assign)
 d seed (the grain of plants)   **i** sesede
 e succeed   **j** procede

7 **Does It End with "ance" or "ence"?** Should *ance* or *ence* be added to the following?

a accord____	**d** resembl____	**g** correspond____
b dilig____	**e** appli____	**h** abund____
c experi____	**f** remembr____	**i** evid____

8 **Do They End with "er," "or," or "ar"?** Should *er, or,* or *ar* be added to the following?

a counsel____	**d** collect____	**g** supervis____
b gramm____	**e** propell____	**h** profess____
c betray____	**f** advertis____	**i** execut____

Communication in Action: *Making Introductions*

How would you introduce each of the following: (1) a young man to an older lady? (2) a boy and girl the same age? (3) a fellow accountant (man) to a very important older business or government executive? (4) a young stenographer (girl, aged twenty) to an older woman? Enact the various situations described.

UNIT 10

Pitfalls in Word Usage

Words Often Confused

An amazing number of words in the English language are confused because they sound or look alike but have different spellings and different meanings. Some of these words are pronounced *exactly alike*, as *break* (to shatter) and *brake* (a device to stop motion). Some *sound somewhat alike*, as *respectively* (in the order given), *respectfully* (courteously), and *respectably* (in a conventionally correct manner). Others *look somewhat alike*. They may contain the same letters but in different order, as *diary* (a daily record) and *dairy* (a business that produces milk, butter, and cheese). One may have one letter where the other has two, as *ad* (the shortened form of *advertisement*) and *add* (to increase). Or they may have other superficial resemblances, as *facetious* (witty) and *fictitious* (like fiction). This unit deals with a few of the groups of words often confused. Your workbook contains additional groups. There are many, many more, however.

How to Study Word Confusions

To master the following groups of words that are often confused:

1. Notice *each letter* in each word in each group; that is, do not merely glance at the words. Careful examination of the members of a word group will reveal the distinguishing differences in the words—whether one or more letters differ, whether the same letters occur but in different order, whether a letter is doubled in one word but not in another, and so on.

2. Read the comments enclosed in parentheses. These will give you valuable help in spotting some of the differences that determine the word to be chosen. For example:

a. Pronunciation. Often the phonetic spelling of a word instantly reveals whether the word is the one sought. (See *loose* and *lose* on page 72.)

b. Accent. Accent alone may be the key to your problem. (See *defer* and *differ* on page 71.)

c. Part of speech. Knowing the part of speech of the word you seek often determines the form to choose. Therefore, note the abbreviations *n., v., adj., adv., prep.* (See *principle, principal* on page 71.)

3. Read the brief definitions thoughtfully. These definitions are intended as *pointers* to the distinctions in meaning. For complete definitions, consult your dictionary.

4. Read thoughtfully the sentences or phrases incorporating the words presented. Illustrations of how the words may be used often reveal the true distinctions between the words more clearly than do the definitions.

5. Study the "Memory Tricks." Experienced writers and editors often employ these devices to help them decide on questioned spellings. (See *advice* on page 69.)

6. Head one section of your personal notebook "Word Confusions," and form the habit of entering there any new group of words that you encounter. Brief definitions and illustrations should be included. Also, enter any additional sentences that you find that illustrate the use of the words presented in these units. Some students

find it helpful to underscore the letters that are the keys to the differences in meaning of the words in a group; for example, a<u>cc</u>ept, <u>e</u>xcept, ex<u>pe</u>ct.

Learning Exercises

Learning Exercises for this unit will be found in the workbook. If you are not using the workbook, write a sentence for each of the words defined in this unit, to show that you understand them.

I

1 accept To approve; receive with favor. "We *accept* your bid."
  except (prep.) Other than. "Everyone *except* Mary passed." (v.) To exclude. "In enforcing this rule, we can *except* no one."
  expect To look forward to. "I *expect* to be graduated in June."
2 accede To comply with. "We gladly *accede* to your request."
  exceed To surpass. "Our department budget *exceeds* $50,000."
3 advice (n.; rhymes with *ice*) Information; recommendation. "I will seek the *advice* of a specialist." **Memory Trick:** Are you cool to adv*ice*?
  advise (v.; sound of *ize*) To counsel. "He *advised* me to consult an attorney."
4 affect (always v.) To influence. "Does the strike *affect* you?" To feign. "She *affects* the manners of a prima donna."
  effect (v.) To bring about. "The new treatments have *effected* a cure." (n.) Result. "The soothing *effect* of music." **Memory Trick:** Recall the expression "cause and effect." If *cause* fits the meaning of your sentence, use *effect*.
5 basis A fundamental principle. "Character is the *basis* for credit."
  bases (pl. both of *basis* and of *base*, the foundation on which something rests) "Respect and trust are the *bases* of a happy marriage." "The *bases* for the statues must be firm."
6 capitol The *building* in which a legislature meets. Capitalized only for the building in Washington, D.C., where Congress meets. **Memory Trick:** Visualize the dome of our beautiful Capit*ol*. Both words contain an *o*.
  capital (for all other uses, both n. and adj.) "*Capital* punishment." "*Capital* letters." "A *capital* idea." "Boston is the *capital* (the city) of Massachusetts." "All his *capital* is in long-term bonds." "The *capital* (top part) of a column."
7 complement Something that completes. "Our camp has its full

complement of counselors." ***Memory Trick:*** *Complement* is derived from *complete*.

compliment (n.) A flattering remark or attention. "Please accept these roses with our *compliments*." (v.) To express approval. "We *compliment* you on your record."

8 formally In a formal manner. "He has not yet *formally* accepted the nomination."

formerly Previously. "He was *formerly* a professor of economics."

II

1 cite To quote; to refer to. "He *cited* many sources for his statistics."

site Location. "The *site* for the new library." ***Memory Trick:*** Connect the *s* in *site* with the *s* in *situation*.

sight (n.) Vision. "Following the accident, he had *sight* in only one eye." (v.) To see. "At last we *sighted* land."

2 council An assembly that deliberates on affairs. "The city *Council*." A member of a council is a *councilor*.

counsel (n.) Advice. "We will seek the *counsel* of a specialist." A lawyer. "The *counsel* for the defendant." A lawyer who conducts cases in court is a *counselor*. (v.) To give advice, especially on important matters. "My uncle *counseled* me not to act hastily in the matter."

consul (kŏn′sul) A government official in a foreign country appointed to look after the interests of his country's citizens there. "I have a letter of introduction to the American *consul* in Rome."

3 desert (dē-zurt′; v.) To abandon. "To *desert* a friend in need." (n.; usually in pl.) Deserved punishment. "He got his just *deserts* for betraying a friend."

desert (dĕz′ert) Barren land.

dessert (dĭ-zurt′) The last course of a meal.

4 dye (n.) A stain or color. (v.) To stain or color. (past, *dyed;* participle, *dyeing*)

die (n.) A tool for molding or shaping; one of a pair of dice. (v.) To cease living; to wither. (past, *died;* participle, *dying*)

5 personal (per′son-al) Belonging to a particular person. "One's *personal* appearance." "*Personal* property."

personnel (per-son-nel′) The staff. "We are proud of the attainments of our *personnel*."

6 precede To go before. "The faculty *preceded* the seniors in procession."

proceed To advance. "Let us *proceed* to the next matter of business." ***Memory Trick:*** Keep in mind the meaning of the prefixes *pre* and *pro*. *Pre* means "before," as in *prewar, pre-school; pro* means "forward," as in *progress*.

7 principle (n. only) General truth; rule of conduct. "The *principles* of mathematics." "A man of high *principles*." **Memory Trick:** Connect the *le* in *rule* with the *le* in *principle*.

principal (for all other meanings) (adj.) Chief. "The *principal* reason for the failure." (n.) A chief person or thing. "*Principal* of our high school." Money on which interest is paid or income received. "I wish to receive a larger interest from my *principal*." One who hires another to act for him. "An agent has power to make contracts for his *principal*."

8 realty Real estate.

reality (rē-ăl'ĭ-tĭ) That which is real. "In *reality*, this material is much more expensive than the other."

III

1 accent (ac'cent; n. and v.) Stress in speaking or writing. "The *accent* is on the first syllable of *interesting*." "*Accent* the first note sharply."

ascent (as-cent') A rising or climbing. "The *ascent* to the summit."

assent (as-sent'; n. and v.) Agree. "We *assent* to the changes suggested in the manuscript." "Please get Mr. Ward's *assent* in writing."

2 choose To select; to prefer. "You may *choose* any one of several items."

chews Masticates.

chose (chōz) Did choose. "Last year the winner *chose* a camera."

3 close (klōz; v.) To shut. "Please *close* the window." (n.) The end. "At the *close* of the summer season." (klōs; adj.) Dense; near; tight. "The air in this room is *close*." "A *close*-fitting jacket." "Their cottage is *close* by."

clothes (klōthz) Wearing apparel.

cloths (klŏths) Fabrics. "A sale of imported *cloths*." "Table-*cloths* and napkins."

4 defer (de-fer') To put off. "I plan to *defer* my vacation for a month." To yield to authority. "We think it wise to *defer* to his judgment in this matter."

differ (dif'fer) To disagree; to be unlike. "The twins *differ* both in temperament and in appearance."

5 lead (lĕd; n.) A heavy metal. (lēd; v.) To guide. "The blind man asked me to *lead* him across the street."

led (lĕd) Did lead. "The drum majorette *led* our school parade."

6 loose (lōōs; adj.) Unfastened; not compact. "A *loose*-leaf note-book." "*Loose* powder." "A *loose* screw." (v.) To set free. "*Loose* the dog."

lose (lōōz; v.) To mislay; fail to win; suffer the loss of. "I'd *lose* my head if it weren't fastened on." "I always *lose* at cards." "Don't *lose* sleep over that small matter."

lost (adj.) Missing. "Keeping within a budget is a *lost* cause in our household!" (v.) Did lose. "Has anyone *lost* a ring?"

7 right (adj.) Correct. "You know that's not the *right* answer!" (n.) Privilege. "Next year I shall have the *right* to vote."

rite Ceremony. "He received the last *rites* of the Church."

write To inscribe. "Please *write* in my autograph album."

wright (usually in compounds) A workman. "A wheel*wright*."

8 stationery Writing paper. *Memory Trick:* Connect the *e* in *paper* with the *e* in *stationery*.

stationary Fixed in position. "A *stationary* wall telephone is bet-ter suited to some locations than a desk phone."

IV

The words in the following groups are often confused because of lack of attention to the pronunciation of the final letters of the words. As you study these words, overemphasize the endings until your ear learns to detect the differences in the sounds.

1 correspondence Letters. "Our *correspondence* has always been promptly handled."

correspondents Persons conducting correspondence. "The letters from our *correspondents* in the Far East are sometimes amus-ing."

corespondents (kō'rē-spŏn'dĕnts) Parties in divorce suits. "Strangely enough, the *corespondents* in the two suits were sisters."

2 commence (com-mence') To begin.

comments (com'ments) Remarks. "He plans to *commence* his talk with several favorable *comments* recently heard."

3 dense Thick, compact. "A *dense* fog drifted in from the sea."

dents Small hollows resulting from a blow. "It will be costly to remove the *dents* from this bracelet."

4 precedence (prē-sēd'ens) Priority in time or rank. "At formal functions, much attention is given to *precedence*."

precedents (prĕs'e-dents) Established rules. "There are no *precedents* to guide us in this case."

5 **presence** Being present; bearing; mien. "Your *presence* is requested." "A dignified *presence*."

   presents Gifts.

6 **residence** A house; dwelling place.

   residents Those living in a place. "They are all *residents* of Houston."

7 **superintendence** Management. "Under the *superintendence* of a district manager."

   superintendents Supervisors. "Mr. Little is attending the convention of school *superintendents* at Atlantic City."

8 **dependence** Reliance; trust. "Put no *dependence* on his promises."

   dependents Persons who rely on others for support. "Since I have no *dependents*, I do not have your problems."

Communication in Action: *Getting the Facts*

A customer, behind in his installments, has been threatened by letter with repossession of his furniture. He comes to you, a clerk in the credit department, waving the letter and shouting, "You can't take my furniture back unless you return the $150 in payments I've made." His installment contract reads: "I, the lessee, hereby rent from the Ace Furniture Company the goods listed above. . . . The lessors agree that, if at the end of the term of the lease, the lessee has fulfilled all covenants, they will convey a free and clear title of the above articles to the lessee." What will you say to this customer? Be sure you understand the contract. *Hint:* Your company does not want to take back the furniture.

3

SPEECH
AS A
COMMUNI-
CATION
ART

UNIT 11

Setting the Stage

How often and for how long do you talk during your waking hours? If you are in school, you recite in class, contribute to discussions, give oral reports. Your success in extracurricular activities depends on the quality of ideas you express in speech. At other times you talk socially with your classmates, if only to ask, "Wodja do lasnight?" If you are in an office, for eight hours of the day you talk to give instructions or explanations, to ask questions, to promote good business relations, to sell goods or services, to sell an idea, or, most important of all, to sell yourself as a person.

You talk much more and much more often than you write; therefore, you are measured more by your speech than by your writing. Your speech is something that is individually and particularly yours; your speech is you. To receive top rating, you need special training in oral communication. The words you use, the way you put them together, your tone, diction, and grammar—all add up to a "you" that can be accurately rated. You need to know how to converse, how to be a good discussion group member. You need to know what to say and how to say it.

Effective speech, however, depends on factors other than the spoken word. For example, the actors in a Broadway play would surely have their lines learned and polished to the highest degree. Now suppose that the plot builds up to a very tender love scene and suppose that the scene is played in a setting of bare mountains and falling snow. With this background the beauty of the words would be lost on an audience. But, of course, you would never see anything like this. Producers and directors are experts in creating surroundings that heighten the effect of words, so this scene would be played in a setting of moonlight, flowers, and soft, dreamy music.

The example just given, although somewhat far-fetched, does illustrate the point that atmosphere effects can contribute much to successful speaking. Therefore, before learning to speak effectively, you need to study the techniques of creating a favorable impression that will set the stage for best reception of what you say. Setting the stage is the topic of this first unit in oral communication.

Now, an impression is, of course, the sum total of many factors, not a step-by-step process. Learning, however, involves studying and mastering separate elements. The elements that merge into the sum total of making a favorable impression are:

1. Dress and grooming
2. Posture and carriage
3. Facial expressions
4. Good manners
5. Mannerisms

Dress and Grooming

Is there such a thing as "business dress"? Indeed there is, and the young man or young woman who chooses and wears clothing appropriate for an office can be sure that one aspect of making a favorable impression is under control.

The young man wears a jacket, a suit jacket or a sport jacket. The sport jacket is of a conservative pattern, in subdued colors. He has too much good taste to wear a "loud" jacket. He wears a necktie, once more exercising good taste in the selection of pattern and color; and the color of his socks matches his tie. He wears shoes, real shoes, not the casual type that he wears during his leisure time. He does not wear the first shirt his hand grabs in the early morning, for he would not spoil the effect of his appearance by wearing to the office a shirt that he puts on for his lighter moments.

The knowledgeable young man also realizes that all the thought and care devoted to suitable clothing will amount to nothing unless he is well groomed. His skin, then, has that scrubbed look. His teeth and breath are clean. His suits are always brushed, clean, and pressed; and his shoes gleam. His nails are clean and clipped; his hair is brushed. He refuses to wear a shirt that shows any sign of soil. He puts a fresh handkerchief into his pocket before leaving home each day. This is the fellow whose appearance is described as "impeccable."

The young lady wears a suit, a skirt and blouse, or a dress that is becoming and fashionable but not striking. Her aim is to be attractively dressed without being showy. Her nail polish is of neutral color; her make-up is not noticeable; her hair shows evidences of good care. Above all, she is clean, fresh, and dainty; and it is a pleasure just to have her in the office.

The hallmark of suitable dress and grooming, both for men and for women, is an unobtrusive attractiveness, refinement, and conservatism.

Posture and Carriage

The effect you wish to create by wearing carefully chosen clothing can be completely destroyed if you do not sit, stand, and walk correctly. The fit and the hang of a garment are right only if posture and carriage are good. It would seem, then, that anyone who takes pride in his appearance would analyze his own sitting, standing, and walking habits and would work hard to make any needed improvements.

The main reason, however, for studying correct posture and carriage is that the way you carry yourself tells stories about your personality and character. Do you sprawl when you sit? Then you are lazy. When you stand, do you habitually rest all your weight on one leg and hip? Then you tire or lose interest quickly and have no drive. When you walk, do you shuffle along with your head down? If so, you must be the kind of person who does not work well with others; and you very definitely show that you have no force of character.

It may well be that the tales told by your posture and carriage are false. For instance, although you do have the habit of lolling in a chair, you are not lazy. But such is the impression you give, and erasing the impression of laziness will be very difficult. You need, accordingly, to study the following discussion of good posture and carriage so that you will be able to make an impression that is favorable—and true!

When you get ready to sit, bend your joints and sit. Do not plop into a chair after the manner of a rag doll. Once in the chair, sit up straight—not rigidly, but not slumped, either. For correct sitting posture the best practice is to be sure that the end of your spine touches the back of the chair. Girls will remember that, except in the privacy of their own homes, ladies cross their legs only at the ankles. A little practice in taking a seat and in sitting correctly will pay dividends.

The person who stands correctly stands tall. His shoulders are in line with the rest of his body, not too far back, not caved in toward his chest. He holds himself erect, but not ramrod-stiff. He has formed the standing habit of distributing his weight evenly on both feet, for he knows that otherwise he will be continually shifting position. The story told by his standing position is that he is an honest, upright person.

There are as many variations in the manner of walking as there are people who walk. There is the swagger type, the rock-and-roll type, the frightened-bunny type, the casual type, and many, many others. You will find that it is impossible to change completely your own distinctive style of walking. You can, however, learn just one thing that will help. With steps neither too long nor too short, neither too fast nor too slow, walk as though you had somewhere to go—and you intended to get there without stopping at way stations! Walking purposefully, you will give an impression of being ambitious, industrious, and self-directing.

Facial Expressions

Part of the education of an aspiring young actor or actress consists of practicing the different facial expressions that reflect the various emotions—joy, fear, pleasure, sorrow, and so on. If, through intelligent practice, the actor can change his facial expression, you, too, can change yours if you so desire. First, of course, you need to know what kind of expression creates a favorable impression. You need some pointers on how to assume such an expression. You need, too, to know where your own shortcomings are. And you need to practice before a mirror.

A pleasant, interested, alive-looking expression is a winning expression. Even a hasty glance at an expression like this would generate a feeling of warmth, of liking. In an interview or in a meeting, conference, or other working situation, pleasant facial expressions promote pleasant relationships. Fortunate, indeed, are those of you who naturally and habitually have this type of facial expression. You are the extroverts, the ones who are interested in and enjoy other people; and you let your interest and enjoyment shine through. You represent, however, a very small minority of our population.

Too many persons by their expressions tell a story of indifference or boredom or discontent or, possibly, tell nothing at all. Some very intelligent people are afflicted with shyness, which they try to hide behind a "dead-pan" or a bored facial expression. These are the ones who will profit by a study of the following discussion.

The eyes are the focal point of facial expression, as you can prove by doing this: Stand in front of a mirror and think of something very pleasant that has happened to you recently. Do you see how your eyes light up and with them your whole face? Now pretend that a salesman is showing you models of small cars and that you are shopping for such a car. If you are good at make-believe, your eyes will reflect your intense interest. With practice, you will find that it is not necessary to smile or grin in order to look pleasant but that it is necessary to *feel* pleasant. However, if you have a warm, attractive smile, use it when the occasion warrants.

Now suppose that you are shy and that you do not look at the person who is talking to you. Since he cannot see your eyes, he is unable to form a favorable opinion of your personality and disposition; and you run the risk of being judged as undesirable. For instance, there are interviewers who will not hire an applicant whose eyes are everywhere except on the interviewer's face. They think that this habit indicates that the applicant is sly, shifty. So, after you have worked to acquire a facial expression that will contribute to your advancement, be sure to look at people. Otherwise, your efforts will have been wasted.

Learning to look pleasant, interested, and alert is purely an individual problem. Only you can study your own expression, and only you can put in the practice time necessary to achieve the results you wish. You are the one who must consciously assume the facial expression that produces a favorable impression. It is you who must remember to look at people when you talk to them. The rewards, also, are yours alone. One of the rewards is that, in a relatively short time, you will find that your improved facial expression will become your habitual expression.

Good Manners

Another and very important factor in creating a favorable impression is the manifestation of good manners. The atmosphere of polish that surrounds the fortunate people who quite naturally do and say the correct thing at the correct time commands the respect and admiration of all who have an opportunity to observe them. These models of good taste and breeding, however, did not reach the state of being natural without learning and practice and without brushing up at intervals. Your own manners may be excellent, but even you may need to study the following discussion and the suggestions given.

The basis of good manners is courtesy, and the basis of courtesy is consideration for others. Without courtesy, good manners are only a veneer. This is the opinion held by many men whose jobs involve rating and grading people. For example, there was the interviewer who, when an applicant entered his office, dropped a book, paper, or pen and watched to see whether that applicant would instinctively pick it up or would walk over it. This was the device he used to rate good manners, the good manners based on natural courtesy rather than on the principles contained in a book of etiquette.

Do not, however, minimize the importance of knowing and observing the rules of etiquette. Natural courtesy, while basic, is not enough for correct behavior. You must know such things as how to make introductions and acknowledge introductions properly. You should know when it is appropriate for a man to shake hands and for a lady to shake hands; when it is proper for a man to stand and when it is proper for a lady to stand. You should, in short, be familiar with all the rules that govern correct social and business relationships. This means that you need to know and to review periodically the contents of an etiquette book. There are some slight differences between social and office etiquette, and these you can learn by studying a book on office etiquette.

Lack of space here prohibits a full discussion of social correctness, but there are two very practical suggestions that can be given. The first has to do with making introductions. Do not try to learn the various rules—presenting a man to a lady, a younger to an older person, and so on. Just determine quickly which of the two people you wish to honor or which is the more important. Then say that person's name *first*. By so doing, you will find your introduction procedures automatically correct. For instance, if you were introducing anybody at all to your mother, you would know immediately which is the more important and would say, "Mother, may I present; Mother, I'd like you to know; or Mother, this is . . . ." If you wished to introduce your boss, Mr. Martin, and a young man who is with you, you would say, "Mr. Martin, ..." You might call this a quick trick that will prevent those first embarrassing moments of silence that occur while you are trying to remember the various methods of presentation.

The second suggestion is that you learn to shake hands in a manner that will give an impression of decision and determination, of having a mind of your own. You will clasp hands firmly, with no pump-handle arm motion. Now "firmly" does not mean "bone crushing." You use just enough hand pressure to avoid having your acquaintance think that he got hold of a dead fish by mistake. Your handclasp may be more important to you than you realize. You may be shaking hands with one of those people who staunchly maintain that a handclasp tells all about character and ability. If this act tells a story, let that tale be favorable to you.

Mannerisms

The young man who sits at the desk beside yours is tops in grooming, posture, manners, and facial expressions, isn't he? But what about his habit of cracking his knuckles? How long do you think you can stand this continual pop, pop, pop? And what about the new girl who, when she comes to tell you something, stands behind you and breathes down your neck? And so it goes. A sincere, ambitious young person works very hard to improve himself and still is defeated by some defect of which he is not aware.

Logically, then, a finishing touch to your study of the elements of creating a favorable impression is a study of your own mannerisms. In your stage setting there must be nothing to detract from the impression you have worked so hard to produce. You will find that the recommended self-study is quite difficult because you may have distracting, annoying, or tiresome habits and not perceive that you have them. For best results, study first the people around you. Watch to see if they have any behavior quirks. Whenever you observe a mannerism that you think is objectionable, say to yourself, "Do I do that?" After you have had practice in looking for these faults in others, you will gradually see any faults that you yourself may have. Successful self-improvement seems to follow the pattern of seeing deficiencies of others before becoming aware of and correcting your own.

Studying your own personal mannerisms and eliminating any that are undesirable are necessary tasks if you wish to protect your investment. There is little profit in presenting a fine appearance and in being polite and well mannered if you consistently do something that rasps the nerves of your colleagues.

Learning Exercises

1 Ask yourself the following questions to determine how you set your stage for speaking. Answer each question with "usually," "sometimes," or "seldom." Check your answers with members of the class to see whether they agree with you. Then, from your answers, make a list of the items that you need to practice.

A. *My Over-All Personality*

1 Am I likable and congenial so that other people want to be around me?

2 Am I optimistic instead of pessimistic or gloomy when presented with a new problem or a new situation?

3 Do I like to be with other people and make the first move to meet new people?

4 Do I look for ways to pay genuine compliments about people to themselves and to others?

5 Am I tolerant of the way other people act or think, avoiding direct criticism or argument?

B. First Impressions

1 Do I take the initiative to meet, greet, and introduce strangers?
2 Am I consciously thinking about the other person's interests and his comforts (instead of my own) when I talk with him?
3 Do I try to find ways of being helpful to the other person when I talk with him?
4 Do I avoid controversial topics when I enter a conversation with a new friend?
5 Do I avoid talking about personal aches and pains, strong personal likes or dislikes, rumors and personal prejudices?

C. My Personal Appearance

1 Do I know what appropriate business dress is?
2 Do I usually feel well dressed without being distracting?
3 Are my clothes clean, pressed, and in good repair when I wear them?
4 Do I practice strict personal rules of cleanliness and good grooming?
5 Do my personal health habits contribute to my appearance?

D. My Facial Expressions

1 When I first meet people, does my facial expression indicate genuine interest instead of feigned interest?
2 Am I usually willing to reveal how I feel through my facial expressions instead of covering my feelings with a noncommittal, dead-pan expression?
3 Do my facial expressions reflect the way I want to be understood?
4 Do I avoid showing indifference toward others in my facial expressions?
5 Do I refrain from reflecting my own personal problems or sad feelings in my facial expressions?

E. My Mannerisms

1 Do I present an attitude of alertness, instead of an "I don't care" attitude, in the way I move about?
2 Do my movements indicate a quiet poise and a purposefulness in living as opposed to an uncertain, frightened, or nervous outlook?
3 Is my posture straight without being stiff?
4 When I walk, is my weight well distributed on both legs?
5 Do I avoid all meaningless, jerking movements of the body and hands when I talk?

2 Designate a day as "Business Dress and Grooming Day." As a result of a class discussion, make a list of "Tips on Business Dress and Grooming" from the good characteristics of dress and grooming you observe among your classmates.

3 In pantomime, try to express before the class some mannerisms of walk, hand movements, or facial expressions that distract and impede communication. Then, express the opposite positive characteristic that would help you set a positive stage for your speech. Was the class able to guess the point you were trying to make?

Vocabulary and Spelling Refreshers

Special refresher exercises designed to help you improve and build your vocabulary and spelling skills appear following the Learning Exercises beginning with this unit and continuing to the end of the textbook. Completion of these exercises is most important to your progress and to your future success in your job.

In each unit, the first of these special exercises lists "Words Often Confused." Two groups of such words are given; for example, *feet, feat; grate, great.* For each of these groups, you are to—

1. Look up *both* words in your dictionary. Note, first, whether there is a difference in pronunciation. Then read the definitions carefully.

2. For each word write a meaningful sentence—one that reveals the use of the word in its correct meaning. For example:

> **Meaningful:** To have completed four years of college work in three years is a feat indeed.
> **Not meaningful:** He accomplished a great feat.

Following the "Words Often Confused" exercise are two other types of special exercises. These deal with the problems of word usage and of spelling. Instructions accompany each of these.

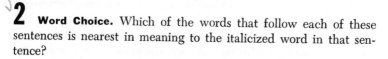

1 **Words Often Confused.** Later, latter; biannual, biennial.

2 **Word Choice.** Which of the words that follow each of these sentences is nearest in meaning to the italicized word in that sentence?

> **a** Her reply to his question was most *perfunctory.* (secretive, exhaustive, mechanical, insolent)

b The suggestion that he is well fitted for the job is *ludicrous*. (imposing, ridiculous, irresponsible, indefinite)

c Do not *procrastinate* longer if you expect to win. (delay, criticize, daydream, rebel)

3 **Geographic Spelling Demons.** Which of the following place names are misspelled?

a Mississippi   **c** Gloucester, Mass.   **e** Harrisburg, Pa.
b Ashville, N. C.   **d** Phillipines   **f** Pittsburg, Pa.

Communication in Action: *Handling a Difficult Telephone Caller*

A policyholder in the insurance company where you work telephones, asking for your boss, Mr. Halleck. You tell the caller that Mr. Halleck is out of the office for the day. The policyholder insists on telling you his troubles. He is irate because your company purchased three new typewriters from a competing office machines firm. He wonders why, since he is a policyholder in your company, he is not given more consideration; and he threatens to cancel his insurance. Exactly what would you say to the caller? Write a summary of the conversation for your employer.

UNIT 12

Making Yourself Understood

Olga is an exchange student from Sweden—young, attractive, demure—with a wholesome appearance, a pleasant expression—the kind of person you'd thoroughly enjoy knowing. Her voice is almost musical as she speaks. But, beyond the nodding acknowledgment of your introduction, you and she are at a loss to develop the warm, friendly relationship you both desire. Although her voice is beautiful (and yours is pleasant, too), her words are not intelligible to you, as yours are not to her. You see, Olga does not speak English; and you do not speak her language. This much is clear from your unsatisfactory encounter with Olga: good human relations require more than just a beautiful voice; they also require intelligible speech.

The problem of being understood, though, is not confined, as in Olga's case, to those with a language barrier. Careless speakers everywhere are not understood or are misunderstood, although they profess to speak English. Consider these gems of unintelligible English: "Jeet?" "Warejugo?" "Wadjuhav?" Translated, the questions were intended to mean—as you have probably guessed: "Did you eat?" "Where did you go?" "What did you have?" These examples are exaggerated; only the speech of a few completely uneducated persons would be so unintelligible. But are you sure that your listeners can always clearly understand (or what is even more important, will not misunderstand) you? Any carelessness in your speaking should be found and eliminated immediately; for any fault of speech that causes others to misunderstand you will detract from your effectiveness in both your business and your social life.

As an employee in business, you cannot afford to be misunderstood. Any unintelligible words that you speak detract from the prestige, the good will, and the profits of your company. For example, the young man who greets customers with a mumbled "Wadjuwan?" will soon find himself transferred to the stock room. Thus isolated from customers, he will not be able to hurt the company through poor human relations. A single careless lapse of intelligibility is just as disastrous. Consider the case of the customer

Lew Merrim, Monkmeyer Press Photo Service

Every employee in a business office must possess the ability to make himself understood. Practice the principles outlined in these units so that *you* may be ready to meet the challenge!

who canceled a large order because it was not delivered on the twenty-second of the month, as he understood it to be promised. In a careless moment the salesman had slurred "twenty-seventh," which was misunderstood as "twenty-second." Yes, business employees must command language that is so clear and so precise that customers cannot misunderstand. Speech that is perfectly intelligible promotes and increases good human relations.

Clear and immediately understandable speech is important in your personal and social relations, too. Have you ever angered a friend or hurt the feelings of an acquaintance because what you said was misunderstood? Most people have. Sometimes, of course, these misunderstandings are avoided when your friends ask you to repeat a careless statement. Your friends and acquaintances may find themselves constantly using such expressions as "What did you say?" or "Will you repeat that?" Often, however, they do not ask; and your careless statements go unchallenged. They assume that they understand you by what they have heard. But the point is this: if your speech were clear and immediately understandable to begin with, such situations would not occur.

To return to the story of Olga, the problem of intelligible speech in this illustration was caused by the fact that you and she did not have the same vocabulary. At least 98 per cent of unintelligible speech, however, involves a physical problem. The difficulty stems from the careless use of the physical tools of speech: the jaw, the lips, and the tongue. In other words, if you know how to relax your jaw, work your lips, and free your tongue, you can be sure of intelligible speech. The proper use of these tools is the foundation of clear and accurate diction that will contribute to your success in speaking for business. It's important, therefore, that you put into practice immediately what you learn here. Be sure to make your speech crystal clear by using properly a hinged jaw, limber lips, and an active tongue.

Hinged Jaw

A rigid jaw is a common fault with those who muffle their speech. You see, all sounds issue through the mouth; and sounds forced through a locked jaw are bound to be muffled and indistinguishable. Try this: lock your jaw tight and pronounce these words—*open, able, ideal, bound.* You probably had difficulty understanding yourself!

In intelligible speech your jaw moves freely between an open and a closed position as the various vowels are sounded. An effective speaker unhinges his jaw to the utmost on such diphthong sounds as *ow* but moves the jaw almost shut when he sounds the *oo* in *boom.* To get the free-moving feeling of a relaxed jaw, practice is necessary. First, try out individually or in a group the following words to be sure you have unlocked your jaw.

open	mine	able	round
dough	responsible	ideal	brown

You usually talk in complete thoughts, so the best way to learn this free-moving jaw action is to practice phrases and sentences. If these are intelligently and faithfully practiced, your speech will never again suffer from a rigid jaw!

down and out	Name the day to harvest the hay.
high in the sky	The dime is mine to find a blind for his yacht.
out of bounds	The honest Yankee yelled for help.
yelps and yells	The quality of mind determines its power.
around the house	Round and round he goes in honest confusion.
pot of gold	The long shadows fade into darkness.
down the hatch	The cake dough was baked and baked and
going home	baked and baked.
	Home is where the heart is.

Limber Lips

Lazy lips are frequently the cause of unintelligible speech. Poor speakers use only one lip position, but good speakers use a variety of lip positions called for by the different spoken words. For instance, *who, lose,* and *shoe* should be said with rounded lips. *Key, see,* and *cat* must be said with the lips widely stretched. *Few, boys, use,* and *how* require two different lip positions. The lips jut out for *shoe* and *church.*

Practice the following phrases and sentences, using maximum lip movement. Limber lips will soon banish the unintelligible sounds of lazy lips.

friend in need	Peter Piper picked a peck of pickled peppers.
office merger	She sells seashells by the seashore.
triumphant march	How now, brown cow?
British viewpoint	The bond of friendship was broken.
mimeograph stencil	Which was the witch?
rapidly weighed	For the sake of safety, sound your horn.
passive resistance	"Hippety, hippety, hop," he said, "the mouse
watered stock	ran up the clock."
	The whistling west wind whipped the whispering trees.

Active Tongue

The last, but equally important, of the mouth tools to be discussed is the tongue; for intelligible speech is a combination of hinged jaw,

limber lips, and active tongue. Effective use of the tongue depends
to a great extent on the teeth, which act as a backstop or baffle for
the tongue. For example, keep your tongue away from your teeth
and say "this." Now repeat the word, this time pressing your tongue
against your teeth, and notice the improved clarity. To get the feel
of an active tongue, say, "the tip of the tongue, the tip of the tongue,
the tip of the tongue." Your tongue moved with snakelike rapidity,
didn't it?

Now that you know what a free-moving tongue feels like, practice
the following phrases and sentences. Be sure that you use an active
tongue.

actually colder

attempted assault and
battery

automobile battery

loose-fitting clothes

zest of children

health, wealth, and
happiness

through thick and thin

this and that and those
and them

thirty thick thistles

Nothing was lost but a delightful time.

Needles, pins, spools of thread, and lovely
linen laces were his stock in trade.

Her tale was not strictly factual; yet not
fictional either.

Thirty thousand thermos bottles were
auctioned.

The sixth letter was smoothly dictated.

The third-rate theaters appealed to the
holiday crowd of shoppers.

It was a delightful time to be alone at
home.

Linger a little longer, lovely lady.

Slow and Easy

Rate is the speed at which a person talks, and your habitual speaking rate reveals much about the "you" behind your voice. Rate can
also determine whether oral communication is understandable or
not, so that speaking at the correct rate of speech is of utmost
importance. The general tendency among many young speakers,
and some older speakers too, is to try to talk as fast as they think.
This, of course, is not only impossible but is a major threat to intelligible speech. Prove it to yourself by saying the following three
sentences at top speed.

We do not have three-ply thread in stock.
Mr. Melvin is forever talking about health and wealth.
A postscript is needed for the sixth letter you transcribed.

Supposing that these messages were given at the rate you just used,
can you see that a listener would not be able to understand: (1)
what is not in stock, (2) what "Mr. Whosit" is talking about, or
(3) what has to be added to what? So check your speed. Slow down
to a rate that makes your every word intelligible.

Equally as bad as too rapid a rate of speech is the fault of ignoring caution signs as you talk. Some words are more difficult to enunciate clearly than others. They require an even slower rate, to allow maximum use of jaw, lips, and tongue. You will be surprised to know that most of these words are short, three- to five-letter words. They usually include one or more sounds that are difficult to distinguish. Thus, *ache* requires both the long *a* sound and a definite hard *k*. A person who ignores the caution signs of these difficult words is likely to have an "*a*' in his '*ed.*"

Most of your practice so far has been in phrases and sentences. Yet, if you learn to pronounce the following words out of context so that each one is intelligible, you have arrived! You will be able to recognize the caution signs that warn you to slow down and move your jaw, lips, and tongue to their maximum use.

ache	corn	fife	jig	nap	peat	tang
at	darn	gas	kite	nick	race	tent
balk	earn	grow	lay	oils	rogue	vamp
beau	else	heed	map	our	scab	wag
climb	fill	jam	nab	path	tan	wield

At this point in your study of speech, you already have many advantages not possessed by the average person. For example, you know how to use your jaw, lips, tongue, and teeth in the most effective way. With the additional practice provided in the following exercises, you should be able to bring out distinctly every sound you utter. Not many persons can do this. You know that too much speed in talking will prevent you from speaking distinctly, and you also know what sounds are difficult to say and difficult to understand. Therefore, you know that in general you must proceed at an easy speed; you know where the pitfalls are and can spot the combinations of sounds that demand a still slower speed. You have a fine start toward being a person who is listened to with respect.

Learning Exercises

1 Your employer calls long distance for a list of the customers who have been in touch with the office since he left. Give him the following names and telephone numbers for him to call. Remember: hinged jaw, limber lips, active tongue. **Note:** You may want to spell difficult names. For example: "Monoghan Dictating Sales (M-o-n-o-g-h-a-n) of New Orleans, Louisiana. Mr. Raymond Zulauf (Z-u-l-a-u-f), the Personnel Director, would like you to call at NOrmandy (N-O)3-3434."

Company and City	Person Calling	Telephone Number
Atomic Office Equipment Sales New York City	Warren Morrissey	HAzelwood 7-0331 Ext. 2535
Cahaw Copymaker Dallas, Texas	Victor Swoverland	TUxedo 4-3200
Ideson and Skinner Chicago, Illinois	Mrs. Marcella Hotchkiss, Secretary to Mr. Ideson	PLeasant 3-0388
Office Electronics Detroit, Michigan	Mr. Merle C. Dowson, Purchasing Agent	LOgan 2-1763
W-D Office Machines Company Kansas City, Missouri	Mr. J. C. Dulgeroff, Partner	FAirlane 3-2421

2 In the shipping department, you are reading the quantities and stock numbers of an order as the shipping clerk checks the merchandise to be trucked to customers. Pair off, one of you reading from the packing slip and the other checking the merchandise. Be sure you use good diction. Be sure, too, that the packing slips agree with the merchandise that is ready to be shipped.

From the packing slips:		Merchandise ready to be shipped:	
Quantity	Stock Number	Quantity	Stock Number
6 boxes	29 x 4028	52 yards	66 x 2738
3 dozen	29 x 370	15 feet	37 x MT9212
52 yards	66 x 2739	5 each	1Y x 1580L
15 feet	37 x MT9212	3 dozen	29 x 370
4 each	1Y x 1580L	6 boxes	29 x 4028

3 Make a list of run-together phrases, such as "Jeet?" (page 85), that you have heard—phrases or sentences that are unintelligible or difficult for the listener to translate. Be ready to enact a conversation in class in which you use some of these jumbled phrases. Then repeat the conversation, this time using good diction. What elements made your diction in the first conversation poor? What elements contributed to your good diction in the second conversation? Discuss.

4 Below is an extension of the list of short words that must be pronounced with caution to be understood. Dictate any ten of these (mix them up) for the rest of the class to write as a spelling list. Pronounce each word once only and allow three to four seconds for each to be written. See how many in the class were able to understand all the words dictated.

aid	dab	fifth	job	need	pitch	tap
air	dams	gab	kick	new	pump	tell
awe	deaf	gem	knee	nip	rap	touch
bait	earl	gill	law	oft	rave	tuck
barge	elk	hack	lathe	or	rug	vast
cape	fame	hit	merge	owe	sheik	waif

Vocabulary and Spelling Refreshers

1 **Words Often Confused.** Lesson, lessen; incite, insight.

2 **Matching Synonyms.** For each word in group A there is a word in group B that means very nearly the same thing. Match the words.

A	B
a discordant	1 Unstable
b incessant	2 Ridiculous
c absurd	3 Inharmonious
d careless	4 Negligent
e artificial	5 Abusive
	6 Diffident
	7 Unnatural
	8 Unceasing

3 **Supply the Missing Letters.** What letter should appear in the blank space in each of these words?

a perc_late   c sep_rate   e p_rsuade
b attend_nce   d controver_y   f vet__ran

Communication in Action: *Sharing the Load*

You are one of two stenographers with equal responsibility for operating a lawyer's office. Among other jobs, you have taken the responsibility for the files; your co-worker, for telephone calls. This morning the boss asks for 26 folders to be pulled from the files—and he needs them immediately. Your co-worker is not busy. What would you say to her to sell her on the idea of helping you?

4

GRAMMAR
REVIEW

UNIT   13

The Sentence

The basic element in the communication of thoughts, ideas, and messages is the sentence. As a baby, you learned first to say isolated words; but, until you had matured enough to put words into sentences, you were unable to make known what was in your mind. As you grew older, gained added facility in the use of the language, and could make better sentences, your efforts to communicate became more successful At the age of five or thereabouts, you went to school; and there, year after year, you studied some form of communication.

English is taught, studied, and learned for the purpose of improving communication. Any courses involving reading have as their objective improvement in *receiving* communications. Courses in speaking or writing are offered to improve the *sending* of communications. Because communication is the primary purpose of language and because the sentence is the core of communications, the logical starting place for your study of grammar is mastery of the sentence essentials that have use value. In this unit, therefore, you will learn the sentence principles that can be directly applied to the clear, correct, and polished transmission of communications.

Definition

In elementary school you learned that a sentence is a group of words expressing a complete thought, and this definition cannot be improved upon. Many students, however, learn a definition and can state it glibly—but they do not think it through. A little reflection would reveal that, to be a sentence, a group of words must mean something. Naturally, then, communication will be disrupted and confusion will arise if no meaning is received from what is supposed to be a sentence. It is, therefore, important that the words you write as sentences express a complete thought.

✳ *Quick Trick*   To enable you to see at a glance whether or not a group of words is a sentence, consider whether the words make or do not make sense. If they make sense, there is a sentence; if not, no sentence. Just remember this: no sense— no sentence. For instance:

> **All bills must be paid within 30 days.**   These words make sense, have meaning, express a complete thought. Therefore, this is a sentence.

> **As we are not in position to advertise now.**   Here is an example of a "no sense" group of words. Because the words do not make sense, do not express a complete thought, this group of words is not a sentence.

1   *Class Practice*   Throughout the entire grammar section, oral class practices and error hunts are provided; for no matter how well you think you understand what has been taught, a little practice helps to fix a principle in your mind. Therefore, in the following groups of words tell which are sentences and which are not. Just say, "Sense" or "No sense." For additional practice, make sense out of the "no sense" groups by adding words that would make them sentences.

1. The typists say that posture chairs are very comfortable.
2. Promotion is the result of honest effort.
3. Although the note is not yet due.
4. Because of lack of warehouse space.
5. Since we are not ready to advertise the new product.
6. The stapler is a "must" in any office.
7. Planned for quick reproduction of transcripts.
8. That telephone operator has a pleasant voice.

Subject and Predicate

In view of all the years you have studied grammar, the statement that every sentence is composed of a subject and a predicate is probably entirely unnecessary. This topic must be reviewed, however, because it is the foundation for principles that will be presented in Units 20, 21, and 22.

The important point here is the subject; for if you are able to select the subject, you will then know that the rest of the sentence is the predicate. The subject is that part of the sentence that shows *who is speaking* or is *spoken to* or *the person or thing spoken about.* A subject may be a single word or a group of words; as:

> **I am going to the bank this morning.**   *I* is the subject of the sentence, the *person speaking.*

You are to report to Mr. Bond. *You* is the subject, the *person spoken to.*

The typist whom we hired last week is very efficient. *The typist whom we hired last week* is the subject of the sentence, the *person spoken about.*

Our out-of-date typewriters have been sold. *Our out-of-date typewriters* is the subject, the *things spoken about.*

2 *Class Practice* Now, for a little practice, select the complete subject in each of the following sentences. Keep in mind the fact that the rest of the sentence is the predicate.

1. Machines are in use in more and more offices.
2. Preliminary examinations are to be given tomorrow.
3. You will be pleased with the new carbon paper.
4. Mr. Edwards has decided to resign.
5. The purpose of the meeting is to determine the reason for increased cost of sales.
6. Many persons in their late teens are obtaining good office positions.
7. I am not sure about the wording of that order.
8. Improvements in electric typewriters are frequently being made.

Simple and Compound Subjects

You have now reviewed and practiced selecting the complete subject of a sentence. The next step is to refresh your memory with regard to selecting the simple or compound subject. Do not lightly assume that you already know all about simple and compound subjects, for the principles presented in Units 20, 21, and 22 are based on your ability to select such subjects quickly and accurately.

A simple subject consists of one element. A compound subject consists of two or more words that are equally important, joined most frequently by the conjunctions *and, or,* or *nor.* To find the simple subject, look for the single most important word in the subject. If there are two or more most important words joined by a conjunction, that sentence will have a compound subject; as:

The girl in the blue dress is a new employee. *The girl in the blue dress* is the complete subject. The most important single word is *girl;* therefore, *girl* is the simple subject.

The debits and credits in the trial balance must be equal. *The debits and credits in the trial balance* is the complete subject. *Debits and credits* are the most important words, equally important, and are joined by the conjunction *and. Debits and credits* is the compound subject.

3 *Class Practice*   In Class Practice 2, each sentence has a simple subject. Name those simple subjects.

4 *Class Practice*   See if you can select without error the simple and the compound subjects in the following sentences.

1. Jean Bennett is a graduate of our school.
2. Jean Bennett and her sisters are graduates of our school.
3. The stencil duplicator or the fluid duplicator may be used for this job.
4. The machine equipped with tape is a listing machine.
5. A few weeks spent in practice will increase your speed.
6. An outgoing personality and good manners are needed for success in business.
7. The tone of a person's voice could arouse resentment in a customer.
8. A desk in the outer office has been reserved for Mr. Ames.

Normal and Inverted Sentence Order

You will avoid many communication errors if you know the difference between normal and inverted sentence order and if you have learned to change inverted to normal order. A sentence is in normal order when the subject is written before the predicate. Obviously, then, when the subject does not precede the predicate, the sentence is in inverted order. To change inverted to normal order, rearrange the words so that the complete subject is written first, followed by the complete predicate. You will find that most questions are in inverted order. Close study of the following illustrations, together with subsequent practice, will prevent your making some rather common errors in grammar and punctuation.

The president of our company announced a blanket increase in salaries.   Since *the president of our company* is the subject of the sentence and since the subject precedes the predicate, this sentence is in normal order.

Somewhere during shipping, the package disappeared.   Here we are talking about *the package;* therefore, *the package* is the subject of the sentence. Since the subject does not precede the predicate, the sentence is in inverted order. Changed to normal order, it reads: "The package disappeared somewhere during shipping."

Whom are you talking about?   This is a question and is in inverted order. The subject is *you,* but *you* does not precede the predicate. The sentence written in normal order is: "You are talking about whom."

Caution. Do not be disturbed by the fact that the change from inverted to normal order may sound odd or may result in a different meaning. Questions, for instance, are statements when changed to normal order. Concentrate on being able to recognize inverted order and on being able to change to normal order, thus providing yourself with a technique that will help you to speak and write correctly.

5 *Class Practice*   Practice what you have learned by indicating which of the following sentences are in normal order and which are in inverted order. Then change to normal order all the sentences that are here written in inverted order.

1. At the present time we are not quoting prices.
2. In the files you will find much valuable information.
3. Where are your letterheads?
4. A crowd of tired-looking girls surged out of the elevator.
5. To the beginning worker, the first day on the job is confusing.
6. Soon after his arrival, the telephones began to ring continuously.
7. When should those letters be signed?
8. Rich furnishings are to be observed in some offices.

Learning Exercises

1 On a separate sheet of paper, for each of the following sentences: (*a*) write the complete subject, and (*b*) draw a line under the simple or the compound subject.

Example: The sharpest pencils in the entire office are on Mr. Smith's desk.

Your paper: The sharpest <u>pencils</u> in the entire office

1 Students who are graduated from our business course are well trained.
2 Time and tide wait for no man or woman.
3 In the morning June works very slowly.
4 The clerks in the brightly lighted office look very happy.
5 Federal and state activities have necessitated the employment of additional stenographers.
6 Hundreds of packages of seeds were shipped today.
7 Paper and other supplies are stored in a special room.
8 Members of the office force have been invited to the picnic.
9 By using a flashlight, Mr. Aker was able to find his pen.
10 Steel industries or ironworks can be operated efficiently in that city.

11 In front of the receptionist stood two callers who did not have appointments.

12 Mr. Gunner and his daughter work in the same office.

13 At five o'clock the gong sounded for closing time.

14 Does the type on that typewriter stick in damp weather?

15 Bombing and strafing planes were their wartime products.

16 A reference manual and a dictionary are tools of the stenographer's trade.

17 Bars of chocolate and boxes of candy will be on sale today.

18 An expert typist or a trained secretary is needed to help Miss Nichols.

19 A course for high-speed shorthand writers is being offered this year.

20 Are you going to the office party?

2 Some of the following groups of words are sentences; others are not. Some sentences are in inverted order. On a separate sheet of paper write the complete subject for each of the following items and draw a line under the simple or compound subject. Your preliminary work will consist of changing to normal order any sentences that may be in inverted order and making complete sentences of any "no sense" groups of words.

Examples:

1 A new method of cost accounting is being considered.

2 Has the message about canceling the order been received yet?

3 By sending us your check for $150.

Your paper:

1 A new <u>method</u> of cost accounting (Complete subject with simple subject underlined.)

2 The message about canceling the order has been received yet. The <u>message</u> about canceling the order (Changed to normal order before following directions.)

3 You can expedite delivery of your order by sending us your check for $150. <u>You</u> ("No sense" group written as sentence before following directions.)

1 Since he disliked bookkeeping.

2 Before cutting a stencil, you should clean your type.

3 Would you prefer a blue stencil?

4 Notwithstanding the severity of the weather.

5 Trembling and pale, Nancy went in to take her first dictation.

6 Each spring our office receives a thorough renovation.

7 By your carelessness in reading directions.

8 Did Mr. Evans buzz for his secretary?

9 In the warm sunlight, Mary's fingers seemed to move more slowly over the keys.

10 As we are making a very small profit.

11 Who was the first champion typist?

12 Strong and tanned and happy were the clerks returning from vacation.

13 After being praised by the office manager.

14 Has Mr. Hart been with our firm very long?

15 While I was typing the memorandum.

16 Here are the paper clips you lost.

17 Once a week, each file clerk gets an extra rest period.

18 Seating himself again.

19 Where is the wastebasket that belongs under my desk?

20 As if enjoying the work.

Vocabulary and Spelling Refreshers

1 **Words Often Confused.** Mood, mode; command, commend.

2 **Wanted: Adjectives!** What are the adjective forms for each of the following words?

a continue   **c** invent   **e** season
b deride   **d** work   **f** imagine

3 **"Ise," "ize," or "yze"?** Which of the following words are misspelled?

a apologize   **c** realise   **e** exercise
b merchandise   **d** advertise   **f** analyse

Communication in Action: *Name Game*

How well do you remember names after an introduction? Have six of your classmates select assumed names and introduce themselves to you. You may ask one question of each as you try to fix the name in your memory. Then, introduce each one to another student. *Hint:* Try to associate face, appearance, dress, speech, etc., with names.

UNIT 14

Test 14-15

Verbs

Suppose somebody gave you a secondhand car. Wouldn't you be thrilled? Now suppose you sat in the driver's seat, turned on the ignition and the starter, but nothing happened. You got out and lifted the hood, only to find that your car had no motor. What a letdown! You are the owner of a car, but the car will not go.

The function of a verb in a sentence resembles that of the motor of a car. Without a verb, the sentence will not go. With an incorrect verb, the sentence will not go where it is supposed to go. The verb principles that you will study in this and the following unit will be more easily understood and learned if you think of verbs as the engines of your sentences.

Definition

A verb is a word that asserts or assumes action, a condition, or a state of being. You probably never will be asked to state the definition of a verb; but you surely will need to be able to recognize verbs, to use them, and to be correct in their use. Keep in mind the idea of the verb as the motor of a sentence as you look at the following groups of words. Note that in each group the verb is missing.

> The bird sweetly.
> Mr. Adams his arm.
> Brenda the best file clerk we ever had.

Did you get any message from these words? Did anything happen? Watch them *go* when verbs are supplied; as:

> The bird (sings) sweetly.
> Mr. Adams (broke, raised, scratched, hit) his arm.
> Brenda (was, is, discharged, snubbed) the best file clerk we ever had.

1 *Class Practice* Here is your opportunity to put into practice your understanding of verbs as motors for sentences. If the verb is missing in any of the following groups of words, supply a verb for the group. This can be fun, for different verbs can be used to make the sentence *go* in different directions.

1. The store rest room needs redecorating.
2. Our information booth on the third floor.
3. This book important information about office etiquette.
4. The office boy the food for the coffee break.
5. Sue the pertinent file folders.
6. All tags show the prices clearly marked.
7. The executive the new dictating machine.
8. Reputable manufacturers the goods they have for sale.

Verb Phrase

In some cases, two or more verbs are needed to make the sentence *go*. Whenever this is true, the sentence has a verb phrase. A verb phrase contains a main or principal verb and one or more helping (or auxiliary) verbs. Remember that, in a verb phrase, the *last* verb is the *main* verb. Some of the more common helpers are:

is	may have	may have been
was	might have	might have been
has	will have	will have been
had	could have	could have been
has been	should have	should have been
had been	would have	would have been

A knowledge of helpers and of verb phrases is necessary as background not only for the next topic you will study but also for some later topics. Study very carefully the following illustrations.

Mr. Wood *was answering* the question. Main verb, *answering;* helping verb, *was.*

The caller *has been* here twice this week. Main verb, *been;* helping verb, *has.*

You *should have asked* permission to use the telephone. Main verb, *asked;* helpers, *should* and *have.*

The bulletin *has been read* by the entire staff. Main verb, *read;* helpers, *has* and *been.*

Note that, in the second sentence, *been* is a main verb; but in the last sentence, *been* is a helper. This will present no problem if you have learned that the *last* verb is the *main* verb and the preceding verb or verbs are helpers.

2 *Class Practice* To find out how well you understand the verb-phrase principle, select the verb phrase, the main verb, and the helping verb or verbs in each of the following sentences.

1. Everybody should choose his career early in life.
2. The folders must be placed correctly in the file.
3. Have you written to Mr. James this week?
4. Your manner might be misunderstood by the customers.
5. Can you think of any necessary improvements?
6. You surely have been instructed in mailing routine.
7. Joan is failing in her efforts to keep up her production.
8. The hatrack has been there for years.

Regular and Irregular Verbs

You have observed that some verbs express or imply *present* time (now). Others express *past* time (time fully passed). Still other forms, usually known as *past participles*, refer to time passed but connected with present time. These forms are usually called the *principal parts* of a verb.

A *regular* verb forms the past tense and the past participle by adding *ed*; as: *walk, walked, walked; call, called, called.* Since a mistake in the use of a regular verb is seldom made, the principal parts of regular verbs do not require special study.

Irregular verbs, however, form the past tense and the past participle in various ways—frequently by changing to a different word. Errors in the use of these verbs occur often, particularly in speaking. A list of preferred forms for important irregular verbs is given in the Reference Section (pages 548–549). They must be learned.

The simplest and quickest way to insure that you will be correct in the usage of irregular verbs is to remember that a helper is not used with the past tense but is always used with the past-participle form. Knowing when a helper is correctly used would prevent you from writing or saying something like this: "Julia has drew $10 on her pay." You would have learned that *drew* is the past tense of *draw* and that a helper is not used with the past tense. Since in this sentence there is a helper, *has,* the past participle should be used. *Drawn,* therefore, is the correct verb form.

Study the principal parts of the irregular verbs listed in the Reference Section (pages 548–549). Make sure you know them.

 Error Hunt   A competent proofreader must have an excellent English background, for his job is to see and to correct errors in English. For this error hunt, you are a proofreader who understands the correct use of principal parts of verbs. To show

how competent you are, find and correct all principal-parts errors in the following sentences.

1. Joyce begun to wonder if she would ever finish transcribing.
2. Charles and Eugene done much for office morale.
3. That man was drove by his ambition to become vice-president.
4. The door opened and in come Martha.
5. Have you ever ate in the cafeteria on the first floor?
6. The train had went before he reached the station.
7. Beverly seen the first draft of the monthly bulletin.
8. Mr. Grimes has often spoke to June about her untidy erasures.

Infinitives

A verb preceded by *to* is known as an infinitive; as: *to run, to say, to do, to think, to be.* Careful writers do not place any word or words between the *to* and the verb. Such practice is called "splitting an infinitive." Many English authorities of today, however, do not consider a split infinitive the major error that it formerly was. Indeed, many well-known authors maintain that a split infinitive often adds force to a statement. Be that as it may, you as a beginning worker should, as a rule, avoid splitting infinitives whenever possible. If, however, you are faced with a choice between a split infinitive and an awkward, unnatural construction, choose the split infinitive as the lesser evil.

If you were thinking of writing *to quickly run,* you would know that you should write *to run quickly,* thus avoiding a split infinitive. Consider this sentence: "The beginning worker should be careful not to deliberately split an infinitive." To avoid the split infinitive, the sentence would be written: "The beginning worker should be careful not to split an infinitive deliberately."

3 *Class Practice* See if you can identify the split infinitives in the following sentences. Then tell how you would reword the sentences to avoid splitting those infinitives.

1. Robert was told to thoroughly clean the duplicator.
2. Nancy was forced to quietly wait until Mr. Downs finished telephoning.
3. You would be wise to accurately proofread all typewritten work.
4. We thought the switchboard operator would try to at least be polite.
5. It is impossible to rapidly type in hot, sticky weather.
6. You should begin to, if you wish to succeed, develop good work habits.
7. The undesirable caller was persuaded to finally leave.

Learning Exercises

1 For each of the following sentences: (*a*) list the verb, (*b*) underline the main verb if you have listed a verb phrase, and (*c*) supply a verb for any group of words where the verb is missing.

1 An impatient customer into the store.
2 Vendors of stockings announced the development of a new fabric.
3 The foundry has been purchased by Allen & Brown.
4 The word "parity" appears frequently in the newspapers.
5 The salesman the coveted order.
6 We shall be glad to hear from you shortly.
7 Miss Morrow can take dictation at 140 words a minute.
8 Three telegrams from Mr. Downs have been received today.
9 Manufacturers usually allow a 30-day credit.
10 Delicious punch at the office party last Christmas.
11 For what company did the applicant last work?
12 Wheat is selling rapidly on the Exchange.
13 Do your customers like these linen napkins?
14 Has our request been given special consideration?
15 Our best customer an extension of credit.
16 We surely cannot be at our desks every minute of the day.
17 Will you make arrangements to see Mr. Frink soon?
18 Combinations of colors and designs catch a shopper's eye.
19 Has there been any change in his feeling about the merger?
20 The strike in the factory shipment of goods.

Check. Did you change into normal order all the sentences that were in inverted order? If not, do so now. Accurate selection of verbs and verb phrases depends on making such changes wherever needed.

2 If a sentence in the following exercise is correct, write "OK" on your paper. If it is incorrect, write the correction and give your reason for doing so.

1 Last week Bahn Brothers run an advertisement in the paper.
2 We are sorry that a misunderstanding about your account has arose.
3 Did you know that our president has broke his lease?
4 Angela has driven her own car for years.
5 Were you choosen to represent the office staff?
6 We were late getting home because the wind had blew hard all day.
7 Have you ever sang in a church choir?

8 Please try to never refuse a reasonable request.
9 After we had eaten our lunch, we hurried back to the office.
10 Prices have rose faster than wages.
11 The package you were looking for has came.
12 Steel companies have began to shorten working hours.
13 How much am I bid for this portable typewriter?
14 Have you payed your monthly dues?
15 The space bar on my machine is busted.
16 Some people find it impossible to clearly reason under pressure.
17 The ink in the duplicator has sank to the bottom of the well.
18 Is the murderer to be hanged tonight?
19 Lucille drunk all the coffee in her vacuum bottle.
20 The maintenance man has never spoke good English.

Vocabulary and Spelling Refreshers

1 **Words Often Confused.** Fineness, finesse; leased, least.

2 **Silent Letters**

 a Which of the following words contains a silent letter: listen, February, sophomore, strength?
 b Which of the following words does *not* contain a silent letter: night, island, doubt, candidate?

3 **Does It End with "ancy" or "ency"?** Should *ancy* or *ency* be added to the following to complete the correct spellings?

 a effici_____ c emerg_____ e buoy_____
 b hesit_____ d flu_____ f vac_____

Communication in Action: *Selecting the Right Word*

Assume that the following sentences are taken from an office memorandum. Rewrite them, using correct words for those that have been used incorrectly or misspelled.

"I respectively request that you permit us to put this proceedure into affect at once. Our department likes sufficient staff to procure the datum we need to insure our customers of efficent service. Keeping seperate cost controls on each operation places a heavy bookeeping burden on our employees, but we will try to preform the task as good as possible."

UNIT 15

Verbs (*Continued*)

The sentences that you write in the future will be sure to move and to move in the right direction because: (1) you know that every sentence must have a verb; (2) you know that the particular verb you use will cause your message to move in a particular direction; and (3) you know that correct usage of the irregular verbs will insure that your sentence, in general, will move correctly.

The next question is: Will your sentences move smoothly? Having a motor is one thing, but having a motor that is always tuned up is another. The additional verb principles presented in this unit represent the tools you will need to keep your verb motor tuned up and operating at peak efficiency.

Classification of Verbs

In your previous grammar study you learned to classify verbs as transitive or intransitive. To provide you with a foundation for some later grammar principles, notably those in Units 18 and 19, verbs are here divided into three kinds: (1) "being" verbs, (2) transitive verbs, and (3) intransitive verbs.

"Being" Verbs

If you were to use the verb *to be* in all tenses, you would find the following different forms of the verb.

am	*be*, with a helper (*may be, can be, will be, would be,* and so on)
are	
is	*been*, with a helper or helpers (*would have been, has been, had been,* and *might have been,* for instance)
was	
were	

These are the "being" verbs. Probably the best way to learn the "being" verbs is to memorize and to repeat frequently: *am, are, is, was, were,* helper *be,* helper(s) *been.*

Remember that these verbs are "being" verbs only when they are main verbs; and, as you learned in Unit 14, the main verb is the *last* verb in a verb phrase. For instance:

> **Mr. Goggin *was* not in the office today.** *Was* is the only verb, so of course it is the main verb. You will have no difficulty in identifying the "being" verb when it is one of the single verbs—*am, are, is, was,* or *were.*

> **The winners of the bonus *should have been* Grace and he.** This verb phrase is a "being" verb because *been* is the main, or last, verb.

> **The reports *have been placed* correctly in the files.** Here, *been* is not a "being" verb because *been* is a helper. The last verb in a verb phrase is always the main verb, which in this sentence is *placed.*

> **Who *is going* to the demonstration?** *Going* is the main verb; *is* is a helper. This is not a "being" verb.

1 *Class Practice* To test your ability to recognize "being" verbs, tell which of the following sentences contain "being" verbs. Be sure to name the verb in each sentence.

1. Your typewriter ribbon is worn out.
2. There must be some reason for his failing to check his work.
3. At the bottom of the wastebasket is a dollar bill.
4. When will the salesman be leaving for his trip?
5. The treasurer's reports were read and filed every week.
6. His check should have been in the mail this morning.
7. Next to our office is a large vacant lot.
8. Mr. Evans might be our next purchasing agent.

Transitive and Intransitive Verbs

You remember that a transitive verb is a verb that takes an object; an intransitive verb, a verb that does not take an object. For accuracy and ease in selecting transitive and intransitive verbs, study the following quick trick.

Quick Trick If there can be an answer to the questions "What?" or "Whom?" asked after a verb, that verb is transitive.

If there can be no answer, the verb is intransitive. Your procedure would be: (1) to say the verb, (2) to ask "What?" or "Whom?" and (3) to decide whether you can get an answer to either of these questions. If there is an answer, the verb is transitive. If not, the verb is intransitive. The following illustrations will show you how easy it is to tell whether a verb is transitive or intransitive.

Birds sing sweet songs in the early morning.   Sing what? Answer—*songs. Sing* is a transitive verb.

Birds sing sweetly in the early morning.   Sing what? No answer.
Sing whom? No answer. In this sentence, *sing* is an intransitive verb.

The caller placed Ella in an embarrassing position.   Placed
what? No answer. But placed whom? Yes—*Ella. Placed* is a transitive verb.

Always Transitive. Whenever a past participle has one of the "being"
verbs as a helper—*was done, has been broken, might be chosen, is
burned*—that verb is always transitive because such verb phrases
represent the subject as being acted on. This is automatic; therefore,
in such a situation you need not ask the questions "What?" or
"Whom?" For example:

The statement *should have been sent* yesterday.   *Sent* is a past
participle. *Should have been* is a "being" verb, but here it is used
as a helper. *Should have been sent* is automatically transitive.

Tom *was* not *following* in the footsteps of his father.   Although
there is a "being" verb helper here, the main verb is not a past
participle. For this verb you ask "What?" or "Whom?" Neither question can be answered; so the verb is intransitive.

[2] *Class Practice*   Name the verbs in the following sentences
and identify them as transitive or intransitive. Remember that
you say the verb to yourself and ask "What?" or "Whom?"
Remember to watch for any past participles that have "being"
verb helpers.

1. The rain has been falling gently all day.
2. That customer sent a check with his order.
3. All letters were typed before noon, despite interruptions.
4. Competition in modern times is becoming very keen.
5. Poor references eliminated the applicant before the interview.
6. The mail plane always circles the city before landing.
7. All the floors should have been polished after office hours.
8. The short circuit terrified the girls in the main office.

Troublesome Verbs

Lie, lay; sit, set; and *rise, raise* are frequently referred to as troublesome verbs. The term is very apt, for these verbs are very often misused. You should have little difficulty, however, because you know
their principal parts and you can immediately identify a transitive
or an intransitive verb. In each pair of these troublesome verbs, one
verb is transitive; the other, intransitive. There remains only the

problem of determining which is transitive and which is intransitive. The following quick trick teaches you how to make the differentiation almost immediately.

✳ *Quick Trick*   First, review the principal parts of each pair:

			Participle and Infinitive
lie	lay	lain	(*lying* and *to lie*)
lay	laid	laid	(*laying* and *to lay*)
sit	sat	sat	(*sitting* and *to sit*)
set	set	set	(*setting* and *to set*)
rise	rose	risen	(*rising* and *to rise*)
raise	raised	raised	(*raising* and *to raise*)

In the first pair—*lie, lay*—which is the "I" verb; that is, the verb that has the "I" sound? The answer is *lie*. With what letter of the alphabet does the word *intransitive* start? *I*, isn't it? Then learn that the "I" verb in each pair is intransitive. Make this connection: *I* is the first letter of the word *intransitive; I*-sounding verbs are intransitive.

In the *sit, set* pair, which would you call the "I" verb? Your answer is *sit*. Then *sit* is the intransitive member of the pair. By now you can see that *rise* is the "I" verb in the *rise, raise* pair; and you know that *rise* is an intransitive verb.

Rather obviously, if you know which verb in the pair is intransitive, you know that the other verb must be transitive. Do not forget that a past-participle form with a "being" verb helper is always transitive.

Observe and adopt the line of reasoning set up for you in the following illustrations.

Sue forgot that she (lay, laid) **her notebook in the top drawer.**

1. Which is needed here, a transitive or an intransitive verb? Answer—transitive.
2. Which verb is transitive? Answer—*laid*.
3. Which, then, is correct? Answer—*laid*.

Our dog (lies, lays) **down at the first command.**   Intransitive verb is needed; *lies* is intransitive; *lies* is the correct verb.

Her marginal stops were (sat, set) **for a short letter.**   There is no problem here. *Set* is correct because a past participle with a "being" verb helper is always transitive.

3 *Class Practice*   To practice what you have learned about these troublesome verbs, study the following sentences. For each sentence, determine whether you need a transitive or an intransitive verb and tell why. Then name the correct verb.

1. During my lunch hour, I (lay, laid) on the couch in the clinic.
2. Please (sit, set) the vase on that table.
3. I have (lain, laid) the rough draft in its proper place.
4. The porter is (sitting, setting) the packages on the bench.
5. Our city (lies, lays) on the west bank of the river.
6. By sheer hard work, Mr. Rowe has (risen, raised) to his present position.
7. Those stencils have (lain, laid) in the box for a long time.
8. If you do not (rise, raise) an objection, Mr. Steers will think that you approve.

If, As If, As Though, Wish

The last tuning tool for your verb motor is concerned with the verb that is correctly used with *if, as if, as though,* and *wish.* The principle you need to study is that after these words you will use *were* where you ordinarily would use *was;* like this:

> The applicant acts *as if* she *were* a good worker.
>
> Shirley talks *as though* Jane *were* subnormal.
>
> On a day like this, Ann *wishes* she *were* at the beach.

Use of *was* or *were* after *if* presents a minor problem. *Were* is used if the expression is not true, is doubtful, or is not possible. *Was,* however, is used if the statement is true. The following illustrations will help you use *was* or *were* correctly after *if.*

> *If* I *were* you, I would look for another position.   Could not be possible.
>
> *If* Jack *were* here, he would find the error in a short time.   But Jack is not here.
>
> *If* he *was* here (and he was), I did not see him.

4 *Class Practice*   By selecting the correct verb in each of the following sentences, you will discover how well you understand what verb is used correctly after *if, as if, as though,* and *wish.*

1. I wish that Amy (was, were) going with us.
2. It seemed as though the type (was, were) out of line.
3. Betty acted as if she (was, were) disappointed.
4. If Kay (was, were) in my position, she would make the same decision.
5. If it (was, were) not for the accuracy of the accountants, our profits would not be so large.
6. I wish it (was, were) possible to type without errors.

Learning Exercises

1 On a separate sheet of paper, write the verb that is used in each of the following sentences and indicate whether it is transitive, intransitive, or "being." Use "T" for transitive, "I" for intransitive, and "B" for "being."

1 There were often a dozen or more callers in our small office.
2 Mr. Floss proudly entered his secretary in the competition.
3 Can't something be done about the stale air in this office?
4 Mr. Waters is confident of our support.
5 Our secretaries applied for the proofreading job.
6 Opposition makes Mr. Benton more persistent.
7 Eraser crumbs must be caught in the type basket.
8 Miss Tripp has returned from her vacation.
9 We all like the new chief clerk very much.
10 You should have been here before 8:30.
11 Mr. Talcott was buying only from jobbers.
12 Did you return the original copy?
13 That applicant might be a competent person for the job.
14 We saw the vice-president at lunch.
15 Dirty type was the cause of her sloppy work.
16 Has the strike developed into a serious situation?
17 Because of the heat, all employees were dismissed from work.
18 Some machine operators are not afraid of getting their hands soiled.
19 Are you going to the office picnic?
20 I am not sure about his qualifications for a clerical position.

2 Write "OK" on your paper for any correct sentences in the following. Write the corrections for any incorrect sentences.

1 If it was possible, all typing errors should have been corrected.
2 Very few housewives now set dough to raise.
3 It seemed as though the day was never ending.
4 Just let the stationery lay there.
5 Miss Brimmer always sits the pace for the other typists.
6 That machine looks as if it was ready to fall apart.
7 Has a time limit for this job been sat?
8 The duplicator has been lying idle all day.
9 I wish it was possible to show my deep gratitude.

10 Employers are rising their standards.
11 If I was in your place, I would check those figures.
12 The foundation for increased efficiency has been lain by the time-and-motion consultants.
13 I feel as though I was going to like working here.
14 Our reception room is just like a private setting room.
15 My lunch lay in the locker all last week.
16 Reports make it appear as if she was going to resign.
17 Yeast causes dough to rise.
18 Before noon the men had lain the tile in the lounge.
19 Undoubtedly Edward wishes he were getting a higher salary.
20 Our quotations on office supplies have been risen.

Vocabulary and Spelling Refreshers

1 **Words Often Confused.** Feet, feat; indite, indict.

2 **Overworked Words.** The italicized words in the following sentences have been worn thin by overuse. Substitute a more meaningful word for each.

   a I'm *awfully* sorry I can't go to the dance.
   b I am *crazy* to study psychology.
   c The heat makes me feel *terrible*.
   d It was *nice* of you to invite me.
   e She was *real* pleased with the gift.
   f She is *keen* about her new job.

3 **Check the Spelling**

   a Which of the following words is *misspelled:* signify, testify, liquify, classify?
   b Which of the following words is spelled *correctly:* accomodate, privelege, embarrass, aquiese?

Communication in Action: *Following Company Rules*

An employee in the stenographic pool believes that punctuation is a matter of personal taste. Her letters read as though she puts in commas and semicolons when the mood strikes her—not when they are needed. Her letters are frequently returned by the dictator for retyping. As her supervisor, you have spoken to her twice about punctuation; but apparently the results were negative. You will have to talk with her again. With another student, enact the drama as you think it should unfold. The door has opened and the employee has just entered.

UNIT 16

Nouns — Plurals

One of the difficulties presented by the English language is the correct spelling of the plurals of nouns, an understandable difficulty when you consider that there is no single way of forming plurals. Take, for example, this sentence: "Several cargoes of radios were shipped yesterday." The plural of *cargo* is *cargoes,* but the plural of *radio* is *radios,* although both singular forms end in *o.* Look at this sentence: "Attorneys for the steel industries met for a conference." *Attorney* ends in *y;* the plural is formed by adding *s.* *Industry* also ends in *y,* but its plural is formed by changing the *y* to *i* and adding *es.* There is, indeed, a great need for good, hard study of noun plurals.

The purpose of this unit is to alert you to the fact that plural endings constitute a threat to a perfect spelling record. The least that can be expected from you as a result of your study is that you become aware of the danger signals and that you consult a dictionary when in doubt. Poor spellers are poor because they do not know enough to doubt. You will, therefore, be well rewarded by careful study of the following principles for the formation of plurals of nouns.

Most Commonly Used Plural Endings

Most nouns form the plural by adding *s* to the singular; as:

| table | tables | worker | workers |
| chair | chairs | pencil | pencils |

However, singular nouns ending in *ch, sh, s, x,* and *z* form the plural by adding *es.* You should have little difficulty here, for the plural *es* form can be heard. As you read the following plurals, pronounce them mentally. Do you hear the extra *es* sound?

church	churches	box	boxes
bush	bushes	chintz	chintzes
glass	glasses		

Plurals of Names. As with common nouns, the plurals of most names are formed by adding *s*; but the plurals of names ending in *ch, sh, s, x,* and *z* are formed by adding *es.* There is no reason for the confusion that so many persons experience when they are required to write the plural of a name. Look at the following illustrations and note that the general rule that applies to plurals of common nouns also applies to plurals of names.

pod	pods	Todd	the Todds
paw	paws	Shaw	the Shaws
log	logs	Fogg	the Foggs

Now see how the *es* plural ending applies to names exactly as it does to common nouns.

bench	benches	Lynch	the Lynches
brush	brushes	Nash	the Nashes
gas	gases	Adams	the Adamses
fox	foxes	Tarbox	the Tarboxes
topaz	topazes	Schultz	the Schultzes

Titles with Names. When there is a title with a name, either the name or the title may be pluralized. Never pluralize both the name and the title. Here are some examples.

Mr. Ogden	*Messrs.* Ogden, the *Messrs.* Ogden, or the two Mr. *Ogdens* (*Messrs.* is the abbreviation for *messieurs,* the French word for *Misters.*)
Mrs. Tate	The Mrs. *Tates* or *Mesdames* Tate (*Mesdames* is the French word that means more than one *Mrs.*)
Miss Park	*Misses* Park or the two Miss *Parks*
Doctor Nye	*Doctors* Nye or the Doctor *Nyes*

Error Hunt 1 If you understand how to use the most common plural endings, you will be able to find any errors there may be in the following sentences. You will also be able to recognize the plurals that are correctly written.

1. How many cup of coffee do you drink during the day?
2. What were the Messrs. Palmers doing in the office yesterday?

3. Many businesses failed during the depression years.
4. The Collinses have purchased a new car.
5. The potted bushs in the foyer are covered with dust.
6. Are the Allenses going to open their new store soon?
7. Did you hear that the Smith's have resigned their positions?

Plurals of Nouns Ending in "y"

As you know, the vowels are *a, e, i, o,* and *u.* The remaining letters of the alphabet are consonants. Therefore, you will find it easy to learn that, when a singular noun ends in *y* and the *y* is preceded by a vowel, the plural is formed by adding *s.* If, however, the final *y* is preceded by a consonant, the plural is formed by changing the *y* to *i* and adding *es.* This rule should be committed to memory, for the need for it arises often. The following examples will help you to learn and to remember it.

Final *y* preceded by a vowel:

attorney	attorneys	valley	valleys
monkey	monkeys	turkey	turkeys
toy	toys	key	keys

Final *y* preceded by a consonant:

facility	facilities	community	communities
supply	supplies	lily	lilies
remedy	remedies	laundry	laundries

Note. This rule does not apply to names. All names ending in *y* form the plural by adding *s,* as: *three Marys, the Overys.*

Plurals of Nouns Ending in "o"

When a singular noun ends in *o,* the plural is usually formed by adding *s.* Interestingly enough, all nouns that relate to music add *s* for the plural; as: *pianos, solos, sopranos, trios.* However, some singular nouns ending in an *o* that is preceded by a consonant form the plural by adding *es.* Still others add *s.* This fact is quite confusing to a student who is trying to learn rules. Study the following examples, but keep in mind that the plural of a noun ending in *o* is not to be trusted. If you are not sure, use a dictionary.

Final *o* preceded by a vowel:

studio	studios	folio	folios
cameo	cameos	radio	radios

Final *o* preceded by a consonant and adding *es* for the plural:

echo	echoes	potato	potatoes
hero	heroes	mosquito	mosquitoes

Final *o* preceded by a consonant, but adding *s* for the plural:

memento	mementos	zero	zeros
domino	dominos	lasso	lassos
dynamo	dynamos	albino	albinos

Plurals of Nouns Ending in "f" or "fe"

Some singular nouns ending in *f* or *fe* change the *f* or *fe* to *v* and add *es*. Others simply add *s*. Beware, then, of plurals of nouns ending in *f* or *fe*. When in doubt, consult your dictionary.

Final *f* or *fe* changing to *v* and adding *es*:

knife	knives	life	lives
half	halves	leaf	leaves

Final *f*, adding *s*:

chief	chiefs	proof	proofs
safe	safes	sheriff	sheriffs

1 *Class Practice*   Before you are promoted to the error-hunt level, you should practice the principles presented in the previous three topics. In each of the following sentences, select the word you think is correct and explain why you chose that word.

1. Did you see the (puppys, puppies) on sale at the kennel?
2. Florida (tomatos, tomatoes) are now on the market.
3. During the storm all the (leafs, leaves) were blown from the trees.
4. Many (industrys, industries) are moving to outlying communities.
5. Banana (cargos, cargoes) are profitable this winter.
6. Our (safes, saves) are burglarproof.
7. There are no (chimneys, chimnies) on any of the skyscrapers.
8. The (echos, echoes) in the lobby are very annoying.

Error Hunt 2   Now you should be ready to consolidate all that you have learned about noun plurals. In the following sentences, indicate which are correct and correct those that need correction. Use this text or a dictionary if in doubt.

1. Our unsold turkies were stored in the freezer.
2. We think that the Harris are quite the best people in town.
3. None of your zeros are written correctly.
4. The tornado was hard on rooves of houses.
5. Attornies in large communities have many clients.
6. The Professors Stewart must not be kept waiting.

7. The customer was annoyed because the prooves of her pictures were not ready.
8. All the Anns in the office have joined to form a club.
9. Everyone seems to work better when the skys are blue.
10. The Doctors Grants are in charge of the new clinic.
11. Western heros always carry two guns.
12. No job is without occasional griefs.

Vowel Changes

Some nouns form the plural by changing a vowel instead of adding *s*. A few plurals end in *en*. Here are some examples.
   Vowel change:

woman	women	churchman	churchmen
mouse	mice	tooth	teeth
goose	geese	foot	feet

En ending:

brother	brethren	child	children
ox	oxen		

In a very few words ending in *man,* the plural is formed by adding *s*; as:

German	Germans	Ottoman	Ottomans
talisman	talismans		

Nouns with Two Plurals

A few nouns have two plurals, but these plurals have different meanings; such as:

brother	brothers (blood relatives), brethren (members of a society)
cloth	cloths, clothes (garments)
staff	staffs, staves
index	indexes (to books), indices (symbols)

Apostrophe Used in Plural

Letters, numerals, symbols, signs, and words referred to as words form the plural by adding apostrophe and *s*. *This is the only time that an apostrophe is used in a plural.* Illustrations of this sole use of the apostrophe to denote a plural are:

> **Mr. Clay does not consider *f.o.b.*'s when figuring costs.** Plural of abbreviation consisting of letters.

June received three *A*'s this term.   Plural of a letter.

Life in the *90*'s was very gay.   Plural of a figure.

Be sure to use *&*'s when firms so print their names.   Plural of a symbol.

Mark's theme was full of "*the*'s."   *The*'s is a word referred to as a word.

Knowledge of the only instances in which the apostrophe is used to form a plural is most important to you. It will prevent your making errors that are frequently made by others. You would not, for instance, write a sentence like this: "The Smith's have invested heavily in company stock." *You* would know that the correct plural is *Smiths*, because the apostrophe is used to indicate the plural only of letters, numerals, symbols, signs, and words referred to as words—and *Smith* is not one of these.

Plurals of Compound Nouns

A compound noun as defined here is a noun consisting of two or more words, whether hyphenated or unhyphenated. The plural of a compound noun is formed on the important, or main, word. Study the following compound nouns and their plurals.

personnel manager	personnel *managers*
editor in chief	*editors* in chief
court-martial	*courts*-martial
man-of-war	*men*-of-war
son-in-law	*sons*-in-law
major general	major *generals*
notary public	*notaries* public

Exceptions to English rules are so frequent that you will not be surprised to learn that, in a very few compounds, the plural is added to both parts of the compound; as:

gentleman usher	gentlemen ushers
Knight Templar	Knights Templars

If a compound noun is written as one word, however, the plural is formed at the end, just like the plural of any other noun; like this:

stepchild	stepchildren	handful	handfuls
fisherman	fishermen	bookcase	bookcases

2 *Class Practice*   Now is the time to find out how well you understand the last four rules for forming plurals. First, review the principles. Then select the correct word in each sentence.

1. How many (workmans, workmen) were employed to paint the house?
2. I cannot tell the difference between his (8s, 8's) and his (3s, 3's).
3. The state (senators-elect, senator-elects) were invited to our rally.
4. No (C. O. D.'s, C. O. D.s) will be accepted in the future.
5. What is the price of (gooses, geese) for Christmas?
6. Mr. Cort uses too many ("whiches," "which's") in his dictation.
7. Petite Fashions is owned by my (sister-in-laws, sisters-in-law).
8. An inspirational talk was given to the (brothers, brethren) of the church society.
9. (Womans, Women) are keener shoppers than men.
10. When typing a dash, use two (-s, -'s).

Error Hunt 3 You have just studied, reviewed, and practiced four rules for forming plurals. You should be ready to tell which of the following sentences are correct and to make corrections in the remaining sentences.

1. Use two tablespoonsful of butter in that recipe.
2. All the zs on those new machines are out of line.
3. Retired teachers often become active clubwoman.
4. The 30's are thought of as the depression years.
5. Too many "ands" in a paragraph are boring to the reader.
6. The army record of your courts-martial may affect your chances for civilian employment.
7. Have the Watrous's sent their check yet?
8. Not all lieutenants colonel are so considerate as ours.
9. We received congratulations from the Benson's.
10. Why are there so many jokes about mothers-in-law?

Plurals for Correct Grammar

Knowing how to form the plurals of nouns will help you to spell correctly. To speak and write grammatically, however, you must also know the special rules that govern the singular and plural forms of certain nouns. You must know, for example:

1. That some nouns have exactly the same form in the singular and in the plural; as:

How many reindeer has Santa? *Not* reindeers.

2. That other nouns, even some that end in *s*, are always singular; as:

The news is good today. *Not* news are.

Ewing Galloway

How many times a day—and in how many different ways—does a topnotch employee demonstrate his or her knowledge of the principles of good grammar? Will *you* be ready to apply the principles you are now learning?

   3. That still other nouns are always plural; such as:

Where are my scissors? *Not* where is.

   4. That the plurals of foreign nouns may follow the foreign spelling; as with:

The memoranda for the report are on your desk. *Not* memoranda is.

Same Form, Singular and Plural. Illustrations of nouns that have the same form, whether the meaning is singular or plural, are:

Chinese	deer	odds	sheep
cod	Japanese	politics	vermin
corps	moose	salmon	wheat

When used with numerals, the following nouns usually have the same form in both numbers.

three thousand	four score (years)
two yoke (of oxen)	two dozen (apples)

Always Singular. Here are some nouns which are always singular and with which you must use a singular verb:

statistics (science)	mumps (disease)	milk
mathematics	whereabouts	music

economics (science)	molasses	news
measles (disease)	civics	

Always Plural. Some nouns that are always plural and that therefore always take a plural verb are:

statistics (facts)	auspices	tidings
scales (for weighing)	trousers	grounds
headquarters	proceeds	thanks
credentials	winnings	riches
belongings	premises	antics
hysterics	scissors	goods
		tongs

Foreign Nouns. Some nouns of foreign origin have been given English plurals, some have only foreign plurals, and still others have two plurals—an English and a foreign. Where there is a choice of plurals, the foreign forms are used mainly in formal, scientific, and technical matter. If you are in doubt as to the plural of a foreign noun, consult your dictionary. The following words are used frequently in business.

Singular	*Foreign Plural*	*English Plural*
addendum	addenda	
alumna (fem.)	alumnae	
alumnus (masc.)	alumni	
analysis	analyses	
basis	bases	
crisis	crises	
criterion	criteria	criterions
datum	data	
formula	formulae	formulas
index	indices	indexes
memorandum	memoranda	memorandums
parenthesis	parentheses	
terminus	termini	terminuses

Note. Among some modern writers there is a tendency to use *data* in most cases as a collective noun with a singular idea. These writers, therefore, use a singular verb with *data.*

3 *Class Practice*   Test your understanding of the principles just presented by selecting the correct word in each of the following sentences.

1. Two (dozen, dozens) oranges were given to the first ten customers.
2. The data for the meeting (is, are) missing.
3. At school, economics (was, were) interesting to me.

4. In your opinion, (is, are) the bases of his argument weak?
5. The goods (was, were) completely sold by ten o'clock.
6. The Mesdames Craig (is, are) employed in our store.
7. (Credential, Credentials) presented by Julia (was, were) given to the personnel manager.
8. For some people, politics (makes, make) a fascinating career.

✓ *Error Hunt 4*   In these sentences, can you tell which plurals are correct? Can you correct those that are incorrect? If so, you have a sound basis for home study and for working the Learning Exercises. A dictionary may be used if needed.

1. Crises is forever arising in our office.
2. Riches has undoubtedly spoiled the contest winner.
3. Analysis of problems is beyond Mr. Perry.
4. We received notice that the premises is to be vacated May 1.
5. The terminus of that railroad is Chicago.
6. Are the whereabouts of the chief clerk known?
7. Sanitoria for tubercular patients are plentiful in this state.
8. All the drum corpses in the state were asked to compete.

Learning Exercises

1 For each correct sentence in the following group, write "OK" on your paper. For each incorrect sentence, write your correction.

1 We simply must keep flys out of the lunchroom.
2 Who were the runner-ups in the office tennis league?
3 Please ask the Burtchs to call at our credit department.
4 All the storeses on this street have been painted.
5 Chintzes are the drapery fashion this season.
6 Be sure to dot your "is."
7 The scissors is in my top left drawer.
8 The NATO force is made up of the armys of many nations.
9 Is the data ready for Mr. Dolan?
10 The president added the names of his three son-in-laws to the payroll.
11 Dwarves were employed to model our children's clothes.
12 A short course for bailiffs is being given Monday evenings.
13 We must work evening's during the Christmas rush.
14 Is the mansion being converted into studioes?
15 The styli has been lost.

16 Our errand boy cannot reach the top shelfs in the stockroom.
17 All the saleswoman in the store must wear black dresses.
18 Mr. Cabot said that the memoranda is to be filed.
19 There are three Samuels' in our family.
20 Measles account for our shortage of help.

2 The following sentences review the grammar principles you have studied so far. Beginning with this unit and continuing through Unit 26, each Learning Exercise 2 will be a cumulative review. Directions for working all these exercises are: If a sentence is correct, write "OK" on your paper. If it is incorrect, write the correction.

1 In an emergency, you can always depend on the Emerson's.
2 The new girl admitted that she had never did any filing before.
3 Erasers with brushs on them save much time.
4 Very few people know when to use *thats* and when to use *whiches.*
5 Alaska was one of the territorys of the United States.
6 Be sure to carefully brush away all eraser crumbs.
7 Many old-fashioned remedys are still effective.
8 The Atom Smasher bowlers are quarters finalist in the tournament.
9 Candelabra is needed for the altar of the chapel.
10 Why do you capitalize your *a.m.*s?
11 I feel as though I was going to be ill.
12 Has her belongings been taken out of her locker?
13 Chicago lies about a thousand miles from New York.
14 The Mesdames Page is here to see you, Mr. North.
15 Files belonging to my two son-in-laws are out of date.
16 What are the Ellis' going to do with their electric typewriters?
17 Where did you lie the carbon copies?
18 We need more sopranoes for the office glee club.
19 Foxeshole were dug very quickly during battle.
20 We no longer carry pianoes in stock.

Vocabulary and Spelling Refreshers

1 **Words Often Confused.** Adverse, averse; preposition, proposition.

2 Suffixes

a Does the suffix *ish* in *bookish, bluish, girlish, devilish* impart to the words the meaning of: resembling, full of, capable of, or made of?

b Does the suffix *ee* in *employee, refugee, mortgagee, nominee* impart to the words the meaning of: a native of, state or quality of, the recipient of an action, or having the characteristics of?

3 How Do You Spell?

a The verb meaning "to go before"?
b The next number after one?
c The adverb formed from *full*?
d The state whose capital is Dover?

Communication in Action: *Word Problems*

Answer the following questions from an employment test:

1. The auditor noted a *discrepancy* in the figures. This means: (*a*) the figures are incorrect, (*b*) the company made too large a profit, (*c*) the figures are illegible, (*d*) the books are in balance.

2. *Insolvent* is nearest in meaning to: (*a*) rich, (*b*) indebted, (*c*) complacent, (*d*) secure, (*e*) impudent.

UNIT 17

Nouns — Possessive Case

A noun or a pronoun is in the possessive case when that word is used to show ownership. This, of course, you know. Do you also know that the proper use of the apostrophe is the chief reason for studying possessive case? Do you know that the apostrophe is the signal of ownership? Many, many writers, even experienced secretaries, are uncertain about the possessive case. There seems to be a rather general correspondence "blackout" as far as correct apostrophe use is concerned.

Only five apostrophe rules are presented in this unit, but ability to apply the five rules will enable you to handle apostrophes with confidence. Mastery of these principles, as with all other grammar principles, depends on clear understanding, concentrated study, and much practice.

Principal Use of the Apostrophe

The apostrophe is used most often to show possession as applied to a noun; for example: *clerk's* salary, a *day's* notice, *bookkeeper's* office, *child's* toy. The rule that governs this most frequent use of the apostrophe has been considerably simplified and consists of the following two parts.

1. If the word denoting ownership *does not* end in *s*, add apostrophe and *s*; as:

> **The man's hat was lost in the fire.** *Man* does not end in *s*; therefore, use apostrophe and *s*.

> **The lady's child is not well behaved.** *Lady* does not end in *s*; therefore, the apostrophe and *s* are added.

2. If the word denoting ownership *does* end in *s*, add *only* the apostrophe. Study the following examples.

> **Do you belong to any of the girls' clubs in the city?** *Girls* ends in *s*; therefore, add only the apostrophe.

> **Our ladies' lounge is on the fifth floor.** *Ladies* ends in *s*. For this reason, only the apostrophe is added.

Exception. An apostrophe and *s* are added to a noun ending in *s* if an added syllable is heard when pronouncing the possessive. For example:

> **The actress's behavior was very childish.** Pronounce *actress's*. Do you hear the extra "ses"? That is the reason for adding the apostrophe and *s*.

Note: Not all authorities agree on this exception.

The rule is very simple, but many students are unable to tell whether the ownership word ends in *s*. They have difficulty, for instance, deciding whether the word in question is *lady* or *ladies*. Understanding and use of the following quick trick will enable you to see immediately whether or not the ownership word ends in *s*.

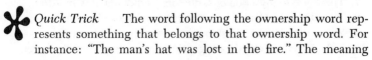 *Quick Trick* The word following the ownership word represents something that belongs to that ownership word. For instance: "The man's hat was lost in the fire." The meaning

here is *the hat belonging to the man*. *Man*, then, is the ownership word; and, since it does not end in *s*, an apostrophe and *s* are added. Another example: "Six months' interest is due tomorrow." The meaning is *interest of six months*. *Months* ends in *s*, which is the reason for adding only the apostrophe.

The quick trick is to say the word following the ownership word and then say "belonging to" or "of the" ownership word. Thus you isolate the word about which you have doubts.

To fix this quick trick in your mind, give close attention to the following illustrations. Ability to use the quick trick, combined with knowledge of the rule, will solve your major apostrophe problem.

> **How complete is your stock of mens topcoats?** Topcoats "belonging to" *men*. *Men* does not end in *s*, so the apostrophe and *s* are added—*men's topcoats*.

> **The** (secretarys, secretaries) **typewriter is seldom oiled.** Typewriter "of the" or "belonging to" the *secretary*. *Secretary* does not end in *s*; therefore, the apostrophe and *s* are added—*secretary's typewriter*.

> **The** (secretarys, secretaries) **typewriters have been exchanged for electric machines.** Typewriters "belonging to" or "of" *secretaries*. *Secretaries* does end in *s*, so only the apostrophe is added—*secretaries' typewriters*.

Note: A modern trend is to omit the apostrophe in names of organizations and institutions except when the name ends in *men;* as: *Lions Club, State Teachers College,* but *Businessmen's Club.*

1 *Class Practice* In the following sentences both apostrophe choices are given so that you can see the two possibilities for the use of the apostrophe. Review the rule, study the quick trick, and then select the correct word in each sentence.

1. (Children's, Childrens') toys are now displayed in the stores.
2. Mr. (North's, Norths') son is living in the (boy's, boys') dormitory.
3. I will give you my answer in three (week's, weeks') time.
4. The (boy's, boys') bicycles are in (everybody's, everybodys') way.
5. A (hero's, heroes') role is usually played by a famous star.
6. Our sale also includes (women's, womens') dresses and (girl's, girls') coats.
7. There are many (doctor's, doctors') offices in this building.
8. The (Olsen's, Olsens') new skyscraper is solidly built.
9. You must use the (customer's, customers') entrance.
10. Bill (Perry's, Perrys') resignation was accepted with regret.

Error Hunt 1   For practice on an advanced level, study the following sentences and see whether you can identify and correct any apostrophe errors.

1. The fishermens' boats were gaily decorated for the occasion.
2. Where is the patron's cafeteria?
3. Daniel Fuller's last pay check has not been cashed.
4. Mr. Greene can now loaf to his hearts' content.
5. Did the police recover the thief's tools?
6. The alto's voices were not strong enough to balance the chorus.
7. Have you seen the Burgess' swimming pool?
8. We are having difficulty finding stars to fill the heroine's roles for our next three pictures.

Possessive of a Compound

The possessive of a compound is formed on the *last word* of the compound. For placement of the apostrophe with this last word, follow the rule you have just learned; like this:

His father-in-law's business is flourishing.   *Law* is the last word and does not end in *s.*

The senator-elect's campaign has begun.   Campaign "of the" *senator-elect. Elect,* the last word, does not end in *s.*

Checking the timecards is someone else's job.   Job "of" *someone else.* The last word of the compound does not end in *s;* therefore, *someone else's job.*

Mr. Silva is president of the newly formed personnel managers' association.   Association "of" *personnel managers.* The last word of the compound, *managers,* does end in *s.*

Joint or Separate Ownership

Joint ownership is indicated by placing the apostrophe with the last word in the combination; as:

Jack and Bill's desk is usually cluttered with papers.   Jack and Bill share the same desk, as indicated by placing the apostrophe with the last word only.

Have you received Sue and Julia's supply list?   Sue and Julia together are making out one supply list.

Separate ownership is indicated by placing the apostrophe with each member of the combination. You might find it helpful to remember that separate apostrophes are used to show separate ownership. See how the preceding sentences have been changed to show separate ownership.

Jack's and Bill's desks are usually cluttered with papers. Jack's desk and Bill's desk. Each has a desk of his own. Note that the plurals *desks* and *are* are required.

Have you received Sue's and Julia's supply lists? Sue has a list and Julia has a list. Note the plural *lists*.

Possessive Before a Gerund

A gerund is a verb form ending in *ing*, used as a noun; as: "*Swimming* is good exercise." "Ray enjoys *walking* to work." A noun or a pronoun that precedes a gerund must be in the possessive case. For instance:

Can you imagine *Ray's* being late? The possessive *Ray's* must be used before the gerund *being*.

You can depend on *his* doing a thorough job. *Doing* is a gerund; therefore, the possessive *his* precedes it.

2 *Class Practice*   To fix in your mind the possessive-case principles that apply to compound nouns, joint and separate ownership, and gerunds, select the correct word in each of the following sentences.

1. You should not use (someone's else, someone else's) supplies.
2. There are no applications for the position of (editor's in chief, editor in chief's) secretary.
3. I was amazed at (Dick, Dick's) doing so well on the test.
4. (Peter's and David's, Peter and David's) locker is jammed.
5. Mr. Baker was much surprised at (Rose, Rose's) performing so poorly.
6. (Him, His) coming was not expected.
7. (Betty's and Kay's, Betty and Kay's) hair has been stylishly arranged.
8. Tom managed to reach the (runner's-up, runner-up's) position last week.

✓ *Error Hunt 2*   If the preceding practice achieved its purpose, you should be ready to proofread for errors in possessive-case principles applying to compound nouns, joint or separate ownership, and gerunds. Prove your readiness by making whatever corrections are needed in the following sentences.

1. Lucy is joining her brother's-in-law counseling service.
2. Hill & Forbes products are sold in all leading stores.
3. I disapprove of you being transferred to the sales department.
4. The secretary-treasurer's position will be filled at the next meeting of the Board.

5. Not many voters recognize our twin cities need for a more adequate water supply.
6. Burnham & Case's hardware store now stocks paints.
7. In the competition, our drum corps performance was rated best.
8. There is no telephone in Bob's and Henry's office.
9. What do you think of Dick's winning the suggestion award?

Possessives of Personal Pronouns

Possessives of personal pronouns never take an apostrophe. But many people violate this principle when using the personal-pronoun possessives *yours, hers, its, ours, theirs,* and when using *whose,* the possessive form of *who.* Look at the following illustrations.

Every incoming letter has *its* own place. *Its,* "belonging to" *it.* Possessives of personal pronouns never take an apostrophe.

If it is misplaced, the fault is *yours.* *Not* your's.

Alice, however, insists that the mistake is *hers.* *Not* her's or hers'.

Confusions in Pronoun Possessives. Errors are often made in the use of pronoun possessives because they sound like other words that have an entirely different meaning (called *homonyms*). The most frequently confused are:

Its. The personal pronoun possessive *its,* meaning *belonging to it,* is often used for *it's,* meaning *it is*—or vice versa. If the difference in the two forms is understood, the error will not be made. Reading for meaning is explained in the following illustration.

***It's* a fact that every job has *its* discouragements.** "*It is* a fact that every job has discouragements *belonging to it.*"

Their. There are three words with this sound: *their, they're,* and *there. Their* means *belonging to them. They're* means *they are.* If the meaning is neither of these, *there* is the correct word to use.

You will find that *there* will be no difficulty about payment. *There* is correct because the meaning is neither *belonging to them* nor *they are.*

Your. *Your* and *you're* sound alike, but the meanings are different. *Your* means *belonging to you; you're* means *you are.* For instance:

When *you're* working in an office, *your* attitudes change. "When *you are* working in an office, the attitudes *belonging to you* change."

Our. Clearly pronounced, *our* and *are* do not have the same sound; but because of careless pronunciation, they are often confused. *Our* means *belonging to us. Are,* as you will remember, is one of the "being" verbs. To illustrate:

> **When *are* you going to present *our* petition?** "When *are* (the verb) you going to present the petition *belonging to us?*"

Whose. *Whose* is a possessive pronoun meaning *belonging to whom.* The possessive must not be confused with *who's,* meaning *who is.* For example:

> **Who's the girl *whose* application was misfiled?** "*Who is* the girl . . . application *belonging to whom?*"

✓ *Error Hunt 3* Without preliminary practice, see how many errors you can find in the following sentences. All errors will be in the use of the possessives of personal pronouns.

1. There incoming mail is delivered at nine o'clock.
2. Who's eraser is that?
3. Judith never admits that a mistake is her's.
4. You know that it's your duty to be punctual.
5. What are those folder tabs doing lying their on the floor?
6. We are looking forward to are holiday.
7. When your typing a stencil, be careful about your stroking.
8. Do you know who's making up the assignments?

Learning Exercises

1 These sentences were constructed to help you differentiate between plurals and possessives. If the quick trick, *belonging to* or *of the,* does not make sense, the word in question is a plural, not a possessive. On a separate sheet of paper, write the correct word for each choice given you.

1 Why have you never joined a (publisher's, publishers') association?

2 Mr. Wheeler's two (daughter-in-law's, daughters-in-law, daughter-in-laws) were graduated from college.

3 (Children's, Childrens') (bicycles, bicycles') will be reduced next week.

4 Mr. Main's (letters, letters') are always well written.

5 The (secretary's, secretaries', secretarys, secretaries) desks are covered with all their paper and supplies.

6 The latest trade (journals, journal's) are in the bookcase by the (president's, presidents', presidents) filing cabinet.

7 All the secretaries must use the (lady's, ladies', ladies) lounge on this floor.

8 (Bookkeepers, Bookkeepers') like them are hard to find.

9 The (girl's, girls', girls) bowling teams defeated the men's teams.

10 When resigning your position, you should give two (week's, weeks', weeks) notice.

11 Right near the main entrance is a fashionable (lady's, ladies', ladies) hat bar.

12 Your carbon copies are full of (streaks, streak's, streaks').

13 The (Browns, Brown's, Browns') have bought a new car and have sold their old car to the Burnses.

14 Are all employees required to use a special (employees, employee's, employees') cafeteria?

15 (Womens, Women's, Womens') office duties usually require much detail work.

16 Production (methods, methods') have changed considerably in the last decade.

17 Those (vendors, vendors') have extended many courtesies to our company.

18 (Ruths, Ruth's, Ruths') notebooks are full of beautifully written shorthand.

19 The (sandwiches, sandwiches') sold in the cafeteria are a little stale.

20 The (Jone's, Joneses', Joneses) credit is poor.

2 Follow directions given in Unit 16, Learning Exercise 2.

1 The boss's wives accompanied their husbands to the convention.

2 Why didn't you put yours' in Mr. Pike's personal file?

3 The Fritzes were pleased to hear of my promotion.

4 The Poe's attended the banquet given by the Rawlings Company.

5 Was the shift key broke before you arrived?

6 We do not stock misse's coats.

7 Mr. Foley is interested in my attending evening school.

8 John and Stanley's shorthand notes are illegible.

9 Did you see my shorthand pen laying on the table?

10 It's difficult for you to fully control your facial expressions.

11 The secretarys desks' should be tidied before the girls leave.

12 I wish I was able to type as fast as Betty.

13 Were the Boston chief's of police reports typed in this office?

14 Mr. Jordan surely was angry when he laid down the law to us.

15 If I was you, I would ask to be transferred.

16 Your very careful about your letterheads and carbons.

17 The sales manager had went before I realized it.

18 Do not answer anybody's else telephone ring.

19 The boys' broke the window while playing football.

20 There are five Peters listed as employees with our firm.

Vocabulary and Spelling Refreshers

1 **Words Often Confused.** Finely, finally, finale; expensive, expansive.

2 **How's Your Pronunciation?**

a The following words are spelled as they are often pronounced. Which one is pronounced *correctly?*

vetran   tremenjus
incidently   purkolater

b The following words are spelled as they are often pronounced. Which one is pronounced *incorrectly?*

temprament   rekogniz
lukshoori   partner

3 **One or Two l's?** Some of the following words are preferably spelled with one *l*; some with two. Which should be changed?

a cancellation   c traveler   e marvellous
b cancelled   d skilful   f installment

Communication in Action: *The Error Is Yours*

You proofread twice some material you typed on a stencil before it was duplicated. But there it is—a misspelled word on each of 1,000 copies. You discover the error only after most of the copies are folded, inserted in envelopes to customers, and ready to mail. No one knows about the error except you. What do you need to know before deciding a plan of action? Should you tell your employer? If so, when?

Section 2   **Pronouns and Predicate Agreement**

UNIT   18

Pronouns — Nominative and Objective Case

Errors in grammar may be divided into two classes, major errors and minor errors. A person who makes only minor errors may be accepted socially and may be entrusted with some kinds of business jobs. On the other hand, a person who makes major errors in grammar reveals his lack of education, of polish. He is the employee who does not advance on the job.

One of the major errors is the use of an incorrect pronoun, such as *he* for *him* or *them* for *they.* In some sentences *he* or *they* would be the correct form; in others, *him* or *them.* The educated business correspondent does not guess which is the correct pronoun, for his education will have included the training that enables him to avoid making this major error in grammar.

The selection of the correct pronoun case form—nominative or objective—is the subject of this unit. *Case* refers to the form of a noun or a pronoun that indicates its relation to other words in the sentence. In English grammar there are three cases: nominative, objective, and possessive. Since the nominative- and objective-case forms of nouns are the same, your study in this unit is limited to the correct use of pronouns.

To train for immediate identification and quick application, you will learn three rules. These rules are for the nominative case only. You may ask, "Why only the nominative case?" Because, if you have at your fingertips or at the tip of your tongue the rules for the use of the nominative case, you will at the same time know when to use the objective case. If the nominative-case form cannot be correctly used, the objective-case form must be correct. (Rules for the use of the objective case are given on page 138.) The rules that govern correct pronoun usage have been considerably simplified here; but remember that absolute mastery of this usage depends on conscientious, hard study and practice—in class and out of class.

Nominative- and Objective-Case Forms of Pronouns

The personal pronouns and *who* have, as noted previously, three cases. In Unit 17 you studied the possessive case of these pronouns. The principles to be presented in this unit and in Unit 19 have as their foundation a knowledge of nominative- and objective-case forms of personal pronouns and of *who*. As you study the following pronouns, you will see that the nominative form of the pronoun is the name of the pronoun. For instance, the nominative-case form of the pronoun called "they" is *they;* of "I," *I;* of "he," *he.* Since you know the nominative-case form for each pronoun, you really need to learn only the objective-case forms for the following six pronouns.

Nominative		*Objective*	
I	we	me	us
he	they	him	them
she	who	her	whom

If you are not already familiar with these forms, be sure that you study them. *You* and *it* are not included in the list of pronouns because the forms of these pronouns are the same in the nominative and in the objective case.

Nominative Case

Although there are several rules for the use of the nominative case, you need to learn only three. Knowledge of these rules will prevent your making major errors in the case forms of pronouns. The three essential rules for the use of the nominative case are:

Subject of a Predicate Verb. In Unit 13 you had practice in selecting subjects of sentences; so you will be able to see immediately the subject of a sentence or of a clause. Now you know that the subject of a verb is in the nominative case.

   I **like apples.**   Why do we say *I* and not *me? I* is the nominative-case form, and the subject of a verb is in the nominative case.

   They **are fine workers.**   The nominative *they,* rather than the objective *them,* is correct because *they* is the subject of the predicate verb.

Predicate Nominative. A predicate nominative is a noun or a pronoun that completes the meaning of a "being" verb. In Unit 15 you learned the "being" verbs as: *am, are, is, was, were,* helper *be,* and helper(s) *been.* With this background, you will be able almost automatically to use the nominative case of a pronoun that completes the meaning of a "being" verb. Some illustrations are:

> **Mr. Bente said that the candidates for the office might be** (they, them). *Might be* is a "being" verb. A pronoun that completes the meaning of a "being" verb must be in the nominative case. Therefore, *they* is correct because it is a predicate nominative.

> **Yes, this is** (she, her). Do you see *is?* Then you know that *she* is correct because it is a predicate nominative.

Complement of the Infinitive "To Be" When That "To Be" Has No Subject of Its Own. This is the only rule that is new to you; and, to help you, the following analysis is made:

1. This rule applies *only* to the infinitive *to be.* Do not try to use the rule in *any other situation.*

2. The infinitive *to be* will have a subject of its own only when a noun or a pronoun immediately precedes it.

For application of this rule, study the following sentences.

> **Who would wish to be** (I, me)? Do you see *to be?* Is there a noun or a pronoun directly before it? No? Then this *to be* has no subject of its own, and the nominative *I* is correct.

> **The receptionist mistakenly thought the visitors to be** (we, us). Do you see *to be?* Is there a noun or a pronoun directly before it? Yes, *visitors.* This *to be* does have a subject of its own, *visitors;* and the nominative-case form after it would be incorrect. Obviously, the objective *us* is correct in this sentence.

 Quick Trick   For a memory hook on which to hang the *to be* rule, make this connection:

> *NO* subject——*NO*minative case

NO is the word you must remember, and *NO* starts the word *NOminative.* Think this over. You will be amazed to see that the quick trick promotes immediate application of the *to be* rule.

1 *Class Practice*   Select the correct pronoun in each of the following sentences. If you select the nominative-case form, give the reason for your choice. You need not give a reason for selecting the objective-case form; your only reason would be that the pronoun could not be in the nominative case. When making your choice, follow this reasoning process: Is the pronoun the subject of a predicate verb? a predicate nominative?

the complement of a no-subject *to be?* If the pronoun is one of these three, the nominative case is correct. If the answer to the three questions is "No," the objective-case form must be correct.

1. Dorothy is often taken to be (I, me).
2. (She, Her) is going to the store.
3. If you were (I, me), would you look for another position?
4. Mr. Sims thought the blonde to be (she, her).
5. Why did you think it was (we, us)?
6. Who would ever wish to be (I, me)?
7. The large, awkward boys in the machine shop were (they, them).
8. Why did you say that it was (I, me) who was ill?
9. Who's there? It is (he, him).
10. The producer would not allow me to be (he, him) in the drama.

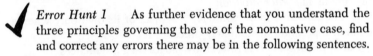

Error Hunt 1   As further evidence that you understand the three principles governing the use of the nominative case, find and correct any errors there may be in the following sentences.

1. Whom is going to need the typewriter first?
2. It would be me who would make a mistake like that!
3. I should certainly not like to be her!
4. The most enthusiastic supporters of the plan were us.
5. The fastest checker seems to be her.
6. If it had not been him who told the story, I would have believed it.
7. It seems to be they over there in the corner.
8. Was it them who left the message?

Pronouns in Compounds

Many pronoun errors are made when the pronoun is part of a compound. For example: *Sue and (she, her) tabulated the data. The girls sat in front of Ruth and (I, me).* You will select the correct pronoun immediately if you learn the following quick trick.

Quick Trick   Whenever a compound contains a pronoun—*Mary and she, Mr. Jopson and me, Francis or him*—mentally omit everything in the compound except the pronoun. Then read the sentence again and see how the correct form pops right out. This quick trick will also make your speech more polished. For instance:

> **Sam and (I, me) will carry out the invoice extensions.**   Omit *Sam and,* and you must say: "I will carry out . . ."

Mr. Sears told Sam and (I, me) to carry out the extensions. Once more, omit *Sam and;* and you must say or write: "Mr. Sears told me to carry out . . ." Do you see the value of this quick trick?

Pronouns in Restrictive Appositives

When a pronoun occurs in a restrictive appositive—*we girls, us fellows, we teachers*—writers and speakers seem to guess at, rather than know, the correct case form of the pronoun. You will have no difficulty with pronouns in restrictive appositives if you learn and use the quick trick given here.

Quick Trick   When you are about to use a pronoun in a restrictive appositive, mentally omit the noun but retain the pronoun. Read or say the sentence using only the pronoun, and the correct form will almost say itself. For example:

(We, Us) **men must stick together.**   Say the sentence, mentally omitting *men;* and you have: "(We, Us) must stick together." The correct form *we*, subject of the predicate verb, is immediately apparent.

Would you like (we, us) **boys to shovel a path for you?**   If you omit *boys*, you would surely say: "Would you like us to shovel a path for you?"

2 *Class Practice*   The first five sentences afford practice in using the quick trick for compounds; the remaining three, practice in using the quick trick for restrictive appositives. How rapidly can you select the correct pronoun?

1. Give the request to Mr. Avery or (she, her).
2. Thelma and (I, me) agree on most political issues.
3. Was that George or (he, him) in the private office?
4. The partners and (they, them) are discussing bankruptcy proceedings.
5. Mr. Todd asked his secretary to call Sarah and (I, me).
6. You students sometimes give (we, us) teachers a little trouble.
7. (We, Us) girls will be glad to work overtime tonight.
8. Every one of (we, us) clerks will do more work than the others.

Error Hunt 2   Now that you have practiced using the quick tricks, are you ready to proofread for pronoun errors in compounds and in restrictive appositives? If so, you will be able to correct whatever errors there are in the following sentences.

1. I told both Cora and she to be here on time.
2. The principal asked we teachers to read the daily bulletin.

3. I think that us girls have a chance to succeed.
4. Mr. Fortin appointed Owen and I to be tellers.
5. Could you persuade Eileen and she to check their work?
6. The manager and us two girls missed the last bus.
7. I encouraged Helen and her to take the lessons, too.
8. I wish you would let us bookkeepers find our own errors.

Objective Case of Pronouns

The objective-case forms of personal pronouns and of *who* are used when the pronoun is:

1. The object of a verb, of a preposition, or of an infinitive
2. The subject of an infinitive
3. The complement of the infinitive *to be* when that *to be* does have a subject of its own

Learning Exercises

1 Use the following short forms to indicate your reasons for selecting nominative-case forms: *S.o.v.* (for subject of verb); *P.n.* (for predicate nominative); or *To be, no subject* (meaning that this *to be* has no subject of its own).

1 The idea struck Agnes and (I, me) at the same time.
2 In her dress of gold, Alice was taken to be (she, her).
3 My brother and (I, me) were served with a summons.
4 What made you think it to be (he, him)?
5 It must have been (we, us) who have been neglecting this duty.
6 Mr. Banks selected both Susan and (she, her) as assistants.
7 Have you forgotten your childhood playmate? I am (he, him).
8 It surely ought to be (they, them) who qualify for the position.
9 I would not care to be (he, him), with all his money.
10 All secrets must be kept between you and (I, me).
11 It really was (they, them) who found the error.
12 When I was a child, I longed to be (he, him).
13 Are you absolutely sure that the visitor was (he, him)?
14 The men on the second shift would like to be (we, us), just for today.
15 Young bookkeepers like (he, him) need advice.
16 I mistook the telephone operator to be (she, her).

17 The agency sent (we, us) bachelors several invitations.
18 The coach and (we, us) boys leave on the afternoon plane.
19 Why have you been avoiding (we, us) scientists?
20 If I were (he, him), I should give the report to Mr. Tate.

 Follow the usual directions.

1 Harriet feels that most mother-in-laws are difficult to know.
2 That letter was written to Mr. Baird and he.
3 Ross failed to fully understand my instructions.
4 Do you know who's record is up for review?
5 Where are Mr. Barr and him going to get the machinery we need?
6 The coffee had went long before noon.
7 I wish Ray had lain the report where I could find it.
8 I cannot imagine Mark's failing to ring in this morning.
9 Us beginners in business have much to learn.
10 Did you say that you and him were not informed of the change?
11 Executive's courses in human relations will be offered soon.
12 What makes your secretary long to be her?
13 Roger rushed in as though he were afraid of being late.
14 Please ask Natalie and she to prepare the agenda for today's conference.
15 Barr and Brecks invention will speed the firing of ballistic missiles.
16 Next year we shall be able to test our counselor's-at-law advice.
17 The hardest workers in the office last week were us file clerks.
18 All the vallies in the graph showed clearly.
19 It might have been he who lost the mailing list.
20 Information about fall-out has found it's way into many homes.

Vocabulary and Spelling Refreshers

1 **Words Often Confused.** Sale, sail; intelligent, intelligible.

2 **From Colloquial to Formal.** Each of the following sentences contains an expression that, though permissible in informal spoken

English, should be replaced by a more acceptable expression in written or formal matter. What are the expressions? Suggest substitutions.

a As soon as I am through with this filing, I will help you.
b She baked a tasty meat loaf.
c His check was no good.
d My brother is now located in San Francisco.

3 **Plurals.** What are the plurals of the following?

a teaspoonful c company e memorandum
b gas d mouse f radio

Communication in Action: *Short Sentences*

Simplify the following involved sentence taken from a rough draft of a report you are asked to revise:

"There are more misplaced papers in small offices, in proportion to the volume handled, than in large organizations and at first this is difficult to understand when you consider that the chances for error are greater in a large organization where more papers are handled and more people are involved, however, the realization of this error possibility causes large organizations to give adequate attention to the important aspects of filing routine, with a resulting increase in speed and accuracy of filing."

UNIT 19

Pronouns — Case   (*Continued*)

In Unit 18 you learned to select the correct case form of a pronoun. You now have the background that will enable you, in almost all situations, to use correctly pronouns that have different forms in the nominative and in the objective case. To put the finishing touches on your training in correct choice of pronoun-case forms, however, you must be able to use *who, whom* correctly. In this unit, then, you will learn three additional rules for *personal*-pronoun case usage and two specific principles for selecting *who, whoever* or *whom, whomever.*

Case of Pronoun After "than" or "as"

When a noun or a pronoun follows *than* or *as* in a statement of comparison and that noun or pronoun appears in an incomplete clause, the correct form may be determined by supplying mentally the words that are not expressed. The following examples show you how to supply the words that complete the meaning of the sentence.

> **Charles says that he has more experience than** (I, me). If you complete the meaning of this sentence, you will have: "Charles says that he has more experience than *I have.*" *I* is, of course, correct. It is the subject of an understood verb.

> **Unnecessary noise disturbs Mr. Reid as much as** (I, me). Supplying the missing words would give you: "Unnecessary noise disturbs Mr. Reid as much as *unnecessary noise* (or *it) disturbs me.*" *Me* is the correct form. Why? Because not one of the rules for nominative case can be applied.

1 *Class Practice* Be sure that you supply mentally any missing words in the following sentences. In some cases, selection of the correct pronoun depends on voice emphasis. Emphasis in writing is shown by italicizing the words to be stressed. When you read a sentence containing italics, put extra emphasis on the italicized word or words.

1. You are much quicker at adding figures than (we, us).
2. I do hope they give *you* better treatment than (we, us).
3. I do hope *they* give you better treatment than (we, us).
4. Martha can do that job just as well as (she, her).
5. Do you think you have been as faithful as (he, him)?
6. Our office force works much harder than (they, them).

Spelling Pitfall. In the early units of this book, it was emphasized that mispronunciation or careless pronunciation is a frequent cause of spelling errors. Incorrect pronunciation is probably responsible for the fact that *than* is so often spelled with an *e.* If you tie in the *a* in *compare* with the *a* in *than,* you will always know that *than* is used in comparisons and *then* in all other situations.

"Self"-Ending Pronouns

Myself, yourself, himself, and *themselves* are illustrations of *self*-ending pronouns. Case-conscious writers who have not had the grammar training that you have had frequently use the *self* pronoun (called an *intensive* pronoun) when they are not sure of the correct case of a pronoun. For instance, "Be sure to write to Bill and *myself*" should be stated "Be sure to write to Bill and *me*." The *self* pronouns should be used (1) to emphasize, or (2) to reflect nouns or pronouns *already expressed*.

To Emphasize. A *self*-ending pronoun is used to add force to a statement; as:

> **Mary told me the news.** This is a simple statement.

> **Mary herself told me the news.** Do you see how the *herself* adds power to the statement?

When using a *self*-ending pronoun to emphasize, you must take care to place that pronoun where it will perform its emphasizing function. Carelessness in placement of the pronoun may lead to distortion of a message. For instance:

> **We are not yet ready to ship ourselves.** The correct message, of course, is: "We ourselves are not yet ready to ship."

> **Did you know that the home economics teacher cannot sew herself?** The message correctly written is not at all funny: "Did you know that the home economics teacher herself cannot sew?"

To Reflect. A *self* pronoun is also used to reflect some noun or pronoun that has already been named; as:

> **Jack mentally gave himself a pat on the back.** *Himself*, back to *Jack*.

> **Public officials should not vote themselves increases in salary.** *Themselves*, back to *public officials*.

Self-ending pronouns, then, are used only to emphasize or to reflect; and you will not use them in place of the correct nominative- or objective-case form of a pronoun.

2 *Class Practice* Selecting the proper pronoun in the following sentences will help you to learn the correct uses of the *self* pronouns.

1. Both Sue and (myself, I, me) have been working steadily all day.
2. Would you like Ann and (myself, I, me) to mail those letters?
3. The man who can laugh at (himself, he, him) possesses the highest form of humor.
4. Mrs. Beck and (myself, I, me) are happy to accept your invitation.
5. Many executives literally work (themselves, they, them) to death.

Error Hunt 1   If the preceding practice fixed in your mind the correct uses of the *self* pronouns, you will be able to correct errors in the following sentences.

1. Wait a minute. I am going to eat myself.
2. Helen and I will treat ourselves to a good lunch.
3. Mr. Curtis asked Mark and myself to share the switchboard duty.
4. Both Paul and myself like to operate a calculator.
5. The president himself issued that order.

Case of Appositives

An appositive is a word or a group of words used to explain, or to give additional information about, a preceding word or phrase. For example:

> **Mr. Barnes,** *the author and lecturer,* **is one of my friends.**   *The author and lecturer* gives additional information about *Mr. Barnes;* therefore, *the author and lecturer* is an appositive.

Did you notice that there was a comma before and a comma after the appositive? An important punctuation rule is: An appositive is set off by commas.

Appositive Pronoun Rule. When the appositive is a noun, no problem exists; but an error can be made in using pronouns as appositives. The case rule for appositives is this: An appositive is in the same case as the word with which it is in apposition. Concentrate on the following illustrations and explanations.

> **These junior executives, Alfred and** (he, him), **are pleasant co-workers.**   This appositive is in apposition with *junior executives,* so the case of the pronoun will be the same as the case of *junior executives. Junior executives* is in the nominative case because it is the subject of the verb; therefore, *he* is the correct pronoun.

> **Mr. Bell frequently compliments our junior executives, Alfred and** (he, him).   The appositive is once more in apposition with *junior executives.* However, in this sentence *junior executives* is in the objective case, so *him* is correct.

> **The shirkers are known to be those clerks, Alma and** (she, her).   The appositive *Alma and* (*she, her*) is in apposition with *clerks. Clerks* is in the nominative case because it is the complement of a no-subject *to be.* The correct pronoun, therefore, is *she.*

Quick Trick   To speed the use of the correct pronoun in an appositive, try this: Whenever the case form of a pronoun in an appositive must be determined, cross out the word or words with which it is in apposition. The correct pronoun will stand out immediately. For example:

These junior executives, Alfred and (he, him), **are pleasant co-workers.** Cross out *these junior executives,* and the sentence reads: "Alfred and (he, him) are pleasant co-workers." *He* is quickly revealed as the proper pronoun.

Mr. Bell frequently compliments our junior executives, Alfred and (he, him). Once more, cross out *our junior executives.* You could also cross out the first part of the compound, *Alfred and.* You would have left: "Mr. Bell frequently compliments *him.*"

The shirkers are known to be those clerks, Alma and (she, her). After crossing out as instructed, you will have: "The shirkers are known to be Alma and *she.*"

Note. Sometimes nouns that ordinarily would be in the possessive are followed by an explanatory word, an appositive. In such cases, the apostrophe or the apostrophe and *s* is added only to the explanatory word; thus:

That is Miss Forbes, the file clerk's, responsibility. Note that the sign of the possessive is added only to the appositive.

3 *Class Practice* Before selecting the correct pronoun in each of the following sentences, review the case rule for appositives and the quick trick.

1. Our good neighbors, Pauline and (she, her), invited us to dinner.
2. The successful applicants were the first two, Barney and (he, him).
3. Mr. Niles put us, Brian and (I, me), in charge of the office.
4. The culprits, (he, him) and (I, me), were punished.
5. Mr. Park placed them, Duncan and (he, him), on probation.

Who, Whom in an Interrogative Sentence

In almost all instances, a question containing a *who* or a *whom* will be in inverted order. Your first job will be to change the order from inverted to normal, after which you will be able to see at a glance which form is correct. You already know how to make this change, for you studied inverted and normal order in Unit 13.

Give close attention to the following illustrations.

(Who, Whom) is the man wearing the sport jacket? Changing to normal order: "The man wearing the sport jacket is (who, whom)." *Who* is correct because it is a predicate nominative.

(Who, Whom) shall I ask to sit at this desk? Normal order: "I shall ask (who, whom) to sit at this desk." *Whom* is correct because no rule for nominative case can be applied.

(Who, Whom) **do you take me for?** "You do take me for *whom.*" No nominative-case rule applies.

(Who, Whom) **are you supposed to be?** "You are supposed to be *who.*" *Who* is the complement of a *to be* that does not have a subject of its own.

Some *who, whom* questions are not in inverted order; but with your background, these will be obvious to you. For instance:

(Whoever, Whomever) **in the world would believe your story?** There is no way that the order can be changed, so *whoever* stands out as correct because it is the subject of a verb.

(Who, Whom) **is supposed to revise the filing system?** Once more, the order cannot be changed. *Who* is correct because it is the subject of the verb.

Quick Trick For rapid selection of the correct pronoun, do this: Mentally substitute *he* or *she* for *who; him* or *her* for *whom.* Test the quick trick by applying it to the four illustrative sentences previously given.

(Who, Whom) **is the man wearing the sport jacket?** "The man wearing the sport jacket is *he.*"

(Who, Whom) **shall I ask to sit at this desk?** "I shall ask *him* to sit at this desk."

(Who, Whom) **do you take me for?** "You do take me for *him.*"

(Who, Whom) **are you supposed to be?** "You are supposed to be *he.*"

4 *Class Practice* If you understand how to choose the correct form of *who* or *whom* when used in a question, you will have no difficulty with the following practice sentences. If the pronoun you choose is in the nominative case, give the reason for your choice.

1. (Who, Whom) did you bring with you?
2. (Who, Whom) will Mr. Ash have to help him?
3. (Who, Whom) is assigned to inspect the rockets?
4. (Who, Whom) did you meet at the conference?
5. (Who, Whom) will Mr. Abbott send to Dallas?

Error Hunt 2 After practicing the previous *who, whom* questions, you surely will be able to detect any errors in the following questions.

1. Who is the better typist, Jane or she?
2. Who do you believe to be the better typist?
3. Who did they take Jerome to be?

4. Whom would you wish to be?
5. Who does he outrank in seniority?

Who, Whom in a Clause

The technique for determining the correct *who, whom* pronoun when that pronoun occurs in a clause within a sentence consists of two steps.

Step 1. Isolate, or take out, the clause. When isolating a clause, the proper procedure is to start with the word *who* or *whom;* as:

>**I do not know** (who, whom) **the applicant could have been.** Step 1—isolate the clause: "(who, whom) the applicant could have been."

>**The new typist is a girl** (who, whom) **everyone likes.** Step 1—isolate the clause: "(who, whom) everyone likes."

>**Be courteous to** (whoever, whomever) **calls on the telephone.** The clause is: "(whoever, whomever) calls on the telephone."

>**Bess talks to** (whoever, whomever) **she meets on the bus.** The clause: "(whoever, whomever) she meets on the bus."

There are two reasons for the wealth of Step 1 examples given here. First, many students neglect to use this very basic technique, with the result that they never learn how to select the correct pronoun. Second, some students cannot isolate the clause. They do not understand that the very first word in the isolation process is always the *who, whoever, whom,* or *whomever.* If you are still a little hazy about Step 1, go over the illustrations again.

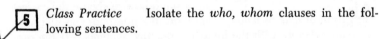 **5** *Class Practice*   Isolate the *who, whom* clauses in the following sentences.

1. My question is addressed to (whoever, whomever) has the data.
2. Philip Jones, (who, whom) you met yesterday, has received the trophy.
3. Philip Jones, (who, whom) was introduced to you yesterday, has received the trophy.
4. (Whoever, Whomever) draws the short straw will win the prize.
5. Do you know (who, whom) will be selected to help Mr. Coe plan the advertising campaign?
6. Mr. Coe did not tell me (who, whom) he has selected to help him plan the advertising campaign.

Step 2. When you have isolated the clause, look to see if it is in order. If not, arrange the clause so that it is in normal order. This will be easy if you remember that a verb can have only one simple subject. If a subject noun or pronoun—plus a *who, whoever, whom, whomever*—appears before the verb, the clause is out of order. For instance, consider the example clauses that were isolated in Step 1.

(who, whom) **the applicant could have been.** Do you see *applicant* and *who, whom* before the verb? This is your cue that the clause is out of order. The correct order is: "the applicant could have been (who, whom)."

(who, whom) **everyone likes.** Do you have a subject plus a *who* pronoun? Yes, *everyone* and (*who, whom*). The normal order is: "everyone likes (who, whom)."

(whoever, whomever) **calls on the telephone.** Since the *whoever, whomever* is the only pronoun before the verb, this clause is in normal order; and no change in order can be made.

(whoever, whomever) **she meets on the bus.** There are two pronouns before the verb, *she* and (*whoever, whomever*). The correct order is: "she meets (whoever, whomever) on the bus."

6 *Class Practice* Using the clauses you isolated in Class Practice 5, indicate those that are already in normal order and change the others from inverted to normal order.

7 *Class Practice* In Class Practice 5 you isolated the clauses. In Class Practice 6 you rearranged the order where necessary. Now select the correct pronoun, giving your reason whenever you select a nominative-case form. Mentally substituting *he* for *who* and *him* for *whom* will be of great help to you here.

Error Hunt 3 If you are perfectly clear about the techniques described in this section, you should be able to select the correct *who, whom* pronoun immediately. Prove it by making any needed corrections in the following sentences.

1. Do you know who they will select?
2. Do you know who will be selected?
3. You are one of those who I saw at the dance.
4. Will you send whoever Mr. Peters says to send?
5. You may give the records to whoever you choose.
6. You may give the records to whoever asks for them.

Pitfall. Sometimes confusion arises because a parenthetical clause—such as *I think, he says, we believe*—occurs within a *who, whom* clause. Whenever you see a clause like this, just omit it. You will then avoid the pitfall. To illustrate:

Is that the man (who, whom) **you said I should introduce to Dick?**

1. Isolate the *who, whom* clause: "(who, whom) you said I should introduce to Dick."

2. Omit the parenthetical clause, *you said:* "(who, whom) I should introduce to Dick."

3. Arrange resulting clause in normal order: "I should introduce (who, whom) to Dick."

4. Select the correct pronoun: "I should introduce *whom* (him) to Dick."

8 *Class Practice*   Identify and omit the "extra" clauses within the following *who, whom* clauses. Then select the correct pronoun. Give your reason if you choose a nominative-case form.

1. We invited Nigel, (who, whom) everyone knows is so popular.
2. Ralph is a man (who, whom) I believe will do satisfactory work.
3. Gilda is one stenographer (who, whom) I am sure can take Mr. Lyle's dictation.
4. I left the pen with the girl (who, whom) I thought had charge of lost and found articles.
5. You should select (whoever, whomever) you believe will best fit into our office atmosphere.

Error Hunt 4   Now see if you can find the *who, whom* errors in the following sentences. Omit any "extra" clause within a clause.

1. The advancement will be given to whoever we think deserves it.
2. Otto has a habit of flattering persons whom he thinks might be useful to him.
3. I listed the names of all whom she said had the necessary initiative.
4. The door opened and in came Ann, who we all thought was ill.
5. Has Horace, whom I believe finished school this month, obtained a position yet?

Learning Exercises

1   The following sentences furnish practice in applying the five additional pronoun principles presented in this unit. On a separate sheet of paper, write the correct pronoun for each sentence. If you select the nominative-case form, give the reason for your choice.

1 Did you think that Sandra was older than (I, me)?
2 (Yourself, You) and your family are to be our special guests.

3 The messages might have been from them, Mr. Nye and (he, him).

4 On closer acquaintance, I find that I like *Harold* better than (he, him).

5 The guide explained to Flora and (myself, I, me) all about shipping room procedures.

6 The prom co-chairmen, Ronald and (he, him), have called a meeting of the committee.

7 Julia wears more jewelry than (I, me).

8 Mr. Dixon always helps those less fortunate than (he, him).

9 My very best friends are they, Anita and (she, her).

10 Would you trust *Gertrude* rather than (she, her)?

11 The carnival manager asked Edna and (myself, I, me) to sell tickets.

12 We, Vincent and (myself, I, me), are civil engineers.

13 You know just as much about the atom as (he, him).

14 The only students who know anything about grammar seem to be Gladys and (myself, I, me).

15 Mr. Thorp (than, then) rang for his secretary.

16 They are not so careful about detail work as (we, us).

17 Mr. Scott has been very kind to my sister and (myself, I, me).

18 That assignment was given to us, Dennis and (myself, I, me).

19 At the masquerade party, Mr. Howe is sure to recognize Bertha and (myself, I, me).

20 Nobody else in this office has so much concentration as (I, me).

21 Tell me (who, whom) you would like to have for an assistant.

22 (Whoever, Whomever) has the right attitude toward work should get along well in an office.

23 (Who, Whom) do you think you are?

24 Tell (whoever, whomever) is the first arrival to open all doors.

25 Are you the person (who, whom) I have to see?

2 Follow the usual directions. Be sure to give your reason for each nominative-case selection.

1 Where are the experienced teachers, Miss Tate and her?

2 Who was the winner, Hiram or he?

3 Mr. Pine said that he knew it was her all the time.

4 Whom would Jane want to be in the drama?

5 Bill says that it is not who you are, but whom you know, that helps a person to succeed.
6 Etta brung flowers to Mr. Morey's desk.
7 Who do you suppose will get the order for jet planes?
8 Mr. Becker is better able to write the speech than me.
9 We found it difficult to determine whom was most worthy of promotion.
10 Mr. Percy's package has lain in the office for a week.
11 If Norman was you, he would spend that money for a new car.
12 We found it difficult to decide who to select for the promotion.
13 Have you noticed that mens' hats have narrow brims this year?
14 Whoever we select for the advancement will be criticized by other members of the staff.
15 Albin told his friends, Bruce and him, to ask for application forms.
16 Please ask her whom the chairman is to be.
17 Whom did you take me to be, Ellis or him?
18 Mr. Field always makes change's after letters have been transcribed.
19 To properly erase, you must know erasing techniques.
20 We shall be glad to receive whoever is sent by the committee.
21 The Ross's have made many personnel changes this year.
22 Why don't you ask whomever is interested for help with the drive?
23 All complaints should be sent to whoever is in charge at your local office.
24 The little boy said that the "Es" on his report card meant "Excellent."
25 Whoever I found in need of help was promptly given that help.

Vocabulary and Spelling Refreshers

1 Words Often Confused. Lean, lien; deference, difference.

2 Complete These Proportions

a *True* is to *false* as *perfect* is to _____
b *Familiar* is to *strange* as *major* is to _____

   c *Abundant* is to *scarce* as *natural* is to _____
   d *Conservative* is to *radical* as *valuable* is to _____

3 **E Plus.** In the following words, what happens to the final silent *e* when the endings shown are added?

   a arrange + ing   **c** expose + ure   **e** concise + ness
   b change + less   **d** advertise + er   **f** hope + ful

Communication in Action: *Right Meeting, Wrong Report*

You are at a staff meeting. As the meeting progresses, it becomes apparent that you did not understand exactly the type of report you were to give at the meeting. What will you do when you are called upon? (*a*) Give the report you prepared? (*b*) Reveal your mistake to the group and ask for more time? (*c*) Blame your supervisor for giving you the wrong information? (*d*) Bluff your way, hoping no one will notice? (*e*) Or what?

UNIT 20

Predicate Agreement — with Simple Subject

Would you say or write, "All our file clerks is experts"? Indeed, you would not! If you read this sentence in a letter, you would recognize it immediately as a major error in grammar. However, you probably do not know why the sentence is incorrect. It is because of lack of predicate agreement. You also do not know that varying principles apply to agreement when the kinds of subjects differ. When you have learned the principles of agreement presented in this unit and in Units 21 and 22, you will be able to avoid making errors in predicate agreement.

    The practice you had in Unit 13 will help you with these units on agreement. In that unit, you learned how to select the simple subject. You know that the predicate is the part of the sentence that remains after the complete subject has been determined. You know how to change a sentence from inverted to normal order. Thus you already have some of the background knowledge that is needed for these units on agreement.

For best results in the learning of grammar, make it a rule to concentrate on and understand each separate topic thoroughly before attacking the next. This procedure is particularly important when you are studying the principles governing predicate agreement. Keep this in mind when you work on the *general* principle and the two *specific* agreement principles presented in this lesson.

General Agreement Principle

A predicate must agree in number and person with the simple subject. Here you have the general agreement principle for all sentences that have a simple subject. For example:

> **The girls who work in the main office** (is, are) **all expert calculator operators.** The simple subject is *girls*, and you would say *girls are.*

> **Any man possessed of many talents** (is, are) **likely to be successful.** The simple subject is *man*, so you must say *man is.*

You will learn the several agreement rules better if you start by thinking of this general rule in terms of a covering umbrella:

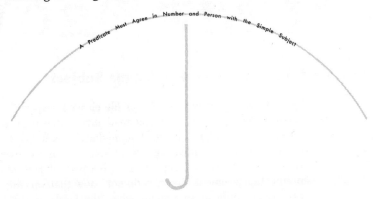

A Predicate Must Agree in Number and Person with the Simple Subject

The Umbrella Fabric

No umbrella will last long if the fabric is weak. To make your "cloth" the strongest that can be purchased, four allied topics are brought to your attention here. These are the supporting topics; and, if you fail to understand even one of these, your umbrella will be too weak to hold up in this unit and in Units 21 and 22. Impress upon your mind the following.

Predicate Verb and Pronoun(s). The general rule states that "a predicate must agree." This means that the *predicate verb* and any *predicate pronoun* or *pronouns* referring to the simple subject must agree with that subject. For instance:

> **Our matron** (likes, like) **to have** (his, her, their) **opinions respected.** The simple subject is *matron,* so you would say *matron likes.* The gender of *matron* is feminine; therefore, the correct pronoun is *her.* Your selection would be: *likes* and *her,* to agree with *matron.*

> **The office, together with the furnishings,** (has, have) **been cleaned for** (his, her, its, their) **open house.** The simple subject is *office,* a singular noun of neuter gender. Your selection, therefore, would be: *has, its,* to agree with *office.*

Correct Pronoun Choice. This you already know: The masculine pronoun (*he, his, him*) is used when referring to a simple subject known to be of masculine gender; a feminine pronoun (*she, hers, her*), to a subject known to be feminine in gender; a neuter pronoun (*it, its*), to a simple subject of neuter gender; and a plural pronoun (*they, their(s), them* and *we, our(s), us*), to a simple subject that is plural in number. Now comes the new rule: When the gender could be either masculine or feminine, use the masculine pronoun *he, his,* or *him.* Remember: Whenever you are in doubt as to the gender of the simple subject, use the masculine pronoun in referring to that subject. See the following illustrative sentences.

> **Every citizen** (is, are) **entitled to take** (his, her, its) **opinions to the polls with** (him, her, it). The simple subject is *citizen,* which might be masculine or feminine. Your selection would therefore be *is, his,* and *him,* to agree with *citizen.*

> **Nobody** (knows, know) **what the future has in store for** (him, her, it) **or for** (his, her, its) **children.** The gender of *nobody* cannot be determined, so the correct choices would be *knows, him,* and *his,* to agree with *nobody.*

Verbs Ending in "s" or "es." Notice that the form of the verb changes in the present tense and in the present perfect tense when the subject is in the third person singular—*he, she,* or *it.* In the present tense, third person singular, *s* or *es* is added to the verb. In the present perfect tense, the helper changes from *have* to *has.* You would, therefore, say:

> I, you, we, or they sing; but he, she, or it *sings.*

> I, you, we, or they do; but he, she, or it *does.*

> Girls have talked; but the *girl has talked. Has* in the present perfect tense, third person singular.

> **Contestants guess; but the *contestant guesses* or the *contestant has guessed*.**

Many students have learned so thoroughly that a *noun* adds *s* or *es* to form the *plural* that they overlook the fact that a *verb* ending in *s* or *es* is *singular* in number. If you do not know when a verb is singular and when it is plural, you will not be able to make a predicate agree with the subject.

Inverted Order. In Unit 13 you learned how to change the order of a sentence from inverted to normal. The point is repeated here because, if you do not apply this learning, you will make many errors in verb and pronoun agreement. Consider the following illustrations.

> **Where** (is, are) **all the bargains that you said would be offered this week?** The correct verb is *are*, as would be evidenced by mentally changing to normal order: "The *bargains* . . . *are* where."

> **In the offices** (was, were) **the missing girl.** Mentally change to normal order: "The missing *girl was* . . ." Do you see how important it is to change a sentence from inverted to normal order?

1 *Class Practice* Select the correct words in the following sentences and state your answers this way:

> *The sentence:* If a stranger (calls, call), treat (him, them) courteously.
> *Your answer:* *Calls* and *him*, to agree with *stranger*.

1. One of you (is, are) surely not telling the truth about (his, their) absence.
2. The key to the desks (is, are) hidden in (its, their) usual nook.
3. Here (comes, come) two of my best friends, (his, their) eyes shining with joy.
4. The file on Evans & Company (doesn't, don't) seem to be in (his, its, their) proper place.
5. Every single one of them (has, have) (his, her, its, their) work done on time.
6. You, as well as I, (am, is, are) to blame for misreading the directions.
7. In our storerooms (is, are) a variety of office supplies.

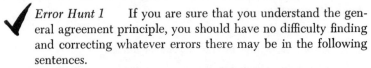 *Error Hunt 1* If you are sure that you understand the general agreement principle, you should have no difficulty finding and correcting whatever errors there may be in the following sentences.

1. Has every girl brought their walking shoes?

2. Not one of those doctors carries his prescription blanks with him.
3. Behind the microphones are seated the principal speaker.
4. Did you hear that not one of the candidates have agreed to state their platform?
5. Where in the world is the gloves I was wearing this morning?
6. The Ocean Beach parking lot don't accommodate many cars.
7. Each one of the players has signed his contract for next season.

Specific Agreement Principles

You have mastered the *general* rule governing predicate agreement. Now, here are two *specific*, special rules. Be sure that you understand the first principle before starting to learn the second.

Collective-Noun Simple Subject. A collective noun is a word that refers to a group or collection of persons or things; such as: *class, faculty, herd, committee, jury, company, audience,* and like words. The correct number, singular or plural, of a collective noun is not always easily recognized. If the group or collection is considered as acting as a whole, the subject is singular; if considered as acting separately, the subject is plural. For example:

> **The jury gave** (its, their) **verdict almost immediately.** *Jury* is a collective noun. The singular pronoun *its* is correct because here the jury is acting as a whole, as a unit.

> **The jury** (is, are) **arguing vehemently.** To argue, more than one person is needed. The plural verb *are* is correct because the jury must be considered as acting separately.

Do not try to apply this principle to any kind of simple subject but a collective noun. Whether to use a singular or a plural predicate when you have a collective-noun subject is one rib—but a separate rib—of the umbrella covered by the general principle.

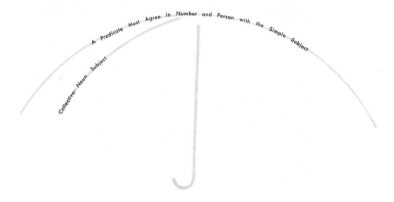

2 *Class Practice*　　If the word or words you select are singular, name them and say, "to agree with the collective-noun subject (whatever it may be)." If you select a plural, state that plural form and indicate the word or words that caused you to decide that the collective noun must be considered as acting separately.

1. Every nation (looks, look) to (its, their) leaders for guidance.
2. Mr. Blake's audience (was, were) so small that the committee (was, were) embarrassed.
3. The public (has, have) widely divergent views on education.
4. The group (was, were) evidently at odds among themselves.
5. Our company (has, have) just completed (its, their) twentieth annual report.

✓ *Error Hunt 2*　　This is your opportunity to find out how well you understand predicate agreement when the simple subject is a collective noun. Make any needed corrections.

1. The Lions Club will hold their meeting on Monday.
2. Mr. Niles said that each group must make its own rules.
3. Did you know that the Nye Corporation have installed several electronic devices?
4. Surely the City Council has discussed this question among themselves!
5. The committee is handing in their various reports.

Part, Portion, or Amount Subject. When the simple subject is a word that indicates part, portion, or amount, the number of the predicate cannot be selected until you know: part of what? portion of what? amount of what? For instance:

All (is, are) **gone.**　　Which is correct, *is* or *are?* Can you see that you must have more information before you are able to make the correct selection?

All the money is gone; but *all the dimes are* gone.

Half (has, have) **been eaten.**　　Once more, you cannot use the correct verb until you know *half of what.*

Half the cake has been eaten; but *half the cakes have been eaten.*

Here is the principle you are to learn: When the simple subject is a word that means part, portion, or amount, the number of the predicate is determined by the meaning of the complete subject, not of the simple subject alone.

Again you are warned not to use this principle except with part, portion, or amount subjects. This is another—and separate—rib for your agreement umbrella.

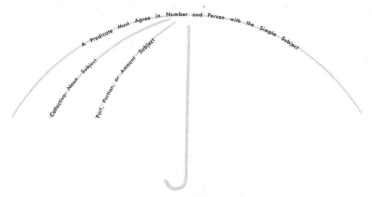

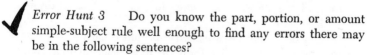

3 | *Class Practice*   After you have selected the correct word or words, be sure to indicate the word that influenced your choice.

> *Example:* Nine-tenths of our office (is, are) adequately lighted.
>
> *Answer:*   *Is,* because of *office.*

1. One-fifth of the clerks (has, have) returned to (its, their) respective offices.
2. Some of the reports (has, have) reached my ears.
3. Two-thirds of the beam (has, have) rotted away.
4. Part of the papers (was, were) in (its, their) folders and part (was, were) not.
5. Three-quarters of all stenographers tested (was, were) poor in spelling.
6. Half the machines (has, have) been moved from (its, their) original positions, and (it, they) must be returned.

Error Hunt 3   Do you know the part, portion, or amount simple-subject rule well enough to find any errors there may be in the following sentences?

1. Four-fifths of the job were finished two hours before the deadline.
2. Most of the money has been invested in bonds.
3. Some of the avenues has been repaved.
4. All the cafeteria have been renovated.
5. Two-thirds of the nuclear physicists has his advanced degrees.
6. Half the rolls are attractively arranged in their boxes.

Learning Exercises

1 For all agreement sentences, indicate your answer, followed by a dash and the word or words with which the answer agrees. Your work, on a separate sheet of paper, will look like this:

Example: The man (is, are) taking the package with (him, them).
Answer: Is, him—man. (You have selected *is* and *him* as correct because they agree with man.)

1 All travelers (stops, stop) at Mount Vernon on (its, their) way south.
2 As long ago as last month, the council (was, were) ready with (its, their) findings.
3 All employees of the State (takes, take) (its, their) vacations in July.
4 Do both companies (shows, show) increases in (its, their) inventories?
5 Every single officer of the Women's League (has, have) paid (his, her, its) dues.
6 In this modern age, nine-tenths of the offices (is, are) well furnished.
7 The outstanding bargain of the sale (is, are) the TV sets.
8 That family (does, do) (its, their) best to make a living.
9 One of our expert saleswomen (is, are) prepared to demonstrate (his, her, its) specialty.
10 Every city in the United States (is, are) conducting civil defense practices.
11 All the gasoline in the tanks (was, were) drawn off by vandals.
12 The committee (was, were) discharged because (it, they) disagreed on every point.
13 For how long (has, have) the two of them been married?
14 Half the offices (was, were) in (its, their) usual disorganized state.
15 Our best seller (is, are) broad-brimmed hats.
16 The revolutions that formerly took place in that country (was, were) a source of much distress to the farmers.
17 The jury (has, have) evidently been expressing (its, their) different views rather forcefully.
18 After the introductory remarks (comes, come) the real action.
19 Some of the machines on our order (has, have) not been received.
20 Mr. Jones said that his salesmen (was, were) out of town.

2 Follow the usual directions.

1 The football heroes, Carl and he, are very popular.
2 Every one of those tours were planned for a person of limited income.
3 Us industrialists must protest the added excise tax.
4 The committee have as their complement seven members.
5 Emily talks as though she were nervous.
6 The foundations of the problem goes back a few years.
7 No other girl in the office speaks so clearly as her.
8 The Board of Education recognize the need for increased school facilities.
9 All contracts will be given to whoever, in the opinion of the trustees, submits the best bid.
10 The day's routine had already began by the time we arrived.
11 In the corner by the window is the confidential files.
12 Has each of you women administrative assistants brought her notebook?
13 Plant worker's holidays are more frequent now than in past years.
14 The Board of Directors was all at the meeting yesterday.
15 The boy was instructed to leave the package with whomever answered the bell.
16 We found the other girls lying on the beach.
17 Ruth, together with Gloria and Nancy, are typing away busily.
18 Winners in the competition were those business college graduates, Dick and him.
19 Every gem, as well as all the paste pieces, was examined for flaws.
20 Your invited to visit us on Monday, June 2.

Vocabulary and Spelling Refreshers

1 **Words Often Confused.** Staid, stayed; facilitate, felicitate.

2 **Some Foreign Expressions.** Some foreign words and phrases frequently used in English are italicized in the following sentences. Translate them.

a Does the French word *résumé* mean: (1) something resumed, (2) a conversation, (3) a summary, (4) the main dish of a meal?

b Does the Latin phrase *pro rata* mean: (1) for the rats, (2) according to the rates, (3) concerning, (4) proportionately?

c Which of these means "for each person": (1) *per annum*, (2) *per capita*, (3) *per diem*, (4) *per se?*

3 **"Ei" or "ie"?** Fill the blank spaces in these sentences with either *ei* or *ie*, whichever completes the words correctly.

a The conc___ted manner of your n___ce was the ch___f reason for her dismissal, I bel___ve.

b My fr___nd s___zed every l___sure moment to ach___ve his ambition.

c The long-awaited for___gn fre___ght shipment has just been rec___ved at the p___r.

Communication in Action: *Celluloid-Collar Writing*

In cleaning out some very old files you find the following letter, which is over fifty years old. Rewrite it in modern language.

"Your letter of recent date received and contents duly noted. As per our agreement, enclosed please find my check in the amount of ten dollars ($10). I wish to advise that this is payment in full for membership dues for A.S.M.E. Please favor me with the date of the national meeting. I remain, Yours truly,"

UNIT   21

Predicate Agreement — with Simple Subject
(*Continued*)

In Unit 20 you learned the general agreement principle and two specific principles. Much emphasis was placed on the fact that the specific principles have no relation one to the other but are separate and distinct rules. In this unit you will learn the four remaining specific principles governing agreement with a simple subject, the four remaining separate ribs for your agreement umbrella.

"A Number," "The Number" Subject. *A number* has a plural mean-ing, and the predicate must be plural; *the number* has a singular meaning, and the predicate must be singular. An adjective between the *a* or *the* and *number* does not affect this principle. For instance:

> **A number of people** (has, have) **been asking for you, Mr. Steele.** *Have,* because *a number* is plural.

> **The number of available stenographers** (is, are) **fewer than the Government needs.** *Is,* because *the number* is singular.

> **A great number of young men** (thinks, think) **that earning** (his, their) **living is of no importance.** *Think, their,* to agree with the plural *a number.* Note that the adjective *great* is disregarded.

Quick Trick When confronted with the choice of correct predicate for *a* or *the number,* you will have no time to sit and think about which is which. This quick trick will enable you to use them correctly—fast! Look at the following:

Plural	*Singular*
a	the

Which is the shorter word, *plural* or *singular?* Which is the shorter word, *a* or *the?* The shorter word *a* goes with the shorter word *plural.* The longer word *the* goes with the longer word *singular.* Therefore, *a number* is plural; and *the number* is singular.

Your agreement umbrella now looks like this:

Class Practice To practice agreement of the predicate with *a number* and *the number* subjects, select the correct words in the following sentences.

1. A number of mysterious accidents (has, have) occurred in our factory.
2. The large number of absences (has, have) held up production.

3. A great number of citizens (is, are) prone to criticize without knowing (his, their) facts.
4. A number of books (is, are) missing from the library.
5. The number of men who idle away their time (is, are) amazing.

Foreign-Noun Subject. In Unit 16 you studied plurals of nouns, among which were plurals of foreign nouns. You will remember that, in some cases, a foreign noun ending in *um* is singular and the plural of that noun ends in *a*; such as: *memorandum, memoranda.* A foreign noun ending in *is* takes an *es* ending for the plural; as in: *crisis, crises.* A *us* singular ending becomes *i* in the plural; as in: *alumnus, alumni.* Perhaps the most important thing you learned was that, if you are not sure whether the noun is singular or plural, you should use your dictionary. When a foreign noun is the simple subject, you must know whether it is singular or plural. Otherwise, how can you make the predicate agree with the simple subject? Consider the following sentences.

> **An analysis of mailing-list returns** (was, were) **made.** *Was* is correct because *analysis* is singular.

> **Analyses of mailing-list returns** (was, were) **made.** *Were* is correct because *analyses* is plural.

Your agreement umbrella adds another separate, distinct rib.

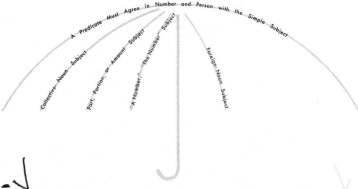

2 *Class Practice* Practice agreement of the predicate with a foreign-noun subject by selecting the correct words in the following sentences.

1. Put the parentheses in (its, their) proper (place, places).
2. The data (has, have) been carefully checked and can be found in (its, their) assigned drawer.

3. A very serious crisis (has, have) arisen in the Middle East.
4. (Is, Are) the sanitorium open for inspection?
5. Analyses of the production lag (is, are) ready for the meeting.

✔ *Error Hunt 1*   The two agreement principles just presented, *a number, the number* and *foreign-noun* subjects, are so simple that you surely will be able to detect any errors in these sentences.

1. The agenda is ready for presentation on Monday.
2. The number of poor spellers in all walks of life are appalling.
3. The bases for your thinking is unsound.
4. The number of mediocre workers are greater than one would think.
5. The alumni of the University is having its reunion Friday.
6. A large number of credit sales are returned every day.

"There" at Beginning of Sentence or Clause. If a sentence or a clause begins with *there—there is, there are, there has been, there have been,* and like expressions—the subject follows the verb. Whenever you see a sentence or a clause beginning with the word *there,* look for the subject *after* the verb and see to it that the predicate agrees with the subject. The following illustrations will help to make this principle clear.

> **There** (is, are) **various ways of setting up a letter.**   The subject *ways* comes after the verb, which is *are* to agree with *ways.*

> **Mr. Coe said that there** (was, were) **several letters still to be typed.**   *Were,* to agree with the subject *letters.* Note that this sentence illustrates *there* at the beginning of a clause.

Now you have another separate rib to add to your umbrella.

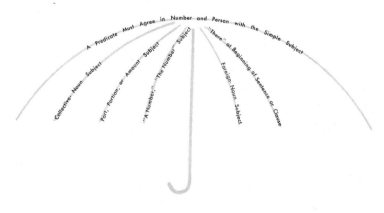

3 *Class Practice*   If you understand what to do when you see a sentence or a clause beginning with *there,* you will be able immediately to select the correct words in the following sentences.

1. There (is, are) always two sides to every question.
2. Have you been told that there (is, are) a right way to do every job?
3. Joe says that there (has, have) been ten men in the machine shop today.
4. (Is, Are) there eight or ten reams in that package?
5. The economist noted that there (is, are) plenty of jobs for everyone.

Indefinite-Word Subject. The indefinite words *each, either, neither, everyone, everybody, someone, somebody, anyone, anybody, nobody, no one,* and *a person* are singular in meaning. Therefore, whenever one of these indefinite words is the subject of a sentence, the predicate will be singular. For example:

> **Nobody** (is, are) **to take** (his, their) **confidential reports home** **with** (him, them).   *Is, his, him,* to agree with the singular subject *nobody.*

> **Neither of the proposed solutions** (is, are) **good.**   *Is,* to agree with the singular subject *neither.*

> **A person** (is, are) **not always able to have what** (he, they) (desires, desire).   *Is, he, desires,* to agree with the singular subject *a person.*

This is your last specific rule for agreement of the predicate with a simple subject. Keep in mind the picture of your finished umbrella. You will then remember that, although the predicate must agree

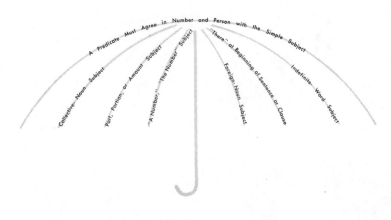

A Predicate Must Agree in Number and Person with the Simple Subject

Collective-Noun Subject

"Part," "Portion," or "Amount" Subject

"A Number," "The Number" Subject

"There" at Beginning of Sentence or Clause

Foreign-Noun Subject

Indefinite-Word Subject

with the simple subject, there are different kinds of subjects. For each separate type of simple subject there is a specific principle that applies only to that particular subject.

4 *Class Practice*   Take one more good look at the indefinite words listed and then select the correct words in the following sentences.

1. Neither of the girls (has, have) finished transcribing (his, her, its, their) notes.
2. Everyone who visits the exhibition (is, are) given a souvenir to take home with (him, her, it, them).
3. Nobody out of the entire group of listeners (seems, seem) interested in the speaker's ideas.
4. Each of the ten men already (has, have) (his, her, its, their) (mind, minds) made up.
5. Either of the synonyms (is, are) applicable here.

Error Hunt 2   Do you know what to do when you see the word *there* beginning a sentence or a clause? Do you know the indefinite words that are always singular? Then find the errors in the following sentences.

1. Neither of us are expected to work Saturday.
2. Did you realize that there are only a few silver dollars in circulation?
3. Nobody but Mary and me ever volunteer for the difficult jobs.
4. Somebody has to take their turn at the reception desk.
5. I looked in the warehouse, and there was only one bale of cotton left.

Learning Exercises

1   Using a separate sheet of paper, select the correct word or words in each of the following sentences and indicate the simple subject with which the predicate agrees.

1 The focus of our thoughts (has, have) been on the strong points in the program.
2 Neither of the men (is, are) able to tie (his, their) bow tie.
3 Because of a lack of responsibility, a great number of working hours (is, are) lost every day.
4 Each of the three leaders (has, have) been trying to get (his, their) (message, messages) to the public.
5 Where (is, are) the styli supposed to be?

6 There (has, have) been several service calls this morning.

7 Either of the typists (works, work) well under pressure.

8 A number of reasons (has, have) been given for the decision.

9 Neither of those executives (is, are) in (his, their) (office, offices) when you need (him, them).

10 That opening parenthesis mark (is, are) not correctly placed.

11 You will find that there (is, are) two mistakes in the letter.

12 Everybody in this office (knows, know) that (he, she, they) (is, are) to help reduce overhead.

13 The large number of graduates this year (is, are) impressive.

14 Mr. Hyde's order is that everyone (is, are) to use (his, her, their) own supplies.

15 Arthur cannot do the work because the needed data (is, are) not available.

16 There (was, were) ten orders that came in the morning mail.

17 The report is that someone (has, have) lost (his, their) notes on atomic power.

18 Usually, the number of applicants (is, are) not very great.

19 Neither of the files (has, have) to be revised.

20 The analyses of claims made during the last three months (was, were) of help to the purchasing department manager.

2 Follow the usual directions.

1 Many heroes have fell on the field of battle.

2 The number of office workers who patronize our cafeteria are truly gratifying.

3 Mr. Niles sent for the three of us—Jim, Clyde, and I.

4 You must have laid the special delivery letter on top of the chute.

5 If a person does not enjoy working here, they should resign.

6 I will provide help for whomever is in need of assistance.

7 Both Fred and myself are eligible for the promotion.

8 Are the memoranda in their usual neat form?

9 The jury was arguing among themselves as to whether it should postpone the verdict.

10 Today, there is more jobs than people to fill them.

11 There are only two private secretaries in our firm, Miss Carey and I.

12 Someone has left their shorthand notebooks on my desk.

13 Meet me at Peck's and Harding's office.

14 Behind our flag stand many patriotic citizens.

15 I reminded you that there was two appointments that have been canceled.
16 Do you know who the prospective buyer could be?
17 Have you seen the Nashes' new delivery truck?
18 Some bacteria are found in all liquids.
19 Neither of the women would admit that they lost their receipt.
20 Be sure to leave instructions for whomever is to take your place.

Vocabulary and Spelling Refreshers

1 **Words Often Confused.** Billed, build; deduce, deduct.

2 **Some Business Terms.** Which of the numbered items in the following sentences correctly matches the italicized business term in each sentence?

a *Agenda* means: (1) a list of the officers of a corporation, (2) a summary of the company's financial condition at the end of the year, (3) the items of business to be transacted at a meeting, (4) the history of the company.
b A *charter* is: (1) a person who draws charts, (2) a document granting a corporation rights or privileges, (3) a seal attached to legal documents, (4) bylaws.
c "The decline of the market wiped out thousands of dollars of *paper profits*." Does this mean: (1) profits listed in newspapers, (2) profits of paper manufacturers, (3) unrealized profits, (4) profits on the sale of paper and stationery?

3 **How Do You Spell?**

a The *ing*-ending form of *to sue*?
b More than one basis?
c The state of being unable to pay one's debts?
d The past tense of *see*, as in "I _____ him yesterday"?

Communication in Action: *Relaying an Important Message*

You receive this telephone message: "Tell Mr. Mason I've been called out of town and can't see him until Thursday." Mr. Mason, your boss, is on the way to the airport to board a plane to the city of the caller. The plane is to leave in 45 minutes. How would you relay this urgent message to your boss? List two alternate methods in case your first attempt fails.

UNIT 22

Predicate Agreement — with Compound Subject

In Units 20 and 21 you learned the principles of predicate agreement with different kinds of simple subjects. However, a subject may be simple or it may be compound. What would you do about predicate agreement if your sentence contained a compound subject?

This unit completes the "agreement" story. Here you will learn to use the correct predicate when you have singular or plural subjects joined by *and* or by *or* or *nor*. Mastery of these principles, plus one rule that does not belong with either the simple or the compound subject, is the task you have ahead of you.

Subjects Joined by "and"

A subject joined by *and* takes a plural predicate; as:

> The letter *and* the envelope *have* been separated.

> Jack *and* Owen *have their* plans made.

You would, perhaps, almost automatically use a plural predicate when you have a subject joined by *and*. There are, however, two instances where a subject joined by *and* takes a *singular* predicate. You must know about and watch for these exceptions.

Exception 1. When a subject joined by *and* denotes the same person or thing, a singular predicate is used. Understanding of this exception will prepare you for one of the topics presented in Unit 23.

> Pie *and* ice cream *is* my favorite dessert. This is one dessert, consisting of a piece of pie with a scoop of ice cream on top of it.

Exception 2. When a subject joined by *and* is modified by *each, every,* or *many a,* a singular predicate is used. For instance:

> *Many a* **young man** *and* **woman** *has* **risen in the profession.** The singular verb *has* is correct because the subject joined by *and* is modified by *many a.*

> *Every* **file clerk, typist,** *and* **stenographer** *is* **expected to have certain basic training as part of** *his* **educational background.** The singular verb *is* and the singular pronoun *his* are correct because the subject joined by *and* is modified by *every.*

Class Practice   Now that you know the rule and the two exceptions governing the predicate to be used with a subject joined by *and,* you will be able to select the correct words in the following sentences.

1. Each accountant, stenographer, and clerk (is, are) happy to be of service to you.
2. Accuracy and speed (is, are) both important to the typist.
3. Many a girl and boy (has, have) been eager to advance (himself, herself, themselves).
4. Joe and Tom (avails, avail) (himself, themselves) of all (his, their) opportunities.
5. Ham and eggs (makes, make) a substantial breakfast dish.
6. Both the workers and the work (is, are) wholly unorganized.

Subjects Joined by "or" or "nor"

When a subject is joined by *or* or *nor,* match the predicate with that part of the subject nearer (or nearest) the verb. For example:

> **Neither the parents** *nor the child was* **watching the traffic signals.** Do you see the *nor* joining the subject nouns? Do you see that *child* is nearer the verb? Then *was* is correct, to agree with *child.*

> **Neither the child** *nor the parents were* **watching the traffic signals.** Here we have the same sentence—with one important exception. This time, *parents* is nearer the verb, so *were* is used to match with *parents.*

Quick Trick   When the subject is joined by *or* or *nor,* start with the second or last part of the subject and read the rest of the sentence; like this:

> **Either Bill or the other men** (is, are) **to be asked to show** (his, their) **workshop products.** *Men* is the part of the subject nearer the verb. Starting with *men,* the sentence reads: "*Men are* to be asked to show *their* workshop products." *Are* and *their,* to agree with *men.*

Neither Mark nor Peter (has, have) (his, their) (mind, minds) **on** (his, their) **work.** *Peter* is the part of the subject nearer the verb. Starting with *Peter*, the selection would be: "*Peter has his mind on his* work." Your answer would be: *has, his, mind,* and *his,* to agree with *Peter.*

Correct predicate use with compound subjects is a matter of seeing *and* or *or, nor.* When *and* is seen, the *and* rule or exceptions are applied. When *or* or *nor* is seen, the *or, nor* rule must be applied. Take time now to fix in your mind each compound-subject rule. Then do the following class practice, which illustrates the correct predicate to be used when the subject is joined by *or* or *nor.*

2 *Class Practice*   How well you understand the agreement of a predicate with a subject joined by *or* or *nor* will be revealed to you as you select the correct words in the following sentences.

1. Neither Wanda nor the two boys (was, were) responsible for the ink spot.
2. Either you or he (is, are) to be transferred to the main office.
3. Neither Ann nor I (am, is, are) ready to start filing.
4. Neither Thomas nor David (avails, avail) (himself, themselves) of all (his, their) opportunities.
5. Either the saleswomen or Frank (has, have) to have (his, her, their) timecards checked.
6. Neither Leo nor the twins (does, do) good work after (his, their) lunch hour.

Error Hunt 1   Make the necessary corrections in the following sentences. You can do this only if you are clear in your mind as to (*a*) the correct predicate to be used for singular or plural subjects joined by *and* and (*b*) the correct predicate to be used for a subject joined by *or* or *nor.* This is the time to make sure that you can distinguish between these two rules.

1. Each pencil, paper, and pen are to be returned to the box.
2. Jane and I are ready to type the lists now.
3. Mercury or alcohol are used in most thermometers.
4. The hours and salary mentioned in the advertisement is not satisfactory to me.
5. The comma or the semicolon are usually required between the parts of a compound sentence.
6. Neither she nor you is in danger of overworking.
7. English and history provides the student with a knowledge of his own language and country.

Relative-Pronoun Clause

The principle that governs agreement of a clause introduced by a relative pronoun might be called an "orphan" rule, for it cannot be classified under agreement with the simple or with the compound subject. Before learning the rule that applies to a clause introduced by a relative pronoun, you must consider some preliminaries.

1. The relative pronouns are *who, which,* and *that.* Say these to yourself again and again, for you must be able to recognize a relative pronoun on sight.

2. A relative pronoun is called "relative" because it relates back to a word that is called an "antecedent."

3. The antecedent is usually the noun or the pronoun occurring immediately before the relative pronoun.

The following illustrations will help you to recognize a relative pronoun and to identify its antecedent. This you must be able to do before you can apply the principle.

Ellen is one of those stenographers who think their methods are the most efficient. Do you see a relative pronoun? Name it. How do you know that it is a *relative* pronoun? Your answer should be: *Who* is a relative pronoun because it relates back to its antecedent *stenographers.*

Where can I buy one of those erasers that have brushes attached to them? If you answer the questions asked in the first illustration, your answer will be: *That* is a relative pronoun because it relates to its antecedent *erasers.*

In the following sentences, can you see that *who, which,* and *that* are *not* relative pronouns? They cannot be, because they do not relate to anything. They have no antecedents.

Who is that man carrying the brown brief case? *Who* is not a relative pronoun because it has no antecedent.

Do you know which word is correct? *Which* here is not a relative pronoun.

Mr. Reid said that the man has much in his favor. There is no relative pronoun in this sentence.

Now that you have this basic information, you are ready for the rule that governs predicate agreement of clauses introduced by relative pronouns. Here is the rule: The predicate of a clause introduced by a relative pronoun agrees with the antecedent of that pronoun, *not* with the relative pronoun itself. You will apply the principle more quickly if you cross out the relative pronoun and use the antecedent as the subject of the clause; like this:

Ralph is one of those students who (thinks, think) (he, they) **can get along without doing** (his, their) **homework.** Omit *who.* Start with the antecedent *students* and make your selections: "*Students think they* can get along without doing *their* homework."

Your written answer would be: *think, they, their—students.* Interpreted, the answer means: *think, they,* and *their,* to agree with the antecedent *students.* You might find it helpful to know that the clause that follows *one of those* is always plural.

Use this procedure with the two illustrative sentences previously given, and you will have:

Ellen is one of those stenographers who (thinks, think) (his, her, their) **methods are the most efficient.** "*Stenographers think their* methods are the most efficient." *Think, their—stenographers.*

Where can I buy one of those erasers that (has, have) (a brush, brushes) **attached to** (it, them). "*Erasers have brushes* attached to *them.*" *Have, brushes, them—erasers.*

3 *Class Practice* Before you select the correct words in this class practice, answer these questions: Can you identify a relative pronoun? Can you select the antecedent? Do you know that the predicate of a relative-pronoun clause agrees with the antecedent? Will you omit the relative pronoun, start with the antecedent, and choose the words that agree with the antecedent?

1. My sister is one of those reckless drivers who (is, are) always taking chances.
2. Your duty is to paint the fence posts, which (is, are) being delivered today.
3. The lion is one animal that (is, are) known for the restless padding of (his, its, their) (cages, cage).
4. Mr. Barker bought one of those lawn mowers that (does, do) not break up the turf with (its, their) sharp knives.
5. Sam is one of those men who (makes, make) friends wherever (he, they) (goes, go).

✓ *Error Hunt 2* If you can make the necessary corrections in the following sentences, you will know that you *really* understand the relative-pronoun agreement principle.

1. It was his favorite pipes that was destroyed in the fire.
2. Judith is the kind of file clerk who think they own the files.
3. Responsibility is given to those people who has this very desirable trait.

4. The boss called my attention to some raised capitals, which is found in many typed communications.
5. Mr. Floyd is one of those golf enthusiasts who are always talking about their last game.

/3? – /7 5

Learning Exercises

1 On a separate sheet of paper, select the correct word or words in each of the following sentences; draw a dash; and write the noun, nouns, or pronoun with which your choice agrees.

1 Either you or Ann (is, are) to deliver the message.
2 On upper Ohio Avenue (is, are) the best drugstore and the best department store in the city.
3 Jack is one of those beginners who (thinks, think) (he, they) (knows, know) everything.
4 Neither Edward nor the other bookkeepers (gives, give) (his, their) services willingly.
5 Bacon and eggs (is, are) my most satisfactory breakfast dish.
6 Eric is a man who (takes, take) excellent care of (his, their) property.
7 Either the President or the Vice-President (is, are) usually in Washington.
8 Each chair, desk, and cabinet (is, are) in need of repair.
9 Let's read one of those books that (was, were) recommended by the librarian.
10 Bill said that there (was, were) present only Jane, Ann, and she.
11 Is it John and George who (has, have) the latest filing equipment?
12 Ruby and Thelma (is, are) taking (her, their) work home with (her, them).
13 You know very well that it is not I who (brings, bring) in the mail.
14 Either the manager or the members of the board (has, have) been approached about that directive.
15 A block and tackle (is, are) of great help to construction workers.
16 You will please mail the letters that (is, are) on the table.
17 Neither you nor Arlene (is, are) studying hard enough.
18 Every man, woman, and child (was, were) frightened when the plane broke the sound barrier.

19 Marshall Field is one of the few firms that (is, are) known throughout the United States.

20 Either Mr. Spears or Mr. Blinn must give (his, their) full time to the sales campaign.

2 Follow the usual directions.

1 Their will be a long holiday weekend for us in July.

2 Everyone is judged by the quality of their work.

3 Mr. Ayres has great respect for whomever he thinks is dependable.

4 Each man and woman is obligated to do a good job.

5 We women take just as much pride in our work as them.

6 Is that book one of the five that was recommended by Julia?

7 Production of plastic materials has risen steadily.

8 How would you like to have to pay the Quinns' heavy overhead?

9 Bread and butter are my favorite afterschool snack.

10 Mr. Craig is one of the salesmen who calls regularly on Ray.

11 Here are the folders you asked me to get for you.

12 Many an executive and a secretary have refused to read mimeographed letters.

13 You can trust Jack and myself to do our best for you.

14 High grades are given to whoever earns them.

15 Either Betty or the male accountants has to take his examination in order to be upgraded.

16 It seemed as if the day were unusually long.

17 Mr. Page is one of the best accountants that has ever worked for us.

18 At the concert last night, the musician's leader was unable to conduct them.

19 It is a shame that neither the teachers nor the principal was at the dance.

20 A committee to promote the morale of office workers were appointed by the president.

Vocabulary and Spelling Refreshers

1 Words Often Confused. Fair, fare; undo, undue.

2 Choose the Definition

a If your dictator told you to *delete* the second paragraph of a letter, would you: (1) indent it, (2) enclose it in quotation marks, (3) omit it?

b A *centimeter* is: (1) an insect having many legs, (2) a unit of measure, (3) a meter that counts cents.

c A *presentiment* is: (1) the sending of something in advance, (2) a representation, (3) a premonition.

3 **One Out of Three Is Right.** Which spelling in each of the following groups is right?

a succeed, sucsede, succede
b mimiced, mimicked, mimmiced
c conscientous, conseinshus, conscientious
d auxillary, auxiliary, auxillaree
e maintainance, mantenance, maintenance

Communication in Action: *The Chronic Complainer*

You work in the purchasing department. Seated at the desk immediately behind you is an older man who is a chronic complainer. He mumbles constantly about his aches and pains, the poor lighting, the unfairness of the manager, overwork, the shortcomings of other employees, and so on. For a while you overlook the problem, but it is beginning to affect your work. What would you do? Would you talk to him? to the supervisor? What would you say?

Section 3   Other Parts of Speech

UNIT 23

Adjectives

To refresh your memory: An adjective is a word that modifies a noun or a pronoun. Adjectives are picture-making words. For instance, if you read the sentence, "The man trudged down the street," you would know how the man walked; but you would have no picture of the man. Consider this: "The unkempt, weary old man trudged down the street." Now you can *see* that elderly, untidy, tired man.

The study of adjectives for the purpose of defining, learning the kinds, and exploring the picture-making possibilities would be valuable to you as a means of making your writing more descriptive. However, you are studying "use" grammar; therefore, you are asked to learn only those principles that will help you to avoid making errors in the use of adjectives. To be a master of the correct *use* of adjectives, you will need to have at your command all the rules presented in this lesson.

Comparison of Adjectives

Most adjectives are inflected, or modified, to express different degrees of quality. This modification is called "comparison." There are three forms or degrees of adjective comparison: (1) *positive,* used when the adjective is not compared with anything else; (2) *comparative,* used to express a higher or a lower degree than is expressed by the positive degree; and (3) *superlative,* used to denote the highest or lowest degree. Adjectives may be compared in any one of the three following ways.

1. By adding *er* to the positive to form the comparative degree and *est* to the positive to form the superlative degree; as:

Positive	Comparative	Superlative
fine	finer	finest
friendly	friendlier	friendliest

2. By adding the words *more* or *less* to the positive to form the comparative degree and *most* or *least* to the positive to form the superlative degree; as:

Positive	Comparative	Superlative
trusting	more (or *less*) trusting	most (or *least*) trusting
efficient	more (or *less*) efficient	most (or *least*) efficient

Adjectives of one syllable are compared by adding *er, est*; adjectives of three or more syllables, by adding *more, less* or *most, least.* Adjectives of two syllables are sometimes compared by adding *er, est* and sometimes by adding *more, less* or *most, least.* Your ear will tell you which form of comparison to use. You surely would not say, "The electric typewriter is *usefuler* than the manual machine." But you would say, "The new electric typewriter is the *prettiest* machine in the office."

3. By changing the form of the word completely; as:

Positive	Comparative	Superlative
much, many	more	most
little	less	least
good	better	best
bad	worse	worst

Double Comparison

Adjectives may be compared in any *one* of three ways. A common error, double comparison, occurs when two comparisons are used at the same time. Some examples of correct usage are:

Mr. Grayson is a kinder (*not* more kinder) man than Mr. Hall.

I think that this is the worst (*not* worsest, *not* most worse, *not* most worstest) of all the ideas.

Choice of Comparative or Superlative Degree

When referring to two persons, places, or things, use the comparative degree; but when referring to more than two persons, places, or things, use the superlative degree. Study the following illustrations.

Both courses are good, but I think this is the *better*. *Both* signifies *two;* therefore, the comparative degree must be used.

All courses are good, but I think this is the *best*. *All* means *more than two;* therefore, the superlative degree is correct.

1 *Class Practice* If you can select the correct words in the following sentences, you will be able to avoid double comparisons and you will know the correct degree to use when referring to *two* in number and to *more than two* in number. In each case, give the reason for your selection.

1. Which picture is the (larger, more larger), hers or mine?
2. Both girls have lovely skin, but Barbara's is the (smoother, smoothest).
3. Who is the (most efficient, most efficientest, efficientest) secretary in the organization?
4. Heather cannot make up her mind which is the (better, best) occupation for her, bookkeeper or secretary.
5. Heather cannot make up her mind which is the (better, best) occupation for her—nurse, laboratory technician, or dental assistant.

"Other" in Comparisons

When a particular person or thing is compared with the group of which it is a part, the comparative degree is used; and the word *other* is inserted. Here are some examples.

There are more office workers in New York than in any *other* city in the world. Since New York is a city in the world, failure to use the word *other* would mean that New York has more office workers than New York.

In some respects, secretarial work is different from any *other* kind of office work. Secretarial work is a kind of office work. Failure to use the word *other* to set off secretarial work from the group to which it belongs would result in comparing secretarial work with itself.

When using the superlative degree, however, *other* is not used. But some caution is required here. Use *all* after the superlative, not *any*. Study the following illustrations.

Sandra is the *most* industrious *of all* our clerks.   *Not:* Sandra is the *most* industrious *of any* of our clerks.

I like your idea *best of all* those submitted.   *Not:* I like your idea *best of any* that were submitted.

Adjectives That Cannot Be Compared

There are some adjectives, called "absolute" adjectives, that cannot be compared because in the positive degree they are already tops. For instance: If you had a *full* glass of water, your friend could not have a glass that was *fuller;* nor could someone have the *fullest* glass of all. Some examples of absolute adjectives are:

complete	level	round
conclusive	perfect	spotless
correct	perpendicular	supreme
dead	perpetual	unanimous
eternal	right	unique
immaculate		

Sometimes there is need to indicate the degree to which a person or thing approaches the top represented by the positive degree. In such case, use *more nearly* or *most nearly*. For example: Three of your classmates have drawn circles. You could say that "John's is *more nearly* round than Tony's" or that "Bill's is the *most nearly* round."

2 *Class Practice*   Now is the time to take stock to see if you understand *other* in comparison and if you know what to do about adjectives that cannot be compared. Select the correct word in each of the following sentences and give the reason for your choice.

1. (No, No other) manufacturing company has a better reputation than ours.
2. Mr. Hill's office is the (emptiest, most nearly empty) of furniture.
3. Jan works longer hours than (any, any other) girl in the bank.

4. This is the (most, most nearly) unique letter setup that I have ever seen.

5. Dora does the best mimeoscope work of (all the, any of the) girls in the duplicating room.

> ✓ *Error Hunt 1*   Speaking of taking stock, it is time that you tested your understanding of the four principles presented so far in this unit. Do this by finding whatever errors there may be in the following sentences.

1. The story about the returned goods is funnier than any story Mr. Loft has ever told.
2. Which master carbon is the best, the black or the purple?
3. Your letters are neat, but I think mine are more neater.
4. Brenda has the calmest disposition of all the girls who have worked for Mr. Larke.
5. Both girls are efficient, but Diane is the most poised.

Omission of the Modifier

When a modifier such as *a, the,* or *my* is repeated before each noun in a series, it is unmistakably clear that two or more persons or things are meant. If the modifier is not repeated, only one person or thing is meant. For example:

> **A stenographer and musician.**   Here we have one person who is both a stenographer and a musician.

> **A stenographer and *a* musician.**   There are two persons, one a stenographer; the other, a musician.

The first exception to the rule for using a plural predicate with a subject joined by *and,* the exception you learned in Unit 22, is: When a subject joined by *and* denotes the same person or thing, a singular predicate is used. The subjects just given as examples are used in the following sentences to show you what effect the omission or repetition of the modifier has on the predicate.

> **A stenographer and musician *is* prepared to offer *his* services.**

> **A stenographer and a musician *have* signified *their* willingness to contribute *their* services.**

Compound Adjectives

A compound adjective is a hyphenated adjective occurring *before* the noun, such as the following:

air-conditioned bank	middle-aged man	twenty-second floor
first-class typist	sixty-day note	up-to-date methods
high-grade goods	ten-story building	well-known person

Whether or not to hyphenate is a puzzler for most students. So that you will know immediately when to use the hyphen, follow these instructions, step by step:

> *Example:* **Highway 66 is a well paved road.**

Your problem is whether or not to hyphenate *well paved*. What noun is modified? *Road*. What kind of road? *Well paved*. In order to answer the question "What kind of?" you used more than one word. In such a case, you do hyphenate.

> **Ralph always has a know it all expression on his face.** What kind of expression? *know it all*. You needed more than one word to answer the question "What kind of?" so the sentence is correctly written: "Ralph always has a *know-it-all* expression on his face."

3 *Class Practice*   Fix in your mind the rules governing the omission of a modifier and the hyphenation of compound adjectives by selecting the correct words in the following sentences.

1. A black and a gold fountain pen (has, have) been found in the ladies' lounge.
2. It is too bad that your building is so far (out of the way, out-of-the-way).
3. Do you ever receive any (short wave, short-wave) broadcasting?
4. The army and the navy (was, were) somewhat lax at Bell Harbor.
5. The secretary-treasurer of the company (has, have) (his, their) (office, offices) on the tenth floor.
6. Most of the broadcasting from that station is (short wave, short-wave).

 Error Hunt 2   The fact that you were able to select the correct words in the preceding class practice does not mean that you thoroughly understand these particular two principles. If you can find the errors in the following sentences, however, you will know that you have a fine foundation for the learning exercises.

1. A blue and a red blouse is to be put away for that customer.
2. China is sold on the twenty first floor.
3. The cab and the driver is waiting for Mr. Evans.
4. Hit or miss methods caused the failure of that firm.
5. Englishwomen are noted for their pink-and-white complexions.
6. There are good workers and not so good workers in our office.
7. The red-and-black ribbon was removed from your typewriter.
8. A blue-and-red blouse are to be put away for Mrs. Graves.

Adjectives and the Polished Grammarian

There are two common adjective errors that are made primarily in speech. That you may not be guilty of these illiteracies, either in speaking or in writing, study carefully the following presentation.

Those and Them. *Those* is an adjective; *them* is a pronoun. Use *those* if there is a following noun; use *them* if there is no following noun. For instance:

> **Please take those papers** (*not* them papers) **to Mr. Hall.** The noun *papers* follows the word in question, so the adjective *those* is correct.

> **Please take them to Mr. Hall.** *Them* is correct because there is no following noun.

You understand, of course, that the adjectives *these* and *those* are equally correct, the choice being a matter of position. *These carbons* would be used when the carbons are near the speaker. *Those carbons* are at a distance from the speaker.

Kind(s) or Sort(s). *Kind* and *sort* are singular nouns; *kinds* and *sorts*, plural nouns. A singular adjective must be used with the singular noun; a plural adjective with the plural noun. For example:

> **The careful employee does not make** (this, these) **kind of error.** *This kind* is correct. *Kind* is singular and must be modified by the singular adjective *this*.

> **Why does Julia make** (that, those) **sorts of errors?** The plural noun *sorts* must be modified by the plural adjective *those*. *Those sorts* is correct.

4 *Class Practice* How well do you understand the difference between *those* and *them* and the correct adjective to use with *kind(s)* and *sort(s)*? Selecting the appropriate words in these sentences will help you to remember the principles.

1. Did you deposit (those, them) checks for Mr. Martin?
2. Cynthia likes this (kind, kinds) of letterhead best of all.
3. Why do you always use those (kind, kinds) of paper clips?
4. I should like you to get (those, them) for me immediately.
5. Those (sort, sorts) of machines were discarded by Mr. Hamil.
6. You ought not to associate with these (kind, kinds) of people.
7. Please pick up (these, them) business reference books.
8. What is the name of that (kind, kinds) of type cleaner?
9. Have you filed (those, them) sales letters yet?

Learning Exercises

1 Before you select the correct words in the following sentences, be sure that you have taken time to study all the principles in this unit.

1 This is the (valuablest, most valuable, most nearly valuable) proposal that I have ever received.
2 The clothing sold in that store is (low priced, low-priced).
3 Why did you buy the (costliest, most costliest) ring in the showcase?
4 The shipment contained only (those, them) sizes specified in your order.
5 The famous author and lecturer (gives, give) (his, their) (talk, talks) this evening.
6 Of the two cities we visited, we thought Dallas was the (cleaner, cleanest).
7 Adjectives are (picture making, picture-making) words.
8 Please hold the tape in a (more, more nearly) perpendicular position.
9 Will (that, those) kind of blanket be warm enough for camp use?
10 Marge has (lovelier, more lovely, more lovelier) manners than she.
11 You should use stainless steel, for it will resist rust and pitting better than (any, any other) metal.
12 Mr. Fyfe is really a much (happier, more happy, more happier) person than he looks.
13 You returned two books, but you surely do not expect full credit for (those, them).
14 In our main office, the receptionist sits at the desk (nearer, nearest) the entrance.
15 A red and a black typewriter ribbon (was, were) missing from the shipment.
16 Only (up to date, up-to-date) accounting procedures are used.
17 With the windows closed, the office became a little (warmer, more warm, more warmer).
18 Have you tried (that, those) kinds of cookies?
19 Why is it that a scholar and gentleman (is, are) specified for that position?
20 I wish you would learn to work (faster, more fast, more faster).

2 Follow the usual directions.

1 A new baby's outclinic has been opened at the hospital.
2 Do these kinds of oranges come from Florida?
3 The sales group are meeting in Parlor A.
4 Please do not order any more of them carbons.
5 Whom would you like to see take part in the discussion?
6 Just telephone my secretary or I for an appointment.
7 Owena is the most friendliest girl in our sorority.
8 Where shall I set these boxes?
9 Of the three buildings, ours is nearer the corner.
10 Celia's spelling grade was the most perfect.
11 Are the runners up Bill and myself?
12 Our company pays higher wages than any other firm in the state.
13 None of the accused men was actually guilty.
14 Our office sent two delegates, Dick and he, to the convention.
15 That file clerk and typist has little time for conversation.
16 Whom was the last person to leave this office?
17 Pride in work is more important than any other quality a worker can have.
18 Have you heard that there selling the warehouse?
19 Sue likes the new electric better than any machine we have.
20 Probably George, accompanied by his friends, has gone to the library.

Vocabulary and Spelling Refreshers

1 Words Often Confused. Shoot, chute; desolate, dissolute.

2 Pronunciation

a In which of the following words is the *u not* pronounced as in *human?*

gratitude   student
utterance   revenue

b In which of the following words is the *ou not* pronounced like the *oo* in *noon?*

souvenir   acoustics
cantaloupe   coupon

3 **They All Rhyme with "Hole."** Here are definitions of five words that rhyme with *hole*. How are these "ole" words spelled?

  a A black, solid mineral used as a fuel
  b One and only
  c A round, deep, hollow dish
  d To have one's name recorded on a list
  e The spiritual part of a person

Communication in Action: *Social Etiquette*

Discuss the following statements. Are they correct or incorrect? Consult a modern etiquette book in the library if you need help.

1. When walking on the sidewalk, the boy should always walk on the "outside" of the girl—that is, nearest the street.

2. A woman should never extend her hand when being introduced to a man.

3. At the formal dinner table, never begin eating until your hostess begins.

UNIT 24

Adverbs

Before you begin to study adverbs for the purpose of avoiding errors, take a minute or two to gather together the adverb knowledge you already have. You are familiar with the definition: An adverb is a word that describes, explains, or limits a verb, an adjective, or another adverb. You know that adverbs and adjectives follow the same rules for comparison. You know that, while it is true that most words ending in *ly* are adverbs, it is also true that some adverbs do not end in *ly*. As a foundation for this lesson, the most important bit of knowledge that you have gained previously is that an adverb usually answers one of the following questions: When? Where? How? Why? How much or how little? To what extent?

The reason you remember these questions is that they helped you to identify adverbs quickly. If the queries have receded to the back of your memory, reread them now and fix them in your mind. You are going to need them. Then roll up your mental sleeves and get ready to learn the principles that will enable you to use adverbs correctly.

Kinds of Adverbs

Classified according to use, adverbs are simple or conjunctive.

Simple Adverb. A simple adverb is used as a modifier only, and this unit is concerned primarily with simple adverbs. Some of the most common simple adverbs are:

soon	quite	immediately	never
too	very	clearly	now
here	nearly	always	then

Conjunctive Adverb. A conjunctive adverb both connects a subordinate clause to the main clause and acts as a regular adverb in that subordinate clause. Knowledge of this twofold use will be helpful to you when you study punctuation. Some of the most commonly used conjunctive adverbs are:

after	however	therefore	when
as	moreover	since	while
before	then	thus	yet

Study the following illustrations of simple and conjunctive adverbs.

> We can *easily* drive that distance in an hour. *Easily* is a simple (or modifying) adverb and answers the questions *"How?"* or *"To what extent?"*
>
> *Since* you did not send us your check, we will cancel the order. *Since* is a conjunctive adverb that introduces the clause *since you did not send us your check.*
>
> Time passes *quickly when* one is busy. *Quickly* is a modifying adverb answering the question *"How?" When* is a conjunctive adverb introducing the clause *when one is busy.*

1 *Class Practice* Stop here to get some practice in identifying adverbs. Use the adverb questions and see how quickly you can select the correct words in these sentences.

1. You will remember that we asked you to fill our order (immediate, immediately).

2. The wind blew (furious, furiously), and all ships made for the harbor.
3. I knew it was Bob, for he always tramps so (noisy, noisily).
4. The snow fell (quiet, quietly), and by morning the streets were covered.
5. When the farmer entered the barn, the cattle lowed (soft, softly).
6. Jet planes fly (swifter, more swiftly) than the older models.

Position of the Adverb

An adverb should be placed as near as possible to the word it modifies. Failure to do this may cause the meaning of a sentence to be obscured or even entirely changed. For instance:

Only **my boss sold his car last week.** Nobody else sold a car, only my boss. The car dealers must have had a poor week.

My *only* **boss sold his car last week.** Lucky me! Some people have several bosses, but I have only one.

My boss *only* **sold his car last week.** He didn't trade it in, polish it, repair it, or anything except *sell* it.

My boss sold *only* **his car last week.** He didn't sell his house, his ring, his clothes—only his car.

My boss sold his *only* **car last week.** Some people have two or three cars, but my boss owned only one.

My boss sold his car *only* **last week.** It was just last week that he sold his car.

 Error Hunt 1   Yes, correct placement of the adverb is a help in making a message clear. To express precise meanings, what changes would you make in the following sentences?

1. After payday, George has a cent hardly to his name.
2. This is the first time I have met him only.
3. I knew the dessert was a success when Dick took three helpings alone.
4. The building lot was not even sold for $3,000.
5. We just expect to leave in five minutes.

Adverb or Adjective after Verb

Some writers do not know whether to use an adverb or an adjective after linking verbs, such as: *seem, appear, sound, feel, taste,* and *smell.* You will always be sure which is correct if you understand that in some sentences the verbs are action verbs and in other sentences the same verbs are no-action verbs. Since you will be greatly hampered unless you understand this double function—action and no-action—of some verbs, you will do well to study very carefully the following illustrations.

The milk *tastes sour*. *Tastes* is a no-action verb here. If it were an action verb, the milk would have a tongue and would be tasting with it.

Kate *tastes* all hot liquids *cautiously* before drinking. Now this same verb *tastes* is an action verb. Kate has a tongue and is using it. Can you see her actually doing the tasting?

Robert *feels* so *bad* when June is ill. Is Robert actually feeling or touching? No. Since the subject is not performing any action, *feels* is a no-action verb here.

Until the lights are turned on, Robert *feels* his way *carefully* through the rooms. Can you see the difference? Here you get the picture of Robert performing an action—feeling, groping his way through the dark rooms. In this sentence, *feels* is an action verb.

If you can distinguish between an action and a no-action verb, you are ready to learn this principle: An *action* verb is modified by an *adverb*, but a *no-action* verb takes a predicate *adjective*.

Quick Trick Look at the following pairs.

Action	**No-Action**
Adverb	Adjective

Isn't it a coincidence that *action* and *adverb* have the same number of letters and that *no-action* and *adjective* also have the same number of letters? This hookup will enable you to remember which is which.

2 *Class Practice* To be sure that you are clear in your mind about *action—adverb* and *no-action—adjective*, select the correct words in the following sentences.

1. A receptionist must have a voice that sounds (clear, clearly) over the telephone.
2. Because of the heat, even our best stenographers looked (dejected, dejectedly).
3. The stenographers looked (dejected, dejectedly) about the office at all the letters that had to be rewritten.
4. Jerry thought that the coffee tasted (strong, strongly).
5. The trucks appeared very (sudden, suddenly) at the entrance to the store.
6. Mr. Park appears (belligerent, belligerently) this morning.

✓ *Error Hunt 2*   If the preceding class practice did what it was supposed to do, you should be able with confidence to make any necessary corrections in these sentences.

1. Your work seems satisfactorily in all respects.
2. The disappointed customer looked angry.
3. Ella said that she felt confidently about winning the contest.
4. I thought she seemed happily to make the appointment.
5. The disappointed customer looked angrily at the bare counters.
6. Throw away the peaches that taste badly.
7. Don't the bells sound beautifully on the clear night air?

Adverb and Adjective Confusions

The word pairs that you study in this section are sources of frequent errors. To provide you with facility in their use, a rather full discussion is given. Start by remembering that, in each pair, the first named is an adjective; the second, an adverb.

Sure, Surely; Real, Really. The choice of *sure* or *surely*, or of *real* or *really*, depends on whether you need an adjective or an adverb. *Sure* and *real* are adjectives; *surely* and *really* are adverbs. For rapid selection of the correct word, remember this: If you can substitute the word *very* or *certainly*, the correct word is *surely* or *really*. *Very* and *certainly* end in *y*, and so do *surely* and *really*. If you cannot make the substitution, use *sure* or *real*. For example:

> **Is this a *sure* way to succeed?**   *Sure* is correct because *very* or *certainly* cannot be substituted.

> **You *surely* have been a success here.**   This is correct because you can say *you certainly have been* . . . .

> **Mr. Sanders has a *real* affection for his friends.**   You would not say he has a *very* or a *certainly* affection.

> **Mary does her best work in a *really* efficient atmosphere.**   She does her best work in a *very* efficient atmosphere.

Good, Well. *Good* is the adjective and *well* is the adverb, except when referring to health. If the question "How?" can be answered, use *well*; if not, use *good*. However, when speaking of health, always use *well*. Say, "I don't feel *well* (not good)." To illustrate:

> **Is this a *good* time to ask about a salary increase?**   *Good* is an adjective modifying the noun *time*. It does not answer the question "How?"

> **The addressograph is now working *well*.**   Working how? *Well*.

> **You do not look *well* today.**   Referring to health, use *well*.

Some, Somewhat. Some is an adjective and *somewhat* is an adverb. For quick application, do this: Use *somewhat* if you can substitute the words *a little bit;* otherwise, use *some.* Study the following examples.

> **Lillian was *somewhat* hesitant about asking for an appointment.** *A little bit* hesitant.

> **I should like to order *some* stationery for my own use.** *Some,* because *a little bit* cannot be substituted.

Most, Almost. Most is an adjective, the superlative of *much* or *many;* as: *many, more, most. Almost* is an adverb meaning *not quite* or *very nearly.* Do not fall into the rather common error of thinking that *most* is a contraction for *almost.* For example:

> **Before I knew it, we were *almost* there.** *Not quite* or *very nearly* there.

> ***Most* employees have spent *almost* all their pay shortly after they receive it.** Many, more, *most* employees have spent *very nearly* all their pay . . . .

Adverb Confusion

Both *never* and *not* are adverbs, but their meanings are quite different. *Never* means "not ever; at no time; not in any degree, way, or condition." It is a strong word. *Not* is simply a word that expresses negation. *Never* is used all too frequently and incorrectly instead of *not.* For instance:

> **We have not received your check.** *Not:* We never received your check.

> **Mr. Hanley did not order us to arrange the names geographically.** *Not:* Mr. Hanley never ordered us . . . .

> **We have never offered a special discount to any of our customers.** *Never* is correctly used in this sentence.

3 | *Class Practice*   To fix in your mind the differences between the pairs discussed in this section and between *never* and *not,* select the correct words in the following sentences.

1. The (real, really) story is (real, really) shocking.
2. Bill has (most, almost) finished (most, almost) of his work.
3. You (did not tell, never told) us to ship C. O. D.
4. (Some, Somewhat) typists are (some, somewhat) careless about proofreading.
5. The (good, well) secretary performs (good, well) even under trying circumstances.

6. You are (sure, surely) justified in making a complaint when you are (sure, surely) of your facts.
7. (Good, Well) work cannot be done (good, well) when the worker is not feeling (good, well).

Avoiding Double Negatives

Scarcely, only, hardly, but, and *never* are negative in meaning; and *no other negative* should be used with them. For example:

> **It is so foggy that you *can scarcely* see the white lines on the road.** *Not* you cannot scarcely.

> **I *have only* one comment to make.** *Not* haven't only.

> **Why *doesn't* the manager *ever* use the front entrance?** *Not* why doesn't the manager never.

4 *Class Practice* Select the correct words in these sentences and remember that your aim is to avoid double negatives.

1. I couldn't (help but think, help thinking) of all the hours Mr. Baird spends on his work.
2. Alice said that she (wasn't, was) scarcely sixteen when she was graduated from high school.
3. Roy (didn't earn but, earned but) $400 last summer.
4. Diane (hasn't, has), according to the latest information, hardly a relative left in the world.
5. Mr. Harper (didn't give, gave) only $5 to the Community Chest.

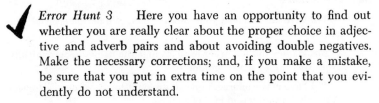 *Error Hunt 3* Here you have an opportunity to find out whether you are really clear about the proper choice in adjective and adverb pairs and about avoiding double negatives. Make the necessary corrections; and, if you make a mistake, be sure that you put in extra time on the point that you evidently do not understand.

1. Catherine is wearing a real pretty dress today.
2. Did you notice that Joan couldn't help but smile at Jim's foolish antics?
3. If you do not feel good, ask for permission to go home.
4. Bill complains that he has learned scarcely anything in that course.
5. Mr. St. Cyr's letters are some longer than Mr. Cabot's.
6. Mr. Homer said that he hasn't, with all his medical care, never been really well since his boyhood.
7. Are you most ready to type that report?
8. It's sure a good thing for you that you checked those figures.

Learning Exercises

V

1 Before you select the correct words in the following sentences, study all the topics presented in this unit. Write your answers on a separate sheet of paper.

1 The experienced mason spreads cement (even, evenly).
2 We were (sure, surely) glad to see Mr. Acton's secretary return to the office.
3 The sale was so successful that the grocer (has, hasn't) scarcely a pound of sugar left.
4 Bess (hardly needs, needs hardly) ten more points to win the contest.
5 Judith felt the cloth (careful, carefully) before making her purchase.
6 Mr. Harkin's reply was that he (had, hadn't) only one comment to make.
7 Mr. Nash is (real, really) delighted that you are able to come to work.
8 At the camp, fresh milk was delivered (regular, regularly).
9 Rufus always tastes hot food (cautious, cautiously) before taking a mouthful.
10 Such an arrangement (could, couldn't) hardly satisfy even the best of employers.
11 Our supervisor can do all the office jobs very (good, well).
12 Edith said that the coffee tasted (bitter, bitterly).
13 There (are, aren't) but five more days before Christmas.
14 Bad news seems to travel (quicker, more quickly) than good news.
15 Frances looked (beautiful, beautifully) in her Easter suit.
16 Miss Doe doesn't (never, ever) take her full lunch hour.
17 In some situations, Natalie does not act very (good, well).
18 The audience (only seems to be applauding, seems to be applauding only) for Mr. Rusch.
19 We were glad we sent for the new doctor. He looked (capable, capably).
20 Mr. Park's son has grown (some, somewhat) taller since his last trip home.

2 Follow the usual directions.

1 Danny, along with two other boys, was selected to represent the purchasing department.

2 Are the messenger boy's bicycles their own property?

3 That house needs a coat of paint very much.

4 Who did you ask for the key to my supply room?

5 Mr. Exeter is one of those men who are conscientious about completing their assignments on time.

6 The boss had no criticism of the efficiency of we personal shoppers.

7 In the files were the data for the specifications.

8 We checkers felt badly about the error.

9 My salary has been risen twice in the six months I have worked here.

10 Because the announcer does not talk clear, I miss much of the news.

11 Three-quarters of the mechanics were in no condition to work in that intense heat.

12 Both Sam and myself need to use a calculator.

13 My plan is really much more simpler than it sounds.

14 Almost all clerks will give you the best of service.

15 About four o'clock, the important records are lain in the safe.

16 Each letterhead, envelope, and carbon copy needs to be handled very carefully.

17 Do you object to the boy walking on the grass?

18 Neither the duplicated copies nor the original have been folded.

19 Everyone whom they talked with liked the plan.

20 Why did the Lewises' decide to sell their business?

Vocabulary and Spelling Refreshers

1 **Words Often Confused.** Disburse, disperse; equable, equitable.

2 **Synonyms.** Match each word in column A with the term in column B that is nearest it in meaning.

A	B
a repetitious	1 With rainbowlike colors
b iridescent	2 Enduring
c obscure	3 Unreal
d permanent	4 Transitory
e axiomatic	5 Monotonous doing or saying
	6 Critical
	7 Indistinct
	8 Self-evident

3 **Adding "ed."** How are each of these words spelled when *ed* is added?

a admit **c** develop **e** refer
b acquaint **d** appall **f** embarrass

Communication in Action: *Grooming*

There was an unfortunate occurrence in your office yesterday. One of the newer office workers was sent home because she had arrived with her hair in curlers and a scarf over her head. It has always been an unwritten rule that both men and women in your office dress in an acceptable manner for business. Prepare a one-minute talk on one phase of good grooming: make-up, appropriate clothing, matching colors in dress, grooming accessories, cleanliness, men's wear, and so on.

UNIT 25

Prepositions

As you already know, a preposition is a connecting word that shows the relation between a noun or a pronoun and some other word in the sentence. You know that a preposition is always followed by a noun or a pronoun and that the preposition and the noun or pronoun, together with any modifiers, are called a *prepositional phrase*. There are, however, additional facts that you should know in order to avoid making preposition errors.

To be sure that you have a clear recall of prepositions, study the following list of some prepositions in common use. Perhaps you can add to the list.

about	below	except	of	up
above	beside	for	off	upon
after	between	from	on	until
among	but (meaning	in	over	with
at	"except")	into	to	
before	by	like	under	

Words Requiring Specific Prepositions

Certain words require specific prepositions following them. Other words require one preposition for one meaning and an entirely different preposition in another situation. Many students in whose homes a language other than English is spoken have difficulty with prepositions. To promote your use of the exact, correct preposition, study those listed in the Reference Section (pages 549–550).

For Special Study

From the longer listing of words that require specific prepositions, nine have been selected for your special study. These words are used frequently in business communications and, of course, call for your concentrated attention.

Agree with (a person), *to* (a plan). Use *agree with* when the object of the preposition is a person; use *agree to* when the object is not a person; as:

> Mr. Taylor *agreed with* the other members of the committee.

> Mr. Taylor *agreed to* the proposal made by the committee.

Angry with (persons), *at* (things or conditions). Use *angry with* when the object of the preposition is a person; use *angry at* when the object is not a person. For instance:

> Are you *angry with me* or *with the other girls?*

> I get so *angry at my machine* when I make an error.

Part from (a person), *with* (a thing). Use *part from* when the object of the preposition is a person; use *part with* when the object is not a person; as:

> Alice *parted from Bill* at the bus stop.

> Sue hates to *part with her stationery.*

Discrepancy in (one thing), *between* (two things). Use *discrepancy in* when the object of the preposition is singular; use *discrepancy between* when the object denotes exactly two in number. To illustrate:

> Did you note any *discrepancy in the Polaris report?*

> There is a discrepancy *between your total and mine.*

In Regard to; With Regard to; As Regards. The three phrases are equally correct. It makes no difference whether you write *in regard to the plan, with regard to the plan,* or *as regards the plan.* The common error is the use of *regards* with *in* or *with*. If you use *regards,* then the word ending in *s* (*as*) must be used before it. Look at the following examples.

> **We should like to talk with you** *with regard* (or *in regard*) **to your proposal.** Not *with regards* or *in regards.*

> *As regards* **personnel policies, Mr. Ames has no authority.** This is correct because both words—*as* and *regards*—end in *s.*

Different from; Identical with; Plan to; Retroactive to. No tips can be given to help you master the correct prepositions in these phrases. You will have to go over them again and again and plant them firmly in your mind. Before you start to memorize, study the following illustrations.

> **Your ideas about proper dress are very** *different from* **mine.** *Not* different than.

> **Bob's problem is** *identical with* **mine.** *Not* identical to.

> **You should** *plan to join* **some of the office activities.** *Not* plan on joining.

> **Do you think Maria is** *planning to apply* **for the secretarial position?** *Not* planning on applying.

> **Is the directive** *retroactive to* **January 1?** *Not* retroactive from.

1 *Class Practice* The following sentences should help you with the particular prepositions selected for special study. Perhaps you should review these nine before you do this practice.

1. Did you see how angry Mr. Lynch was (with, at) the way Sally treated that customer?
2. The blouse Ella bought is identical (with, to) Jean's.
3. Our city editor plans (to put, on putting) out a special edition.
4. Mr. Saunders' views are seemingly exactly (opposite to, opposite) Mr. Price's.
5. Why isn't the salary increase retroactive (to, from) May 15?
6. Mr. Burke wishes to see you (in regard, in regards) to taking inventory.
7. Has your mother ever parted (from, with) any of the letters your father wrote to her?
8. The discrepancy (in, between) what Mr. Hayes says and what he does is very apparent.
9. In what way is Lee's personality different (from, than) Jane's?

✓ *Error Hunt 1* Some of these sentences illustrate prepositions taken from the Reference Section list. If you need to use your book as you look for errors, feel free to do so.

1. Our old product is much inferior to the new one.
2. Mr. Emmet becomes so angry at people who do not listen to him!
3. Do you agree with accepting her as a member in good standing?
4. Lucy's boss is not planning on making any promotions just yet.
5. All employees should be glad to conform with established policies.
6. The second statement is different than the first.
7. In a democracy, citizens are supposed to abide with any fair decision that is made.
8. At the end of the year, most teachers are loath to part with their pupils.
9. Gracious compliance to office rules will be appreciated by your employer.
10. In his younger days, Mr. Ellis was employed for $15 a week.

Correct Preposition Usage

In order to be correct in the use of prepositions, you must sometimes make a choice between two prepositions. Then, too, there are times when a certain preposition should be expressed and other times when that same preposition should be omitted. This introduction may make correct preposition usage sound more difficult than it really is, as you will discover by studying the following seven principles.

Between, Among. Between is commonly used when referring to *two* persons, places, or objects; *among*, when referring to *more than two*. For instance:

Between you and *me,* I think he should apologize.

The work was divided *between* the *two* clerks.

The work was divided *among* the *three* clerks.

Between may also express the relation of one thing to each and all of several related things; as:

An agreement has just been reached *between* our company and the retailers, jobbers, and wholesalers handling our product.

Beside, Besides. Beside means *by the side of,* and *besides* means *in addition to;* as:

Stack the finished letters *beside* the tray for outgoing mail. Meaning *by the side of* the tray.

Who, *besides* Bill, is being promoted? Meaning who, *in addition to Bill.*

Inside, Outside. Do not use *of* after *inside* or *outside.* When referring to time, use *within*, not *inside of.* For example:

> **You will find the receptionist's desk just *inside* the door.** *Not* inside of.

> **Do you do much work *outside* office hours?** *Not* outside of.

> **May we have your check *within* a week.** *Not* inside of a week.

All, Both. Use *of* after *all* or *both* only when *all* or *both* is followed by a *pronoun.* Omit *of* if either word is followed by a *noun;* thus:

> **All of us are eager to make all the money we can.** All *of* before the pronoun *us,* but no *of* before the noun *money.*

> **Both of them reported that both the machines were in need of repair.** *Both of them,* but *both the machines.*

At, To; In, Into. *At* and *in* denote position. *To* and *into* signify motion. Study these illustrations.

> **Mr. King was *at* his desk early this morning.** Can you see him in place there *at* his desk?

> **Mr. King went *to* his office early this morning.** Can you see him moving toward his office?

> **The lost letter was *in* the wrong tray, as I discovered when I went *into* the office.** The letter was right there *in* position. I was moving; therefore, I went *into* the office.

Note. When either *at* or *in* refers to a place, use *in* for larger places; *at* for smaller; as:

> **Rita lives *in* Chicago and works *at* the Marshall Field store.**

Behind, In Back Of. Use *behind*, not *in back of.* Oddly enough, *in front of* is correct. For instance:

> **Mr. Higgins likes best to work *behind* closed doors, so his secretary stands guard *in front of* his office.** Queer language, English, isn't it? *In back of* is incorrect, but *in front of* is correct.

From, Off. *From* is used when referring to persons; *off*, when referring to things; as:

> **Borrow a pen *from* Jim, if you can get him to take his feet *off* the desk long enough to lend you one.** *From* Jim—*person; off* the desk—*thing.*

2 *Class Practice* By selecting the correct words in the following sentences, you can discover just how well you understand the use of correct prepositions.

1. Was Mr. Hake (at, to) the bank when you went (in, into) town yesterday?
2. Nobody (beside, besides) Patrick would stand (beside, besides) Mr. Ryan in the controversy.
3. (Both of, Both) us realize that (all of, all) the other offices close during the very hot weather.
4. Take some money (from, off) the table and buy some coffee (from, off) Jake.
5. Pete's desk is just (behind, in back of) David's.
6. Personality is said to be (outside, outside of) a person, while character is (inside, inside of) a person.
7. Just (between, among) the two of us, do you think Lora is popular (between, among) her many acquaintances?

Preposition Illiteracies

Certain preposition errors are indicative of lack of education or of gross carelessness. If you recognize these errors and avoid making them, you will better impress your business and social associates. The illiteracies are:

Of, Have. *Of* is a preposition; *have* is a verb. Writing or saying *of* when *have* is correct is a common error. As with many other errors, this one may be charged to mispronunciation. For instance, people say, "You shuduf paid your bill." Is it any wonder that the written sentence frequently is, "You should of (for *have*) paid your bill"? Think this over and remember to use *have*, not *of*, when that verb should be used.

Where . . . At; Where . . . To. Neither *at* nor *to* should be used with *where.* For example:

Do you know where John is now? *Not* where John is *at.*

Where in the world did that girl go? *Not* where in the world did that girl go *to.*

Help, Help From. Do not use *from* after *help;* as:

Edith cannot help asking all these questions. *Not* cannot help *from* asking . . . .

It is evident that Henry just cannot help throwing his money away. *Not* cannot help *from* throwing . . . .

Opposite, Opposite To. *To* after *opposite* is incorrect.

Arthur's desk is opposite mine. *Not* opposite *to* mine.

The Davises' office building is opposite ours. *Not* opposite *to* ours.

Off, Off Of* or *Off From. *Of* or *from* after the word *off* is incorrect.

Did you push the atlas off the shelf? *Not* off *of.*

You may take the stapler off my desk. *Not* off *of.*

✓ **Borrow a dollar from Judith.** *Not* off *from* Judith or off *of* Judith.

3 *Class Practice* The following practice sentences will help you to learn to avoid preposition illiteracies.

1. If you know where Mr. Collins' folder (is, is at), please get it for me.
2. Why did you shove the packages (off, off of) the receiving table?
3. Eva could hardly (help, help from) laughing at the man's silly question.
4. The apartment house (opposite, opposite to) the Schultzes has some vacant suites.
5. Donald's entry should not (have, of) won the prize.

✓ *Error Hunt 2* To consolidate your learning with regard to (1) choosing the correct preposition, and (2) avoiding serious preposition errors, correct the errors in these sentences.

1. Your choice lies between Sue, Ann, and her.
2. Everybody borrows paper clips off of Grover.
3. The customer was so rude that I could scarcely help from losing my temper.
4. There are many men besides us who are loyal to the company for which they work.
5. You should of consulted the post office guide.
6. Do you think I can find Mr. Keane to home today?
7. Surely, more than one person in this office knows where the petty cash box is at!
8. Both the plans are satisfactory to all of us.
9. Go into the private office, and just inside of the door you will see the new table.
10. We will let you know our decision inside of a week.

Learning Exercises

1 On the basis of your study of the topics presented in this unit, make your selection of the correct words in the following sentences. Use a separate sheet of paper.

1 Your debit total should be identical (to, with) the credit total.

2 The fence was made of posts, with a space between (each, each two).

3 Why were you so angry (at, with) Mr. Lynd this morning?

4 (Beside, Besides) Gavin, two other salesmen exceeded their quotas.

5 One of the covenants of the League of Nations was that nations would not enter (upon, into) private agreements.

6 Had I known how hot the weather was going to be, I wouldn't (of, have) gone.

7 If Sonja could have a new machine, she would gladly part (from, with) her old one.

8 During an air raid, nonofficials must stay (inside of, inside) special shelters.

9 Discrepancies (in, between) Bill's and Jack's statements were obvious to all of us.

10 Would it be convenient (for, to) you to see me this morning?

11 Did you mean that (all, all of) the envelopes must be re-typed?

12 When Mr. Loft tears through the office, I often wonder where (he is going, he is going to).

13 We are writing you (in regards, in regard) to your request for an extension of credit.

14 Isabel can be found anywhere except (to, at) her desk.

15 Kay is so punctual that no one ever has to wait (on, for) her.

16 You can get the data (off, from, off of) Mr. Flynn's secretary.

17 In several respects, Joyce's story is different (from, than) Warren's.

18 (In back of, Behind) our summer camp is a spring of cool water.

19 It seemed that Pete just couldn't (help from, help) inter-rupting Mr. Austin.

20 The contract calls for the completion of the building (within, inside of) a year.

2 Follow the usual directions.

1 Nylon does not feel very softly to the touch.

2 On days like this, I wish I were lying on the beach.

3 In our office, one clerk does nothing beside filing.

4 Edwin receives a higher salary than him.

5 There is the man who we thought was too ill to work.

6 Had we not been delayed, we surely would of been here sooner.

7 Are the Baileys' moving their machinery to the new location?

8 Our best customers, Mr. Bell and he, have gone out of business.

9 All of the telegrams received this morning contained cancellations.

10 This vase is expensive because it is made of hand-blown glass.

11 The Boy Scout troop are preparing for the court of awards.

12 When the parade passed our building, Mr. Adams was talking to Henry and myself.

13 Some of the applicants for the position of head scientist is married.

14 John is quite different from his brother, isn't he?

15 To which of our artists, Eric or he, did I give the layout?

16 Dick, as well as Frank, receive frequent praise for superior performance.

17 Have you arranged for Mr. Burdick to sit at the speaker's table?

18 Did you hear that our secretary and treasurer has been offered a better position?

19 Owena parted from the other girls immediately after lunch.

20 Does anyone know whom was elected mayor?

Vocabulary and Spelling Refreshers

1 **Words Often Confused.** Pact, packed; facetious, fictitious.

2 **What Did She Mean?** Mary described the singer whom she had heard last evening with, "I enjoyed listening to him. His voice is so *redundant.*" What did she mean to say?

3 **Find and Correct.** The following sentence contains five misspelled words. Find them. How should they be spelled? "It was a privilige to recomend him for the goverment begining bookeeping position."

Communication in Action: *Understanding Big Words*

You may have to use a dictionary to understand the following excerpt from a magazine article. Can you summarize in two sentences the major idea of the paragraph?

"Nostalgia for 'the Grand Old Days' of U. S. selling merely obscures the vital question: Just where does responsibility for the enfeebled selling of today really lie—with the boss or with his salesmen? Like it or not, a new day is upon us, one in which the shortcomings of management cast a far more ominous shadow than those of the salesmen. In too many companies, management itself has imposed a ceiling on selling through cretinous psychology, myopic price policies, somnolent reaction to the market, and archaic product." (From an article in *Fortune,* August, 1958.)

UNIT 26

Conjunctions

From your previous grammar study you will remember that a conjunction is a word used to connect words, phrases, or clauses. For example:

> The letter *and* the envelope are on your desk.   Connecting *words*.

> You will find them on the blotter *or* in the tray. Connecting *phrases*.

> They were there this morning, *but* I am sure they are not there now.   Connecting *clauses*.

You will also remember that you studied co-ordinate, correlative, and subordinate conjunctions. Co-ordinate conjunctions connect words, phrases, or clauses of equal grammatical value; correlative conjunctions are conjunctions that are used in pairs; and subordinate conjunctions connect clauses of unequal grammatical rank. In this unit you will study the correct usage of co-ordinate and correlative conjunctions, and you will become familiar with the more common subordinate conjunctions to prepare you for the punctuation principles in Part 5.

Co-ordinate Conjunctions

Co-ordinate conjunctions connect *like* grammar elements such as: two or more *words,* two or more *phrases,* or two or more *clauses*. Study the following list of some of the most common co-ordinate conjunctions.

accordingly	hence	now
also	however	or
and	likewise	so
as well as	moreover	so then
besides	neither	therefore
but	nevertheless	thus
consequently	nor	wherefore
either	notwithstanding	yet

A study of conjunctions used in business correspondence would probably show that the most frequently used co-ordinate conjunctions are *and, but, or,* and *nor*.

Correlative Conjunctions

Correlative conjunctions are conjunctions used in pairs; as:

both .... and	not only .... but also
either .... or	whether .... or
neither ...... nor	

Note that *or* is used with *either* and *nor* is used with *neither*.

As with co-ordinate conjunctions, correlatives connect words, phrases, or clauses of equal grammatical value. For instance:

Either an eraser or a white pencil may be used to correct a master. A *pair* of conjunctions is needed to express the meaning, and the pair connects nouns.

Subordinate Conjunctions

Subordinate conjunctions connect *clauses* of *unequal* rank or grammatical value, as illustrated in the following sentences.

Please type this letter *whenever* you have time. *Whenever you have time* is a subordinate clause.

While we are about it, we may as well cover all the machines. This sentence starts with the subordinate clause *while we are about it*.

Since we are junior clerks, we must expect to do routine work. This sentence also starts with a subordinate clause, *since we are junior clerks*.

Some of the common subordinate conjunctions are listed here. Study them carefully, for you will need to recognize them on sight in order to punctuate quickly and accurately.

after	inasmuch as	then
although	in case that	though
as	in order that	unless
as if	on condition that	until
as soon as	otherwise	when
as though	provided (*not* providing)	whenever
because	since	where
before	so that	whereas
even if	supposing	wherever
for	than	whether
how	that	while
if	till	why

1 *Class Practice* Do you know and can you recognize the different kinds of conjunctions? You can find out by selecting the conjunction in each of the following sentences and classifying it as *co-ordinate, correlative,* or *subordinate.*

1. Is this your own work, or did someone else do it for you?
2. When Mr. Hyde enters the office, everybody becomes very busy.
3. Bring me both the originals and the carbons of the letters to salesmen.
4. If Henry is late just once more, he will find himself out of a job.
5. Branch offices are located in Boston, Chicago, and Dallas.
6. Be sure that all corrections appear not only on the original but also on all carbons.

Parallel Structure

Parallel ideas should be expressed in parallel structure; for example, in expressing co-ordinate ideas, a noun should be paralleled with a noun, an adjective with an adjective, a phrase with a phrase, and so on. This principle is often violated, especially in written English. Study the following examples of correct parallel structure.

> **Michael works quickly and quietly.** Co-ordinate conjunction *and* connecting adverbs.

> **He can be found at his desk or in Mr. Fry's office.** Co-ordinate conjunction *or* connecting phrases.

Because parallel structure (sometimes called "parallelism") must be used with co-ordinate and correlative conjunctions and because you are studying these conjunctions, right now is the time to learn the principle of parallel structure. Give your concentrated attention to this topic, for it is part of the background you will need when you study business correspondence.

With Co-ordinate Conjunctions. First, review the co-ordinate conjunctions listed for you at the beginning of this unit. Then learn that co-ordinate conjunctions must connect *like* elements. For instance, if *and* has a noun or nouns before it, a noun or nouns must also come after. Just remember that the elements that are written before and after a co-ordinate conjunction must match. Study the following illustrations and explanations.

> **Martin is honest, capable, and ought to be promoted.** *And* is a co-ordinate conjunction. *Before* the *and* in this sentence there are two adjectives; but *after* the *and,* there is a verb. The two sides of the co-ordinate conjunction do not match.

> **Martin is honest, capable, and worthy of promotion.** This is parallel structure, for there is a match—adjective, adjective, *and,* adjective.

> **Martin is honest and capable, and he ought to be promoted.** Here is another matching possibility—clause, *and,* clause.

> **Our firm is noted for its excellent reputation and because it treats the employees fairly.** Do you see that the two sides of the co-ordinate conjunction do not match? The construction is: prepositional phrase, *and,* subordinate clause. Can you make the match?

2 *Class Practice* In the following pairs of sentences, one represents a violation of parallel structure; the other is correct. Select the correct sentence and tell why it is correct.

1. Our office is well ventilated and well lighted.
   Our office is well ventilated and with plenty of light.
2. The executive told us that we should learn the vocabulary of the business and to keep a shorthand notebook of these words.
   The executive told us to learn the vocabulary of the business and to keep a shorthand notebook of these words.
3. Finding a vacancy is one thing, but preparing for an interview is quite another.
   Finding a vacancy is one thing, but to prepare for an interview is quite another.
4. A girl cannot be beautiful if she has big ears, flat feet, or with a pug nose.
   A girl cannot be beautiful if she has big ears, flat feet, or a pug nose.

With Correlative Conjunctions. Remember that correlative conjunctions are conjunctions used in *pairs.* Parallel structure demands that whatever kind of element is written *after* the *first* member of the pair must match the element that is written *after* the *second* member of the pair. The following illustrations and explanations will make this clear.

> I *both* need the originals *and* the carbons. *Both . . . and* is a correlative conjunction. In this sentence there is a *verb* after *both* and a *noun* after *and*. Thus there is no match.

> I need *both* the originals *and* the carbons. Now there is a match—*both, noun; and, noun.*

> You must *either* go to the post office *or* to the bank. The structure here is not parallel because *either* is followed by a verb and *or* is followed by a prepositional phrase. There is no match.

> You must go *either* to the post office *or* to the bank. This matches—*either, prepositional phrase; or, prepositional phrase.*

3 | *Class Practice*   As in Class Practice 2, one of the following pairs of sentences is correct; the other, incorrect. Select the correct sentence and tell why it is correct.

1. That department store has neither a good stock of dresses nor hats.
   That department store has a good stock of neither dresses nor hats.
2. Miss Cone is one of those women who talk either too much or too little.
   Miss Cone is one of those women who either talk too much or too little.
3. Ronald has neither the personality nor has he the background for that job.
   Ronald has neither the personality nor the background for that job.
4. Jack was undecided whether he should take the test now or to wait until next week.
   Jack was undecided whether to take the test now or to wait until next week.

✓ *Error Hunt 1*   If you thoroughly understand parallel structure with co-ordinate and correlative conjunctions, you should be able to find any errors there may be in the following sentences. When you make a correction, tell why you make it.

1. I agreed to accept the increase and that I would try to be worthy of Mr. Dunn's confidence.
2. The wastebaskets have been emptied by neither the office boy nor the porter.
3. Mr. Dean is the man who managed the business and later rising to the position of president.
4. Writing advertising copy is more interesting than to work with figures.
5. Every business person not only must be courteous but also tactful.

Correct Usage

There are some conjunction errors that are made so frequently that they merit special study. There is no quick trick that will help you to avoid making these errors. Your problem is that of memorizing and of retaining what you have memorized. The errors you will wish to avoid are:

And, for But. Whenever there is a contrasting or opposing idea, no matter how faint the contrast or opposition, use the conjunction *but*—not *and*. For example:

> You are young, *but* I am old.   Not *and*.

> Albert is neat, *but* Henry has the better personality.   Not *and*.

> I should like to go with you, *but* I must finish this work first. Not *and*.

And Which or And Who, for Which or Who. And should not be used with *which* or with *who;* as in the following:

> In the morning mail was the announcement, *which* made Andrea's engagement official.   Not *and which*.

> Yesterday I met the head salesman, *whom* you have often mentioned.   Not *and whom*.

Because, Where, and Like, for That. To be correct, you must say the *reason is that*, not the *reason is because*. You *read in the paper that* or *see by the notice that*, not *where*. You *pretend that*, not *pretend like*. If necessary, reread the preceding three sentences. Then study the following illustrations.

> The *reason* the girl failed is *that* she was poorly prepared. *Reason is that*, not *because*.

> Did you *read* in the paper *that* our company is going to expand? *Read that*, not *where*.

> *Pretend that* you do not see her.   *Pretend that*, not *like*.

Being That, for Since, Because, or As. Using *being that* for *since, because,* or *as* is really an illiteracy. There is no such conjunction.

> *Because* the ability to speak well is so important, you should devote more time to English grammar.   Not *being that* the ability . . . .

> A caller entered; and, *as* I was nearest the door, I greeted him. Not *being that* I was . . . .

Like, for As or As If or As Though. When *like* is used as a preposition, it takes an object and, of course, should not be used to introduce a clause. A preposition takes a noun or a pronoun object; a conjunction is used to introduce a clause. Therefore, do not use *like* when *as, as if,* or *as though* would be correct. For instance:

> **Wardens taste good,** *as* **a cigarette should.** Not *like.*
>
> **You type** *as if* **you were angry.** Not *like you were* . . . .
>
> **It looks** *as though* **it would be a good day tomorrow.** Not *like it would be* . . . .
>
> **The children look** *like* **their mother and me.** This is correct.

Without or Except, for Unless. This error is the same type as that discussed in the preceding paragraph. The prepositions *without* and *except* are sometimes used when the conjunction *unless* would be correct. Study the following illustrations.

> **Do not make any changes** *unless* **you tell me first.** Not *without you tell me* . . . . *Without* would be used correctly as a preposition if the sentence read: "Do not make any changes *without telling me* first."
>
> **You may not leave** *unless* **Mr. Pike gives you permission.** Not *except Mr. Pike gives* . . . . The sentence would also be correct if written: "You may not leave *without Mr. Pike's permission.*"

As . . . As, for So . . . As. The correlative *as . . . as* should be used when the statement made is positive; such as: "Helen transcribes just as fast as I do." The correlative *so . . . as* should be used when the statement made is negative; such as: "Helen does *not* transcribe *so* fast *as* I do."

> **This duplicated report is** *as* **clear** *as* **it possibly could be.** *As . . . as* for a positive statement.
>
> **Duplicated reports have** *never* **been** *so* **clear** *as* **they should be.** *So . . . as* for a negative statement.

4 *Class Practice* So many different points of correct usage have been discussed that you should take a little time to study them before you work this class practice. After a review of the seven topics, select the correct words in these sentences.

1. Mr. Ames looked (like he was, as if he were) keeping his temper with difficulty.
2. The reason for the change in position is (because, that) business now demands desirable personality traits.
3. Do not leave (without, unless) you first turn out the lights.
4. Pretend (that, like) you do not notice the new clerk's nervousness.
5. I intended to close the books this morning, (and, but) Mr. Bohn needed me for some special work.

6. Edna's car was not equipped with snow tires, (and which, which) delayed our arrival.
7. I saw by the daily bulletin (that, where) no shift will work on Saturday.
8. (Being that, Since) the bus would be a little late, we decided to have some lunch.

✓ *Error Hunt 2*   This is the "proof of the pudding." If you can without difficulty make the necessary corrections in these sentences, you will have little difficulty with your home study of correct usage principles.

1. You look like your mother did when she was young.
2. Are you pretending like you're too busy to talk to me?
3. Mr. Wood has changed my working hours, and which is all right with me.
4. You are not so familiar with conjunctions as you are with verbs.
5. Being that your quotation was too high, the contract has been awarded to Harvey.
6. The reason Vera went home was because she was ill.

Learning Exercises

1 After you have studied every point that was made in this unit, select the correct words in the following sentences. Write your answers on a separate sheet of paper.

1 Next Saturday (either we shall go, we shall go either) fishing or swimming.
2 The package was delivered to the Hotel Royal, (and which, which) was not the correct address.
3 Miss Alison (neither wants, wants neither) your help nor your pity.
4 We are going to take inventory tomorrow, (and, but) a more important job is scheduled for today.
5 The reason I refused to buy the house was (because, that) it was too expensive.
6 Writing a speech is sometimes easier than (to deliver, delivering) it before an audience.
7 I saw by the notice on the clock (that, where) the plant will close during the first week in August.
8 Miss Dane always (pretends like, pretends that) she is very efficient.

9 (It is our policy not, It is not our policy) to frighten witnesses, but to win their confidence.

10 (Being that, As) his jaw was broken in the accident, a wiring job had to be done.

11 Use that machine (like, as) you were instructed.

12 Our boss enjoys winter sports like sleighing, skiing, and (to skate, skating).

13 Blanton's store will not be able to continue in business (except, unless) there is an upturn in the recession.

14 The cost of building the school was not (as, so) great as was estimated.

15 The studio couch (was neither the, neither was the) regulation size nor the right color.

16 Was the retirement party for Mr. O'Neil, (and whom, whom) we all like so much?

17 Personality is important, (and, but) it alone will not bring success.

18 Eleanor is pretty and (with good manners, well mannered).

19 Did you know that the reason Mr. Perry sent for you was (that, because) he needed your signature?

20 Maria read in last night's paper (where, that) Miss Hyde is taking another trip.

2 Follow the usual directions.

1 Who is Mr. Phelps interviewing now?

2 I both like to teach and to work in an office.

3 Whom the next president would be was a closely guarded secret.

4 Mr. Blake prefers to deal with Hake & Company rather than they.

5 All the Harrises' children have college degrees.

6 Simon works like he was a machine.

7 The rest of the money have been locked in the safe.

8 Our vice-president's speech was well received.

9 Either of the salutations are correct for this letter.

10 No other duplicator works as well as our old model.

11 The letter I have been looking for was lying under the tray.

12 The reason you made that mistake is because you are not familiar with business reference books.

13 The applause was for the baseball players, Hugh and him.

14 Everyone seems to think that Tom and myself have plenty of time to chat.

15 Roger told me that he saw by the confidential report where our company is rated among the top ten.
16 Whomever you suggest will be hired by me.
17 Jan is quiet, ladylike, and should be pleasant to have around.
18 I like my typewriter better than her's.
19 The mob was gathered around the speaker.
20 Is Mr. Beebe a graduate of a four-year college?

Vocabulary and Spelling Refreshers

1 **Words Often Confused.** Fate, fete; census, senses.

2 **One Word for a Phrase.** Each of the following phrases may be replaced by a single word that conveys the same thought. What are the words?

a Without meaning to
b Of his own free will
c With great emphasis
d Without thinking
e From time to time
f Lost consciousness

3 **How Are These Sounds Spelled?** Substitute for the following italicized phonetic spellings the correct spelling of the words. All the sounds are spelled by using one or the other of two groups of letters.

a Greek is no longer *taut* in most high schools.
b As I *fot* my way through the snowbanks, I *thaut* I should miss my bus.
c Brooklyn is one of the five *buros* of Greater New York.
d The police *kot* the fugitive after they had searched the house *thoroly*.
e As the delivery entrance was closed, my furniture was *brot* *thru* the *wrot*-iron gates of the front entrance.

Communication in Action: *A Club Project*

The Girls Club in your company plans to take orders for Christmas trees from employees in the plant. The proceeds are to be used for food baskets to be given to needy families. Write an announcement to go into your monthly employee magazine, describing the why, what, where, when, how, and who (make up your own set of circumstances) for purchasing a tree. Appeal to the employees to purchase their trees from the Club.

5

REVIEW
OF
PUNCTUATION,
ABBREVIA-
TIONS,
AND FIGURES

UNIT 27

The Period

In the writing process, the period is a full stop, much like a red traffic signal. It is a warning to the reader that one line of cars must halt in order to let another line move. Knowledge of when to use this red light, and when not to use it, is most important to the writer who wishes to make his message clear. For better and quicker understanding, your study of the use of the period is divided into two main topics: when to use a period, and when *not* to use a period.

Use a Period

Four situations involving the use of periods are discussed and illustrated in this unit. Understanding of these uses will allow you to flash the red light that signals your correspondent that he must come to a full stop.

Declarative and Imperative Sentences. In previous grammar courses you learned that a declarative sentence is a statement and that an imperative sentence is a command or an entreaty. You also learned that a period is used at the end of a declarative or an imperative sentence. The following illustrations will refresh your memory.

> **The mail has not yet come in.** Declarative sentence.

> **Please bring in the mail.**   Imperative sentence.

Sometimes a writer does not realize that an indirect question is a statement and, therefore, does not use the correct punctuation. For instance:

> **Mr. Ryan asked, "Have the letters been mailed?"** This is a direct question, for Mr. Ryan's actual words are used.

Mr. Ryan asked whether the letters had been mailed. This is an *indirect* question, really a statement. A period is therefore used.

Requests Phrased as Questions. Sometimes a request or a suggestion is written in question form—only for the sake of courtesy. Such a request or suggestion should end with a period, not a question mark. Sentences like the following often occur in the last paragraph of a business letter.

May we have your reply immediately. No question is intended here. Actually, the words *mean:* "Get busy and reply to this letter."

Will you please verify this information. Just because "verify this information" would sound too abrupt and dictatorial, the request was phrased politely.

The Period Fault. The period fault is the placing of a period at the end of a group of words that rightly belong in either a preceding or a following sentence. Do you remember selecting "no sense" groups of words in Unit 13? If not, turn back to that unit now and refresh your memory. This was your foundation for avoiding the period fault. Here is an illustration:

Mr. Lloyd stayed at the office until eight o'clock. Hoping thus to get his work done. Does "hoping thus to get his work done" make sense? No? Then it is not a sentence, and this use of the period is a period fault. The sentence correctly written is: "Mr. Lloyd stayed at the office until eight o'clock, hoping thus to get his work done."

The use of a period after condensed expressions—such as answers to questions or phrases that lead into another thought—is not a period fault. These expressions do not rightly belong in another sentence. If a condensed expression is declarative or imperative, it is followed by a period. For instance:

Are we planning to reduce our sales staff? Not for a few weeks. "Not for a few weeks" is the answer to a question. Since this group of words does not belong in another sentence, it is correctly followed by a period and can stand alone.

One part of our problem has been solved. Now, for the next part. "Now, for the next part" is a transitional phrase leading into the next topic. It correctly stands alone, although it is not a complete thought.

The Comma Fault. The comma fault is the use of a *comma* where a *period* should be used. When this error is made, there is no full stop at the end of a complete, finished thought. Instead, two different thoughts are hitched together. The result is one cloudy message, not two clear, distinct, separate messages. For example:

> **Miss Niles is an excellent teacher, she received her education and training at our state university.** Do you see that the red light should have flashed after *teacher?* Yes, the first line of cars should have been halted so that a *different* line could move.

1 *Class Practice*   Right here seems to be a good place to stop to see how well you have assimilated the principles that have to do with the use of a period at the end of a sentence. Select the correct marks of punctuation and tell why you make your choices.

1. We have received your check for $100 (period, comma) (as, As) well as your letter about the $10 balance that remains.
2. Mr. Doe asked how much I could afford to pay (period, question mark)
3. Will you please send us a check for your order No. 434 before the end of the month (period, question mark)
4. Our chief editor is very much in demand as a speaker (period, comma) (he, He) has had a great deal of lecturing experience.
5. Will you have your check certified before mailing it to us (period, question mark)
6. We must expect many cancellations of orders for towels (period, comma) (since, Since) we have not stamped the goods as irregular.

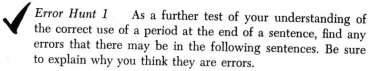 *Error Hunt 1*   As a further test of your understanding of the correct use of a period at the end of a sentence, find any errors that there may be in the following sentences. Be sure to explain why you think they are errors.

1. I get so annoyed by that old question of whether the hen or the egg came first?
2. For years we have ordered parts from you, they have always given satisfaction.
3. Please send Mr. Spears the references he requested.
4. Many members of the staff are attending the play tonight, they like comedies.
5. We are returning your affidavit dated June 1. This paper being unsuited to our needs.
6. Will you please fill in and return the enclosed form soon.
7. A last-minute demand for gloves was noted. With suedes and double-woven cottons wanted.

Do Not Use a Period

Five specific instances where periods should not be used are:

After Headings or Titles; After Roman Numerals Written with Names. A period should not follow any centered heading; for example:

    Unit 27: The Period   (Chapter heading)

    Swiss Family Robinson   (Centered title)

No period should follow a roman numeral used with a name or with a title. For instance:

    Elizabeth II is surely loved by the British.

    I think that Chapter IV is the most exciting chapter in the book.

In tabulations or outlines, however, roman numerals *are* followed by periods, as shown in the skeleton outline below.

After Numbers or Letters Enclosed in Parentheses. "Enclosed in parentheses" are the important words in this heading, as illustrated in the following skeleton outline.

    (Do use period)   **I.**
                      A.
                      B.
                          1.
                          2.
                              a.
                              b.
    (But—do *not* use period)   **(1)**
                                 (2)
                                      (a)
                                      (b)

After Items in Tabulated Lists or in Outlines. This "do not use" is illustrated for you here.

    Unit 27 is divided into the following main parts:
      1. When to use a period
      2. When not to use a period

Note that there are no periods at the end of the listed items. If, however, each item is a complete sentence, a period should be used; as in:

    The important points for you to remember are:
      1. A period brings the reader to a full stop.
      2. Correct uses of the period are part of a writer's stock in trade.

After a Sentence That Ends with an Abbreviation. Only one period is needed at the close of a sentence ending in an abbreviation in order to indicate a full stop. For instance:

The consultant expects to arrive before 10 a.m. *Not* 10 a.m..

After Even Amounts of Dollars. Except in tabulations, do not use a period or two zeros after even amounts of dollars. For instance:

The price of the table is $98.60. The cost to you will be $95 if you send a check with your order. Note $95, *not* $95. or $95.00.

✓ *Error Hunt 2*   You are omitting the usual class practice because the points just presented are not very difficult—or are they? You will have the answer when you have found whatever errors there may be in the following sentences.

1. The following are headings or titles. Indicate the punctuation you would use.

   The Edge of Night
   Business English and Communication
   Use of the Period

2. The prices of the various chairs are $58.40, $78.00, and $98.89.
3. "The Wives of Henry VIII." was an excellent play.
4. We are sending you our check for $10, which represents the difference between the $80 due on your account and the $90 check you sent us.
5. Before you transcribe, assemble such needed supplies as paper, carbon, eraser, etc.
6. By now, you know that you learn best when you: (*a.*) study and learn one principle at a time, (*b.*) study all principles before attempting to work a homework assignment, and (*c.*) review frequently.

Learning Exercises

1 Using a separate sheet of paper, write your selection of the correct alternate in each of the following sentences, together with the reason for your choice. For example, suppose the sentence to be: *Our prices are all (f.o.b.., f.o.b.)* Your answer would look something like this:

f.o.b.   Only one period should be used at the end of a sentence.

1 Mr. Evans asked how I knew the story was true (period, question mark)

2 According to instructions from the merchandise manager, all coats marked ($150.00, $150) or higher are to be moved to the ($120.00, $120) rack.

3 The package fell into the wastebasket (period, comma) (where, Where) it remained until the porter cleaned the office.

4 You must hurry, for the safe deposit vaults close at 3 (p.m., p.m..)

5 Will you please write us about your procedure for sending statements to customers (period, question mark)

6 Before Chapter (III., III), the story was rather dull.

7 The letter had been filed (period, comma) Jean could not find it.

8 My supervisor questioned me about the revised price list (period, question mark)

9 We are extending our store hours (period, comma) (although, Although) the increase in business may not justify the increase in overhead.

10 Will you please have your check in the mail by noon on Monday (period, question mark)

11 The customer asked whether the cafeteria was open on Tuesdays (period, question mark)

12 Will you please return the report to me as soon as you have read it (period, question mark)

13 We are sending you a check for the ($49.00, $49, $49.) due on our order of June 15.

14 Our typist is well satisfied with your carbon paper (period, comma) (she, She) has asked us to order twelve more boxes.

15 Before you take that long trip, you should become a member of the (A.A.A.., A.A.A.)

2 Some of the following sentences are correct; others are incorrect. On a separate sheet of paper, indicate your corrections and explain in your own words why you are making them.

1 Before preparing for air-raid activities. Everybody should read instructions.

2 We have decided to engage the services of a C. P. A..

3 You must increase your typing speed, you must work harder than you have been working.

4 Please ship collect. As we do not wish to wait until you investigate our credit references.

5 Will you please return the enclosed papers to me within twenty-four hours after their receipt?

6 Just send a check for $46., and the mattress will be shipped immediately.

7 May we have Mr. James's references by Monday of next week?

8 Making decisions takes time, we must wait another week before answering your question.

9 Remember that the price quoted is f.o.b.

10 If you wish to paint a clear picture. You must master the principles of punctuation.

11 To carry through the theme of your story, Chapter IX. must be rewritten.

12 May we have your specifications before the bids are advertised.

13 Was George V. the father of Elizabeth II?

14 Our salesman called on Mr. Lane, this customer is very difficult.

15 George III hired Hessian mercenaries to fight our early settlers.

Vocabulary and Spelling Refreshers

1 **Words Often Confused.** Recent, resent; reference, reverence.

2 **Pick the Grammatical Term.** Choose the correct definition for the italicized word in each of the following sentences.

   a An *idiom* is an expression: (1) that is used by illiterate persons, (2) that cannot be explained by the usual rules of grammar, (3) that is now considered obsolete.

   b An *antecedent* is a word: (1) that just precedes another word, (2) that has a meaning opposite to the meaning of another word, (3) to which another word refers.

   c A *suffix* is: (1) a syllable or word joined at the beginning of a word to change its meaning, (2) a syllable or word joined at the end of a word to change its meaning, (3) the second element of a compound word.

   d A *direct question* is: (1) a question used in its original form, (2) an impertinent question, (3) a request in question form.

3 **Geographic Spelling Demons.** Which of the following place names are misspelled?

a Albuquerque, N. Mex.
b Bismark, N. Dak. *Bismarck*
c Bowlder, Colo. *Boulder*
d Champagne, Ill *Champaigne*
e Raleigh, N. C. ✓
f Sacramento, Calif. *Sacramento*

Communication in Action: *Storyteller*

A good conversationalist has a knack for selecting incidents of human interest to tell: the strange or extraordinary happening, the embarrassing moment, the ordinary happening with a humorous twist, and so on. From your own personal experience, select one such event to tell your class. Limit yourself to one minute. Relate your story as though you were giving an after-dinner talk.

UNIT 28

The Question Mark and the Exclamation Point

The question mark and the exclamation point are the two remaining full stops in your study of punctuation traffic signals. Like the period, they are red lights. Fewer errors are made in the use of these punctuation marks than are made in the use of the period, probably because there are fewer rules regarding their application. Even though the principles relating to these "Stop" signs are relatively few, you will not be able always to convey a clear message unless you know how to use the question mark and the exclamation point correctly. Principles governing their use are as follows:

The Question Mark

In this section you will study the use of the question mark after a direct question; after a short, direct question following a statement; and in a series of queries. You will, in addition, review two related principles that you studied in the preceding unit.

After a Direct Question. A question mark is used after every *direct* question. This you have known for years, but the following illustrations may bring the principle to the fore-front of your mind.

> **When shall we release the advertising?**
>
> **What kind of type is used in this book?**

After a Short, Direct Question Following a Statement. Sometimes a sentence will begin as a statement but will end in a question, usually a short question. The correct end punctuation is a question mark; as in these sentences:

> **You will bring the book tomorrow, will you not?**
>
> **Mr. Baxter expects to go to the meeting, doesn't he?**

In Series of Questions. If a sentence contains a series of questions, use a question mark after each member of the series. Do not capital-ize the separate items. For example:

> **Who is to make the decision—the office manager? the advertis-ing manager? the sales manager?**

Review of Related Rules. In the preceding unit you learned that a period, not a question mark, is the correct punctuation after an in-direct question and after a sentence written in the form of a question just for the sake of courtesy. These principles are reviewed here to be sure that you will not use a question mark when you should use a period. Study the following illustrations.

> **Where are you going, Miss Staples?**   This is a direct question, and the question mark is needed.
>
> **Mr. Peabody asked her where she was going.**   This is an indirect question. Since it is really a statement, the period is correct.
>
> **May I have my bill just as soon as you can get it to me.**   This is not a question, but a request. In fact, it is practically an order. The period is, therefore, correct.

1 *Class Practice*   Indicate the correct punctuation for the fol-lowing sentences and explain the reason for each selection you make.

1. You expect to take the cash to the bank before closing time, do you not (period, question mark)
2. Will you please let me have the first draft by noon tomorrow (period, question mark)
3. Would you like to live in Boston (period, question mark) in Chicago (period, question mark) in Seattle (period, question mark)

4. Mr. Towne asked her how much difference there was between the debit and credit totals (period, question mark)
5. What address did you type on that envelope (period, question mark)

The Exclamation Point

You have often read and heard that an exclamation point is used to express strong emotion. Only the writer, however, can use it accurately because only the writer knows whether the words are a question or an exclamation. For instance:

> **Who ever heard of such a thing!**   Now the writer is thoroughly exasperated, as he shows you by using the exclamation point.
>
> **Where in the world has that girl gone?**   No strong feeling here—just a question.
>
> **Where in the world has that girl gone!**   Whew! Is she going to hear something when she gets back!

Although the use of the exclamation point depends on the emotion the *writer* wishes to express, that writer should be familiar with the rules for correct use of this mark of punctuation.

After a Single Word or a Short Phrase. The exclamation point may be used after a single word or a short phrase. The sentence that follows the exclamation, however, is punctuated in the usual way, as illustrated in these sentences.

> **Congratulations! You surely deserve the promotion.**   *Congratulations* is the exclamation. It is followed by a statement.
>
> **Whew! Is she going to hear something when she gets back!**   *Whew* is an exclamation, as is also the following sentence.
>
> **Well, now! Where do we go from here?**   *Well, now* shows strong feeling. The following sentence is a question.

After the Word "Oh." The exclamation point is used directly after *oh* when *oh* is the exclamation. If the entire group of words containing *oh* is the exclamation, *oh* is followed by a comma. In studying the following illustrations, note that *oh* is capitalized only at the beginning of a sentence.

> **Oh! What a relief!**   Both the *oh* and *what a relief* are exclamations.
>
> **But, oh, so sad!**   The entire group of words is the exclamation.

2 | *Class Practice*   What is the correct punctuation for each of the following sentences? Why do you think so?

1. No loitering on these premises (period, exclamation point) This means you (period, exclamation point)
2. Great Scott (period, exclamation point) Are you sure that letter was mailed on Tuesday (question mark, exclamation point)
3. Stop (period, exclamation point) You are using the wrong copy (period, exclamation point)
4. Not on your life (period, exclamation point) Saturday has always been my day of rest (period, exclamation point)
5. Oh (period, exclamation point) How could you find time to do that (question mark, exclamation point)
6. What delightful news (period, exclamation point) You must come and tell me all about it (period, exclamation point)

Learning Exercises

1 Both this group of exercises and the next contain sentences that review the use of the period. On a separate sheet of paper, indicate your selection and give the reason for your choice.

1 Is there any difference between a bookkeeper and an accountant (period, question mark)
2 What a tremendous saving we made by changing to electric typewriters (period, question mark, exclamation point)
3 If the fault does not lie with the shipping department, where does it lie (period, question mark, exclamation point)
4 Will you please send this remittance before April 15 (period, question mark)
5 Of what value to a salesman is a knowledge of psychology (period, question mark)
6 If businessmen did not have integrity (period, comma) (there, There) would be no business.
7 Does your company carry hospitalization insurance for its employees (period, question mark)
8 Oh (period, question mark, exclamation point) Where did you learn the wonderful news (period, question mark, exclamation point)
9 Can you guarantee that shipment will be made before the first of the month (period, question mark)
10 Our check was mailed on Monday (period, comma) (You, you) should have received it by Wednesday.
11 Do you think you will be able to send your remittance by April 15 (period, question mark)

12 Harry will be sure to lock up when he leaves, will he not (period, question mark)

13 When are you planning to hold your anniversary sale (period, question mark)

14 Do you spend your leisure time in playing golf (period, question mark) in relaxing (period, question mark) in puttering around the yard (period, question mark, exclamation point)

15 Mr. Perry asked me to find out what the largest city in Iowa is (period, question mark)

2 Using a separate sheet of paper, make the necessary corrections in these sentences. Explain why each correction is made. If you do not make a correction, explain this, too.

1 Mr. Abbey wants to know where the new warehouse is located.

2 What a pleasure it is to see a letter properly punctuated?

3 If we follow these instructions, how can we reduce our inventory.

4 Atlases are now in our library, we needed them very much.

5 In your opinion, were his data accurate.

6 You are sure that no letters remain to be filed, aren't you.

7 What interesting news did you see in the trade journal!

8 Well! Are you satisfied now?

9 The manufacturer asked whether it is a fact that previous generations were more industrious than the present generation.

10 Will you please let us have your answer by January 1?

11 Sara will be able to finish those letters this afternoon, won't she.

12 Here, now! How often have I told you to clean your keys daily.

13 How do you like typing? filing. answering the telephone.

14 Bill came to work for us only a year ago, his advancement has been remarkably rapid.

15 Will you please use the enclosed envelope when replying to this letter?

Vocabulary and Spelling Refreshers

1 **Words Often Confused.** Expand, expend; assistance, assistants.

2 **From Positive to Negative.** By adding a short prefix to each of these words, change the word to one having a negative meaning.

    a normal   **c** proper   **e** literate
    b engage   **d** noble   **f** enchanted

3 **Adding "ing."** How are the following pairs of words spelled when *ing* is added?

    a hop, hope   **c** mop, mope   **e** bar, bare
    b plane, plan   **d** dote, dot   **f** pine, pin

Communication in Action: *Taking Notes*

Your instructor will read a short article. Pay close attention, taking appropriate notes as you listen. From your notes, write a brief summary of the article.

UNIT 29

The Semicolon, Colon, Dash

The semicolon, the colon, and the dash are *partial* stops. In terms of driving procedures, you might think of these marks as traffic signs that say, "Yield." You do not come to a full stop, but you do slow almost to a stop. Partial stops, therefore, show that, while the thought of a sentence is continuous, there is a break in that thought. Study carefully the following uses of these punctuation marks. You will find partial stop signals helpful when you are writing a message that must be clear to the reader—as every message should be.

Semicolon

When the eye sees a semicolon, the mind receives a signal to take a deep breath, a little rest; for the semicolon is a sign that tells the reader to come to a partial stop.

The partial stop signaled by the semicolon is used mainly in compound sentences.

Now, a compound sentence is a sentence that has two or more independent clauses. In other words, if a sentence has two or more parts, each of which makes sense when standing alone, the sentence is compound. Because the clauses in a compound sentence are of equal value or rank, the connective used is a co-ordinate or a correlative conjunction. Turn to Unit 26 and review co-ordinate and correlative conjunctions. Then, to be sure that you can recognize a compound sentence on sight, study the following illustrations and explanations.

Telephones rang incessantly, and the switchboard operators could not get a moment's rest. Here there are two parts, each of which would make sense if it stood alone: *telephones rang incessantly* and *the switchboard operators could not get a moment's rest.* The connective is the co-ordinate conjunction *and.*

Mr. Kerr does not wish to be a candidate, but he will serve if elected. Two complete thoughts connected by the co-ordinate conjunction *but.*

Although a co-ordinate conjunction is usually the connective used in a compound sentence, a correlative may be used. Consider this sentence: "Either this machine is not properly adjusted, or we do not know how to operate it." There are two parts to the sentence, and each one makes sense all by itself. The connective is the correlative *either . . . or.*

Now that you can recognize a compound sentence, you are ready to study four uses of semicolons in compound sentences.

No Conjunction Joining the Clauses. If the connecting conjunction is omitted in a compound sentence, a semicolon is used to show that omission. For example:

The bell rang; the light flashed; the whistles blew. No conjunctions connect these three complete thoughts. Semicolons are the signals that conjunctions are omitted.

Second Clause Starting with an Introductory Word. In some compound sentences, the second part starts with an introductory word. Some of the common introductory words are:

accordingly	consequently	moreover
again	furthermore	nevertheless
also	however	otherwise
besides	indeed	therefore

A semicolon signals the break before a word that introduces the second clause. Study these illustrations.

> **Miss Hughes understands bookkeeping; therefore, she has a foundation for learning to operate a calculator.** Since the second clause is introduced by *therefore,* a semicolon shows the partial stopping place between clauses.

> **The samples of material you sent are of excellent quality; however, the designs are too flamboyant.** *However* introduces the second complete thought, so a semicolon is used to show the break between the clauses.

At Least One Comma in Either Clause. If a compound sentence contains a comma or commas in either clause, a semicolon is used to separate the clauses. Be sure that you understand the following: (*a*) There may be only one comma in either clause, or (*b*) there may be commas in both clauses. In either case, a semicolon is needed between the clauses. For example:

> **If you need replacements, write us immediately; and we will send them in the very next shipment.** A semicolon separates the clauses because there is a comma in the first clause.

> **I think we can get the five o'clock train; but, if we miss that, there is one at six o'clock.** Here there are two commas in the second clause; therefore, a semicolon is used to separate the clauses.

When One or Both Clauses Are Very Long. Remembering that the semicolon is a partial stop sign, you can understand its use in a long sentence. There must be some stopping place that will clearly separate the parts of the sentence. In the following illustration, can you see that you would be lost in a maze of words if the semicolon were not used?

> **We feel somewhat embarrassed in making the following request of a customer who has been so prompt about paying his bills for so many years; but this record is the very thing that leads us to feel that our last statement has either gone astray or been overlooked.**

Semicolon Before Explanatory or Enumerating Words. A semicolon is also used to signal the approach of words that explain or enumerate. Some of these words are: *as, for example, for instance, namely, that is,* and *that is to say.* Again, the semicolon fulfills its function as a partial stop by furnishing the rest period needed by the reader before he gives his attention to the words that follow the colon. For instance:

The most common typing error is the striking of a nearby key for the letter desired; as: *k* for *l*, *v* for *b*, and so on. The semicolon says, "Take a little rest and then look at the illustrations."

1 *Class Practice* Checkup time! Make correct choices in the following sentences and give reasons for your choices.

1. Concord was the home of four famous authors (semicolon, comma, period) namely, Thoreau, Alcott, Emerson, and Hawthorne.
2. One brother sold stationery (comma, semicolon) another operated an employment agency.
3. Miss Thorne is the senior member of the staff (semicolon, comma) therefore, she should be given first consideration.
4. Since your order arrived only this morning, we shall be unable to ship today (comma, semicolon) but we can promise to put the merchandise on the truck within three days.
5. We were obliged to refuse delivery of our order No. 825 (comma, semicolon) however, we are sending a reorder that contains more explicit specifications.

Colon

Whenever you hear a fanfare of trumpets—ta-te-ta-ta te-ta!—what is your response? You automatically prepare yourself for something that you know is coming, don't you? A colon is the written blare of trumpets that say: "Now, hear this! Here comes something for your special consideration." The various uses of the colon are:

Colon Before Listed Items. A listing that follows a colon is sometimes written as a part of the sentence; as:

To make neat corrections, the typist needs the following tools: a piece of blotter, a typewriter eraser, a piece of artgum, and an erasing shield.

Sometimes, however, a listing is tabulated. For example:

The most important factors to be considered in selecting filing equipment are the following:
1. **Durability**
2. **Safety from fire**
3. **Adaptability**
4. **Convenience**
5. **Price**

Some of the expressions that precede a colon are: *as, as follows, the following, thus,* and *these.* In the preceding sentence, why is there a colon after *are?* It was the fanfare that announced the coming of something important to you, a listing of words and phrases commonly used before colons, wasn't it?

The most important rule connected with the colon is this: Use a colon before a listing whenever you wish to make that listing stand out as important. For example:

> **The duties of the general clerical worker usually include filing, typing, record keeping, and opening mail.** There is no strength here. The reader's eye moves rapidly from start to finish of the sentence, without registering anything in particular.

> **Duties of the general clerical worker are these: filing, typing, record keeping, and opening mail.** When the reader's eye sees the colon, his mind registers, "Here comes something important. I must pay attention."

Also, a colon may be used before a complete sentence if you wish to place strong emphasis on that sentence; as:

> **The most important rule for the colon is this: Use a colon before any words that you wish to emphasize.**

Right here is probably the best place to learn the rule for capitalization after a colon. The rule, stated simply, is: The first word of a complete sentence following a colon will be capitalized if the writer wishes to emphasize the statement or if the sentence states a formal rule.

In the following illustrations, see how the colon performs its role of trumpet tooting.

> **You should remember that the person who practices the Golden Rule finds himself comfortable to live with.** Is the point strongly made?

> **Remember this: The person who practices the Golden Rule finds himself comfortable to live with.** Do you feel and see the strength here? Do you know why *The* is capitalized?

Period Instead of Colon. If the last words in a sentence do not directly *lead into* a listing or a statement, use a period after those words, not a colon. For instance:

> **Your cashbook balance may not agree with the actual cash balance for one of the following reasons, which are here enumerated in the most convenient order for rechecking purposes.** The *last word or words* do not lead directly into the listing; therefore, a period, not a colon, is the correct mark of punctuation.

A period, not a colon, would also be used if another sentence follows the sentence containing the lead-in; as:

> **If you do the family buying, keep the following rules in mind. By heeding them, you can help to "stretch" your income. (1) Take a shopping list with you. (2) Examine each article carefully before buying it. (3) Consider the cost of upkeep and of repairs of substantial items.** The sentence immediately before the listing does not *lead into* the listing.

2 *Class Practice*   Make your selections in the following sentences and explain your reasons.

1. In your order you failed to specify the following (no punctuation, colon) the length and width of the floor, the height of the ceiling, and the number of doors and windows.
2. The following suggestions are recommended for your study. You will be well repaid for your time (period, colon)
3. Please send the following items (period, comma, colon) one set of dishes, one tablecloth, and a dozen matching napkins.
4. You are invited to consider the following facts, which are the result of an extensive study by our staff (colon, period)
5. I simply must have these (no punctuation, colon) a room for the night, some warm clothing, and a good dinner.
6. The office training areas, as enumerated in the following outline, should be included in all clerical practice courses (colon, period)

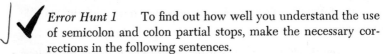

Error Hunt 1   To find out how well you understand the use of semicolon and colon partial stops, make the necessary corrections in the following sentences.

1. The successful candidates were the following. Mayor Thomas, General Holmes, and Councilman Kirby.
2. The house was dilapidated; the yard was neglected; the front gate hung by one hinge.
3. I have finished all my business, accordingly, I shall be able to sail tomorrow.
4. Both jobs can be filled by a man already in our employ, namely, Fred Jackson.
5. The question that Mr. Alton very much needs to ask himself is this, Am I improving or destroying the morale of the personnel?
6. Your merchandise has been deteriorating steadily in quality, moreover, your service is very slow.
7. The following words are often misspelled. *Receive, separate, accommodate,* and *chief.*

Dash

Forcefulness is the trade-mark of the dash. The writer uses it to snip off the message abruptly, so that the following words burst upon the reader. Probably you will understand this use better if you consider the message of each partial stop. The semicolon says, "Now take a good, deep breath before you go on with this thought." The colon says, "Ta-ta-te-ta tedah!" The dash says, "Snip—WHAM!" The difference between the colon and the dash is that the colon gives warning, leads into something; but the dash cuts off the message, without warning, just to make the following words conspicuous. You, too, can be a forceful writer—by using the dash effectively!

Dash Instead of Semicolon or Colon. If you are in doubt as to whether to use a semicolon or a dash or whether to use a colon or a dash, you must first of all decide what effect you wish your words to have. Is this just an ordinary, straight-from-the-shoulder message? If so, use the colon or the semicolon. Would you like certain words to crash upon the reader's consciousness? If so, use the dash. For example:

> **The box for petty cash contains coins of all denominations; as: pennies, nickels, dimes, quarters, and half dollars.** The colon warns the reader that a listing is coming. This is a good sentence, but the following sentence is stronger.

> **The box for petty cash contains coins of all denominations— pennies, nickels, dimes, quarters, and half dollars.** Do you see that the use of the dash, with no introductory word, makes the listing more forceful?

Forceful Expression, Forceful Summarizing, and Forceful Repetition. Remember that the dash is the partial stop that you, the writer, use to make your words stand out in the mind of the reader. Is there a certain fact or message that you feel *must* be made to register? If so, use the dash before stating that fact or message; like this:

> **Bill just walked in and asked for an increase in salary—and got it.** The point you wish to make forcefully is the amazing result of Bill's casual request—*and got it.*

Will a review, a summing up of what you have just said, cause the reader to pay particular attention to your words? Then use the dash before that review; as follows:

> **The monotonous checking operations, the tiresome copying and recopying, the constant addition of new material—all were forgotten when the finished report was so enthusiastically received.** Your "punch line" summary of the drudgeries—*all were forgotten when the finished report was so enthusiastically received.*

If you strike the same note a second time, will the reader receive and retain a deeper impression? Use of a dash will strengthen the repetition. For instance:

> **Congratulations! You have made a fine record—a very fine record, indeed.** The outstanding thing about the reader very definitely is his *fine record*—as you show by the repetition after the dash.

With Afterthoughts. The dash may be used before words that really are an afterthought, although a good writer does not have afterthoughts. He plans his writing. You, as a finished writer, might use a dash before a *planned* afterthought to add variety to your writing, to soften a statement that could give offense, or to prepare the reader for some topic that will be discussed in a later letter. For example:

> **We are unable to adopt your suggestion—that is, without further study.** To soften the refusal.

> **On the other hand, the budget of the purchasing department shows—but we won't go into that now.** "But we will later, so get prepared for it."

Punctuating Material Within Dashes. No other mark of punctuation is used *before* words that are set off by dashes.

You need to know, however, the principles governing punctuation of words enclosed in dashes and punctuation at the close of a sentence that ends with "dashed" material.

Punctuating "Dashed" Material at End of Sentence. Whenever "dashed" material ends a sentence, the regular end-of-sentence punctuation should be used—not the ending dash. For instance:

> **Who is the tall girl in the outer office—the one in the blue dress?** This is an interrogative sentence.

> **What a gift for a bride—or for yourself!** Exclamation point at the end of an exclamatory expression.

Commas Within Material ·Set Off by Dashes. When commas are needed within the material that is set off by dashes, those commas are used where indicated. For example:

> **Most employees—and John, of course, is no exception—do not like to work overtime.** *Of course* set off by commas.

Question Mark and Exclamation Point with "Dashed" Words. The question mark and the exclamation point are the *only* punctuation marks that are used *before* the *ending* dash. No other marks are correct. Here are some illustrations of this principle.

Their cashier—what did you say his name is?—entered an incorrect total on the deposit slip. The words within the dashes ask a question.

Here are pure-silk ties—yes, think of it!—for as little as $4.98. An exclamatory expression is enclosed in dashes.

3 *Class Practice* In each of the following sentences tell where you would use a dash and why you would use it.

1. Louis is reasonably sure of a promotion though promotions are unusual at this season because of his work on the project.
2. When Mr. Lewis arrived, George, no, it was Ray, met him.
3. This is a "super" opportunity, one that we cannot afford to neglect, according to our broker.
4. Two of the attendants were on duty, you know, the ones who were there last Friday.
5. Tickets for the play can be obtained at the box office, yes, also at the agencies.
6. Tennis, rowing, hockey, these are Mr. Fort's favorite sports.

Error Hunt 2 You can test your knowledge of the correct punctuation to use with "dashed" words by finding whatever errors there are in these sentences. Justify every correction.

1. I cannot reconcile these two claims—or any of the others, for that matter,—can you?
2. Did you receive our designer's sample color schemes—two for your living room and three for your bedroom.
3. So far as I am concerned, her word is good—and always will be!
4. With your health, intelligence, and youth, you should never think of failure—never.
5. Your letter—was it dated June 3—was very welcome.
6. We cooked supper—bacon, potatoes, and beans, of course,—over a sputtering campfire.
7. Yesterday—and what a day it was—went so fast that I just could not find time to answer your letter.

Learning Exercises

1 Each of the following sentences contains one or more question marks enclosed in parentheses. On a separate sheet of paper, indicate whether you would use a colon, a semicolon, a dash, or another mark of punctuation at the point where the question mark occurs.

1 You have a choice of these three models (?) the table model, the console, and the two-door cabinet.

2 When you have complicated tabulation jobs (?) for example, payrolls, personnel analyses, market surveys (?) call on us.

3 Mr. James was handicapped by entering college a month late (?) furthermore, he lacked sufficient funds.

4 The qualities that I admire in Ethel are these (?) her industry, her graciousness, and her integrity.

5 I prefer transcribing letters to typing tabulations (?) but, since my job involves both duties, I give them equal attention.

6 Mr. Knapp operates his office on the barber shop principle (?) first come, first served.

7 A good sales letter will do the following (?) attract attention, create desire, and motivate action.

8 Little Tommy has decided to become a musher—(?) one who drives sled dogs.

9 Miss Bates is a victim of wanderlust (?) that is, she yearns to see more of the world.

10 You, too, can have color television—and for only 10 cents a day (?).

11 Department stores are so called because they are divided into various departments (?) men's clothing, household furnishings, yard goods, jewelry, and many others.

12 My complaints are as follows (?) no instructions for assembling the unit, wrong nails, and insufficient amount of tar paper.

13 Shorthand and typing skills, punctuation, spelling, grammar (?) these are "musts" for the good secretary.

14 Miss Ames has been with us only a month (?) therefore, she is not acquainted with all the personnel.

15 Please send me another atlas (?) an atlas without missing pages.

2 On a separate sheet of paper, indicate corrections for any of the following sentences that may be incorrect. This is a punctuation review.

1 Your machine is very satisfactory, in fact, we think it is the best on the market.

2 Lucy asked how ice skating differs from roller skating?

3 Your letter went to Mr. Martin, then he referred your request to Mr. Carlin.

4 Mr. Jenkins has worked long and faithfully on the missile project—and for what?

5 If Edna had joined the army, she would have had a very different kind of life; because she enjoys meeting people.

6 Will you please send me very soon a copy of your latest price list.

7 Miss Ash started as a pool stenographer, then she became secretary to Mr. Perry.

8 We shall be glad to change your billing date to the second week of the month. If that would be more convenient to you.

9 Harry seems to have only one pleasure—eating.

10 The housewares exhibit will be held in our store, very likely there will be a large attendance.

11 Poise, confidence, awareness, security. All these have women acquired now that they are permitted to work for wages.

12 The plasterers began their work. The concrete blocks having hardened.

13 Our state is considering several ways of raising money; : increasing property taxes, levying an income tax, and increasing the sales tax.

14 Will you please send a recent photograph with your data sheet?

15 Our most respected executives—Mr. Lee, Mr. Archer, and Mr. Blinn,—will represent us at the annual meeting.

Vocabulary and Spelling Refreshers

1 **Words Often Confused.** Peace, piece; specie, species.

2 **Wanted: Singulars.** What are the singular forms of the following plural nouns?

a parentheses	**c** passers-by	**e** p.m.'s
b teeth	**d** notaries public	**f** flies

3 **Spot the Prefix.** Column A lists six words containing prefixes. Column B lists the meanings of many of the most commonly used prefixes. Match the meaning with the word containing the prefix defined.

A	B
a subway	**1** Before
b contradict	**2** Against
c postscript	**3** Around
d inconvenient	**4** Between, among
e antedate	**5** One
f interstate	**6** Beyond
	7 Under
	8 Above
	9 After
	10 Not

Communication in Action: *Writing a Radio Announcement*

As a public service, your local radio station devotes 30 minutes daily to announcing community events of public interest. Up to one minute is allowed for each event. Write a one-minute announcement of the play, "Charley's Aunt," a comedy that is to be presented by the dramatic club of your school. Supply your own details as to time, place, etc.

Section 2   Punctuation — the Comma

UNIT 30

The Comma

Commas are the "Slow" signs that guide your reader into absorbing one part of a thought before going on to another part. Unless you use commas correctly, your message will not be clear to the reader. Confusion leads to waste of time and money. Additional letters must be written, goods may be delayed, and friendly relations with customers are threatened. To show you how garbled a message can be if a comma is used incorrectly, here is a copy of a newspaper announcement.

Because of the holiday, tomorrow the stores of Anton will remain open tonight until 8:30. Use of the comma after *tomorrow* would have slowed down the reader at that point—*because of the holiday tomorrow*. As the sentence is written, the reader must back up and reread.

Failure to use a comma when the reader should be "slowed down" also causes confusion, as illustrated in the following sentence.

In order to balance the statement would have to be rewritten. A second reading is necessary here. If the reader is slowed down after *in order to balance,* the message is perfectly clear.

Training in the use of the comma is provided here and in the next two units. Your ability to slow down the reader will enable you to make your messages crystal clear. In addition, "Keep Moving" pointers are given at the end of each unit. These are broad arrows that indicate that the traffic must *not* be slowed.

Compound Sentence

In a compound sentence, a comma is used before *and, or, nor,* or *but* when one of these conjunctions separates the *main* clauses of the sentence. This principle can be simplified if you will do this: Concentrate on four words—*and, or, nor, but.* Whenever in the future you see or hear one of these words, a bell should ring in your mind. The bell says, "Look to see if there is an *expressed* subject after this word." If there *is* an expressed subject, use a comma before the *and, or, nor,* or *but.* In other words: no subject, no comma.

If you are in doubt as to whether the clause that follows the conjunction contains an expressed subject, cross out the conjunction and all words preceding it. Then read only the words that follow the conjunction. If those words make sense, there must be an expressed subject.

Now study the following illustrations to fix in your mind the use of the comma in a compound sentence.

We have ordered radios from you before, and they have always given satisfaction. There is a comma before *and* because the following main clause contains an expressed subject. *They have always given satisfaction* makes sense, so there must be an expressed subject.

Your check must reach us before the first, or we shall take legal steps to collect the balance of your account. *We* is the expressed subject in the second clause.

A machine may cost $100, but in a month it may be difficult to realize $75 on this same machine. *It* is the expressed subject in the clause following *but.*

We wired him at his hotel and asked him to call you. *Asked him to call you* are the words following the conjunction. They do not make sense, so there is no expressed subject. No subject, no comma.

The correspondence with Wood Products and that with the Dover Company is to be transferred to the new file. *That with the Dover Company is to be transferred to the new file* are the words following *and*. Since they do not make sense, there is no expressed subject. No subject, no comma.

Very Short Clauses. If the clauses of a compound sentence are very short, the comma may be omitted; as:

We wired him but we received no answer.

Clara likes the office and she is happy there.

Semicolon Exceptions. In Unit 29 you studied the uses of the semicolon, and you learned three uses that concerned compound sentences. Turn now to Unit 29 and review those semicolon principles so that the compound-sentence package may be neatly wrapped.

1 *Class Practice*   In the following sentences, tell where you would insert commas or semicolons and explain why you do so.

1. If you ask John, he will open the door for you but he refuses to leave it unguarded.
2. All of us were interested in the blueprints for the new car but it was the motor that particularly interested Peter.
3. Bess typed all the letters left behind by Alice and still had time to transcribe her own letters.
4. In the morning the porter cleans the entrance to the office building but in the afternoon, of course, his wife has to repeat the process.
5. The seniors toured Washington and visited Mount Vernon and the Naval Academy.
6. Marvin went to school but he was late.
7. Checking is my job operating the addressograph is yours.

Series

A series consists of a minimum of three succeeding items, which may be three words, three phrases, or three clauses. A comma is used to separate the parts of a series; and, according to latest and best business practice, a comma is used before the conjunction that precedes the last item in a series. For example:

The dress makes up well in orlon, nylon, or rayon acetate. Series of words. Note the comma before *or*.

Our offices are located in New York, in Chicago, in Boston, and in Dallas.   Series of phrases.

Type the letter, sign it in my absence, but do not mail it until tomorrow.   Series of clauses.

The art department will offer the following courses: figure sketching, fashion design, interior decoration, and advertising and commercial art.   Use of the comma after *decoration* tells the reader that advertising and commercial art is one course.

Repeated Conjunctions. When the conjunction is repeated before each item of a series, no commas are used to separate the items; thus:

At our camp you will have an entire week of swimming or boating or fishing or just sitting.

End of Series. No comma is used at the end of a series unless the sentence structure demands a comma at that point. Such occurrences are rare. For instance:

The four periods of prosperity, crisis, recession, and recovery constitute the business cycle.   A comma after the ending item *recovery* would be incorrect.

A jurist, an economist, and an explorer, each known for his contribution to society, were the speakers.   The sentence structure demands a comma after *explorer*. However, no comma would be used if the sentence were written: "A jurist, an economist, and an explorer were the speakers."

"Etc." Ending a Series. If a series ending in *etc.* occurs in the body of a sentence, a comma is placed *after,* as well as before, the *etc.* If *etc.* ends the sentence, the period denoting the abbreviation is the ending punctuation mark. Watch that you do not fall into the common error of writing *and etc.* (*Et cetera*) is the Latin for *and so forth,* and writing *and etc.* would be saying *and and so forth.* Study the following illustrations.

There is a temporary embargo on butter, milk, eggs, ice cream, etc., both in and out of the city.

A meeting has been called to discuss increase in wages, decrease in working hours, expansion of fringe benefits, etc.

Semicolons in a Series. In Unit 29 you learned that a semicolon is used to separate the main clauses of a compound sentence when the clauses are long or when they contain one or more commas. A semicolon rather than a comma is used because a comma does not provide a long enough break to prevent confusion in the message. It is logical, then, that the semicolon should be used in a *series* when the items are very long or when the items contain commas. For example:

> Goods must be transported to the place where they are to be consumed; sometimes they have to be stored for a time; often they must be rearranged into shipping units; and the good must be culled from the damaged and spoiled. With so many words, a partial stop between items is needed.

> The population of the city is made up of the following groups: native-born, 75%; English, 5%; German, 10%; French, 2%; Russian, 2%; all others, 6%. Visualize commas used here instead of semicolons, and you can imagine the perplexed state of the reader.

2 *Class Practice* Practice what you have learned about the use of the comma in series by telling where you would insert the punctuation in the following sentences.

1. You can get the data from Bill or Jack or Harry.
2. Books papers pencils magazines etc. were strewn on the floor.
3. Ann swept the floor with an old, worn-out broom Mary dusted the furniture when Ann finished sweeping and Henry chopped stove-length sticks for the fireplace.
4. Please check all invoices statements bills of lading etc.
5. The hail beat against the windows rattled on the roof and flattened the flowers in the garden.
6. This is what you must do: Prepare a data sheet, with photograph attached write a covering letter of application and tell Miss Atwood when she may expect to receive the material.

Introductory Word, Phrase, or Clause

As a sign to the reader to slow down, a comma is used after an introductory word, phrase, or clause. Without the comma, there is no clearly marked separation between the introduction and the main thought or message. Specifically, the rules are these:

Introductory Word. Use a comma to set off an introductory word, the most common of which are the following:

accordingly	fortunately	naturally	otherwise
actually	further	next	perhaps
also	however	nevertheless	personally
besides	indeed	no	say
consequently	meanwhile	now	theoretically
finally	moreover	obviously	therefore
first	namely	originally	yes

The one-syllable adverbial connectives *hence, still, then, yet, thus,* and *so* usually do not require a comma after them unless the connective demands special emphasis; as:

> **Several of the items you ordered are out of stock; *so* we are holding the entire order.**

> **You shouldn't be without this soap powder another day; *so,* the first thing tomorrow morning ask your grocer to send you a package.** The *so* in this sentence is used to emphasize the message that follows and is, therefore, set off by a comma.

An introductory word may occur at the beginning of a sentence, or it may introduce a clause within the sentence; as:

> **However, we do feel that the slight price increase is justified.** At the beginning of a sentence.

> **Our production costs are mounting steadily; consequently, our prices must be increased comparably.** Introductory *consequently* with second clause of the sentence.

Do not take it for granted that these words are always introductory and, therefore, are always followed by commas. Sometimes the word modifies a word that follows. In this case, you would not use a comma after the word. The following illustrations should help to make this point clear.

> **However, we shall be very happy to contribute to the Community Chest.** *However* is introductory in this sentence.

> **However worthy the cause, we feel that we can contribute only to the Community Chest.** *However* here is part of the message, *however worthy the cause.* It is not introductory and is not followed by a comma.

Introductory Phrase. When a phrase—prepositional, infinitive, or participial—is used as an introduction to the thought that follows, place a comma after that phrase; like this:

> **For various good reasons, we have decided to change our style of letterhead.** Introductory prepositional phrase.

> **Speaking before a special committee, the treasurer gave reasons for decreasing the dividend.** Introductory participial phrase.

> **To mention just one objection, our office is too small to accommodate such a large machine.** Introductory infinitive phrase.

Whether or not to use a comma after an initial prepositional phrase is something of a problem. If the phrase is very short or if it flows into the main thought, do not use a comma. If it is a long phrase or if it is obviously introductory, use a comma. Study carefully the following illustrations and explanations.

> **In the spring we plan to open a new store.**   Short phrase that flows into the main thought—no comma.

> **With the addition of the new wing, the building will cost more than we had planned.**   Not only is this phrase long, but it is also obviously introductory to the main thought.

Introductory Clause. An introductory clause is a subordinate clause that precedes the main thought. Study the following list of conjunctions that introduce subordinate clauses. You will then be able to recognize an introductory clause on sight, because the conjunction will signal you that such a clause is coming.

after	even if	provided	until
although	for	since	when
as	how	so that	whenever
as if	if	supposing	where
as soon as	inasmuch as	then	whereas
as though	in case that	till	wherever
because	in order that	though	whether
before	otherwise	unless	while

Use a comma to slow the reader after an introductory clause; as:

> **Although Mr. Ash has lived in the city for many years, his greatest ambition is to own a farm.**   Introductory clause beginning with *although*. Note the comma after the clause.

> **When the messenger returns, please ask him to deliver the package.**   *When* clause ends with a comma.

3   *Class Practice*   In the following sentences, tell where you would place commas to set off introductory words, phrases, or clauses.

1. Your suggestion was very valuable; therefore, we are writing to thank you for it.
2. Having forgotten the previous unfortunate experience, Mr. Dove ordered a year's supply of stationery.
3. When I give the signal, start to type.
4. Personally, I would not risk hiring a man without references.
5. To tell you the truth, I had completely forgotten the time.
6. Perhaps you would like us to send you some swatches of the new dress materials.
7. We concede that your proposal would do much for us; nevertheless, we do not feel that we are in a position to adopt it.

Subordinate Clause Following Main Clause

There is no question about using a comma after an introductory clause, but there may be a question about using the comma before a subordinate clause that *follows* a main clause. If this clause is an essential part of the message, no comma is used. If it is not necessary to the meaning—just "tacked on"—a comma is used. To illustrate:

> **She plans to go home if he comes before six.** No comma here because her going home is entirely contingent upon his arriving before six.

> **We should appreciate your sending us the home address of your sales manager, if you will be so kind.** *If you will be so kind* is not essential; therefore, the comma is used.

 Error Hunt Study these sentences and tell whether or not they are correctly punctuated. Then make any necessary corrections.

1. This item should be charged to selling expense¸if you wish to be technical about it.
2. Since I do not write shorthand¸ I shall be unable to take notes of incoming telegrams.
3. You must not leave¸unless¸you have permission to do so.
4. The slight improvement is only temporary¸ as we all realize.
5. Many of our appliances are of advanced styling; for instance, the combined freezer and refrigerator. O. K.

Keep Moving

Have you ever been at the wheel of a car in a congested traffic area? When the officer signaled for your line to move, he waved his arms madly and probably shouted, "Come on, come on! Keep moving!" He knew that, if one of the cars slowed down, the traffic would be snarled. Now, a written message, too, is snarled if commas slow the reader at the wrong places. A writer, then, must know when *not* to use the "Slow" sign, must know when to keep a thought moving. For instance, he must observe these rules:

1. *Do Not Separate the Parts of a Compound by a SINGLE Comma.* A compound that is composed of two parts may have two or more commas between those parts, but it may not be separated by only *one* comma. For example:

> **The president and the treasurer will discuss cost of sales.** A single comma separating the two-part compound *the president and the treasurer* would be incorrect.

The president and, of course, the treasurer will discuss cost of sales. Here the compound is separated by two commas, which is correct. The "Keep Moving" sign says that a *single* comma may not be used.

2. *Do Not Separate a Subject from Its Predicate by a SINGLE Comma.* Never will you use *one* comma between a subject and a predicate. Some illustrations are:

Whoever fails to understand the importance of the SAC fails to realize our position in case of a surprise attack. A comma after *SAC* would violate the "Keep Moving" principle.

The complaint of the new employee, in addition to those of some of the older staff members, was submitted to the grievance committee. This sentence is correct because there are *two* commas in the subject.

3. *Do Not Use a Comma Before the Ampersand (&) in a Firm Name.* For example:

Wool, Sharpe & Wool *Not* Wool, Sharpe, & Wool.

Learning Exercises

1 On a separate sheet of paper, write the correct punctuation for any sentences that are incorrectly punctuated and give your reasons for the corrections. If a sentence is correct, write "OK."

1 We went early and left early.
2 The string, paper clips, rulers etc. on our order No. 432 have not been delivered.
3 We could not possibly get the report out yesterday; moreover, we were not the only ones who did not meet the deadline.
4 The Scouts swam, ate, sang and danced away their week at camp.
5 To think well is admirable, to act well is more so.
6 However, poor the service is we feel that it is better than none.
7 We could not find our tickets, or we would have been at the theater earlier.
8 To hold our trade we must give better service.
9 Digest, the letters we received from Harding, Adams & Polk.
10 Certain foods contain lime; for instance, milk and butter.
11 On Friday we shall celebrate our tenth anniversary.
12 Mr. Beck contributed $100; the staff gave an equal amount.

13 From our office window there is a fine view of the river and on a clear, sunny day even the smaller boats can be seen.

14 If you accept this position, typing letters and envelopes, typing from corrected rough draft setting up and typing tabulations etc. will be some of the duties entrusted to you.

15 Some of the natives of India will not eat anything that is fish flesh or fowl.

2 On a separate sheet of paper, make whatever corrections are necessary and explain in your own words why you make them. Some of these sentences review punctuation principles you have previously studied.

1 Fred is cheerful and carefree, his brother is very reserved.

2 A shopper should never be without a charge plate, or a checkbook, or a reasonable amount of cash.

3 Alice, Bill, Edgar, and I, are always the first to arrive.

4 Please give us a choice of three dates, and if we can possibly arrange to see you, we will make a definite appointment.

5 You may obtain your passport by making application to the local office, or by writing direct to Washington.

6 On our tenth floor you will find a complete stock of chairs, tables, lamps and etc.

7 Unless granted permission, you must not take any materials off my desk.

8 David always did his work better than the rest of us, that is the reason for his rapid promotions.

9 Edna knows very well that she must go, that she would like to go and that she will go.

10 To win the bonus you must exceed your quota by 10 per cent.

11 Will you please send the requested information immediately.

12 We have canceled Mr. Salem's account with us, moreover, we have reported him to the Better Business Bureau.

13 I should like to know whether the new type cleaner is satisfactory?

14 However, fast a train may go, a plane goes much faster.

15 Mr. Ferry handed me the paper, thrust a pen at me and told me to sign on the dotted line.

Vocabulary and Spelling Refreshers

1 **Words Often Confused.** Lightening, lightning, lighting; patience, patients.

2 **Nouns and Adjectives.** What nouns ending in *ty* are related to the following adjectives?

    a rare   **c** entire   **e** facile

    b real   **d** anxious   **f** notorious

3 **Never Trust a "shun"Ending.** To each of the following, add the termination that is pronounced "shun."

    a expan＿＿＿   **c** comple＿＿＿   **e** discus＿＿＿

    b connec＿＿＿   **d** func＿＿＿   **f** suspi＿＿＿

Communication in Action: *Gobbledygook*

High-sounding words and phrases cloud the meaning of your writing and speaking. They are called "gobbledygook." For example, "Extinguish the nocturnal illumination" means, in everyday language, "Turn off the light." Rewrite the following example of gobbledygook so that it is easy to understand.

"It is anticipated that the writer will be reimbursed upon lapse of a reasonable interval of time. The amount of $685 is considerably in arrears, and it is contemplated that compensation will be forthcoming in due course. If complete reimbursement is not feasible immediately, perhaps an arrangement could be consummated whereby intermittent installments would be acceptable."

UNIT 31

The Comma   (*Continued*)

One very important use of commas, the "Slow" signs, is to indicate to the reader which parts of a message are not closely allied with the main thought. In this unit you will learn when to set off words and expressions by commas, thus marking clearly the sentence parts that are not all-important. "Set off" means that, if the expression is in the body of a sentence, there will be a comma *before* such an expression and a comma *after* it. Of course, if the expression ends the sentence, the period or other ending punctuation will take the place of the second comma.

Whether or not to set off words and expressions depends on whether they are restrictive or nonrestrictive. *Non* is a prefix meaning *not;* so all you have to remember is that *nonrestrictive* means *not necessary.* By the same token, *restrictive* means *necessary.* The punctuation rule states that nonrestrictive elements must be set off by commas. Simplified, this means that, when you are in doubt, you ask yourself two questions: Are these words necessary to the meaning? Could I omit them and still have a clear message? If the words are not necessary, if you could omit them without affecting the clarity of the message, these words are set off by commas; otherwise, no commas are used.

The use of the comma with unnecessary elements is divided here into three sections: interrupting, parenthetic, and explanatory words and expressions. In every case, however, keep in mind the basic fact that all words not absolutely necessary to the meaning are set off by commas.

Interrupting

An interrupting element does exactly what the name indicates—interrupts the message. An interruption, however, makes no contribution to the message; it might be called "excess baggage." Now, all "excess baggage" words are set off by commas, as illustrated in the following sentences.

> **The sales tax, moreover, went into effect in April.** Read the sentence, omitting *moreover.* Is this word necessary? Can you omit it without clouding the message? Yes. That is why it is set off by commas.

> **A check for the full amount of your bill would, therefore, be very welcome.** Read this sentence and slow down before and after *therefore.* Now read it and omit *therefore.* Can you see that the *therefore* in this sentence is "excess baggage," totally unnecessary? It is, therefore, set off by commas.

Words ordinarily considered interrupting may occasionally be written without commas for special effect. However, you will be wise to follow the more acceptable pattern in your writing.

Parenthetic

An expression inserted in a sentence by way of comment is a parenthetic expression, *if the meaning of the sentence is complete without it.* The words may be used to qualify or to amend the message. The aim of the writer may be to take away some of the sting of his words. The words may also be used to point out a contrast. Whatever the reason for their use, parenthetic expressions are set off by commas. You will have no problem with such expressions, for all you have to do is to apply your test. If the meaning is clear without using the words, set them off by commas. Study the following illustrations and explanations.

The incident, as far as I am concerned, is closed. *As far as I am concerned* qualifies the message. Apply your test questions: (1) Are these words necessary to the meaning? (2) Can you omit them and still have a clear message? The expression is not necessary to the meaning and can be omitted without affecting the message; therefore, the words are set off by commas.

The great hope of preventing, or at least controlling, future wars lies in the United Nations. Read the sentence, omitting the words set off by commas. Do you need these amending words for clarity? No, you do not; and they are correctly set off by commas.

The mailing list must be checked very carefully, not just inspected casually, if the revision is to be of any use. Apply your test. You find that the words expressing a contrasting thought are not necessary words; so they are correctly set off by commas.

Actually, you do not have to analyze these expressions to see whether they are qualifying, amending, contrasting, or whatever. All you have to do is recognize that they are "excess baggage" words and set them off by commas.

1 *Class Practice* Now see if you do recognize words and expressions that are set off by commas because they are not necessary to the meaning of a sentence. Indicate the punctuation in the following sentences and tell why you would use that punctuation.

1. On this decision then rests our authority to proceed.
2. We are, of course, prepared to stand behind our guarantee.
3. The rumor, we are convinced is, without foundation.
4. The due date on your note, however, was July 8.
5. The ceramics factory, is according to my information, operating three shifts daily.
6. The samples were definitely shoddy, and we are therefore requesting you to cancel our order.
7. We are asking you, therefore, to cancel our order.

✔ *Error Hunt 1*   You have just had practice in setting off by commas all "excess baggage" words. You should be ready, therefore, to find any errors there may be in the following sentences. Tell why you make the corrections.

1. The new model, it is generally conceded, contains the best features of preceding cars in addition to some new features.
2. George Edsen, it is reported, will be a candidate at the coming mayoralty election.
3. We will, though it is against our rule, allow the discount.
4. The new posture chairs are very desirable for, but not absolutely necessary to the comfort of the typists.
5. The rest of the typewriters, too, are to be serviced when your repairman calls.
6. You can obtain the information, fortunately, from our office in Seattle.
7. Errors like these cost money. You will, therefore, check all figures three times.
8. All stenographers, not clerks, are to work seven hours a day.
9. The restrictions regarding credit, as you can well imagine, have seriously affected installment buying.
10. Shipments, however, are to be made according to the current schedule.

Explanatory

Some sentences contain words that are not necessary to the meaning but do give additional information. Your comma problem in explanatory elements is to recognize them as such and to set them off by commas. This is not easy, as you can see.

> **Mr. Anderson, who has had twenty years' experience in the shoe business, will join our staff on March 1.**   Omission of the words set off by commas leaves: "Mr. Anderson will join our staff on March 1." This makes perfect sense; so you know that the words set off by commas were used just to give additional information.

Now attack the problem from another angle. You have written the following sentence, and you wonder whether you should have used commas.

> **The salesman who joined our staff on March 1 has had twenty years' experience in the shoe business.**

Should you have used commas to set off *who joined our staff on March 1?* If you did, you would have left: *The salesman has had twenty years' experience in the shoe business.* You would leave yourself wide open to the natural question, "What, or which, sales-man?" The clause in question is needed to identify the salesman about whom you are talking; so no commas are used.

2 *Class Practice*   Decide which of these sentences contain words that are not essential to the meaning and which contain words that are essential. In the sentences where additional, unnecessary information is given, indicate the places where you would use commas.

1. In the South where temperatures are milder there is no demand for the heavier line of coats.
2. In sections where temperatures are milder there is no demand for the heavier line of coats.
3. We received their bid after the time for filing bids had expired.
4. We received their bid this afternoon which was after the time for filing bids had expired.
5. The results of the mailing are as disappointing as you prophe-sied they would be.
6. The results of the test mailing are disappointing as you prophe-sied they would be.

That, Which. Careful writers make a distinction between the use of *that* and *which*. Clauses that are *not* necessary to the meaning are introduced by *which*, and clauses that *are* necessary are introduced by *that*. For example:

> **We are sending you our new catalogue, which contains all the new items we manufacture.** *Which* introduces a clause that gives additional information. Note the comma.

> **The catalogue that we are sending you will give you an idea of the many new items that we are featuring.** *That* introduces a clause needed for identification. Note that no commas are used.

Appositives. In Unit 19 you studied the correct case form for ap-positives; and the signposts you used to recognize appositives were the commas that set them off. You already know, then, that an ap-positive is set off by commas; and you know that appositives give additional information.

There are, however, some instances where the identifying term is very, very closely connected with the principal term; and in such cases commas are not used. For these closely connected terms, use your test. If the term is needed for identification, no commas are used. If the words can be omitted without affecting the meaning of the sentence, set them off by commas. The following examples show you when to use commas and when not to use them.

Our representative, Mr. Charles Daniels, will call on Monday. Omit the words set off by commas and you have: "Our representative will call on Monday." This is a clear message, and the commas were used correctly.

In 1917, the year of our entry into World War I, the production of rayon in the United States was 6,700,000 pounds. *The year of our entry into World War I* is in no way essential to the message. It is, therefore, set off by commas.

My sister Eileen works for the new plastics company. If you omit *Eileen,* your reader will not know which sister you mean. *Eileen* is necessary for identification, and that is why this word is not set off by commas.

William the Conqueror found the English people very uncooperative. Omission of *the Conqueror* would leave the reader wondering which William you meant. This closely connected term is needed for identification and, therefore, is not set off by commas.

Degrees, Titles, and Other Explanatory Terms. *Ph. D.* after a person's name gives additional information about that person—indicates that he is a doctor of philosophy. *Inc.* after a firm name tells you that the company has been incorporated. *Jr.* after a man's name gives the information that this man is the son, not the father by the same name. Because degrees, titles, *Inc., Ltd.,* etc., give additional information, they are set off by commas. Some illustrations are:

The newest book on the subject is by John Doe, M. D., who is a former member of the faculty at the University.

Amos Garfield, Jr., was elected president of the board.

Make the check out to William Seton & Company, Inc., and send it by registered mail.

Calendar Dates. Whenever the year is included in a date, set off that year by commas—that is, use a comma before *and* after the year. Really, the year is explanatory, telling which May 1 or April 10 is meant or which May or April is meant, if the day is not given; as:

July 14, 1960, is a date that I shall never forget.

Are you thinking of May, 1958, or May, 1968?

States, Cities. If the name of a city is followed by the name of its state, the name of the state is set off by commas. The name of the state is explanatory, indicating which Springfield or which Columbus is meant; thus:

Rochester, New York, is my home town. *New York* tells which Rochester of all the Rochesters is my home town.

Would you rather live in Lincoln, Nebraska, than in Lincoln, Iowa?

3 *Class Practice*   Some of these practice sentences contain "additional information" words, words that should be set off by commas. Other sentences contain words essential to the meaning, words that are not set off by commas. Take a few minutes to study them and then tell where you would insert commas and why.

1. Judith herself told me the good news.
2. My pocket dictionary which never failed to help me out of a difficulty has been mislaid.
3. Please call at our main office in Dayton Ohio for your registration card.
4. A student who works his way through college appreciates his education. O.
5. Send the tax notice to Edward Bessette, Jr. rather than to Edward Bessette, Sr.
6. The manuscript which was beautifully typed was accepted for publication.
7. An appointment for July 18, 1965 has been made for you.
8. Harold was in spite of this failure a studious and an intelligent young man.
9. Philip Black, D. D. S. is the way he prefers his name to be written.
10. Our earliest caller the woman in the black suit arrived before the office staff.

Error Hunt 2   On the assumption that the previous class practice has made clear to you the use of commas with words that give additional information, you are invited to prove it by finding whatever errors there are in the following sentences.

1. I am returning your article, which I read last evening and thoroughly enjoyed.
2. The books, that contain the records, are in Mr. Boyd's file.
3. Our manager sensing the situation sent out of the office the stranger who was causing the trouble.
4. Mr. Gibson my next-door neighbor has formed a car pool.
5. This is the book that I told you about yesterday.
6. Stonington, Maine is a smaller town than Stonington, Indiana.
7. The words appearing in red ink fairly shout their message. O.

8. Joe's friend who was also his cousin made the arrangements.

Keep Moving

The line of traffic that must be kept moving, explained in this unit, might be called twin sister to the "Keep Moving" principle you learned in Unit 30. That principle was that a subject must not be separated from its predicate by a *single* comma. Now learn the companion rule: A verb should not be separated from its object or complement by a *single* comma. There should be either two commas or no comma. To help you to avoid a very common error, study the following examples.

> **I am returning to you for your files the record for the plaintiff in the case of Martin vs. Larsen.** A comma after *files* would be incorrect.

> **Please send us within the next week or two the first draft of your plan for increasing sales in the cosmetics department.** A comma after *two* would violate this "Keep Moving" principle.

Learning Exercises

1 Keeping in mind the general rule that you set off by commas any words or expressions not essential to the meaning and that you do not use commas with words or expressions that are necessary to the meaning, punctuate these sentences. Indicate on your paper your reasons for making the corrections.

1 We cannot however approve such action until we know more about the circumstances.
2 Fred Wills who has been largely responsible for the success of the sale has asked me to type his report.
3 Yours is a legitimate though somewhat unusual excuse.
4 Many adults like some children fear to meet new situations.
5 John P. Quirk, LL. D. is a professor at Eli University.
6 Excise taxes by the way are to remain at their present level.
7 Under the circumstances therefore we do not feel that we can make an exception in your case.
8 July 4, 1776 is a date that is known to every American.
9 Charles the only son Mr. Coe had at home has joined the army.
10 The biography of the poet Shelley is now published in a paperback edition.
11 Our offices are in Dallas, Texas and Chicago, Illinois.

12 Ceramics, Inc. is the name of the firm that has bought the Barrows Building.

13 Then too he feels that Bill will advise us about the contract.

14 The cellar or basement of his new house is very dry.

15 The machine, although old and ugly does a very satisfactory job.

2 Beginning with this unit and ending with Unit 37, the second learning exercise will be a cumulative review of the principles presented in Part 5. For each Learning Exercise 2, you are to write "OK" on your paper if a sentence is correctly written. If a sentence is incorrect, write your corrections and give reasons for making them.

1 Perhaps Mr. Bates was too ill to attend the meeting.

2 Place all bills face up, that is, with the portraits on top.

3 Our guest entertained us with many exciting stories of World War II, he had been a newspaper correspondent.

4 Books, and papers, and pencils were strewn on the floor.

5 A man should be judged by what he does, not by who his ancestors were.

6 James will go to the bank, and make the deposit for you.

7 The really happy person knows, that work is a blessing.

8 Elsa works as a typist during the day, and attends school at night.

9 In the summer, when June cannot skate or ski she plays tennis and golf.

10 However, gratifying the attendance may be at the next meeting, it will probably fall short of the goal we have set.

11 Your service has always been excellent; and we are, therefore, recommending your transportation facilities to Evans & Bates.

12 You can expect to be happy in almost any job. If you are interested and conscientious.

13 The regulations state that any employee, who is frequently tardy, may receive a low rating.

14 Although Marcia was willing to work on other holidays, she refused to work on Labor Day.

15 You have been one of our best customers, therefore, we are happy to extend your credit for another thirty days.

Vocabulary and Spelling Refreshers

1 **Words Often Confused.** Hole, whole; explicit, implicit.

2 **Don't Be "All In."** In each of the following sentences, *all* is misused in some way. Substitute the correct forms.

    a This procedure is universally followed by all.
    b I did not sleep all night.
    c He is an all-around technician.
    d All of the members voted "Yes" to the proposal.
    e This is all the farther I will walk.

3 **How Is "uhble" Spelled?** How are the following words spelled when the "uhble"-sounding suffix is added?

    a detest____   **c** inexhaust____   **e** siz____
    b indestruct____   **d** unspeak____   **f** reduc____

Communication in Action: *Testing Your Tact*

Marge has just returned from vacation. She begins to give you the full details of her two weeks of relaxation and fun. You're mildly interested; but you have a long letter to type, and your boss is waiting impatiently for it. How would you handle the situation? Exactly what would you say?

UNIT 32

The Comma *(Concluded)*

This final unit on the use of the comma presents some important principles that are not related to any of the others you have studied. For best results, concentrate on each separate use and understand that use thoroughly before proceeding to the next principle. The unit is planned and arranged to help you with this study method. When you have learned these five additional uses, you will have achieved mastery of the comma. Your message then cannot be misinterpreted, for you will know how to use the "Slow" signs that will guide your reader into understanding the thoughts expressed by your words—as you wish him to understand them.

With Modifying Adjectives

If you use two or more adjectives to modify a noun, separate the adjectives by commas—if each one separately modifies the noun. For instance:

> **The blue, red, and yellow sweaters belong to the three girls taking the entrance test.** *Blue* modifies *sweaters; red* modifies *sweaters; yellow* modifies *sweaters.*

> **The 1916 automobile was a high, cumbersome vehicle.** The automobile was a *high vehicle* and was also a *cumbersome vehicle.*

Quick Trick . When you are in doubt as to whether to use a comma in a situation like this, try a quick trick: If you can mentally use correctly the word *and* between the adjectives, a comma should be used. If not, no comma should be inserted. Using this quick trick with the preceding illustrations, you would know that the commas are correct because you could say, "The blue *and* red *and* yellow sweaters," "A high *and* cumbersome vehicle."

Another advantage of knowing this quick trick is that you will avoid the common error of placing a comma after the last modifying adjective. You know that it would have been incorrect to write: "the blue, red, and yellow, sweaters." You would then be saying: "the blue *and* red *and* yellow *and* sweaters." Suppose you punctuated the second sentence thus: "The 1916 automobile was a high, cumbersome, vehicle." You would be saying: "The 1916 automobile was a high *and* cumbersome *and* vehicle."

As you know when to use the comma with modifiers, you should, at the same time, know when *not* to use it. For example:

> **From our spring one can always get a glass of clear, cold water.** You know that this is correct, for you can get a glass of clear *and* cold water. What about the next sentence?

> **Our spring is noted throughout the neighborhood for its cold running water.** Why is there no comma after *cold?* Because the meaning is not cold *and* running water. Our spring is noted for its cold—what? Running water, isn't it? *Cold,* then, modifies the idea of *running water;* and no comma is placed between *cold* and *running.*

1 *Class Practice* These sentences provide you with the practice necessary to be sure that you understand when to use, and when not to use, a comma with modifiers. Punctuate the sentences correctly.

1. Eva got the information from a polite,helpful man at the reservations desk.
2. You have been recommended as a progressive ,wide-awake dealer.
3. We never offer shopworn,defective goods for sale.
4. Miss Harding is wearing a bright,pretty scarf.
5. Our department store is a modern ,well-stocked, and well-run business.
6. At last the wearisome,monotonous checking job was finished.
7. Mr. Ahern is a short, stout good-natured man.
8. A detailed,comprehensive report is required.

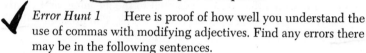 *Error Hunt 1*   Here is proof of how well you understand the use of commas with modifying adjectives. Find any errors there may be in the following sentences.

1. Mr. Ladd is a true, loyal, honorable, man.
2. The article was written by a renowned mining engineer.
3. Our visitor had a long pointed head.
4. The new cabinets are beautiful practical roomy models.
5. A feeble, old, man was begging on the corner.
6. Miss Harding is wearing a bright nylon scarf.
7. The people who can least afford to do so eat desserts topped with sweet thick snowy whipped cream.
8. Two heavy square-wooden boxes were delivered at the office this morning.

To Indicate Omissions

Writers sometimes omit words without confusing the message, for the omitted words are clearly understood from the sense of the sentence. However, whenever such words are left out, a comma is used to slow down the reader, so that he knows there is an omission. To illustrate:

> **Men's overcoats are marked down to $49.50; boys', to $39.50.** The comma slows you down for the omission. The meaning, very clearly, is: *boys' overcoats are marked down to $39.50.*

> **To err is human; to forgive, divine.**   To forgive *is* divine, but the comma slows you down for and indicates the omission of *is.*

In Direct Address

Names or terms used in speaking directly to a particular person or group of persons are said to be used in direct address. Any names, words, or phrases used in direct address are set off by commas; as:

For you, Mrs. Gordon, we are happy to exchange the blouse. Speaking directly to *Mrs. Gordon*.

It is my privilege, members of the Rotary Club, to introduce Dr. William F. Jackson. Speaking directly to *members of the Rotary Club*.

There is no more important question in the whole field of politics, my friend, than that of taxation. Speaking directly to *my friend*.

Very probably you would automatically set off by commas any words used in direct address, even without being familiar with the term "direct address." You have already learned to set off by commas any words that are not essential to the meaning, and words used in direct address are not necessary words. The preceding illustrative sentences make perfect sense when written:

For you, we are happy to exchange the blouse.

It is my privilege to introduce Dr. William F. Jackson.

There is no more important question in the whole field of politics than that of taxation.

2 *Class Practice* To clarify your understanding of the use of the comma to indicate omissions and to set off words used in direct address, punctuate the following sentences.

1. We are gratified to tell you that in May our sales jumped 15 per cent; in June 20 per cent; and in July another 20 per cent.
2. Will you teach me to operate the machine Harold?
3. Something has been added. What we are not sure.
4. Yes sir, I will have the data for you by Monday.
5. The reports show that in 1959 the company had fifteen salesmen; in 1960 forty; and in 1961 seventy-five.
6. We wish Mr. Downes that we were able to grant your request.

Error Hunt 2 If you can find whatever errors there are in these sentences, you will prove to yourself that you have a fine understanding of the two comma rules you practiced in the preceding sentences.

1. You can readily understand gentlemen that our expenses, too, are increasing.
2. The price of the first table is $100; of the second $90; and of the third $75.
3. Do you agree with me Mr. Bates that we must revise our accounting procedures?
4. The average person when young is venturesome; when old, less daring.

5. We are glad to offer you courteous reader an opportunity to buy these books at a 10 per cent discount.

In Repeated Expressions

Sometimes, effective writing can be achieved by repeating a thought or an idea. If you should repeat for emphasis, use a comma to set off the repetition; like this:

> **Yours is a splendid idea, a splendid idea.** Repetition of *a splendid idea* for emphasis.

> **Such a discount policy is foolishness, utter foolishness.** Repetition of *foolishness* for emphasis.

In Numbers and Between Unrelated Numbers

Use a comma to separate thousands, millions, billions, and so on, in numbers of four or more digits; as: *3,874; 35,500;* and *$1,500,000.*

When two unrelated numbers are written together, they should be separated by a comma. Otherwise, there would be no slowing down between the numbers. For example:

> **In 1960, 1,736 persons requested free samples of our soap.** Without the separating comma, the two separate numbers would run together, with resultant confusion.

3 *Class Practice* In the light of your study of commas with repeated expressions, in numbers, and between unrelated numbers, punctuate these sentences.

1. Never never draw a check before filling in the stub.
2. In the year 1929 387 companies in this kind of business failed.
3. We are pleased with your report really pleased.
4. There are more than 3500 accounts on our books.
5. You must always always observe the rules of the office where you work.
6. In 1959 3498 of our 3500 accounts were settled promptly.

✓ *Error Hunt 3* Now, find any repeated-expression or number errors in the following sentences.

1. Out of a total loss of $4,000, $500 was due to bad debts.
2. You will find Miss Byrne an intelligent girl, unusually intelligent.
3. Our total sales for the year amounted to $22,894,532.78.
4. Of the total tax amounting to $43,968 $41,878 has already been paid.
5. Above all, this project needs to be better organized much better organized.

Keep Moving

You have just learned when to use a comma in numbers. You do *not,* however, use the comma in years, page numbers, house and telephone numbers, serial numbers, and decimal fractions. These are written as follows:

in 1960	1212 Elm Street	policy No. 387546
page 1468	Jefferson 6-2288	5.7236

It is also necessary to keep moving when writing weights, capacities, or measurements that refer to *one* weight, *one* capacity, or *one* measurement. For instance:

My roast weighed 5 pounds 4½ ounces. No comma is used, because this is *one* weight.

We made the flight in 4 hours 50 minutes 10 seconds. No commas, because this is *one* time unit.

Learning Exercises

1 The following sentences afford practice in using all the comma principles presented in this unit. On a separate sheet of paper, indicate where you would place commas and tell why you do so.

1 The typist has long hours of sitting; the file clerk long hours of standing.
2 We can allow only our customary regular discount.
3 That contestant won $98,000 $29,400 of which had to be set aside for income tax.
4 Friday is the deadline for the report Mr. Anderson.
5 The Gila monster is a vicious poisonous lizard.
6 Don't you agree that we have been lenient in this case too lenient?
7 Your policy number has been changed to No. 11,167,099.
8 In England the statesman was revered; in France despised.
9 Alice arranged six golden daffodils in a gray bowl.
10 Mr. Mohr can you spare some time for me this morning?
11 A large number of customers attended the sale an unusually large number.
12 We cannot use the small model that adds only to 99999.
13 My mother was an energetic quick skillful nurse.
14 Jack is the son of a lawyer; James of a doctor.
15 We do hope Mrs. Grant that you will be pleased with the substitution we made for you.

2

Follow the usual directions for working Learning Exercise 2.

1 The last shipment, however, is not up to our standards.
2 Mr. Lee complains that his secretary is slow, and inefficient.
3 The teapots nevertheless did arrive in good condition.
4 Art museums have great cultural value, they help everyone to broaden his education.
5 The treatment was in line with the latest, scientific discoveries.
6 We manufacture locks, bolts, and screws, and we can supply hardware dealers in all parts of the country.
7 The television hero offered his enemy three choices: draw, fight with fists or turn tail.
8 Our interviewer objected to her voice, not to her manner.
9 Will you please pay your future bills by check by check only.
10 A week before business showed a slight improvement.
11 Hosiery, gloves, neckwear, etc., will go on sale next week.
12 Mr. Wilton has been appointed manager of the new company; Mr. Higgins purchasing agent; and Mr. Barr chief accountant.
13 The skirt you ordered is out of stock but we shall be happy to place a special order for you.
14 The lion tamer was a clever, fearless, little man.
15 Many of the china pieces were broken in transit, however, the cups escaped damage.

Vocabulary and Spelling Refreshers

1

Words Often Confused. Manner, manor; emanate, eminent, imminent.

2

Geographic Mishaps. The following geographic names contain some type of error other than spelling. Find the mistakes.

a Juneau, Ala.
b Columbus, O.
c Savannah, Tenn.
d Honolulu, T. H.
e New York City, N. Y.
f Spring Field, Mass.

3

Find the Misspellings. Rewrite the following announcement, correcting the spelling and any errors in grammar. Improve the wording.

Pleas announse to all of the students in your classes that a meeting for a organisation of a proffessional nature will be held on January 10th, 1961 in room 2436 accrost from the lounge at 7:30 p.m. in the evening. All of the students in your classes are wellcome. Any other students are also invited.

Communication in Action: *To Bluff or Not to Bluff*

You are asked to give your opinion about the value of merit ratings, a topic brought up at a staff meeting. The trouble is that you don't know anything about merit ratings. Should you bluff your way through, saying something you hope makes sense; or should you admit that you don't have an informed opinion? What would you say?

Section 3   **Punctuation and Capitalization — Signals**

UNIT   33

Quotation Marks

As you drive along a familiar highway, you pass or see a building, a monument, a gas station, or something else that tells you where you are. They are the signals that orient you, that keep you straight. On a long trip, in strange territory, you watch carefully for signs showing route numbers, particularly the number of the route you are following. If there is a long interval during which you do not see your route number, you become uneasy, fearing that you are off your route. Without signals, a person can very easily become lost.

A writer has at his command various signals that he uses to cue a reader into the proper interpretation of a written message. The writer's signals mark the reader's thinking route and prevent the reader from straying. This unit takes up instruction and training in the signals that you will need to keep a reader on the intended message route. Facility in the use of these signals is essential if your aim is to write in such a way that your precise meaning is clear.

This first unit is concerned with the use of quotation marks. These signals are used principally to tell the reader: "These are the actual words spoken or written by a specific person." This and other uses of quotation marks, together with related pointers, are explained under the following topics.

Direct Quotations

When you record word for word what someone has said or written, enclose the words in quotation marks. If the quotation is brief, use a comma to separate the rest of the expression from the quotation.

> **Mr. Scott's comment was, "That will be satisfactory."** *Before* a brief quotation.

> **"That will be satisfactory," said Mr. Scott.** *After* a brief quotation.

If you wish a quoted sentence to strike the reader forcibly, or if the quotation is a long one, use a colon before the sentence.

> **The letter contained just one sentence: "We are now ready to discuss a new lease with you."** The colon emphasizes the sentence by signaling, "Something important is coming."

> **Secretary Pine, on his return from Europe yesterday, said: "If the free peoples of the world are to remain free, they must rally to a cause that will unite them."** The colon precedes a long direct quotation.

Interruptions in Quotations. If a direct quotation is interrupted, quotation marks are placed around the quoted words only; thus:

> **"Neither the manufacturer nor the jobber," ran the letter, "can supply the goods in time to fill the order."** The interruption is *ran the letter.* Commas set off the interruption.

If the quotation ends with a question mark or an exclamation point, these marks of punctuation are used instead of the comma; as:

> **The sign, "Dangerous Curve Ahead!" could not be overlooked.** Ordinarily, an ending comma for the appositive would be used; but the exclamation point is part of the quotation and is, therefore, used here instead of the comma.

If a semicolon or a period occurs at the interrupting point, place the semicolon or the period *after the interruption.* For example:

"**Our sales staff should be enlarged,**" he recommended; "**our show-rooms should be modernized.**" The interruption in the quoted sentence comes at the point where there is a semicolon; therefore, the semicolon is placed after the interruption.

"**Our sales staff should be enlarged,**" he recommended. "**Also, our showrooms should be modernized.**" This is one quotation, but there are two separate sentences in the quotation. A period indicating the end of the first sentence is placed after the interruption.

When you enclose material in quotation marks, that material must be copied exactly as it is written. Even if you know that the grammar or the punctuation is wrong, you should make no corrections. Otherwise, you would not be quoting.

Punctuation at End of Quotations

Are punctuation marks at the end of quoted words, phrases, and sentences placed inside or outside the quotation mark? Here are the three principles that cover all ending-punctuation situations.

1. *Periods and commas* are always placed *inside* the closing quotation mark; thus:

Our new model reproduces sound from records without "chatter." *Period inside* quotation mark.

To eliminate "chatter," purchase one of our new models. *Comma inside* quotation mark.

2. *Colons and semicolons* are always placed *outside* the closing quotation mark; as:

The following are usually listed under "Assets": **cash, furniture, equipment, and accounts receivable.** *Colon* is placed *outside* the ending quotation mark.

The person who is being sued is known as the "defendant"; the one who is bringing the suit, as the "plaintiff." Note that the *semicolon* is placed *outside,* but the *period* is placed *inside* the ending quotation mark.

Stop here for a moment and review; thus: *periods and commas, inside* quotes; *colons and semicolons, outside* quotes.

3. *Question marks and exclamation points* are sometimes placed inside and sometimes outside closing quotation marks, depending on the following conditions:

a. If the quoted matter is a question or an exclamation, the question mark or the exclamation point is placed *inside* the quotation marks.

I am sending you a copy of my book, "What Are the Flowers Saying?" If you stop to think, placing the question mark inside the quotation mark is only sensible. The question mark is part of the title of the book, and it is the title that is enclosed in quotation marks.

My message to you is "Stand fast!" Again, since the exclamation point is part of the quoted material, it must be placed with the words with which it belongs—*inside* the ending quotation mark.

b. If the *entire sentence* is a question or an exclamation, the question mark or the exclamation point is placed *outside* the ending quotation mark.

What have you done with your "excess baggage"? The question mark here is *not* part of the quotation. It is used to end a sentence that asks a question; therefore, it is placed at the very end—*outside* the ending quotation mark.

Jim is an out-and-out "parasite"! Is the exclamation point part of the quotation? No. Is it the proper punctuation mark for the ending of an exclamatory sentence? Yes. Then it is placed *outside* the quotation mark—at the end of the sentence, where it belongs.

Error Hunt 1 The following sentences were written to help you with quotation marks and with the punctuation used with quotations. If a sentence is correct or if punctuation is omitted or incorrectly placed, say so and tell why you think so.

1. It looks like rain said the farmer. we certainly can use some.
2. Please "rush:" 1 dozen packages mixed flower seeds, 4 lawn mowers, and 6 garden rakes.
3. The purchasing agent said I very much regret the decision.
4. The friendly feeling of the public for a firm is known as "good will;" without it, no business can long endure.
5. "May we look forward to receiving your order soon" is an excellent way to close a sales letter.
6. Is this stock one of the "Blue Chips?"
7. Mr. Jelton said that he very much regretted the decision.
8. Our new textbook "Grammar for Everyone" will be published within six months.

Quoted Expressions and Terms

Quotation marks are used with some expressions and terms to signal that the quoted words have some special significance. You, the writer, can direct the reader's interpretation of your message by plainly marking his route with quotation marks. Follow closely the topics and discussion given here, so that you will be able to quote correctly and effectively.

Words Explained or Defined. Words and phrases accompanied by their definitions or introduced by such expressions as *so-called, known as, termed, marked, entitled, signed, the word,* and similar words and phrases are enclosed in quotation marks. For instance:

> A contest in a court of justice is termed "litigation" by attorneys.

> You should have used the word "but," not "and."

> This is an example of their so-called "hands-off policy."

> Strictly speaking, "manuscript" refers to handwritten documents. *Manuscript* is the word that you wish to stand out.

> "Yours for profits" is an unusual complimentary closing. You draw special attention to this unusual complimentary closing by enclosing it in quotation marks.

> *Note:* This rule applies to material that is to appear in typewritten form, as in letters or reports. If the material is to be set in type, however, expressions of this kind should be underscored and the quotation marks omitted. Underscoring indicates to a printer that the expressions are to be set in italic type.

Terms Unfamiliar to the Reader. Whenever you use terms that you assume are unfamiliar to the reader, those terms should be enclosed in quotation marks. There may be a question as to whether you should use such terms. As your primary aim is to make your message clear to the reader, it may well be that the use of technical or trade terms unfamiliar to the reader will not promote clarity. If you do use them, however, enclose them in quotation marks; as:

> All our newspaper "cuts" become the property of the newspaper using them. *Cut* is a technical term meaning "an engraved block or plate for printing."

> This new locomotive will make it possible to eliminate "pushers" up the westbound grade. *Pusher* is a term peculiar to railroading.

Slang, Humor, Poor Grammar. Sometimes writers use slang or poor grammar just to make their writing more interesting. Too, sometimes writers like to use words that they intend to be interpreted as humorous. In such cases, the slang, poor grammar, or humorous words are enclosed in quotation marks.

When writing to a person who is a total stranger, it is safer not to use slang or poor grammar. Also, perhaps you should not try to be funny. He may not appreciate your humor. In some cases, however, your point will be better made if you do use such words. The following sentences illustrate this use of quotation marks.

> The price quoted in our letter of May 3 was surely a "boner."

> All this is an indication of the fact that the "world do move."

Translations of Foreign Words. Whenever you give a translation of a foreign word, enclose that translation in quotation marks; like this:

> *À la mode* means "after the fashion."

> "As it should be" is the translation of *comme il faut.*

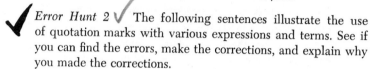 *Error Hunt 2* The following sentences illustrate the use of quotation marks with various expressions and terms. See if you can find the errors, make the corrections, and explain why you made the corrections.

1. In material descriptive of automobiles, the term automotive is frequently used.
2. Remember that the only safe way is to check and double check.
3. The words principal and principle are frequently confused.
4. Sandhogs is the name given to men who work under compressed air, as in driving tunnels.
5. Each letter in the series has been tailor-made to fit a particular situation.
6. This is confidential—to at least a thousand people.
7. Noninterference is the free translation of *laissez faire.*

Quotation Within a Quotation

A quotation within a quotation is enclosed in single quotation marks; as:

> The student reported, "We now know the difference between 'adapt' and 'adopt.' "

Titles

Enclose in quotation marks the following titles: books, parts and chapters of books, plays, lectures, articles, essays, sermons, poems, toasts, mottoes, paintings, sculptures, and names of ships. For example:

> Dr. Henry Van Dyke's "Work" contains much inspiration for those who must work to live.   Title of a book.

> Chapter V, "Inquiry Letters," appears in Part I, which deals with "Business Letter Writing."   Title of a chapter and title of a section of a book.

Professor Gray will address our club on "This Competitive Era." Title of a lecture.

My personal motto is, "I'd rather be ready and not go than go and not be ready." Exact words of a motto.

Did you get reservations for the "Queen Mary"? Name of a ship.

Do *not* enclose in quotation marks the following: names of periodicals (daily, weekly, monthly), documents, annuals, reports, proceedings, and such words as *Preface, Introduction, Contents, Appendix,* or *Index* of a book. For instance:

The New York Day carried the announcement in its March 9 issue. Name of a newspaper is not enclosed in quotation marks.

Have you seen the Report of the Committee on Law Enforcement? Name of a report is not enclosed in quotation marks.

Note. Underscore all titles that are to be *set in type* later. Underscoring indicates to the printer that such titles are to be set in italics.

Error Hunt 3 To be sure that you are clear about quotations within quotations and about titles that should be enclosed in quotation marks, find any errors in the following sentences.

1. Adam Smith's great work is his Wealth of Nations.
2. Please save me your copy of Life.
3. Romeo and Juliet is both a play and an opera.
4. Business first is our motto.
5. "I have read the article, 'The Continuing Business Pattern,'" reported Mr. Pierre.
6. The subscription price of "Today's Post" has not been increased.
7. Mr. Kent's favorite newspaper is the Evening Times.

Learning Exercises

1 On a separate sheet of paper, indicate where quotation and punctuation marks should be inserted in the following sentences. Be prepared to give a reason for every mark you insert.

1 A mechanical conveyor is known in the trade as a conveyer.
2 The general's words were, I will return.
3 His next article will be titled Is Asia Preparing for War?
4 Outline the material on the following pages in Business Advertising 120, 121, 122, and 123.
5 Our lawyer said that he did not wish to bring suit unless it was absolutely necessary.

6 Which paper is delivered to your house, the Morning Record or the Evening Sun?

7 The most important part of the order read like this "Buy 100 shares of General Oil at market."

8 The mere fact that a package is marked Fragile is not enough to guarantee safe transportation.

9 Have you read Bret Harte's The Luck of Roaring Camp

10 The words stationery and stationary are called homonyms.

11 I have read your book, What Is Ahead for Small Business

12 In the column headed "Total" place the total for the month.

13 His secretary asked Shall I mark this cablegram Deferred Rate

14 Look up some synonyms for nice; it is an overworked word.

15 Please do not feel that we are trying to rook you.

2 Follow the usual directions.

1 If Henry can still type that typewriter should suit him.

2 "We, the People of the United States," etc., begins the Preamble to the Constitution of the United States.

3 A group of cold, hungry, Boy Scouts reached camp long after dark.

4 Your credit standing is excellent, and if you wish to purchase goods on open account, we shall be happy to have you do so.

5 I cannot understand the luck that some people have, last year my neighbor won an automobile with an outlay of 10 cents.

6 We are proud of the reputation we enjoy and will do everything in our power to maintain and increase our prestige.

7 Many writers cannot spell the word recommend.

8 No discount is to be taken when a bill is paid in 30 days. As is clearly printed on all our invoices.

9 Trees, shrubs, flowers, etc. are all parched for rain.

10 However successful the results, the methods used are questionable.

11 May we have your answer within a week?

12 He replied that "their company is no longer manufacturing this machine."

13 Mr. Maine urged the applicant to begin drawing his chair nearer and nearer to the prospective employee.

14 Mr. Brant prefers to read his speeches; Mr. Atwater to talk from notes.

15 The report made public by the committee on June 2, shows gross inefficiency at all levels of the bureau.

Vocabulary and Spelling Refreshers

1 **Words Often Confused.** Human, humane; forgo, forego.

2 **Some Business Terms.** In each of the following sentences, choose the definition that really defines the term in italics.

    a To *garnishee* is: (1) to attach wages to pay a debt, (2) to appropriate an employer's money, (3) to try to enforce by legal process, (4) to try to effect an agreement.

    b *One to whom a debt is owed* is: (1) a creditor, (2) a cashier, (3) an auditor, (4) a referee.

    c *One who has authority to represent another in a business transaction with a third person* is: (1) a notary public, (2) a jobber, (3) an agent, (4) a financier.

Communication in Action: *Helping a New Employee*

A new employee, Frank Hart, is assigned to the desk next to yours. Your supervisor was called to a meeting before he could introduce Frank to you or any of the others. Courtesy demands that you take action. What are your responsibilities? Enact a typical introduction. Make a list of other things you could do to be helpful to this person.

UNIT 34

Parentheses and the Apostrophe

If you were asked, "What makes a writer a *good* writer?" what would you answer? Briefly, you would probably say that the good writer is able to express on paper the ideas he has in his mind, that he uses the exact words needed to express his exact thoughts, and that he uses correct grammar. Then, almost in the same breath, you would say that the good writer also knows the mechanics of writing. He is adept at using the full and partial stops, the "Slow" signs, and the signals that direct the reader's interpretation of the written words. Such an answer would be comprehensive and correct, for the ability to write well consists of facility with words *plus* effective use of the writing techniques that make those words meaningful.

In this unit you will study two more signals, parentheses and the apostrophe. When you have learned the uses of these signals, you will have available to you two more devices for insuring clear and accurate interpretation of your written messages.

Parentheses

Parentheses are used mainly to enclose words that give additional information. You will remember that commas and dashes are also used for this purpose; but, while words set off by commas or dashes *may* be omitted, still these words are helpful to the main thought. The peculiar function of parentheses is to tell the reader, "This is something I am repeating or adding, but it has very little connection with the main thought." For instance:

> **We have turned your problem over to our advertising depart-ment, located in Chicago, for expert solution.** *Located in Chicago* is not essential to the meaning, but it may be helpful to the reader to know where the advertising department is located.

> **If we were offering you just a course in salesmanship—even an unusually good one at an unusually good price—it would not be surprising if you did not buy it.** The words enclosed in dashes stand out, which is the purpose of using dashes. The words may be omitted, but such omission would cause the sentence to lose color and emphasis.

> **A real estate mortgage is a written document that pledges title to real property (land and buildings) as security for debts.** *Land and buildings* is added to be sure that the reader understands what is meant by *real property*. The words make no contribution, how-ever, to the *main thought* of the sentence.

One use of parentheses, therefore, is to enclose words that give additional information or explain but that have little or no influ-ence on the main thought of a sentence; such as:

> **You will receive 25 per cent off (our usual trade discount) on these articles.** The words *our usual trade discount* have no bearing at all on the main thought: "You will receive 25 per cent off on these articles."

With Question Marks and Exclamation Points. Some writers enclose a question mark in parentheses (?) to express doubt and an exclamation point (!) to show disbelief, sarcasm, or surprise. For example:

> **The applicant is a Rumanian (?) refugee.** *Meaning:* I am not sure that he is Rumanian. He may be of some other nationality.

> **You will find that this is a harmless (!) treatment.** *Meaning:* I say "harmless," but you will probably find it quite different.

Caution. Question marks and exclamation points enclosed in parentheses have a place in the punctuation repertoire of the good writer. Because he is a *good* writer, however, he has at his command several ways of punctuating a message. He knows the danger of overusing any one method of punctuating. He knows that too frequent use of marks enclosed in parentheses can make his messages very boring, even annoying, to his readers. He uses this device only when it is exactly the right punctuation for some precise situation.

For References. Parentheses have great value for indicating references. Enclose in parentheses the name of an authority for a statement and all references or directions; as:

> **The "Ave Maria" (Schubert) was sung beautifully.** There are several selections called "Ave Maria," written by different composers. *Schubert* in parentheses is necessary for reference purposes.

> **The steps in the retailing process have already been discussed (see page 57).** Directing the reader to page 57 if he wishes to review the steps in the retailing process.

> **Good will: The favor or advantage in the way of custom that a business has acquired beyond the mere value of what it sells. (Branton)** A reader would understand that this is a definition taken from a Branton dictionary.

With Enumerated Items. In Unit 27 you learned that the period is not used after numbers and letters that are enclosed in parentheses. At the same time, you had a preview of this principle: Enumerated items and some items in outlines are enclosed in parentheses, as shown below and in the skeleton outline on page 216.

> **The following instructions are intended for: (1) senior bookkeepers, (2) junior bookkeepers, (3) ledger clerks, and (4) statistical clerks.** Equally correct for enumerating items would be the use of the letters (*a*), (*b*), (*c*), and (*d*).

1 | *Class Practice* In the following sentences, insert parentheses where needed; but, before you do this, perhaps you should solidify the parentheses instruction you have received. Parentheses are used: (1) to indicate additional information not pertinent to the main thought of a sentence; (2) to enclose a question mark to express doubt and an exclamation point to show disbelief, sarcasm, or surprise; (3) to acknowledge authority for a statement made; (4) to enclose references or directions; and (5) to indicate enumerated items and items beyond the fourth level in an outline. Now you ought to be ready to practice.

1. That novel was written toward the close of the nineteenth century 1893.
2. The office of comptroller chief accountant is sometimes filled by a man who has a C. P. A. degree.
3. Insert the carbon pack into your machine be sure that paper edges are even and start typing on line 10.
4. It was in 1899 ? that we started to manufacture marine engines.
5. Your attention has previously been called see Unit 27 to enumerated items and to items in outlines.
6. The population of the United States grew from a total of 3,929,214 in 1790 to a total of 150,697,361 in 1950. U. S. Bureau of the Census.

With Other Marks of Punctuation. This rule is easy: No mark of punctuation should be used *before* the opening parenthesis mark.

> **If there is good reason for writing (and I think there is), we will do so tomorrow.** *Not:* If there is good reason for writing, (and I think there is) we will do so tomorrow.

Parenthetical Words Included in a Sentence. When the words enclosed in parentheses are part of a sentence:

1. Place *after* the end parenthesis mark any regular sentence punctuation—comma, period, question mark, exclamation point, colon, or semicolon. For instance:

> **If you will call us tomorrow (Main 5-2319), we will have the information for you.** The regular sentence punctuation calls for a comma to set off an introductory clause. Note the comma *after* the end parenthesis.

> **Does your firm specialize in office equipment: desks, chairs, tables, files (all makes)?** The sentence is a question; therefore, the question mark is placed *after* the end parenthesis.

2. Place *before* the end parenthesis mark any question mark, exclamation point, or abbreviation period that *belongs with the words enclosed in parentheses;* as:

The Kelly Mills have moved to Chester, Vermont (or is it Maine?). The parenthetical words are a question, so the question mark is placed *before* the end parenthesis. Note that the regular sentence punctuation, the period, is placed *after* the end parenthesis.

The taxi driver (the wretch!) claimed to have no small change. The words enclosed in parentheses are exclamatory; therefore, the exclamation point is placed *before* the end parenthesis mark.

3. The first word of parenthetical words included in a sentence is capitalized only when that first word is a proper noun. This is true even when the words are a complete sentence. For instance:

The account may be withdrawn by giving advance notice (this is usually two weeks). Note that *this* is not capitalized, even though the words are a complete sentence.

Congratulations on the new job (I should say "position")! *I* is always capitalized.

Parenthetical Words Standing Alone. When words enclosed in parentheses are not part of a sentence, but are entirely independent, the first word is capitalized; and the end punctuation is placed *before* the end parenthesis, as illustrated below.

No further action was taken on the Cass case. (See the enclosed annual report for details.) The parenthetical words are not part of a sentence, but are entirely separate and complete. The first word begins with a capital letter, and the end period is placed *before* the end parenthesis.

Please accept my best wishes for your new work. (How does it feel to be boss?) The first word is capitalized. Since the parenthetical words are a question, the question mark is placed *before* the end parenthesis.

2 *Class Practice* Now it is time to practice the punctuation principles just presented. Insert the punctuation mark called for in each of the following sentences.

1. *Comma.* When you reach Buffalo (it will probably be near noon) be sure to telephone the office.
2. *Colon.* Please select one of the following colors (they are all that are offered) gray, blue, or red.
3. *Question mark.* Please send me the proper quality of ribbon (is it No. 1 or No. 2) for my typewriter.
4. *Exclamation point and/or period.* I was delighted to receive a salary increase (and retroactive to January 1)

5. *Question mark.* Would you be interested in our introductory offer of twelve treatments for $25 (regularly $3.50 a treatment)

6. *Semicolon.* President Barr did not mention moving (a great many things required his attention yesterday) but, so far as we are concerned, we can be ready at short notice.

7. *Capital letter and period.* A thrifty person estimates his income and expenditures for a given period. (this is known as "budgeting" and is explained in Chapter V)

3 *Additional Practice*   Check to see whether the capitalization in sentences 1–7 is correct.

The Apostrophe

In Unit 17 you studied the use of the apostrophe to indicate possession. In Unit 16 you learned that the apostrophe is used to form plurals of letters, numerals, symbols, signs, and words used as words. In Unit 33, the preceding lesson, you learned that the apostrophe is used as a single quotation mark. As a brief refresher, these uses are illustrated below:

> **Men's and boys' swimming trunks are sold in our sportswear department.**   Swimming trunks belonging to men and to boys—apostrophe to indicate possession.

> **Your "7's" are not written plainly.**   *7's,* plural of 7.

> **"Then," said the reporter, "the guard called, 'Everybody off!' "** Quotation within a quotation is indicated by the single quotation mark—made by striking the apostrophe key on the typewriter.

Other uses of the apostrophe are as follows.

In Contractions. Use an apostrophe to indicate contractions—shortened forms of one or more words; as: *nat'l* for *national; don't* for *do not;* and *o'clock* for *of the clock.* Some words formerly considered contractions are now recognized as complete words; for example, *phone* and *cello.*

For Omission of Figures. Use the apostrophe to signal the omission of the first figures of a date: *'65* for *1965.*

For Invented Verbs. A verb that is made up from a letter or an abbreviation must be signaled as being an invention by adding an apostrophe and *d* or *ing* to the coined verb; as:

> **I do not approve of your X'ing out words that you have typed.**

> **The order was OK'd before we sent it to you.**

4 *Class Practice*   Practice the several uses of the apostrophe by correctly inserting apostrophes in these sentences.

1. The "Three Rs" are the subject of many magazine articles.
2. We just cant get the shipment out today.
3. Charless mother had previously met the manager of the office.
4. At what time in the 40s did World War II start?
5. I know for a fact that Mr. Alger was born in 99.
6. Many unions require that workers birthdays be paid holidays.
7. One of Miss Doe's duties is the OKing of requisitions.

Learning Exercises

1   On a separate sheet of paper, indicate for these sentences: (1) any needed apostrophes, (2) correct marks of punctuation, and (3) parentheses where parentheses should be used.

1 We cannot consider your recommendation until after July 1 (the beginning of our fiscal year) therefore, please write us after that date.
2 The hurricane of 38 was more disastrous than the blizzard of 88.
3 If you call before eleven on Monday, we shall be able to make a definite appointment for you. (our number is Lyric 6-5448.)
4 I cannot read the name, for it has been Xd out.
5 What amount was entered in the bankbook (passbook)
6 Mr. Acton uses too many "sos" in his speeches.
7 The man repaired my radio free of charge (can you beat it)
8 Whos to be notified to attend the meeting?
9 Mr. Bell is not of legal age (if we can believe the records) but he has been made a member of the city council.
10 Please arrive at the pier in ample time (the ship sails at 10 a.m.)
11 There are two "ts" in *committed.*
12 At this point I recommend do you follow me? that we revert to our old policy.
13 The bank may refuse to honor pay or cash the check when it is presented.
14 Since the Everglades are low (swampy) high winds and rains bring floods.
15 Final reports will be ready Monday (or is it Friday?) and, as soon as they are assembled, we will call you so that you may analyze them.

2 Follow the usual directions for working a second learning exercise.

1 Within the offices had that look of bustling prosperity.
2 We cannot send you the catalogue immediately. As it is not yet off the press.
3 Note these special features (operated from the keyboard): (1) marginal set, (2) tab clear, (3) tab set, and (4) electric carriage return.
4 Bill failed the final examination, and had to take another one the following year.
5 Did you characterize your warehouse as "bursting with activity?"
6 Judith has developed into an excellent proofreader, Miss Akers was her special office teacher.
7 The Empire State Express one of the finest trains in the country runs between New York and Buffalo.
8 I shall be glad to lend you my copy of "Where Do We Go Now"?
9 Show me a typist who X's out errors, and I will show you a person who is not long for the job.
10 It seems to me that these are the character traits, that will make you a valued employee.
11 You are to be commended for an excellent job a really excellent job.
12 The appliance then called "radio," would be a museum piece today.
13 The Japanese beetle is not very troublesome in its native country (Japan); however, in America it is a most destructive insect.
14 Our manager made this strong statement: "Our production is suitable for domestic trade only".
15 "The stock market," reports the financial sheet, "suffered another 'sinking spell' yesterday."

Vocabulary and Spelling Refreshers

1 **Words Often Confused.** Access, excess; forbear, forebear.

2 **Accent Changes the Meaning.** What is the difference in the meaning of:

    a *con'summate* and *consum'mate?*
    b *in'valid* and *inval'id?*
    c *ref'use* and *refuse'?*
    d *en'trance* and *entrance'?*

3   **"Y," "i," or "ie"?** Should *y, i,* or *ie* appear in the blank spaces in order to complete the following words?

a	bus__ness	**c**	occup__ing	**e**	trolle__s
b	dr__ness	**d**	rel__ance	**f**	tr__s

    Communication in Action: *Supervising People*

As department head, you receive the following written report from a supervisor: "I cannot recommend Miss Allison for a salary increase this period. During her first six months as my assistant, she tried very hard. Then she lost interest. Now my work is taking second place to her long coffee breaks and her personal visits and telephone calls. It took three hours yesterday to get a simple, six-page report typed. I request that you talk with her."

    You have asked Miss Allison to come to your office. What will you say to her? Enact the scene with another student.

UNIT 35

Capitalization

You now know that quotation marks, parentheses, and apostrophes are signals used by you, the writer, to direct the reader's attention and thoughts to an important word or words or to indicate to the reader that certain words do not affect the main thought expressed by you. In this unit you will learn how to use the last of the signals that you need in order to make your written messages perfectly clear—the capitalization signal. The principles you are asked to study are basic principles. When starting a new job, you may find that your firm uses some special capitalization that deviates from rules you have learned. Keep in mind the fact that some businesses employ capitalization rules of their own, and check any capitalization about which you are in doubt.

Capital letters are used mainly to signal the reader that a *particular* person, place, or thing is meant. Remember that all-important word *particular*. It may be of help to think of capitalized words as denoting private property. For instance: Your name is capitalized because it is your private property; *Spain* is capitalized because that name is the private property of that country; *Bureau of the Census* is capitalized because that name is the private property of that bureau.

Some of the principles presented in this unit will be review for you; but, since you are now considering capitalization from the point of view of a *particular* person, place, or thing and of private property, the principles you have studied in previous years should be brought into sharp focus, should assume new meaning. The following principles, old and new, are of importance to you; and they merit your best efforts.

First Words

Capitalize the first word of: (1) sentences, (2) groups of words used as sentences, (3) lines of poetry, and (4) items in outlines. For years you have been capitalizing in these four situations, because you have learned rules that say it is correct to do so. Now you understand why it is correct: You wish to signal the reader that something new is beginning. You direct his thoughts to a fresh start.

Names of Persons

To every person in the world, his own name is very important, for it is the one thing that is indisputably his private property. Therefore, if you do not write a person's name as he wishes it to be written, you run the risk of causing ill will. You are about to learn how to capitalize names that present problems, but do not use these rules blindly. If you have any way of checking—files or current incoming letters—be very careful to write a name exactly as written by the person who owns it. Lacking such information, use these rules:

1. *O', Mc, Mac.* The prefixes *O'* and *Mc* are always followed by a capital letter without extra spacing: *O'Neil, McCaffery.* The prefix *Mac* may or may not be followed by a capital, depending on the style used by the owner of the name: *MacNamara, Macmillan.*

2. *D, da, de, della, di, du, la, le, lo, van, von.* Whether or not to capitalize these prefixes depends on these two factors:

a. If only the last name is used, the prefix is capitalized: *Du Pree, De Frias, Von Ribbentrop.*

b. If a first name or a title is used with the last name, the prefixes are not capitalized: *François de la Croix, Madame la Salle, Elsa von Veer.*

1 *Class Practice* In the following sentences, indicate which words should be capitalized and explain why. Criticize spacing.

1. many of our most successful businessmen started out as office boys.
2. will lo priore be in the office on Monday?
3. the manager said, "your sales approach was commented on favorably."
4. mary obrien is my best friend.
5. indeed, yes.
6. mr. de lancy does not approve of chewing gum.

Names of Places

Capitalize names of places as follows:

1. Capitalize names of geographical localities, streets, parks, rivers, and buildings; as: *North Africa, Northwest Street, Central Park,* the *Potomac River,* the *Eagle Building.*

2. Capitalize points of the compass—*North, West, Southeast*—when those names are the private property of the localities mentioned, when they denote a *particular* section of the country. When compass points refer simply to *direction,* they are not capitalized; as:

> **The South is becoming a land of factories.** *South* is a name that is the private property of the section mentioned. It is a *particular* section of the country.

> **We are thinking of going south this winter.** *South* is not capitalized because it indicates *direction.*

3. Capitalize the word *city* only when it is part of the corporate name of a city; as: *Long Island City,* but *the city of Chicago.*

4. Capitalize the word *state* only when it follows the name of a state; as: *Ohio State,* but *the state of Ohio.*

5. Capitalize the word *the* in names of places only when *the* is part of the official name; as: *The Dalles* (a city in Oregon), but *the Maritime Provinces.*

2 *Class Practice* In these sentences, capitalize the names of places that you think should be capitalized.

1. The "Nautilus" traveled under the north pole.
2. Is Kansas city in Illinois or in Missouri?

3. When you go to the Netherlands, be sure to visit the Hague.
4. The west offers a visitor scenery unlike that in any other part of the country.
5. Our offices are in the Globe building.

Other Capitalizations

Names of Organizations. Capitalize the names of particular firms, companies, associations, societies, commissions, committees, bureaus, boards, departments, schools, political parties, conventions, fraternities, clubs, and religious bodies. This may seem like a great deal to remember, and so it would be if you tried to memorize the different kinds of organizations. All you need do, however, is to ask yourself this question: Is this a name that is the private property of a particular organization? Look at the following illustrations.

> **Mr. Fyfe's family attends the First Methodist Church.** The name that is the private property of this particular institution is *First Methodist Church.* That is why it is capitalized.

> **Mr. Fyfe's family attends the first church that was built in this city.** Is there any name here that is the private property of any particular institution? No. Then there is no particular name to capitalize.

Note that some names of organizations are preceded by *the;* then the question of capitalizing the *the* naturally arises. A *the* that precedes a name should be capitalized only when it is part of the recognized official name. If you do not know whether the name in question uses *the* as part of its official title, check to find out.

> **We have an account at The National City Bank of Cleveland.** The official title is *The National City Bank of Cleveland.*

> **That family has been reported to the Child Welfare Committee.** The official title here is *Child Welfare Committee.*

Governmental Bodies. Capitalize names of countries; of international organizations; and of national, state, county, and city bodies and their branches. Once more, for purposes of capitalizing, you need only to determine that the name is the private property of a particular governmental body or branch; as:

> **Dr. John Allen has been employed by the Federal Bureau of Investigation.** Capitalized because the name is the private property of a particular governmental agency.

> **Dr. John Allen has turned the investigation over to a bureau that specializes in such problems.** There is no capitalization because there is no name that is the private property of a particular governmental body or agency.

Commercial Products. Names of commercial products are capitalized—*Griffin Shoe Shine, Master's Coffee, Moon Radio.* The name that is the private property of a particular commercial product, then, is capitalized. Some writers have difficulty recognizing the difference between the proper nouns that are part of the official title of a commercial product and common nouns that name the general class to which the nouns refer. The following illustrations should help to make this difference clear to you.

> **Have you considered looking at the Gelidaire washing machine?** *Washing machine* is not part of the official title; so it is not capitalized.

> **I have heard that the Weston Launderquik does a most satisfactory job.** The name that is the private property of this particular product is *Weston Launderquik.*

Historical Events and Documents. Capitalize names of important historical events; of movements; of periods; and of specific treaties, bills, acts, and laws: *World War II, the Declaration of Independence, the Dark Ages, the Wagner Labor Relations Act.* You should not find this rule too difficult, for you know the key to capitalization. When you wish to indicate a historical event or document, capitalize the name that is the private property of that particular event or document.

Holidays and Religious Days. Names of holidays and of religious days are capitalized—*New Year's, National Education Week, Easter, the Day of Atonement.* Just remember that you capitalize the official name that is the private property of the particular holiday or religious day.

3 *Class Practice* Find out for yourself how well you know and can apply the rules for capitalizing names of things by capitalizing correctly the words in the following sentences.

1. The bureau of home economics will send you a booklet of recipes.
2. Is there a United States army recruiting office in Mystic?
3. We are returning the white and the brown shoe polish purchased on our order No. 423.
4. Did you know that democrat coffee is now packed in tins?
5. How many times has the supreme court reversed its decisions?
6. The social security act has been amended to increase survivor benefits.
7. Alice is planning to attend Chicago university next year.
8. Many pages in history books are devoted to the treaty of Versailles.

In Letter Parts. You need to review two capitalization principles pertaining to letter parts—capitalization of salutations and of complimentary closings. In salutations, the first word and any title are capitalized: *Dear Mr. Bradley*, but *My dear Mr. Bradley*. Only the first word of a complimentary closing is capitalized: *Very truly yours*. Do not dismiss these two rules with the thought that you already know them. Many writers capitalize incorrectly the salutations and complimentary closings of letters.

Headings and Titles of Publications

Many writers (and typists) do not know how to capitalize a manuscript heading or a title of a publication. They know that some words are capitalized and others are not; but when to capitalize and when not to capitalize are complete mysteries. The rule is this: Capitalize all main words; but do not capitalize articles, conjunctions, and short prepositions. By "short prepositions" is meant those consisting of five or fewer letters. By the same token, if the preposition has six or more letters, it will be capitalized. The following examples will help to make this rule clear.

Teaching Principles and Procedures for Gregg Shorthand
And is a conjunction; *for* is a three-letter preposition.

The Case Against War
Against is a preposition of more than five letters and is, therefore, capitalized.

A capitalization problem may arise when a heading or a title contains a hyphenated compound or a compound adjective. Capitalize a hyphenated compound just as you would if it were not a compound. For example:

How to Use High-Speed Tools
Speed is capitalized because it would ordinarily be capitalized.

Laws Enacted by Sixty-Three Congresses
Three would ordinarily be capitalized.

Proper Adjectives

Since proper nouns are capitalized, adjectives derived from proper nouns are capitalized. These are called *proper adjectives*. See the following illustration.

In Mexico, the language used is Spanish. There seems to be no Mexican language as such. *Spanish* is a proper adjective derived from the proper noun *Spain; Mexican,* a proper adjective derived from the proper noun *Mexico*.

Substitutions

We here in the United States have the habit of devising nicknames for persons and places. If somebody or some place attains prolonged prominence, usually by frequent newspaper mention, the real name will often be replaced by some term that describes the person or place. Such a descriptive term is capitalized if: (1) it is generally known and recognized, and (2) you can lift out the term and substitute the name of the actual person or the actual place. For instance:

> **It is said that the Great Emancipator was possessed of a keen sense of humor.** Lincoln is known by the descriptive term *Great Emancipator.* You can lift out *Great Emancipator* in this sentence and rewrite it as: "It is said that Abraham Lincoln was possessed of a keen sense of humor."

> **Mr. Martin has gone to the Windy City for a few days.** *Windy City,* describing *Chicago,* is a term that is generally known. Rewriting the sentence using the actual name of the place: "Mr. Martin has gone to Chicago for a few days."

This principle is not difficult if you think of the descriptive term in the sense of a nickname and if you realize that the term is used and understood by many, many people.

4   *Class Practice*   In the following sentences, capitalize the words that should be capitalized and tell why.

1. How many times have you crossed the canadian border?
2. Anton's book, "the English-speaking nations," will be published in two volumes.
3. The happy warrior was known to be a wise politician.
4. To new employees, Mr. Frye always recommends the book, "success through application of common sense."
5. You really should study the article, "how to read the financial page."
6. Our soldiers were amazed at korean customs.
7. The African Campaign is noted for the brilliance of the desert fox.
8. That is a quotation from "the merchant of venice."

Shortened Forms

Occasionally, instead of writing out a complete name for some person, place, or thing, a writer will use only part of that name. In such a case, he capitalizes the shortened form to indicate that a *particular, specific* person, place, or thing is meant. You will so capitalize whenever you can lift out the shortened form and replace it by the full name that is the private property of the particular person, place, or thing. For example:

> **You are to report to the Admiral immediately upon termination of your leave.** The capitalization of *admiral* is a signal that one *particular* admiral is meant. The sentence could have been written: "You are to report to Admiral James A. West immediately upon . . . ."

> **Orders from the General are that no passes will be issued for a period of two weeks.** Can *general* be lifted out and the full name of a *particular* general be used? Yes, the sentence could have been: "Orders from General Ray T. Webb are that . . . ."

> **Does the trip you mention include four days on the Lakes?** *Lakes* is capitalized because it is the shortened form for *Great Lakes.*

> **Mr. Shaw is the youngest member of the House.** *House* is capitalized to indicate that the *United States House of Representatives* is meant.

> **The right of free speech is guaranteed under the Constitution.** Capitalizing *constitution* signals that the *United States Constitution* is referred to.

5 | *Class Practice*   Before you indicate the capitalization of the words in the following sentences, think about the principle: Capitalize a shortened form when you can replace that form by the full name of a *particular* person, place, or thing.

1. The association voted to contribute to all charity drives.
2. Has the governor issued his Thanksgiving message yet?
3. How many governors attended the White House Conference?
4. Mr. Dodds is a member of the senate and lives in Washington.
5. The ambassador has claimed diplomatic immunity.
6. We have invited a judge, a senator, and a colonel to join our organization.
7. The senator will be glad to help you obtain an appointment to the academy.
8. When you are in San Francisco, be sure to take time to see the bridge.
9. We like to boast that we have the best high school in the state.

Personal and Official Titles

To use capital letters correctly, you need to know the principles that tell you whether to capitalize or not to capitalize titles used with names of persons. These principles are as follows:

Titles PRECEDING Names of Persons. Capitalize professional, business, executive, civic, military, religious, and family titles that *precede* names of persons. More simply, whenever a person has a title that you write *before* his name, capitalize that title; thus:

> The invitation list includes Professor Edward Seton, Chief Justice Fred A. Vine, and Captain Robert McCaffery. Illustrating capitalization of titles written *before* names.

Titles FOLLOWING Names of Persons. Titles written *after* names of persons are always capitalized on envelopes and in inside addresses; for example:

> Mr. John W. Dolan, City Editor
> The Westerly Sun
> Westerly, Ohio

In all other cases where titles *follow* names, capitalize the titles only when they belong to Congressmen and *high* Government officials. Perhaps it will help if you realize that the only people who rate the capitalization of titles written *after* names are Congressmen and Government officials in the highest echelon. Soldier slang for these people would be "Top Brass." For instance:

> Woodrow Wilson, President of the United States, was at one time a college president. There should be no question about capitalizing *president* after the name of the person who bears the title. This is the highest office in the land.

> Andrew W. Mellon, Secretary of State under three Presidents, was a patron of the arts. *Secretary of State* is capitalized, since an office in the Cabinet is a *high* Government position.

Now see what happens when titles are written *after* names of persons who are not in the upper brackets.

> John J. White, mayor of New York, is much interested in fire-fighting procedures. *Mayor* is not capitalized because it is not a *high* Government position.

> We are waiting to hear from Mr. A. B. Ryan, secretary of the Junior Chamber of Commerce. Mr. Ryan is not a top Government official, so *secretary* is not capitalized.

Hyphenated Titles. When *ex-* and *-elect* are joined to titles, they are not capitalized. Although not hyphenated, *former* and *late* also are not capitalized when used with titles. To illustrate:

> Did ex-President Truman receive a pension from the Government?

The welcoming address will be given by Mayor-elect Roy.

Mr. Morgan, the late Secretary of the Treasury, retired to his estate in Oregon.

6 *Class Practice* As a check to see how well you understand capitalization of titles used with names of persons, indicate which words in the following sentences should be capitalized.

1. Recommendations will be solicited from treasurer-elect Sherman.
2. The annual cleanup campaign was announced by Harold Thorpe, health commissioner.
3. David B. Sloan, chairman of the Appropriations Committee, has a new secretary.
4. You will have to ask chairman Grant for a ruling on the question.
5. Mr. Henry W. Powers, treasurer of the Milford Storage Company, is best qualified for the position.

Learning Exercises

1 On a separate sheet of paper, indicate the correct capitalization of words in the following sentences.

1 Our new fashion consultant is Paul De Beaumont.
2 The easter and passover holidays occur at about the same time.
3 One of the notable events of 1952 was president-elect Eisenhower's trip to Korea.
4 Mr. Burgess is a veteran of the battle of the Marne.
5 All my graduate work was done at the university.
6 The democratic national convention will be held in Chicago.
7 If you write a personal letter to the governor, he will probably accept your invitation to speak.
8 Can you recite the poem, "the owl and the pussycat"?
9 For best results do this: check the capitalization of any words that do not conform to the capitalization rules you have learned.
10 Many people will never forget the squire of Hyde Park.
11 The security council of the united nations has great influence on the peace of the world.
12 The nutmeg state is noted for its beautiful scenery.
13 "Results of the twenty-first investigation" was the title of Anderson's report.

14 The people of the far east were grateful for the food sent by the United States.

15 Without exception, the staff members are loyal to the company.

2 Proceed as directed for all final learning exercises.

1 Did Mr. Blaine say, "Turn west" or "Turn left?"

2 The strait of Magellan was named for the man who discovered it.

3 The heading of Chapter X is "The War between the States."

4 We know that you will be interested in this type of job (secretarial); your training has prepared you for it.

5 There is no opening in our office just now, nevertheless, we shall be glad to place your name at the top of our list.

6 The new member of the Cabinet has no comment to make.

7 Mr. Houston handles all our adjustments, he will be glad to discuss your problem with you.

8 Mr. Andrews has invested in some Montana Copper Mines.

9 Chicago, Illinois, is a well-known railroad terminal.

10 Mr. Bergen the new controller has his office on the tenth floor.

11 The author worried about having the book ready for the printer called in additional typists.

12 We very much enjoyed la Follette's speech.

13 Here is an easy way to multiply by 75: first multiply by 100 and divide by 4; then multiply the result obtained by 3.

14 Is the new doctor a member of the Association?

15 The best seller was written by James B. Douglas, former chief justice of the Supreme Court.

Vocabulary and Spelling Refreshers

1 **Words Often Confused.** Weak, week; metal, mettle; medal, meddle.

2 **Find the Synonyms.** Two of the words in each of the following groups are synonymous. Pair the words.

a genuine, commodious, spacious, fabulous
b prestige, knowledge, attainments, renown
c superficial, ridiculous, shallow, serious
d disparage, value, discredit, distrust

3 **Masculine or Feminine?** Indicate whether the following words are masculine or feminine; also give the correct spelling for the word of opposite gender.

a executrix   **c** aviator   **e** heroine
b actor   **d** alumna   **f** host

Communication in Action: *Correcting an Error*

The salesclerk had written $7 on a sales check instead of $9. As cashier, you find the error when the customer comes to pay you. Exactly what will you say to this customer to correct the error and yet retain good will?

Section 4   **Signals — Abbreviations and Figures**

UNIT 36

Abbreviations

An abbreviation is a signal used to tell the reader that a longer word or that several words are indicated by the abbreviation used. In business communications, some terms are always abbreviated; for example, *f.o.b.* for "free on board" and *C. O. D.* for "collect on delivery." Such terms are few, however. For most business writing, abbreviating is frowned upon. This feeling is logical, for the primary aim of business writing is to make a message absolutely clear; and abbreviating is a threat to the clarity of the message. The reader, you see, may not understand the abbreviation you use or may misread it.

If you are thinking of abbreviating a person's name or the name of a company, check the files or current incoming letters to see how the person or the firm wishes the name to be written. If the name on the letterhead is *Blendix Corporation,* you should so write it—

not *Blendix Corp.* Lacking a means of checking, spell out a name rather than abbreviate it. Your motto could well be: "When in doubt, spell it out."

Careful study of principles governing use of abbreviations will increase your skill in effective, as well as correct, signaling. Principles for abbreviating are as follows:

Titles After Names

Always abbreviate the following titles when they are written *after* a name: *Esq.* for "Esquire"; *Jr.; Sr.;* and *academic and religious titles.* Some academic and religious abbreviations are: *B. S.* for "Bachelor of Science"; *Ph. D.* for "Doctor of Philosophy"; and *D. D.* for "Doctor of Divinity."

Titles Before Names

Titles Always Abbreviated. You should always abbreviate the following titles when they are written *before* a person's name: *Mr., Messrs., Mrs.,* and *St.* for "Saint." Since *Miss* is not an abbreviation, it is not included in this list.

Titles Before Full Names. When a title precedes a *full name*, practice differs. In formal usage, such titles should always be spelled out; and many writers prefer to spell them out under all circumstances. In business correspondence, technical writing, tabulations, or wherever brevity is desirable, abbreviated forms are commonly used; as:

Dr. Amos F. Cutler	Prof. William T. Green
Lt. (jg) S. Henry Archer	Supt. T. Alan Crowe

Titles Before Last Names Only. Write in full any titles that you use with just the *last names* of persons. Remember this when you are writing the salutation of a letter. For instance:

Doctor Strong	Governor Farnsworth
Professor Green	Colonel Lathrop
Superintendent Crowe	Captain Winter

Titles of Respect and Dignity. *Reverend* and *Honorable* are titles of respect and dignity used in addressing clergymen and government officials of any rank. Spell out these titles, except in addresses, lists, and notices. *The* will precede the titles in formal usage but may be omitted in addresses, lists, and notices. In the following illustrations, note that a first name or another title follows the *Reverend* or the *Honorable.*

The Reverend Carl Worcester	The Honorable Jay F. Arnold
The Reverend Doctor Worcester	The Honorable Mr. Arnold

Firm Names

As mentioned in the introduction to this unit, a part of a firm name is abbreviated only when you are sure that the abbreviation is used by the company in question. Only when you have so seen it in print would you abbreviate the words *Company, Corporation, Association, Brothers, Railroad, Railway, Manufacturing,* or any other parts of a firm name.

1 *Class Practice* In the following sentences, practice what you have learned so far by indicating words that should be abbreviated and words that should be spelled out.

1. The data were obtained from Prof. Ives.
2. We have received a report from Mr. Jno. D. Macafee describing recent economic developments.
3. The name of the marshall of the parade is General Arnold G. Braintree.
4. When you arrived at the scene of the accident, had a dr. been called?
5. Be sure that you reserve a place on the platform for the Rev. Doctor Cragan.
6. You should have used the salutation "Dear Dr. Cutler."

Names of Associations and Government Agencies

Probably because of the need to save time, abbreviations for names of associations are in increasing use and are considered correct. If you use such abbreviations, you must be sure that they are in general use and will not be misunderstood. Some illustrations of commonly used abbreviations for names of associations are:

A. A. A.	American Automobile Association
A. B. A.	American Bankers Association
N. E. A.	National Education Association
S. P. C. A.	Society for the Prevention of Cruelty to Animals

The business of our Government is conducted by many agencies, with new ones being created to serve increasing needs. The practice in writing abbreviations for these agencies is to write them "solid," with no periods and no spacing. For instance:

SSA	Social Security Administration
FBI	Federal Bureau of Investigation
NLRB	National Labor Relations Board

There is a discernible current trend also toward writing "solid" many well-known abbreviations, including abbreviations of names of associations. If you wish to use this method of abbreviating names of bodies other than Government agencies, check first to be sure that you are correct. You have probably seen some abbreviations like the following written without periods and without spacing.

CIO	Congress of Industrial Organizations
NEA	National Education Association. (The abbreviation was written in a previous illustration as N. E. A. This abbreviation is following the current "solid" writing trend.)
TWA	Trans World Airlines
TWU	Transport Workers Union
WNFC	Radio and television call letters are written "solid."

Plurals of Abbreviations

In Unit 16 you learned to use an apostrophe and *s* to indicate the plural of an abbreviation consisting of letters. You would write: two *C. O. D.'s, f.o.b.'s, C. P. A.'s,* and the like. To form the plurals of most other abbreviations, *s* is added to the singular form; as: *yds., lbs., depts.* Some abbreviations, however, are the same in both singular and plural; as: *oz., in., min., ft.*

Always Abbreviate

A. D. and B. C. in Year Dates. Important historical dates are often accompanied by the abbreviation *A. D.* (for *anno Domini,* "the year of our Lord") or *B. C.* ("before Christ"). Note that *A. D.* is written before the year, but *B. C.* is written after the year; as: *A. D. 1960,* but *400 B. C.*

The Information a.m., p.m., and m. in Statements of Time. Although you will see *a.m., p.m.,* and *m.* written in capital letters, the preference is for small letters with no spacing. Be sure that: (1) you do not use the word *o'clock* with these abbreviations, and (2) you do not use the abbreviations without figures. Study the following illustrations.

> **You will please report at 9 a.m.** Equally correct would be: "You will please report at nine o'clock." The following, however, would be incorrect: "You will please report at 9 o'clock, or 9 o'clock a.m."

> **Harriet is to be married at noon on Saturday.** *Not:* Harriet is to be married at m. on Saturday.

Number as No. Before Numerals, Except at Beginning of a Sentence. Before numerals, *number* is always abbreviated as *No.* At the beginning of a sentence, the word *number,* not the abbreviation, is used. Writing *No.* at the beginning of a sentence could be confusing, for the reader's first impression would be that the word *No* is meant. Some illustrative sentences are:

We are enclosing your policy No. 345987. Illustrating *No.* followed by a numeral.

Number 34567 has been assigned to your latest policy. *Number* spelled out because it begins the sentence.

2 *Class Practice* Now comes checkup time, time to see how well you have assimilated the previous topics. In the following sentences, make the necessary abbreviation corrections and explain your reasons for doing so.

1. Have you ever visited any sessions of the U. N. when you were in New York?
2. Is 10 o'clock p.m. the official closing time for the sessions?
3. There are too many "f.o.b.'s" in your advertising copy.
4. An appointment has been made for you at 1 o'clock on Tuesday.
5. Julius Caesar was assassinated in B. C. 44.
6. No. 3 now moves into first place.
7. Box number 483 weighs 10 pounds.

Never Abbreviate

Names of Cities, Certain States, Certain Months. First on the list of terms that you will never abbreviate are the following: (*a*) Names of cities are never abbreviated, no matter how long the names may be. You will, then, resist the temptation to write *Phila.* for *Philadelphia.* (*b*) Names of the following states are never abbreviated: *Alaska, Hawaii, Idaho, Iowa, Maine, Ohio,* and *Utah.* (*c*) Names of the following months are never abbreviated: *May, June,* and *July.*

Fort, Mount, Point, and Port in Names of Places. Never abbreviate *Fort, Mount, Point,* and *Port* in place names. They are written: *Fort Knox, Mount Desert, Point Pleasant,* and *Port Royal.*

Terms of Measure. Except in technical work and on invoices, spell out the names of the common units of weight, length, capacity, area, volume, temperature, and time. In ordinary business writing you would write: *50 pounds, 7 yards, 4 square miles, 8 dozen,* and the like.

Compass Points. In business communications, a compass point used in a sentence should be spelled out. You would write: "The new building is at the *northeast* corner of Elm and Cutler Streets." Compass directions used in a specialized business, such as real estate, would be written as *N., NE., SSE.,* and so on.

Avoid Abbreviating

Names of Streets and Like Residence Addresses. In the message part of business writing, do not abbreviate names of streets, roads, avenues, and so on. These names are, however, usually abbreviated in lists and may be abbreviated in inside addresses and on envelopes, as shown in the Reference Section (page 550).

Geographical Names. Prefer to spell out names of counties, states and possessions, provinces, and countries. In case of need, you should know the correct abbreviations for our United States states and possessions. These are listed for you in the Reference Section (page 551).

Days and Months. Names of days of the week and months of the year are preferably spelled out. Because of lack of space, as in a table or a list, you may be forced to abbreviate as shown in the Reference Section (page 551). *May, June,* and *July,* however, are *never* abbreviated.

3 *Class Practice*   Using your knowledge of the "Never Abbreviate" and "Avoid Abbreviating" topics just presented, correct the following sentences. Explain each correction you make.

1. Mr. Drake plans to go to Chi. on Monday of next week.
2. We have found that Oct. is our worst month for sales.
3. The state of Alas. was our forty-ninth state.
4. Is the store you mention on the W. side of State Street?
5. Ft. Dodge is one of the principal cities in Iowa.
6. Superintendent Emerson lives at 16 Garden Terr., doesn't he?

Periods Not Used

Chemical Symbols. Chemical symbols, which are becoming increasingly common in modern correspondence, are not followed by periods; as: *Na, O, Fe,* which are the symbols for *sodium, oxygen,* and *iron,* respectively.

IOU and SOS. Contrary to popular belief, *IOU* and *SOS* are not abbreviations; therefore, they are not followed by periods.

Letters Used Instead of Names. Sometimes letters are used to designate a person or a thing, and in such cases no period follows the letter; as: *Mr. B, Exhibit D,* and so on.

Shortened Forms. Because of long and frequent use, certain shortened forms have become accepted as complete words. Some of these forms are *ad* for *advertisement, gym* for *gymnasium, phone* for *telephone,* and *lab* for *laboratory.* Since such shortened forms are regarded as complete words, they are not followed by periods.

Note the following illustrations:

> **Did you know that Na and Cl combine to form salt?**   No period is used after chemical symbols.

> **The SOS was picked up by the Coast Guard.**   *IOU* and *SOS* are not abbreviations and, therefore, are not followed by periods.

> **You really save money by buying Grade A beef.**   No period after letters that substitute for names.

> **The medical secretary should be familiar with terms used in lab work.**   *Lab* is a shortened form that is now regarded as a complete word.

4 *Class Practice*   Now test your understanding of the additional abbreviation principles by correcting the following sentences.

1. I gave my IOU. to the cashier.
2. You will be allowed an additional week for the report on your lab. work.
3. H₂O. constitutes what proportion of the human body?
4. Cancel our order for the Grade B. eggs.

Learning Exercises

1 Each of the following sentences contains an abbreviation error. On a separate paper, indicate your correction of each error and be prepared to justify the correction.

1 The marriage ceremony was performed by the Rev. Doctor Albin.
2 Mr. Ash calls his assistants Miss A. and Miss B., for he can never remember names.
3 Our guest of honor will be the Hon. Charles E. Hyde.
4 The real estate agent asked to have the house approved by the F. H. A.
5 All employees are expected to be ready to start work at 8:30 o'clock a.m.
6 Please let us know the No. of pamphlets you need.

7 The school gym. is the best place for the football rally.
8 Have you asked the V.A. for help in obtaining a duplicate of your army discharge?
9 A new member of the faculty of the University is Albert C. Fowler, Doctor of Philosophy. *Ph.D.*
10 Their new executive officer is Lieutenant (jg) Peter Clinton.
11 The Middle Ages are generally considered to have begun in 400 A. D.
12 F. B. Axton, Junior, is the man who ordered the hampers.
13 Please send us an additional 50 lbs. of the cement you advertised on July 6.
14 Is Pt. Arthur in the eastern part of Texas?
15 Martha Simmons, Master of Arts, is writing an English textbook.

2 Follow instructions given for all second learning exercises.

1 Our firm specializes in the georgian style of architecture.
2 This food has an alkaline (nonacid) reaction in the body.
3 Our present policy regarding transfers has been criticized as biased (unfair); therefore, we are making a change in our rules.
4 "What are your reasons"? challenged the chairman of the meeting.
5 Again we have lost, nevertheless, we are determined to keep trying until we attain the success we think we deserve.
6 I should like very much to accept, however, circumstances force me to decline.
7 The Senator will meet with his constituents on Monday at the City Hall.
8 Without fail, send us your check at once, or we shall be obliged to draw a sight draft on your account.
9 Your erasures, on the other hand, are always very neat.
10 The T.V.A. has proved to be a blessing for the people who live in its vicinity.
11 Many of our executives do not use our teletype, they seem to prefer to use the commercial wire services.
12 Mr. Andrews was born in the green mountain state.
13 The mts. have a grandeur all their own.
14 I am happy to contribute to the fund. Since so many of our group will benefit from it.
15 Mr. Anton L. Daniels, executive director of the Bureau of Social Service, will preside at the meeting.

Vocabulary and Spelling Refreshers

1 **Words Often Confused.** Instance, instants; magnificent, munificent.

2 **What Are the Opposites?** Give a word of opposite meaning for each of the following words.

a different	**c** sensible	**e** receive
b complicated	**d** objective	**f** careful

3 **Do They End with "el" or "le"?**

a lab__	**c** gigg__	**e** tit__
b mod__	**d** nick__	**f** whist__

Communication in Action: *Taking Sides*

One of your co-workers confides, "I don't think Mr. Jones likes me. I was late twice this week—only 15 minutes each time—but he warned me that just one more time and I'll lose part of my pay." You have always felt Mr. Jones to be very fair. Reply to your co-worker.

UNIT 37

Figures

In previous units you learned to use the "Stop" signs and signals that direct a reader's interpretation of your message. If you have mastered all the various topics, you can write with confidence, knowing that your words will not be misunderstood. Your *words* will be clear, but what about the *figures* you use? Figures are not signals; they are the message. Almost unknown is a business letter that does not contain a figure, even if only a date. An error in or an incorrect use of figures could seriously affect the profits of a business. The writer of business communications quite obviously needs special training in the use of figures in order to give a finished writing performance; and without this training he, the writer, may be "finished"— out of a job!

In business correspondence, numbers are more often written in figures than in words. The untrained writer would probably write all his numbers in figures. The trained writer, however, would know when to use words and when to use figures and would thus be able to prevent dollars-and-cents errors, errors that cause actual loss of money.

Numbers Written as Words

Numbers One Through Ten. Numbers from one through ten should be written in words when such numbers are used in isolated instances. If, however, you are writing a series of figures, this rule would not apply. In the following sentences, numbers occur in what is called "isolated instances."

> **Miss St. John has had four years' experience as a secretary.** *Four* is written as a word because it is not a part of a series of quoted figures. It is an isolated instance.

> **The property consisted of three parcels, one containing a building and the other two being vacant.** The three numbers here are below eleven and do not represent a listing. They occur in isolated instances.

Now, however, look at the following illustration.

> **Miss St. John has requisitioned 2 notebooks, 3 erasers, 2 ball-point pens, and 1 box of paper clips.** Do you see the difference? Here you have a listing, so the numbers are not used in isolated instances.

Numbers one through ten in isolated instances *must* be written in words, but numbers from ten to a hundred *may* be written in words. If your eye is offended by: "So far this month, there have been 18 instances of absenteeism," you are privileged to write "eighteen instances."

Approximate Numbers and Even Units. Even or approximate numbers are written in words; as:

> **We have received exactly one thousand applications.** Illustrating a definite even number written in words.

> **About five hundred of our students are veterans.** Illustrating an approximate number written in words.

When spelling out even numbers over one thousand, express the numbers in the fewest possible words; as: *fifteen hundred* (two words), not *one thousand five hundred* (four words); *twenty-five hundred* (three words), not *two thousand five hundred* (four words).

Learning Aid. A general rule for writing isolated numbers will help you to learn quicker and remember longer. Here is the rule: *Write in words all isolated numbers that can be expressed in not more than two or three words.*

Numbers That Begin Sentences. Numbers that occur at the beginning of sentences are written in words; for example:

Twenty-six executives attended the planning session.

From experience, you, of course, know that there is no need to begin a sentence with a figure. The above sentence could have been reworded thus: "There were twenty-six executives at the planning session."

Fractions That Stand Alone; Mixed Numbers. When a fraction stands alone (is not used with a whole number), that fraction is written in words. For instance, you would write:

Because of the recession, our inventory is only about one-half of normal.

Just about one-third of the building is in need of waterproofing.

When spelling out a mixed number (a whole number and a fraction), be sure to use the word *and* to separate the whole number from the fraction; as:

Our turnover is two and one-half times that of the other firms in the city.

Political and Military Divisions; Sessions of Congress. When names of political and military divisions contain numbers, those numbers are written in words. Sessions of Congress are numbered, and those numbers are written in words. Study the following examples.

Mr. Joyce is a candidate for representative from the Fifth Congressional District. *Never* 5th Congressional District.

Our personnel director is very proud of having been a member of the Seventh Armored Division. *Never* 7th Armored Division.

The record of the Eighty-third Congress will stand for all time. *Not* 83d Congress.

√ **1** *Class Practice*   How clear is your understanding of these five occasions where numbers are written in words? To find the answer, correct the following sentences and explain why you make your corrections.

1. About 200 typists are employed by that insurance company.
2. We found that 2 of the dozen shirts you sent us were marked "seconds."
3. The job breakdown shows that ⅖ of her time is spent in checking.
4. Returns from the 5th Ward are always slow in coming in.
5. 110 applications were received for this high-level position.
6. Within an hour after opening for business, we had 10 calls about our advertisement.
7. Marines were assigned to the 2d Division.
8. About 10,000 persons are reported to have left the farms of our state.

Names of Numbered Streets. When streets have numbers one through ten as their names, the numbers are written in words. For example:

> **We often shop in the Fifth Avenue stores.**   *Not* 5th Avenue.

> **There is a transfer point at the Tenth Street substation.**   *Not* 10th Street.

Ages and Time. Use words when writing numbers that represent ages of people if expressed in *years only: twenty-five years of age; sixty years old.* When referring to time units, spell out single, isolated numbers; as: *four years of work; seven months to pay.* These principles are illustrated and explained in the following sentences.

> **In our company any employee who becomes sixty-five years of age is eligible for a pension.**   Illustrating age in years only.

> **The Ohio Rolling Company is celebrating its fortieth year in business.**   Isolated number expressing passage of time.

> **The crisis is expected in three days.**   Isolated number referring to time.

Time of Day. Part of this principle is already known to you. In the last unit you studied the abbreviations *a.m., p.m.,* and *m.* You also observed that, when the word *o'clock* was used, the hour was written in words: *ten o'clock,* not *10 o'clock.* The *word* for the number is used with the word *o'clock.*

To what you have already learned about expressing time, add the principle that time will be written in words whenever that time is a shortened form. "Shortened form" means without the word *o'clock* or the time abbreviations; as: *Be sure to arrive before three.*

Here are some additional illustrations.

> **Mr. Barner does not return from lunch until half past one.** Illustrating the "shortened form." Note the absence of *p.m.* or the word *o'clock.*

> **Mr. Kiddy starts his dictation at ten every morning.** Another illustration of "shortened form."

Centuries and Decades. Numbers referring to centuries or decades are written in words. Some examples are:

> **The United States did not feel the effects of the Industrial Revolution until the nineteenth century.** The number of the century is written in words.

> **Life must have been exciting in the gay nineties.** Illustrating writing in words the number of a decade—*nineties.*

2 *Class Practice*   Test the degree to which you have learned the last four principles by correcting the following sentences. As further proof of your understanding, tell why you make the corrections.

1. A branch of our store is to be opened at West 1st Place.
2. Do you ordinarily begin work at 8 o'clock?
3. Mr. O'Brien has served 30 years as engineer for our company.
4. I can remember only that the Civil War ended sometime in the 60's.
5. A person of 40 may have difficulty in obtaining a position.
6. This will be the 30th year that Mr. Eaton has been on the Boy Scout Court of Honor.
7. At the age of 25, Bill took out an annuity.
8. This firm has been in operation for 18 years.

Numbers Written in Figures

Sums of Money. In business communications generally, sums of money are written in figures. Only in a specialized business, such as the legal business, is money written both ways, in words and in figures. Your instruction for writing sums of money is divided here into: (*a*) dollars, and (*b*) cents.

1. You learned in Unit 27 that the period and two zeros are not used with even sums of money. If, however, you are tabulating, the period and two zeros are used to even the columns. For instance:

Your daughter purchased from us on May 10:

1 Dress	$19.95
1 Blouse	8.45
1 Skirt	14.00
1 Box of pins	.15

Whenever you write a series of sums of money, use the dollar sign with each member of the series; thus: "Our new fall blouses are priced at *$5, $7.50,* and *$10.*"

2. Isolated amounts of cents that appear in a sentence are written in figures followed by the word *cents;* as: "You will take *50 cents* from the petty cash for carfare."

To be consistent, use the dollar sign and the decimal point with amounts under $1 if those amounts occur in a series with other sums made up of dollars and cents; as:

> Just today I spent $4 for stamps, $2 for stencils, and *$.60* for file cards.

The symbol ¢ on your typewriter is used in quotations and in technical communications; such as:

> The Conway Construction Company's last bill contains a charge for 250 cement blocks at 75¢ and 4 bags of cement at 98¢.

Numbers Over Ten. In the previous pages you learned that isolated numbers one through ten *must* be written in words. It would necessarily follow that numbers from ten to one hundred would be written in figures. You may remember that, although numbers over ten and up to one hundred are preferably written in figures, you *may* write them in words. You would be wise to find out which form your employer prefers and use it. For instance:

> By the end of the year we expect to have 11 new designs. This is correct according to the rule.

> By the end of the year we expect to have eleven new designs. Your employer prefers the number spelled out; he feels the word looks better than the figure.

When you write a sentence containing a series of numbers, write *all* numbers in figures, including those under ten and round numbers, for you must be consistent. For example:

> Of the more than 200 members of the graduating class, 59 plan to become nurses; 65, secretaries; 8, dietitians. The remainder have not made known their plans. Note *8* dietitians, not *eight.*

Numbers over one hundred, with the exception of round numbers, are written in figures; as:

> **The book you mention has 212 pages.**
>
> **Last week we sent out 686 sales notices.**

House, Street, Zone Numbers. In business correspondence, house, street, and zone numbers are written in figures.

1. House numbers are written in figures, with the exception of the number *one*. The figure *1* is such a thin mark that it may be overlooked if used as a house number. You will remember that no comma is used in four-digit house numbers. Neither should the abbreviation *No.* nor the sign # be used with house numbers or with R. F. D. numbers. A comprehensive illustration is:

> **The Gay Publishing Company has moved from 3846 Madison Avenue to One Park Place, not 14 Park Place.** Note: (*a*) no comma in 3846; (*b*) One Park Place, *One* written as a word; and (*c*) 14 Park Place, house number written in figures.

2. In the preceding pages you learned that names of streets numbered through ten are written in words. Numbered street names over ten would, then, be written in figures. However, since you are ever on the alert to write in a way that is absolutely clear, you should give special attention to the writing of numbered streets over ten. To separate the building number from the numbered street, an extra space may be left between the street number and the street name; or a hyphen may be used to mark the separation; as: *1718-86th Street.*

Also in the interests of readability, *East, North,* or any other word that precedes the numbered name of a street should be spelled out. To illustrate:

> **Marcia's new address is 1462 East 125th Street.** Can you see the reason for spelling out *East?* If the reader is careless and if the address is written *1462 E. 125th Street,* there is a possibility of error.

Consider just one more item about names of numbered streets. There is a growing trend toward writing these numbers without the *st, th,* and so on. Marcia's address could thus have been written *1462 East 125 Street.* Dispensing with the ordinal endings makes the name of the street stand out, promotes clarity.

3. Postal zone numbers follow the name of the city; and a comma follows, but does not precede, the number. For instance, you would write *New York 17, New York* or *Chicago 65, Illinois.*

3 *Class Practice*   The best learning takes place when a student puts into practice what he has learned. That is why you are given an opportunity here to practice the preceding three principles. Correct the error in each of the following sentences.

1. Is the correct price of the coat $79.00 or $89.00?
2. The most desirable business address in the city is 1 Broad Street.
3. Please send us: 15 reams typing paper, ten gross shorthand notebooks, six boxes erasers, and 24 dozen nylon typewriter ribbons.
4. Address the package to R. F. D. #4, Blaine, Kansas.
5. We shall be happy to sell you gift certificates in the amounts of $5, 10, and 25.
6. Be sure that you note the change in address to Hartford, 4, Connecticut.
7. Blankton's number is 1,826 State Street, not 1,836.
8. Do you think 1333 N. 168th Street is too far out for a business to locate?
9. The postage due on your last order amounts to 38¢.

Age in Years, Months, Days. You have already learned that age expressed in *years only* is written in words. Figures should be used, however, when a person's age is given in years, months, and days; as:

> **At the time of the accident, the insured's age was 45 years 7 months and 5 days.**   Because the time is considered as a single unit, no commas are used in the series.

Time of Day. When the word *o'clock* is written, the *word* representing the time is used. It would logically follow that the figure (which is a short form) would be used with the short forms *a.m., p.m.,* and *m.* You thus have a choice of writing "three o'clock" or "3 p.m." If no minutes are given, it is not necessary to use two ciphers with the number denoting the hour. Study the following illustrations.

> **Our closing time is 5:15 p.m.**   Figures used with *p.m.*

> **All employees must be back from lunch by one o'clock.**   Word *one* used with word *o'clock.* Remember that the use of both *o'clock* and *p.m.* is a serious error. Never "one o'clock p.m."

> **We have been instructed not to make appointments for Mr. Bruce after 4 p.m.**   *Not* 4:00 p.m.

Time Connected with Discount or Interest Rates. For clarity and emphasis, periods of time mentioned with terms of discount or interest rates are written in figures; as:

If you will pay for the goods in 10 days, they will cost you just **$126.** *Ten* in figures to make *10* stand out as the time during which the discount may be taken.

Years of Graduation and Well-Known Years in History. Years of graduation and well-known years in history are usually written in two figures preceded by an apostrophe; as: *the class of '61; the blizzard of '88.*

To Insure Clarity. If one number immediately follows another, a comma should separate the numbers. Better still, the sentence should be worded so that the numbers do *not* immediately follow each other. Consider the following illustrations.

In 1952, 61,637,951 votes were cast in the presidential election. Note the comma separating the numbers. Also note how confusing the sentence is, even with the comma.

In the presidential election of 1952, there were 61,637,951 votes cast. The two numbers are not written together. Note that the rewording prevents confusion.

If two numbers form one item, however, rewording is not possible; and the numbers must follow each other. An example would be *ten 30-inch strips.* In a case like this, one number is written in words; the other, in figures. Usually, the shorter word is spelled out. Here are two illustrations that will help you to understand this principle.

Please get me 75 four-cent stamps. Do you see that this is clearer, and shorter, than *seventy-five 4-cent stamps?*

You should have used two 6-cent stamps on Mr. Coe's letter. This is more readable than *2 six-cent stamps.*

4 *Class Practice* To practice the principles just presented, find and correct the errors in the following sentences.

1. The executive session is called for 8 o'clock p.m.
2. In 1962 125,463 subscribers were added to the mailing list.
3. At the time the policy was written, Mr. Alger's age was 35 years, 8 months, and 3 days.
4. California probably owes its development to the gold rush of forty-nine.
5. What is the interest on $375 for seventy-five days at 6%?
6. The order specified one hundred twenty-four 10-foot beams.
7. Mr. Wilson will be the guest of honor at the reunion of the class of sixty.

Dates

The term "ordinal endings" is frequently used in this section pertaining to dates. Ordinal endings are *st, d,* and *th* following figures; such as: *1st, 2d, 3d, 15th,* and so on. Note particularly *2d* and *3d.* The styles *nd* and *rd* are considered old-fashioned.

Day Following Month. When the day follows the month, that day is written in figures, *without ordinal endings;* as: *April 15, January 2, July 27,* and so on.

Day Preceding Month. When the day precedes the month, the day is written in figures, *with ordinal endings;* as: *the 15th of April, the 2d of January, the 27th of July,* and so on.

Think through the following illustrations and explanations.

> **All bids must be in our office on or before May 16.** Not *16th,* because the day is written *after* the month.

> **Your bid must be in our office on or before the 16th of May.** Here *16th* is correct, because the day is written *before* the month.

5 *Class Practice*   Each of the following sentences contains an error in the writing of a date. Find the errors and correct them, stating your reasons for making the corrections.

1. The Adams salesman visits us each year on April 3d.
2. The reorganization will take place on the eleventh of July.
3. We very much appreciate your order of November 20th.
4. Our sale will end on the 22 of January.
5. This year the annual house furnishings sale will be held on the second of May.
6. Did you read carefully the bulletin issued on January 1st?

Weights and Measures

In ordinary business correspondence, figures are used in expressing weights, measures, distances, and so on; as: *5 pounds, 7 kilowatts, 6 gallons, 2 feet 6 inches.*

Million, Billion

As an aid to clarity, present practice in writing extremely large numbers is to spell out *million, billion,* and so on. For example: "Foreign aid so far this year has amounted to more than *2 billion dollars.*" This number could also be written *$2 billion.*

50th anniversary

Percentages

Percentages that appear in isolated instances in sentences should be written in figures followed by *per cent*. For example:

The 6 per cent method of calculating interest is the simplest to learn. Note *6 per cent.*

Note. Some authorities prefer *per cent* to be written as one word—*percent*. Whichever form you choose to write, be consistent.

When percentages occur frequently, use the % sign and repeat that sign with each figure; like this: *discounts of 2%, 5%, and 10%.*

When percentages occur singly or in pairs, however, they are written in figures, with *per cent* following the second or last figure; as: *Our discounts range from 2 to 10 per cent.*

In ordinary business correspondence, *fractional* percentages are written as common fractions rather than as decimals; as: $33\frac{1}{3}$ *per cent* or $5\frac{1}{2}$%. In *technical* work, however, they are usually expressed decimally; as: 5.5%.

Decimals

Decimals are always expressed in figures, *without* commas; as: *7.5; 0.2568.* In technical writing where exactness is necessary, a cipher is written before the decimal point when there is no whole number.

6 *Class Practice*   By correcting the following sentences, you will test your understanding of the additional principles relating to the use of figures.

1. Economists predict the building of twenty million houses next year.
2. Living costs have increased 30 per cent to 50 per cent.
3. Many items that formerly cost five cents are now priced at 7 cents.
4. Be sure to order 10 5-pound bags for Mrs. Thomas.
5. Jean is four pounds heavier than her sister.
6. The members of some religious denominations contribute ten per cent of their income to the support of their churches.
7. This catfish weighs ten pounds two ounces.
8. Mr. McKenna's new contract calls for a twenty-five % increase.
9. You need a wire that is .05 of an inch in diameter.
10. The thinking, sensible person spends $33\frac{1}{3}$ per cent of his time working; $33\frac{1}{3}$ per cent, sleeping; $13\frac{1}{3}$ per cent, playing; and 20 per cent, improving himself mentally.

Learning Exercises

1   Each of the following sentences contains an error in the use of figures. On a separate sheet of paper, indicate the errors and make the corrections.

   1 Our family is eligible to vote only in the 3d Ward.
   2 Your subscription expires in 2 months.
   3 5,000 questionnaires were sent out on Saturday.
   4 An employee *may* retire at 65, but he *must* retire at 70 years of age.
   5 About 1,000 extra shipfitters are needed to build the new submarine.
   6 Depending on quality and workmanship, we can offer you bedspreads at $8, 10, 15, and 20.
   7 The cost of the manila envelopes is only seven cents each.
   8 Your note will fall due in sixty days.
   9 Do not expect a definite answer from us before the twenty-first of October.
  10 You probably would like to know that 7th Avenue extends to the city limits.
  11 We are making your appointment for 10:00 a.m. on Monday.
  12 We have no 11 o'clock appointments open until after Labor Day.
  13 His age at the time of his death was eighty years six months and fourteen days.
  14 We have received proxies from ⅓ of the stockholders.
  15 We have 3 questions to ask you, 2 of which relate to business and 1 to personal affairs.

2   Proceed as directed for all second learning exercises.

   1 Your letter was dated April 12th, not April 10th.
   2 My next job is to type the speech to be given at the Kiwanis Club meeting.
   3 The Hon. John Faulkner will present the trophies.
   4 Miss Archer has designed 6 new shirt patterns.
   5 Essential secretarial traits may be mentioned here without comment (analysis): tact, initiative, discretion, and poise.
   6 The office force presented the bride with a large, old-fashioned, inlaid, desk.
   7 There are 400 of our employees who rate the salary increase.
   8 The Vikings carried a flag, that bore a black raven on a field of white.

9 The information, not the money, was requested by Mr. Drake.

10 Is the price of the material 75¢ a yard?

11 The good executive listens attentively to all complaints, he realizes that knowing about and preventing dissatisfaction will promote good employee morale.

12 Instead of ten 40 folders were taken from the stock room.

13 16 boxes are exceedingly heavy.

14 Bill wanted to know, whether it would be possible to ship the goods on Monday.

15 We are glad to report that the Company now has ten factories in the South.

Vocabulary and Spelling Refreshers

1 **Words Often Confused.** Deceased, diseased; risky, risqué.

2 **Signs of the Times.** These signs appeared in various places—in stores, in ads, along highways. What's wrong?

   a Tourists accomodated.

   b If Its a Camera You Want, We Have It.

   c Carmel Sunday, 25 cents.

   d Our Vanishing Cream is more effective than any cream.

   e Clearance Sale of Mens' and Boys' Suits.

3 **From Figures into Words.** How are the following figures written in words?

   a 19   **c** $\frac{1}{9}$th   **e** 3,900

   b 90   **d** $2\frac{3}{24}$th   **f** $2\frac{8}{14}$ths

Communication in Action: *Making Facts Meaningful*

Paul believed in giving the facts about his company to anyone who would listen. Often, he was assigned the job of taking visitors through the company plant. Here is part of his talk: "Five years ago, we had only 127 production workers. Today, we have 1,270. Those workers produced 1,635 fans a month. Today, the workers produce 247,000 a year. Five years ago, we were losing $1,000 a week. This year our profits will be about $250,000." Assuming these facts are important, can you give them in such a way that your visitors will grasp them more quickly?

6
WRITING
FOR
BUSINESS

UNIT  38

Making Business Letters Effective

Why Business Letters Are Written

Why do you write letters to your friends and relatives? You write because you wish to exchange news and information—to keep in touch. These letters are substitutes for personal visits. They convey messages; at the same time, they build new friendships or maintain old ones. Business letters are written for much the same reasons as personal letters.

To Convey Messages. Primarily, a business letter is written because the businessman can't afford the time and expense of a personal visit each time he wishes to convey a message. Business letters, too, are substitutes for personal visits. They are "paper representatives" of the writer. Goods and services are exchanged freely throughout the country, and the businessman must depend upon the written word to keep in touch with his customers and business associates. So important is the letter to the businessman that a conservative estimate reveals that 85 per cent of business is conducted either wholly or partially by mail.

To Build Good Will. Good will is a friendly feeling—a feeling of confidence in an organization that makes a customer trade with one particular business rather than with another. Good will is not a tangible thing. However, when a business is sold, the purchaser may pay much more than the worth of the physical assets because of the good reputation of the business. You can see, therefore, that good will is extremely important to a business. You may have a favorite store in which you like to shop. Perhaps you prefer this store because it gives superior service, or it may be more conveniently located than other stores, or the people who run the store may be very pleasant to you each time you go there. These factors all add up to a good feeling on your part towards the store. And this is what the store wants and works hard to maintain. They want you to think of them when you need merchandise.

Building good will—and holding it—is an important job of the business letter. Many of the people to whom you write never enter your place of business, never see you, never talk to you. Their impressions of your business and their attitudes toward it are formed entirely through the letters they receive. A business letter, therefore, is not only a representative; it is also an ambassador.

Kinds of Business Letters

The employee in business writes many types of letters. He may write letters to ask for information, favors, or advice; he may write letters to send information, to collect money, to apologize for a mistake, to say "No" to an unreasonable request, to apply for a job, to sell his products or his company. One could hardly name all the types of letters written—the list is practically endless. Some letters are easier to write than others. For example, you can more easily maintain good will when granting a request than when refusing one. However, you cannot say that one letter is more important than another. Every letter is important.

The following kinds of business letters are among those most frequently written:

"Asking" Letters. "Asking" letters may also be called "please send me" letters. These are the simple requests for information, literature, prices, favors, appointments, and reservations. Secretaries and stenographers often write such letters for their employers.

Another type of "asking" letter is written to order merchandise or service. Many large companies use a form, called a purchase order, to order goods or services; but thousands of small companies place orders by means of letters. A clothing store, for example, may write letters to several suppliers asking them to itemize, right on the letters, the goods they wish shipped. These letters are often the only authorization needed by the supplier to ship the merchandise. Secretaries often write order letters for special office supplies—accounting forms, typewriter ribbons, and reference books, for example.

Letters Answering Requests. Just as a business firm often writes letters asking for something from another organization, it also receives a great many such letters. Most often the replies to these letters are not difficult to write. For example:

> Thank you for your order for 12 gross Velvet Tone
> silk typewriter ribbons. The shipment will leave our
> warehouse today and is being sent by Railway Express.
>
> I feel sure you will find these ribbons to be the
> best you have ever purchased. We should be happy to
> have the privilege of filling all your needs for sta-
> tionery and office supplies.

Form letters and postal cards are often used to acknowledge routine requests for orders if the reply does not require a personal message.

Some letters answering requests are not so easy to write. You may sometimes have to tell a customer that his order will be delayed because the merchandise is out of stock, or you may have to refuse a customer's request for a special favor simply because you cannot possibly grant it. These letters require the utmost tact and courtesy.

Letters answering requests give the letter writer one of his best opportunities for making friends and building good will. They are, therefore, among the most important communications written in business.

Claim and Adjustment Letters. However hard people try to avoid them, mistakes will occur in business. A furniture store receives a shipment of lamps and several are broken. A disappointed mother feels that the tricycle she ordered for her young son does not look new—the paint has been scratched in several places. A shoe store manager receives too many shoes in size 6A and too few in size 5B. These are typical situations in which the person who has been inconvenienced or offended writes a letter in protest. Although these letters are called claim letters, they really are complaint letters. All businesses receive—and send—them.

Letters written in response to claims are called adjustment letters. When the adjustment asked for is not granted (it isn't always; the claim may be unreasonable or unjustified), you must write the claimant a letter refusing to make the adjustment. In order to retain good will, a letter of this type will always give a logical reason for the refusal. Because adjustment letters are among the most difficult to write, they require special understanding of people as well as of the company the writer represents.

Credit and Collection Letters. A large percentage of business transactions in this country are handled on a credit basis. Letters must be written in response to requests for credit. Usually, the responses are favorable: "We are pleased to welcome you as a new charge customer at Elliot's." Sometimes, however, requests for credit must be declined because the applicant is not a good credit risk. These letters, too, call for great skill. One of the easiest ways to offend a person is to tell him that he is a poor credit risk!

A very small percentage of those who are given the privilege of credit violate that privilege. They must be reminded, reasoned with, and sometimes threatened, before they will pay what they owe. Collection letters are among the most challenging to the letter writer—their effectiveness is measured by the amount of money they bring in from forgetful and careless customers.

Sales Letters. A great many different kinds of sales letters are used in business today to encourage people to buy. Most common are the letters written specifically to sell an article of merchandise or a service. However, an increasingly important type of sales letter is the public relations or good will letter. These letters do not attempt to make direct sales; their primary purpose is to make friends and create a good feeling between the company and its customers. In the long run, of course, the desired outcome is an increase in customers —and in sales.

Employment Letters. Employment letters deal with getting a position. They are, of course, written by everyone, not only by those who expect to work in business. Employment letters include letters inquiring about a position, letters of application, letters thanking an employer for an interview, and letters of resignation.

Social-Business Letters. Many letters of a social-business nature are required to maintain friendly relationships with customers and business acquaintances. Typical social-business correspondence includes letters of congratulation, letters of sympathy, invitations, letters of friendship, and thank-you letters. Since they show thoughtfulness on the part of the writer, social-business letters do a great deal to build good will.

Getting Results from Business Letters

Business spends millions of dollars each year corresponding with customers, prospects, dealers, suppliers, and the public at large. Because letter writing is so very costly, many businesses have made special studies to determine the cost of writing letters. Would you be surprised to learn that for many businesses the cost of writing a single letter is over $1.80? Such factors as the executive's time, the stenographer's time, the paper consumed, the postage, and miscellaneous expenses contribute to the total cost. Yes, letter writing is expensive, but letters must be written regardless of the cost. The question the businessman asks himself about the correspondence that goes out from his office every day is, "Will this letter get results?" If it doesn't, a great deal of time and money is being wasted. If his communications get the results he is after, however, the businessman is not so concerned about the cost.

Measuring Results. What is an effective letter? An effective letter gets the most favorable reaction possible from the recipient. Of course you can't expect every reader to be bowled over with joy at every letter he receives. That is why the word *possible* is included in the definition of an effective letter. An effective business letter, however, makes a friend—or keeps one.

Measuring the effectiveness of a business letter usually is not easy. Every reader is different, and a letter that appeals to one reader will not always appeal to *all* readers. The good letter writer knows this and tries very hard to adapt his message to each individual to whom he writes. He is a student of human nature. A good letter writer is essentially a person who understands people—what motivates them, what "ruffles" them. He is usually a tactful person who respects the feelings of those around him. Good letter writing cannot be separated from good human relations. Someone has said that "effective letter writing is good human relations—*on paper.*" This statement may be oversimplified, but there is a great deal of truth in it.

Planning Leads to Better Results

Why Plan? If you were going to take a long trip, would you just hop into your car and take off? Not very likely. If you had not done some preliminary planning, your car might break down shortly after you started; you might run out of money before you reached your destination; and you might waste much valuable time by traveling on the wrong routes. Any number of things could go wrong because you had not planned ahead.

A blueprint helps the carpenter to build a house; a pattern helps the dressmaker to make a dress. Without the blueprint and the pattern, the builder and the dressmaker would be lost. When you write a letter, your "blueprint" can be of great help to you, for an effective letter does not just happen—it is a combination of knowledge, experience, and careful planning.

How to Plan. The first step in any planning process is to gather together all the materials that will be necessary to do the job—the letter to which a reply is being written, for example. A good diction-

ary is a valuable ally, too. Prices, delivery dates, or other information should also be available. The letter writer always makes certain that amounts, order numbers, dates, and names are complete and correct.

After all the materials have been gathered, the writer may refer to them to make a few brief notes before dictating his reply. These notes may be made on the letter to which he is replying or on a scratch pad. From these notes, the writer will either dictate his reply or prepare a rough draft to be typed later by a stenographer or a typist.

The beginning letter writer needs to spend a little more time in planning than an experienced writer. The beginner should first prepare an outline of his letter. This practice will save time and money, for it may prevent the necessity for writing follow-up letters to explain something that is not clear or complete. In addition, an outline helps the writer reduce the number of times he may have to rewrite his letter.

From the outline, the inexperienced letter writer should prepare a rough draft. This rough draft should then be corrected, checked for completeness, and improved upon before the letter is written in final form. Although this procedure may be time-consuming, it provides greater assurance that the letter will more effectively achieve its purpose. As a person gains experience in writing, he will find that less time is necessary in planning.

Both the experienced and the inexperienced letter writer should use the dictionary frequently to check for correct spelling, for the meaning they desire to convey, and for variety in word choice to add interest to the letter.

A Successful Example. An outline for a letter quoting the wholesale price on portable radios might look like this:

1. Acknowledge receipt of Mr. Leonard's inquiry of May 15 regarding the Clarion Portable Radio.
2. Quote price of $15.95 in lots of 50 or more radios.
3. Explain that batteries are not included in the price quoted but are extra.
4. Quote a wholesale price on batteries for portable radios at 65 cents each when purchased in lots of 50 or more batteries.
5. Promise delivery of radios and batteries within five days of the receipt of the order.

Eventually—when you have had more experience in planning and writing business letters, you will need only brief notations to direct you. Your outline then might look like this:

1. Acknowledge inquiry
2. Clarion $15.95 each in lots of 50, no batteries
3. Batteries 65 cents each in lots of 50
4. Five-day delivery

Here is the letter written from the outline:

Gentlemen:

　　We are pleased to answer your questions about the wholesale price of our Clarion Portable Radio.

　　The portable model sells for $15.95 each in lots of 50 or more. Batteries are extra. However, our price for batteries is only 65 cents each in lots of 50 or more.

　　We can give your order immediate attention, and you can expect delivery within five days after we receive your order. May we have an opportunity to demonstrate our excellent product and fine service?

　　　　　　Very truly yours,

Learning Exercises

1
　a List all the types of letters you have received during the past year.
　b List all the types of letters you have sent during the past year.

2 List and describe the types of letters the following might write or send in a typical month.

　a Housewife
　b Dentist
　c College dean or school principal
　d Clothing store owner
　e Manager of a garage
　f Librarian

3 Bring to class as many examples of letters (each person should be able to bring at least four) as you are able to collect at home or from business friends. Be prepared to discuss:

　a The kind of letter it is
　b Why the letter was written
　c The over-all appearance of the letter

4 Divide a sheet of paper into two columns. Label each column as follows.

Message Conveyed
0. *Example:* The price of the radio is $25.95.

Good Will Feature
0. *Example:* We sincerely hope you will give us an opportunity to serve you.

From each letter used in Exercise 3, select one sentence that conveys a message to the reader, as in the above example. In addition, from each of these letters select a sentence or phrase that attempts to develop good will.

5 For each of the following situations, tell the kind of business letter you would write.

> *Example:* To open a charge account, you would write a *credit letter.*

a To obtain a college catalogue
b To sell a power lawn mower
c To report that a radio you ordered was received in damaged condition
d To apply for a position with the Raymore Company
e To congratulate a business acquaintance who has been elected president of the Lions Club
f To answer a customer who wrote you for the price of slip covers
g To open an account to buy on credit
h To order 500 boxes of stationery
i To remind a customer that his account is overdue
j To send a customer a catalogue he requested

6 In each of the preceding letters, what might happen if the letter is not clear or complete or correct?

Vocabulary and Spelling Refreshers

1 **Words Often Confused.** Intense, intents; insoluble, insolvable, insolvent.

2 **Raise or Rise?** Should *raise* or *rise* be chosen for the blank spaces in these sentences? (Some sentences require the past-tense or past-participle forms.)

a John, will you please _____ the shades.
b At what time will the sun _____ tomorrow?
c Last year we _____ both cucumbers and tomatoes in our garden.
d The price of coffee has _____ several times this year because the growers _____ their prices.
e The last speaker _____ a doubt as to the wisdom of the decision.

3 **Spelling Mishaps.** Which of the following frequently used words are here misspelled?

a sandwitch   e questionaire   h amature
b untill   f parallel   i alright
c anonymous   g inoculate   j alledge
d grammer

Communication in Action: *Avoid a Mistake*

You overhear the new salesclerk promise to have a customer's dress delivered to her home the following evening. As an experienced clerk, you know that the alterations will not be completed for three days and that it will take another day to deliver. How can you unobtrusively get the correct information to this customer without causing the new clerk to "lose face"?

UNIT 39

Qualities of Effective Letters

Upon what basis do you select your friends? How do you decide what food to pick from an appetizing display in a cafeteria? How do you decide what suit or dress to buy from a wide selection shown to you? In each case, the person or the article possesses certain qualities or characteristics that appeal to you and that influence your choice. The friend may be very thoughtful of other people—and thoughtfulness is a trait that appeals to you. The salad may just look good—and appearance helps you make the choice. The suit or dress may be a particular style—and style influences your decision in this case. These are only a few of the factors that help us choose one person or thing rather than another. There are, of course, many, many others. We react favorably to some characteristics and unfavorably to others.

And the same is true when you read a letter. The qualities it possesses will influence you to react either favorably or unfavorably. One of the main objectives of all business letters is to get a favorable reaction. "Every person does not like the same things, so how can a letter please everyone?" you may ask. All of us do not like spinach; we do not all like the color yellow; not everyone likes Beethoven's music. Then, can you write a letter that will appeal to *every* reader?

You cannot predict exactly how what you say or write will affect another person. From your own experience in dealing with friends and classmates, however, you know what kind of behavior and personal characteristics affect *most* people favorably. So, too, you know that friendliness usually wins friends, but sarcasm and indifference do not. You know that a "sharp" appearance, a ready smile, and good listening habits usually attract people; shoddiness, glumness, and constant jabber drive them away. There are certain qualities in business letters, too, that will get successful results.

Qualities That Spell Letter Success

If each of your letters meets the following nine requirements, the chances are that you will be a successful letter writer.

1. Creates a favorable first impression
2. Appeals to the reader's point of view
3. Is correct in every detail
4. Is courteous, friendly, and sincere
5. Promotes good will
6. Is clear, complete, and concise
7. Holds together
8. Is well paragraphed
9. Uses modern words

Creates a Favorable First Impression. When you meet a person for the first time, what is the first thing that makes an impression upon you? You will probably answer, "Appearance, of course." Appearance is the first thing nearly everyone notices. And appearance can add to or detract from your first impression. So it is with a letter. Your first impression is often influenced by the letter's appearance, and that impression stays with you as you read the message. If the letter creates a favorable first impression, you will react more favor-

CHAMPION PAPER SPECIALTIES INC.

GENERAL OFFICE, HAMILTON, OHIO

The **C** **hesapeake**
and
P **otomac Telephone Company of Maryland**

320 St. Paul Place · Baltimore 2, Maryland · LExington 9-9900

Home & Highway Magazine

Now printing more than 4 million copies / 7447 Skokie Boulevard, Skokie, Illinois / ORchard 5-2200 (Chicago Oner. COrnelia 7-7700)

EASTERN AIR LINES

INCORPORATED

MEMBER OF THE NATIONAL SAFETY COUNCIL
EASTERN AIR LINES BUILDING
10 ROCKEFELLER PLAZA
NEW YORK 20, NEW YORK

QUAINT AMERICAN · FORSLUND FARMSTEAD

CARL FORSLUND, inc. *Furniture*

122 EAST FULTON STREET · GRAND RAPIDS 2, MICHIGAN

EVINRUDE MOTORS milwaukee 16, wisconsin A DIVISION OF OUTBOARD MARINE CORPORATION

Several attractive letterheads in a variety of designs.

ably to the contents. Therefore, every letter you write should, first of all, look inviting. An attractive platter of food stimulates your appetite to eat; an attractive letter stimulates your desire to read. The factors that help to create a favorable impression include the quality of the stationery, the attractiveness of the letterhead, the neatness of the typing, and the style of the letter.

Appeals to the Reader's Point of View. Many letters are written to get the reader to do something that is of mutual advantage to the reader and to the writer. So, you should put your words together in such a way that the reader will be prompted to act in the way you want him to act. Some people react quickly if their pride is at stake; health or happiness will motivate others; financial gain is still another incentive to get people to act.

Producing an action-getting letter will be easier for the writer who puts himself in the reader's place. As he composes the letter, the writer can pretend that he is the reader asking, "What do *I* get out of this? What will it do for *me?*" The writer will find that he uses the pronoun *you* more often than *I* or *we.* He puts the reader's interest first. He shows how taking the desired action will be to the advantage of the reader.

Suppose you wrote as follows to a customer who was tardy with a payment:

> Please send <u>us</u> your check for $16.89 so that <u>we</u> may balance <u>our</u> books.

Is there anything in this sentence that would move the reader to sit down, write the check, and mail it? No. The typical customer doesn't care whether the company's books are balanced or not. Certainly, he can't see any advantage in it for him. Nearly always there is a better chance of collecting a bill if the customer himself is brought into the picture. For example, here is an appeal to the customer's pride:

> Your check for $16.89 will balance <u>your</u> account and help <u>you</u> to maintain <u>your</u> good credit standing.

Is Correct in Every Detail. Errors in a letter can prevent the letter from doing the job it sets out to do. Of course, errors are never intentional; even so, there is little excuse for them. Reasons for errors fall into two main categories:

1. Carelessness; such as:
   Uneven typing—some letters light, others dark
   Poor margin balance—top and bottom and right and left sides far out of balance

Typographic errors—errors in spacing, strikeovers, raised capital letters

Poor erasing

2. Failure to consult reference sources, resulting in:

Misspelled words and names (All misspellings are very serious; misspelled names are unforgivable.)

Errors in dates, figures, and word choice

Errors in capitalization and punctuation

Errors in selection of words

Some errors, such as those involving dates and amounts of money, can cause a great deal of harm. Such errors not only irritate the reader (especially if they cause him loss of time or money), but they also cause him to lose faith in the company sending the letter. You can see the harmful effect on good will if your letters contain errors. Therefore you know why every letter should be proofread carefully and all errors corrected before it is mailed.

Is Courteous, Friendly, and Sincere. Would you continue shopping in a store where your patronage was not appreciated? You would not be very likely to return often to a store where you did not receive courteous treatment. A famous chain of cigar stores displays this sign at all cash registers: "Your purchases are free if we fail to say 'thank you.'" The owners claim they have never lost any money but have won thousands of friends. They do not take their customers for granted. No doubt you can remember from your own experience some person for whom you were always delighted to do favors. Why? Probably this person always showed his appreciation, and his *expression* of gratitude made you want to help him. Yes, everyone wishes to be treated courteously—to be told that he is appreciated. When you write letters, you should remember this principle: Saying "thank you" for a favor done and "please" for a favor requested is a good way to make and keep friends.

Of course, good manners are not reflected merely in a "please" or "thank you." The *way* in which you say or write "please" or "thank you"—the tone—makes the difference. The tone of your letter tells many things about you—your attitude, your sense of fair play, your desire to be of service. Such expressions as the following help to give your letter a desirable tone:

```
You were most thoughtful to . . . .
We can always rely on you for . . . .
We are indeed happy to
Thank you for . . . .
We appreciate your . . . .
```

```
You are entirely right in saying . . . .
We were gratified to learn that . . . .
We should very much appreciate . . . .
```

Of course, these phrases do not in themselves make a courteous letter. Your letter must "talk" to the reader as if he were a guest in your home.

Friendliness is an important quality of the good letter. Friendliness and courtesy are related, but they are not synonymous terms. You may use courteous words and yet not be very friendly. For example, the person who wrote the following was not actually discourteous. But he does not sound very friendly, does he?

```
We cannot honor your request for a discount. We
can grant discounts only on the regular items listed in
our catalogue. Please send us your check for $2.76.
Thank you.
```

You can inject warmth into your letters by writing as you would talk, by keeping the reader's point of view, and by using friendly sounding words and expressions, such as:

```
Your check arrived this morning. Thank you!
We were very happy to learn that you . . . .
Why not let us add this to your account?
Welcome as a new customer of Baggett's!
You are entirely right, Miss Jasper, the error is
ours . . . .
As a person with a fine credit rating, you . . . .
```

Now let's try to inject a friendly tone in the preceding letter:

```
No doubt, Mrs. Holcomb, you assumed that our usual
discount applied on these rose bushes. Perhaps this was
not entirely clear in our advertisement. I know you
will understand, however, that, because we are selling
these Beverly Beauties below cost, our usual discount
does not apply. May we, therefore, expect your check
for $2.76?
```

Sincerity is another quality your letter should possess. Sincerity means that you really do wish to be of service to your reader—you have a genuine interest in him. Assumed sincerity, however, will show through. Sincerity must be genuine. If you are sincere, the customer will not take the attitude that your courtesy and friendliness are prompted by a selfish desire to get what you want. Rather, your sincerity should make him feel that *he* will benefit by acting as you request. When you are sincere, you mean what you say; and your letter reflects this feeling. To write a sincere letter, you must believe in people, in your company, and in yourself. You must talk

with, not *at,* people. Following are examples of expressions that help
to reflect sincerity:

```
        Please accept my apology for the delay in send-
ing . . . .
        Your problem is quite understandable, and . . . .
        We would like to make an exception in this case;
however . . . .
        I am pleased to explain the situation more
fully . . . .
        Certainly, you have every right to expect better
service; and I . . . .
        I agree with you that two weeks does seem a long
time to . . . .
```

Promotes Good Will. Every letter you write should help to promote
good will for your firm. Good will results from:

1. Good products or services
2. Ethical conduct
3. Superior service to customers
4. Prompt attention to details, such as correspondence

Every letter you write *is* the company insofar as the reader is
concerned. Your letter sells—or unsells—the reader on your firm.

Courtesy The Shaw-Walker Company

The employee who demonstrates the ability to write clearly and effectively
is soon given writing assignments of his own.

The promptness with which you handle correspondence, your thoughtfulness in answering all the reader's questions, your willingness to do the little bit extra for your customers—all influence good will.

A good letter writer must have a thorough knowledge of the products or services sold by his firm and must honestly believe that they and his company are superior. In every sentence and every paragraph in every letter this faith must show through.

Ethical conduct means honest and upright dealings in all situations—and equal fairness to all. A company's reputation for high ethical standards must also include keeping its word, never taking advantage of any other firm or person, and paying its bills promptly.

Customers expect good service; yet, when they receive it, they are flattered. Poor service, on the other hand, loses good will and, eventually, loses customers. Most progressive firms make top service a company policy, for they know that the best in service *all the time* keeps old customers and makes customers out of prospects. Your business letters should stress this "service-mindedness" of your company. One secret of building a reputation for "super" service is prompt *action*. When an order is received, it should be filled immediately. When a request comes in, it should be acted on within forty-eight hours. If a customer has a complaint, it should be attended to without delay.

Failure to reply quickly to a letter is one sure way to destroy good will. Such negligence tells the customer that he is not important enough to get your attention. Therefore, even if you are unable to answer all the writer's questions, you should write, giving what help you can and indicating when the remaining answers will be sent.

Is Clear, Complete, and Concise. Have you ever received a message that you did not understand? How did you feel—confused, and maybe a little angry? What kept the message from being clear? Was something left unsaid? "Meet me tomorrow at 4 p.m.," Jim writes. But Jim doesn't tell you *where* to meet him. So his message is not clear because it is not complete. You can see, then, that completeness contributes to clarity in letter writing, that a clearly written message is vital if your letter is to achieve its purpose. You can't meet Jim if you don't know where to meet him. And Miller Brothers can't fill your order for shirts if you don't tell them the size you want. Incomplete letters can be costly, for they lead to errors and often cause delays in filling orders. Sometimes further correspondence is necessary; and, when time is an important factor, expensive telephone calls must be made or telegraph messages sent.

Clarity is also influenced by the words you use and the way you use them. First, you must have a clear idea in your own mind of what you want to say. Then, you must decide how you are going to say it. In general, the writer should use the simplest everyday expressions—those he is sure the reader will understand. Contrast the following:

```
        It is obligatory that you confirm this outstanding
indebtedness and, if no discrepancies exist, that you
expedite remittance.
        Please let us know if your records and ours do not
agree. If you find that they do, won't you send us your
check right away?
```

A concise letter—a letter that covers the entire subject in the fewest possible words—is more certain to convey the message than a rambling, verbose letter. But guard against thinking, as many people do, that *concise* and *brief* mean the same thing; brevity is only a part of conciseness. To be concise, a message must be both complete *and* brief—but not so brief as to be discourteous. Look at the following letter. What is wrong with it?

```
        Please send me a pair of the desert boots adver-
tised in last Sunday's Sacramento Bee. My check is
enclosed.
```

This letter certainly meets the test for brevity; but could the order be filled? No, because the size (and perhaps color) desired has not been specified. Brevity is desirable; but it must not be used at the expense of clarity or completeness—and this letter is not clear because it is not complete.

Conciseness means saying all that needs to be said and no more. In business, time is money—and few business people have time to read irrelevant details.

Holds Together. A letter should hold together—each part should be related to the other parts of the letter. This cohesiveness helps the reader to follow your line of thinking because you have "led him by the hand" from one point to another. Each sentence flows smoothly into the next, and each paragraph connects with the other. A rambling letter that has no guide lines—like a rambling conversation— is hard to follow. Using such connecting or linking words as the following will help you considerably in achieving cohesiveness:

in the first place	next	on the other hand
furthermore	however	in this way
at any rate	naturally	consequently

equally important	nevertheless	moreover
for instance	of course	on the contrary
finally	therefore	thus

Another way to achieve cohesiveness is to number the points you wish to make and to arrange them as separate paragraphs. In letters where many details are given, subtitles may also be used to set off each paragraph.

Is Well Paragraphed. Good paragraphing is an essential of effective business letters. However, there is no formula for determining how many paragraphs a letter should have. Many believe that every letter, no matter how short, should contain at least two paragraphs. And this is a pretty good rule to follow in most cases. However, the rule does not always work. Consider the following:

```
        Enclosed is my check for $3.60 for a two-year sub-
    scription to Sportsman magazine.
```

This letter is complete (assuming that the writer's name and address are included elsewhere), and there is no need to say more. If you have to contrive a message just to make two paragraphs, then you should forget about the two-paragraph rule.

There are three main guiding principles in paragraphing letters:

1. Hold paragraphs to not more than six or eight typewritten lines. Long paragraphs make your message *look* hard to read, whether it actually is or not.

2. Convey only one principal idea in a paragraph.

3. Don't overparagraph. Too many paragraphs make a letter look choppy and detract from the smoothness of the message. The typical full-page letter contains three or four paragraphs.

Uses Modern Words. Modern words are essential to a modern letter. Study the following list and the lists in the Reference Section (page 551), and be sure to apply this learning in all the letters you write.

Old-Fashioned	*Modern*
Acknowledge receipt of	We received **or** Thank you for
Advise	Say, tell, inform, let us know
Am in receipt of	Have received
And oblige	**Do not use.**
As per, per	As, according to
At an early date	Soon, **or give specific date**
At that time	Then
At this time, at the present time, at the present writing	Now, at present

Old-Fashioned	Modern
Attached hereto	Attached
Beg	**Do not use. We are not beggars.**
Due to the fact that	As, because, since
Duly	**Do not use. Superfluous.**
Enclosed please find	Enclosed is
Esteemed favor	Your welcome letter
Have before me	**Do not use.**
Herewith	**Do not use, except in legal work.**
In re	Regarding, concerning
In the event that	In case, **or** if
In this matter	**Do not use.**
Instant (Inst.)	**Give exact date.**
Kindly	Please
Our check in the amount of	Our check for
Party	Person, **except in legal work**
Proximo	**Give exact date.**
Same	It, they, them, **or whatever is meant**
State	Say, tell
Take pleasure	Pleased, are happy, are glad
Take the liberty of sending you	Will send you
Thank you in advance	**Do not use. A discourteous expression.**
The writer	I, me
Trust	Hope, know, believe
Ultimo	**Give exact date.**
Under date of	On
Under separate cover	By freight, **or whatever the means of sending**
Up to this writing	Previously
Valued (letter or order)	**Do not use.**
We wish to thank you	Thank you
Would ask, remind, say, suggest	**Go ahead and say it without warning.**
Yours received and contents noted	**Unnecessary. The letter must have been received and read if it is being answered.**

Learning Exercises

1 Rewrite the following material. Arrange it in appropriate paragraphs and use connecting words that will give the material cohesiveness.

Your order No. 7432 for pencil sharpeners was
received today. We do not manufacture pencil sharpeners. We cannot fill your order. We looked up the
nearest manufacturer. We found it to be the American
Sharpener Company. Their address is 701 Wharf Street,
Boston, Massachusetts. We are sending you a catalogue
of our products. Perhaps we can be of further service
to you in the future.

2 Each of the sentences below is "writer slanted"—it takes the
writer's point of view. Rewrite each sentence so that it is "reader
slanted" instead.

a We are anxious to receive your order.
b Help us meet our sales quota by sending us your order
now.
c Send your remittance now so that we may balance our
books.
d Your overdue account prevents us from paying our
bills promptly.

3 Criticize the following letter on the basis of the qualities discussed in this unit.

Dear Mrs. Barker:

We do not believe you have any cause for complaint concerning the shipment of your order for
Princess Priscilla blouses. Our seamstresses have
been working night and day trying to catch up on a
multitude of orders. It is not our fault that the
blouses you ordered have been so popular that everyone wants them. Besides, you should have ordered them
earlier. We are just not prepared for the big run on
our stock. One of the problems was that at first the
textile mills were not sending us enough of the yard
goods from which the blouses are made. So, they were
behind; but they have caught up now. If you will just
be patient, we will do our best to get your order
shipped. You ask whether you can have these blouses
in time for Easter. That is a good question. It looks
like we could and I am sure you will, but still one
never knows, do they? As a matter of fact, our production manager said this morning that we will ship
all orders by the end of next week. This means you
would be receiving them two weeks before Easter.

Yours truly,

4 Each of the following messages lacks some important information. Rewrite the message, providing the necessary information that
will make it clear and complete—and correct.

a Meet me at 9 tomorrow.
b Please send 3 doz. lamp bulbs.
c Reserve a room for me for May 15-16 in your hotel.
d I would like your travel agency to plan a trip to California for me for next summer.
e Please let me know how much your typewriters cost.

5 Revise the following sentences, using more effective wording.

1 Due to a recent change in accounting procedures, you will receive your bill on the tenth of the month instead of on the first.
2 We trust that you will agree with us.
3 Please advise as to what disposition you wish to make of order No. 684.
4 We are replacing the broken gasket and will rush same to you.
5 The goods were shipped as per your order of June 5.
6 Thanks for your esteemed favor of April 2.
7 Janet stood inside of the doorway to shield herself from the rain.
8 The rush was over with before five o'clock.
9 I shall not repeat the instructions again.
10 Past experience has taught us that we must collect bills promptly.

Vocabulary and Spelling Refreshers

1 **Words Often Confused.** Deprecate, depreciate; bow, beau, bough.

2 **Know Your Roots.** Many of our most frequently used words are derived from Latin or Greek roots. To each word in the third column add two or more words built on the root in the first column.

Root	Meaning	Words Built on Root
a graph-	write	graphic
b duc-	lead	ductile
c spec-	look at	spectator
d phon-	sound	phonograph
e fin-	end	finish

3 **What Is the Past Tense?** Change the present-tense forms of the verbs within the parentheses to the past-tense forms.

    a It (begin) to snow about seven o'clock.
    b I (hear) the faint sound of bells in the distance.
    c She (choose) a slightly darker shade of blue for her new suit.
    d Tim (swim) to the raft and back several times.
    e I (forget) my report card.
    f My sweater (shrink) when I washed it.

Communication in Action: *Contract for an Orchestra*

You have been asked to arrange for an orchestra to play at the annual Accounting Department dinner dance. Make a list of the information you will need to give and get as you telephone an orchestra leader to engage his group for this event.

UNIT 40

Parts of the Business Letter

First Impressions

When you meet someone for the first time, his dress, the color of his hair and eyes, his smile, and his physical appearance in general all add up to your first impression before even a word is exchanged.

A business letter, too, creates an impression upon the reader even before he reads the message. This impression often sets the reader's mood and can make him more, or less, receptive to the message you are trying to convey. In a business letter, there are four principal elements that help to make that first impression:

1. The stationery—the size and quality of the paper used and the letterhead

2. The format or layout—how the parts of the letter are arranged on the page

3. The quality of the typewriting—the sharpness of the typescript (not a mixture of light and dark strokes), the neatness of erasures, and the over-all neatness of the letter

4. The style of letter used

Parts of the Letter

When a musician writes a song, he is concerned with a number of things—the title, the notes, the key, the "beat," and the verse, to mention but a few. These parts all must fit into their proper place on his sheet of music. The letter writer, too, is concerned with many parts and their arrangement on the page. A picture may be very attractive in itself; if a beautiful frame is placed around it, however, the beauty of the picture is often greatly enhanced. A business letter, too, will convey a more pleasing message if it is attractively "framed."

Look at the illustration on page 334, showing the parts of a business letter. The parts have been numbered and are identified.

Punctuating the Parts of the Letter

There are three commonly used punctuation styles that you may select for business letters. These are:

1. Open
2. Close
3. Mixed

When you use open punctuation, omit commas and periods at the ends of all lines in the date, the inside address, and the signature block. No mark of punctuation follows the salutation and the complimentary closing.

```
                                                    May 15, 19—

    Mr. Robert Lambert, President
    Crawford Manufacturing Company
    1436 Kent Road
    Richfield 27, Missouri

    Dear Mr. Lambert


    _____

    _____

                        Very truly yours

                        James C. Martin
```

When you use close punctuation, insert commas or periods at the ends of lines in the date, the inside address, the complimentary closing, and the signature block, as shown at the top of page 335.

Simmons & Waters (1)

200 Clinton Avenue
Charlotte, North Carolina
Phone: Center 6-0135

September 10, 19-- (2)

(3) Treeman-Hughes Chemicals, Inc.
1458 Hampshire Road
Lincoln 9, Nebraska

ATTENTION: PLANNING ENGINEER (4)

Gentlemen: (5)

Subject: Opportunities in North Carolina (6)

Over a quarter of the $4 billion industrial expansion in the South
during the past ten years went into new chemical facilities. The abundance of raw materials for chemical production, the lower labor rates,
and the economy of transportation in the South are just three of the many
reasons why chemical manufacturers are moving to the South.

Two special reasons will be of particular interest to you: the great
tracts of property suitable for industrial development that are still
available at low real estate prices; and favorable privileges in regard
to taxation of new industrial enterprises. Aren't they worth investigating?
Do read the enclosed pamphlet! (7)

We are pleased to offer you the services of our firm in conducting
your investigation of opportunity for your firm in North Carolina, which
is fast becoming the nation's center for chemical industries. Because we
have been established in this state for three generations, because we are
fully informed of properties throughout the state, because we have already
serviced three other chemical companies and so know well the elements of
prime consideration to you, we believe that we can offer you the most
authoritative assistance available.

We hope that you will consider building in the South and, especially,
building in North Carolina. And we look forward to having the opportunity
to be of service to you.

(8) Very truly yours,

SIMMONS & WATERS (9)

F H Waters

F. H. Waters, President (10)

FHW-tm (11)
Enclosure
(12)

The parts of a business letter are:

1	Heading	**7**	Body
2	Date line	**8**	Complimentary closing
3	Inside address	**9–10**	Signature block
4	Attention line	**11**	Identification initials
5	Salutation	**12**	Enclosure reference
6	Subject line	**13**	Carbon copy notation

Parts 1, 2, 3, 5, 7, 8, 9, 10, and 11 must be included in *every* letter.
Parts 4, 6, 12, and 13 are used only when they are needed.

May 15, 19—.

Mr. Robert Lambert, President,
Crawford Manufacturing Company,
1436 Kent Road,
Richfield, Missouri.

Dear Mr. Lambert:

_____

_____

Very truly yours,

James C. Martin.

With mixed punctuation, you use a colon after the salutation and a comma after the complimentary closing. Although mixed punctuation is very widely used today, there is a growing trend toward simplification and the use of open punctuation.

The Heading. The heading consists of the name of the firm and its address—street, city, zone number, and state. Most businesses use printed or engraved letterheads on which are included the essentials. Some letterheads contain additional data, such as a telephone number, a cable address, and the names of the executives.

Office people become so accustomed to using printed letterheads that they sometimes forget to type the heading when they write personal business letters on plain paper. A personnel manager for a well-known industry once remarked, "I received a splendid letter of application today. I'd certainly hire that girl if only I knew her address."

For a typed heading, use one of the following forms:

1645 Madison Avenue
Middletown 3, Ohio
June 15, 19—

or

JOHN J. FRANKLIN
45 Midtown Avenue
Boise 7, Idaho

June 15, 19—

The Date Line. The date line is usually typed on the second line space below the last line of the letterhead. It may be centered; typed so that it ends flush with the right margin; or, in full-blocked letters, typed flush with the left margin. The date line contains the month, the day of the month, and the year. Do not abbreviate the month or the year and do not use figures alone, like 10/17/60. Do not use *st, nd, rd, th,* or *d* after the day of the month. The correct way to write the date line: September 15, 19—

The Inside Address. The inside address consists of:

1. The name and title of the person to whom the letter is written —Mr. Ralph G. Leeds, President

2. The name of the firm—Leeds Manufacturing Company, Inc. (Do not use abbreviations unless the company uses an abbreviation in its name, such as *Co.* or *Inc.*)

3. The street address—113 Rendale Avenue

4. The city, postal zone, and state—Detroit 6, Michigan

Be particularly careful about the spelling of names. The misspelling of a name is certain to annoy its owner; if you have any doubt regarding the spelling, check it and get it right! Consult original correspondence, mailing lists, the files, or directories like the City Directory.

The inside address is placed at the left margin. In some semisocial letters, the inside address is written below the signature at the left margin.

Sincerely,

Sara Wilkes

Miss Marian Heath
2020 Shelley Street
Bainbridge 3, Maryland

Out of courtesy, the name should always be preceded by a title; such as *Mr., Miss, Mrs., Dr., Prof. (Professor),* or *Hon. (Honorable).* Never use two titles meaning the same thing, one before and one after the name. For example, Dr. Robert Johnson, M. D., is incorrect because both *Dr.* and the *D* in *M. D.* are abbreviations for *doctor.* In letters to business people and to executives, you should, if possible, include the business or executive title that shows the person's connection with the firm or organization. When the title is short enough to be written on the same line with the person's name, it should be preceded by a comma.

Mr. Lawrence Morrison, President
Hopewell Manufacturing Company
2436 Central Boulevard
San Bernardino 8, California

If the firm name is short, you may type the addressee's title on the second line, preceding the firm name.

```
Mr. Alexander Cunningham, Jr.
Secretary, York Company, Inc.
1478 Fifth Avenue
Camden 8, New Jersey
```

Depending upon the length of the other lines, it may be preferable to type the addressee's title on a line by itself.

```
Mr. Adam R. Andrews
Director of Personnel
Ames Manufacturing Company
Chicago 72, Illinois
```

Always spell in full the names of cities, states, counties, and countries. However, *Saint* is usually abbreviated, as in *St. Paul* and *St. Louis.* Another exception is the District of Columbia, which is generally written *D. C.*

The Attention Line. You use an attention line generally when you don't know the name of the person you wish to handle your correspondence but you do know his title. For example:

```
ATTENTION: Sales Manager
```

Or you may know the person's last name but not his first name. You cannot address the letter to him without his first name, but you can direct it to him through the use of an attention line; as:

```
Attention of Mr. Greene
```

The attention line may be typed in three ways (each, two spaces below the inside address):
1. Flush with the left margin
2. Indented the same as the paragraphs in the letter
3. Centered on the page

The attention line may be in all capital letters; it may be underscored; or it may have only *Attention* underscored. The following illustrates the two most common ways of handling the attention line:

```
L. M. Robins Company        L. M. Robins Company
23 Bromley Lane             23 Bromley Lane
Norfolk 9, Virginia         Norfolk 9, Virginia

Attention of Mr. Alley      ATTENTION: SALES MANAGER

Gentlemen:                  Gentlemen:
```

Notice that the inclusion of the attention line does not change the salutation. Since the letter is addressed to the firm, the salutation must be *Gentlemen.* Remember, then, that the salutation agrees with the first line of the inside address, *not* with the attention line.

The Salutation. The salutation always starts at the left margin and, with close or mixed punctuation, is followed by a colon. With open punctuation, *no mark follows the salutation*. In social correspondence, a comma may be used after the salutation.

There are three simple rules to remember about salutations:

1. Abbreviate only the titles *Mr., Mrs.,* and *Messrs.* Other titles, such as *Professor* and *Doctor,* should be written in full.

2. Capitalize *dear* only when it is the *first* word of the salutation—Dear Mr. Lyons; *but* My dear Mr. Jackson.

3. Choose the salutation that is suitable and correct for the firm or the person.

The correct salutation for a firm composed of men or both men and women is *Gentlemen.* For a firm or organization composed entirely of women, use *Mesdames* or *Ladies.* Sometimes *Ms.* is used when the writer does not know whether a woman is Miss or Mrs. Salutations for individuals, in the order of formal to informal, are:

```
Sir:                    Madam:
My dear Sir:            My dear Madam:
My dear Mr. Thorp:      My dear Mrs. Thorp:
Dear Mr. Thorp:         Dear Mrs. Thorp:
```

The Subject Line. A subject line tells the reader at a glance what the letter is about. The subject line is also an aid in filing and in finding a filed letter. However, not all firms use a subject line. When they do use it, its style and position are usually decided by office preference. The line may be typed two spaces below the salutation (at the margin, indented five spaces, or centered); or, if the subject is very short, it may be centered on a line with the salutation. Remember, however, that the subject line is part of the body of the letter; therefore, it never precedes the attention line.

```
Collector of Internal Revenue
1426 Pearl Street
Hartford 2, Connecticut

Dear Sir:
        Subject: Case No. 167
```

or

```
Dear Sir:          Case No. 167
```

The Body of the Letter. The body of the letter contains the message. Since the writing of the message will be treated in later units, only appearance will be discussed here. These four points regarding appearance should be remembered:

1. Provide generous margins of white space so that the letter looks like a picture in a frame. Allow at least an inch each for the right and the left margin.

2. Keep the left margin absolutely even; and keep the right margin as even as possible, with very few divided words.

3. Keep the paragraphs fairly short—never more than six to eight lines long.

4. Be certain the typing is neat—no strikeovers or noticeable erasures.

The Complimentary Closing. The complimentary closing is the leave-taking line—the "so long" or "good-by" of the letter—and should be in keeping with the salutation and with the message contained in the letter. The complimentary closing is typed two spaces below the last line of the body of the letter. And only the first word of the complimentary closing is·capitalized. It is followed by a comma, except when open punctuation is used. The most used forms, ranging from formal to informal, are:

Very truly yours,	Sincerely yours,
Yours very truly,	Very cordially yours,
Very sincerely yours,	Yours very cordially,
Yours very sincerely,	Yours cordially,
Yours sincerely,	Cordially yours,

Notice that the closing *Yours truly* is not included in the list. This closing, although still used by many, is considered abrupt by experienced letter writers. Notice, too, that *yours* is always included in the complimentary closing of business letters.

If you are writing to someone to whom you wish to show great respect, you may use "respectfully" closings—*Yours respectfully* or *Respectfully yours.* You must not, however, make the error of using *respectively* for *respectfully.*

The Signature Block. The signature block may include both the firm name and the name of the dictator of the letter, or it may include just the name of the dictator. The choice of style is determined by the nature of the letter, the position of the dictator, and other considerations. Newcomers should, therefore, inquire as to the style used in a particular office. If the firm name is typed, it is placed in all capitals two spaces below and starting under the first letter of the complimentary closing. In the indented form of letter, however, the firm name would be indented five spaces from the start of the complimentary closing.

```
        Yours very truly,              Yours very truly,

      FAULKNER COMPANY            FAULKNER COMPANY
```

   The name of the person dictating the letter is typed four spaces below the firm name. If a dictator's title is short, it may be placed on the same line as his name; otherwise, it should be placed below his name. Sometimes just the title is used, the signature not being typed. However, since the handwriting of many people is difficult to read, a typed signature should be included. A typed name sometimes appears instead of initials in the space reserved for the identification initials (see page 341). Following are several examples of signature blocks:

```
      Yours very sincerely,           Yours very sincerely,

   ATLAS MANUFACTURING COMPANY
                                         William A. Durfee
                                         Director of Research

   George L. Greene, President
```

```
          Yours very sincerely,


          George L. Greene, President
```

   The title *Mr.* is never typed in the signature block.

Identification Initials. Identification initials are used on business letters only and not in personal correspondence. They identify the person who takes and transcribes the dictation. When the dictator's initials are included, they always precede those of the transcriber and are placed at the left margin. They are typed either on the same line as the last signature line or two lines below the last signature line.

```
                          Very sincerely yours,

                          ATLAS MANUFACTURING COMPANY


      JTA:MG               John T. Arnette, Comptroller
        or
      MG
```

   If no typed signature is used, the dictator's name should be typed in full in the identification data.

```
                         Very sincerely yours,

                         ATLAS MANUFACTURING COMPANY


                         Comptroller
        J. T. Arnette:MG
```

Other ways of typing the identification initials are:

```
    CBD:G       AEL:g       ATR:RCC       lna/rm       abl:r
```

Enclosure Reference. If a letter contains an enclosure—a check, a pamphlet, a copy of another letter—that fact should be indicated by typing the word *Enclosure* one or two lines below the identification data. If there is more than one enclosure, the number should be indicated, as *Enc. 3.* Some typical enclosure forms are:

```
    Enclosure       Encl.       Enc. 3       Enclosure--Check
```

Carbon Copy Notations. If carbon copies are being sent to other persons, the information should be indicated immediately below the identification-data lines; as:

```
    cc to Mr. Andrews       cc T. R. Bennett
    cc Andrews              CC: Mr. T. R. Bennett
```

Sometimes the writer wishes to send a carbon copy to a third person without letting the person to whom he is writing know that he is doing so. This carbon is called a *blind carbon copy* because the person to whom the correspondence is addressed is unaware of the situation. However, to keep a record of the blind carbon copy, the secretary types this on her file copy of the letter:

```
    bcc: R. L. Marney
```

The Second Page

Sometimes letters cannot be completed on one page and must be carried over to a second and, sometimes, even to a third page. For all pages after the initial letterhead, plain paper of equal quality should be used. The same left and right margins should be used, with about a one-inch margin at the top. Also, one of the following headings should be used, with four spaces between the heading and the first line of the letter. For example:

```
    Mr. S. R. Emerson        2        December 1, 19--
    Mr. S. R. Emerson
    Page 2
    December 1, 19--
```

At least three lines must be carried over to the second page. However, at least two lines of a new paragraph must be left at the bottom of the first page. Never hyphenate the last word at the bottom of the first page.

If a third page is necessary, leave the same margin at the bottom of the second page that you left at the bottom of the first page.

The Envelope

The information contained in the envelope address should be identical with that in the inside address. Since the postal authorities prefer that the name of the state be typed on a line by itself, this should be done whenever possible. Some points to remember about envelope addresses are:

1. Avoid two-line addresses. This can be done by typing the state on a separate line.

```
Mr. William Anson
Beaver
Idaho
```

2. Double space three-line addresses; single space addresses containing more than three lines.

3. Type the attention line in the lower left corner of the envelope.

4. If the envelope does not contain a printed return address, be sure to type a return address in the upper left corner—not on the back of the flap.

5. No part of the address should be typed in the upper half of the envelope space. Center the address slightly below the center of the envelope.

```
CENTRAL STATIONERY COMPANY
1213 WEST BROADWAY
YONKERS 14, NEW YORK




                        Allen Paper Company
                        44 Simpson Place
                        Des Moines 8
                        Iowa


ATTENTION: R. E. Beck
```

A correctly addressed envelope.

Learning Exercises

1 The following were selected from actual business letters in the files of a large company. Many of these letter parts contain errors. Rewrite *each*, making corrections wherever necessary.

a Dr. Robert Allen, M. D.
b Dear Prof. Nestor
c September 5th, 19—
d My Dear Agnes,
    h William Smithers
       1463 5 Ave.
       Saint Louis, 8, Mo.
    i Velvet-Smooth Ribbon Company
       83 Lynn Avenue
       New York 7, New York

e Yours very cordially,
f Yours truly,
g Mr. John Bennett
   Beaver, Idaho

    caps Attention: Mr. R. E. Ellwood

    Dear Sir:
    Gentlemen:

2 Write the salutation and complimentary closing for each of the following.

a A letter to a good customer, Edwin Murray, congratulating him on his recent marriage
b A letter to a firm composed exclusively of women, inquiring about a new product it has just distributed
c A letter to a Senator from your state, asking him to support a bill before Congress in which you are particularly interested
d A letter to a friend, inviting him to a party
e A letter to your doctor, thanking him for his recent attention when you were ill

3 Cut five pieces of paper to correct envelope size. Making whatever corrections are necessary in each of the following, prepare the envelope as it should appear.

a Ferris Window Co.
  1283 State St.
  Charlotte, 6 N. C.
b John J. Cotter
  249 Todd Ave.
  New London, Connecticut
    d Cochran Furniture Company
      High Point, North Car.
      Attention/J. M. Smith
    e Doctor L. E. Douglas, M. D.
      Professional Building
      1313 Cary Street
      Norman—2—Oklahoma

c Mr. Thomas Fallon
  President
  Ames Desk Company
  1411 Main St.
  Bridgeport, 11, Conn.

Vocabulary and Spelling Refreshers

1 **Words Often Confused.** Pursue, peruse; populous, populace.

2 **Making Nouns.** Give the nouns that may be formed from the following verbs.

  a compel **c** govern **e** unite
  b refuse **d** annoy **f** denounce

3 **Spell the Words That Are Pronounced—**

  a trāl **c** sēs **e** mōd
  b vāg **d** kwit **f** sēz

Communication in Action: *Attention!*

Robert Micheau speaks quite frequently at staff meetings. He notes, however, that he does not receive the attention of all those present— they look very bored. Suggest ways in which Robert can get the attention he should have when he is speaking. What might he be doing wrong? Outline a plan of action whereby Robert might improve his speaking techniques.

UNIT  41

Style of the Business Letter

Which Style to Use?

Just as we select clothing to suit our individual preferences, we may also select the style of letter we would like to use. Bob Aldrich prefers a shirt with button cuffs, but Bill Williams prefers french cuffs that require the use of cuff links. Both cuff styles are appropriate, but Bob and Bill have different preferences. Life is much more interesting because we are able to make choices, because we all do not have to conform to the same style of dress, the same mode of behavior, or the same beliefs.

Just as Bob and Bill may choose from among several types of shirt cuffs, so too the writer of business letters may select any one of several letter styles to use for his letters. Therefore, you should be familiar with all the commonly used letter styles so that you will be prepared either to use the one that may already have been selected by your firm or, if you are given an opportunity to select the style of your choice, to select the one that best suits you.

There are several business letter styles from which to choose. No business standard exists by which one can point to a letter style and say that it is incorrect. Not any one of these styles is *the* correct one. All of them are used, some more widely than others. Letter make-up is entirely a matter of personal taste and preference. The letter styles used by business today include:

1. Blocked (also called modified block)
2. Semiblocked (also called modified block with indented paragraphs)
3. Indented
4. Full-blocked (also called block or extreme block)
5. Hanging-indented (also called inverted paragraphs)
6. Simplified

Each letter style is discussed briefly below and illustrated in later pages.

Blocked Letters. The blocked style is widely used in business today. The date line ends at the right margin, or it may be centered. Each line of the inside address begins at the left margin. Paragraphs are not indented but begin at the left margin. The complimentary closing, typed signature, and title lines are generally blocked near the center of the page.

Semiblocked Letters. The semiblocked letter is exactly like the blocked letter, with one exception. In the semiblocked letter, paragraphs are indented—usually five spaces.

Indented Letters. The indented style is perhaps the oldest letter form, for it was the style principally used when all letters were handwritten. Each line of the inside address is usually indented five spaces and looks like this:

```
Mr. Clark A. Appleton
    823 Island Road
        Ellsworth
            North Dakota
```

All paragraphs are indented five spaces. (You may, however, work in an office where the preferred practice is to indent ten spaces. If so, follow that preference.) The typed company signature is indented five spaces to the right of the complimentary closing, and the typed signature and/or title of the signer is indented five spaces to the right of the complimentary closing or of the company name.

```
        Very truly yours,                   Sincerely yours,

        MORTGAGE LOAN COMPANY
                                               Credit Manager

              Adam Johnson
```

The most appropriate use for the indented style is in handwritten letters, where the parts will stand out more clearly if they are indented. This style is not recommended for typewritten letters because of the time required to indent.

Full-Blocked Letters. The full-blocked letter saves typing time since the typist does not need to use the tabular key. Each line, including the date line, starts at the left margin. The body of the letter is single spaced, and paragraphs are separated by double spacing. (If the body of the letter were double spaced, there would be no way to distinguish between paragraphs.) Open punctuation is recommended with this letter style because it is in keeping with the timesaving feature of the full-blocked letter.

Hanging-Indented Letters. The hanging-indented style is not widely used except in advertising or sales letters, to attract the reader's attention. The inside address is blocked. And the first line of each paragraph is brought out to the left margin, but the remaining lines in the paragraph are indented—usually five spaces.

Simplified Letters. The National Office Management Association has been promoting the use of what it calls the NOMA Simplified letter. In this style, the full-blocked form is used, with the following changes:

1. Omit the salutation and the complimentary closing.
2. Set up the subject and the typed signature lines in capital letters.
3. Indent five spaces for listings, except when numbers (1, 2, 3) or letters (a, b, c) precede the items. When numbers or letters are used, the listings are blocked. No periods are used after such numbers or letters.

The chief purpose of using the NOMA Simplified letter is to save typing time. The claim is made that in a 96-word letter, 10.7 per cent of typing time is saved. However, you must remember that efficiency is not the sole criterion for selecting a letter style—custom and tradition still carry a great deal of weight. In addition, some writers consider this form a little cold and impersonal.

SONIN PRODUCTS, INC.

BEACON FALLS, CONN.

May 5, 19--

Mr. James Connors
346 Royal Avenue
Windsor, Illinois

Dear Mr. Connors:

Thank you for your letter of May 2 and for your check for $125. We have credited the check to your account.

Your arrangement for payment of the balance of your acccount is perfectly satisfactory. Therefore, we have marked your account to indicate that the next payment will be made on August 1.

We are always pleased to co-operate with our customers and are delighted that we could be of service to you at this time.

Cordially yours,

James Abernathy
Credit Manager

JA:nd

A blocked letter.

FISHER BEARING MANUFACTURING COMPANY

222 FRANKLIN AVENUE   ELLSWORTH, CALIFORNIA   ELLSWORTH 5-5001

January 15, 19--

Mr. Robert J. Leary
Prescott Manufacturing Company
935 Hamilton Drive
Winchester 4, Iowa

Dear Mr. Leary

Subject: Statement of January 2

We are sorry that the statement we sent you on January 2
was not correct. We found that your account had not been
credited for the ten bearings you returned on December 16.

We wish to correct this mistake as quickly as possible.
Therefore, we are enclosing a credit memorandum for the
merchandise returned, as well as a revised statement for
the month. We cannot justify this error and hope that you
will excuse it.

We wonder whether we might impose on you for a favor.
We should like to survey our customers to see what they
think of the service we render them. Will you participate?
Please return the enclosed questionnaire, being frank in
answering each question.

Yours very truly

FISHER BEARING MANUFACTURING CO.

Ralph E. Fisher
Treasurer and Credit Manager

PTR

Enc. 3

On the left, a semi-
blocked letter. On the
right, a full-blocked
letter.

ECR–TV CORPORATION

PRESTON PLAZA   CANTON 1, OHIO

April 15, 19--

Miss Gloria Erdman
1536 Noble Road
Canton 3, Ohio

Dear Miss Erdman:

Thank you for your very kind letter of congratulations
concerning our telecast of the "Great Books" series. We
have shown each participant your letter, and they all
appreciate your kind comments and suggestions.

We have decided to try out your suggestion to eliminate
the audience applause at the conclusion of each participant's
presentation. We hope that this change will add to your
viewing pleasure and to the pleasure of our other viewers
as well.

We value your interest in our program and believe that
you might like to attend our next telecast. Therefore, we
are enclosing two tickets for the April 21 session. We
hope you will enjoy using them.

Cordially yours,

Jack Ames
Program Director

Enclosure

JA-PE

MARTIN

AIRCRAFT CORPORATION
Long Island · New York

July 8, 19--

Mr. John L. Sullivan
Personnel Director
Wisconsin Dairy Company
Madison 12, Wisconsin

REFERENCE FOR MR. A. R. LOWE

Mr. Lowe was employed by us as assistant controller from May 6, 1949, to July 8, 1953. We found him:

1. An excellent accountant

2. An industrious, dependable, efficient worker

3. An employee whose relationships with his co-workers were completely satisfactory

Mr. Lowe resigned voluntarily because he wished to work in a city where he would have an opportunity to attend evening classes, thereby furthering his education.

We are happy to recommend him to you.

James W. Ellis

JAMES W. ELLIS--PERSONNEL DIRECTOR

JE:an

A hanging-indented letter on the left. On the right, a Simplified letter.

RIVER & EVEY

9 PARK AVENUE, NEW YORK 16

April 5, 19--

Mrs. Harold A. Williams
4675 Country Drive
Rye, New York

Dear Mrs. Williams:

As the owner of a brand new home, you probably would like some help with your decorating problems. Are you familiar with our complete decorating service?

We have a complete staff of experts in every phase of home decoration. Our floor- and window-covering specialist has available hundreds of samples of rugs and drapery materials from which you may select the colors and textures best suited to each room in your home. Our paint and paper specialist will bring to you samples of our many paint and paper patterns that you can try out right in your own home. Our furniture specialist will show you the many beautiful pieces of furniture for every room in your home that we have available in stock. In addition, she has photographs of thousands of other pieces of furniture that may be ordered from the leading manufacturers in the country. And to give you the kind of kitchen you have always dreamed of, our kitchen expert will help you plan a kitchen that is both practical and a joy to work in.

All these experts are at your service--and at no charge to you! They will help you with your selections; order those items we do not carry in stock; and arrange to have your painting and papering done, your draperies made and hung, your rugs laid, your equipment installed, and your furniture properly placed. They can help make home decorating a pleasure for you.

Won't you telephone us at RYrnak 4-3798, Ext. 13, today? Our home decorating experts can then begin working for you tomorrow.

Very cordially yours,
(Miss) Helen Laramee
Head Decorator

HL:ev

Style Accessories

As important as the letter style are the accessories used. These refer to:

1. The stationery
2. The letterhead design
3. The quality of the typewriting

These three accessories and the letter style together contribute to the first impression made by a letter upon its reader. Therefore, considerable care should be taken to see that they create the desired effect.

Stationery. Good-quality stationery is a good investment. It gives the impression that the firm attaches importance to its correspondence, while poor-quality paper may give the reader the opposite impression of the company sending it. Thus, cheap stationery may endanger prestige.

The size, color, and quality of stationery selected is a matter of individual preference. Frequently, the type of business the firm is engaged in will determine what size, color, and weight of paper should be selected. For most uses, white bond paper is preferred, although a conservative tinted paper would be acceptable in some instances. For example, a florist or gardening supply house may wish to use light-green stationery instead of white. A bond paper with some rag content is of better quality than very lightweight paper with no rag content. Again, however, there are circumstances when lightweight paper may be very appropriate. Certainly, if a firm sends multipage letters or many airmail letters, a thinner paper may be more appropriate, and more economical, than a heavier paper. The second sheet should be of plain paper that matches the letterhead stationery in quality and color.

Envelopes should also be of the same quality and color as the letterhead paper.

Carbon copies for the files are typed on inexpensive paper that is firm enough to give a good carbon impression. Either onionskin or a lightweight yellow second-sheet paper is generally used.

Letterhead Design. The letterhead expresses the artistic taste of the firm using it. The letterhead information should appear in a space of not more than $2\frac{1}{2}$ inches. It should be set up in a style suitable to the company and to the nature of its business. It should be designed by a professional designer, just as clothes and automobiles are. Advertising agencies and some stationers employ professional designers who can design a letterhead that will be most appropriate for a particular business.

Typewriting Quality. The quality of the typescript is governed by three factors: the evenness of touch, the typewriter ribbon, and the neatness of erasures. An even touch will produce typescript of even density—not a sprinkling of light and dark letters across the page. The use of an electric typewriter guarantees consistent density of typescript, since each key strikes the paper with the same force regardless of how much or how little pressure is used by the typist. Cleaning the type keys regularly will prevent dirt-filled letters from marring the appearance of a letter.

A good-quality ribbon should be used, one that is suited to the kind of typewriter you use—standard, noiseless, or electric. When the ribbon has been used so frequently that there is insufficient ink to produce clear typescript, the ribbon should be replaced. Ribbons come in a variety of colors, but black is the color most frequently used. If tinted stationery is used, a matching colored ribbon might be used. For example, the florist who uses a very light-green stationery may prefer to use a dark-green ribbon.

Of course, erasures should be kept to a minimum. And, if there are noticeable erasures, the letter should be rewritten. Some erasures are usually necessary, but these should be made so neatly that they are not noticeable. Good erasing tools are as essential to the typist as a good set of tools is to the carpenter or the plumber. A good typing eraser and a typing shield that will prevent the smudging of adjacent letters help to make the erasing process easier and neater.

Learning Exercises

1 If your employer permitted you to use whatever letter style you preferred, which would you use? Why?

2 Design a letterhead that you think would be suitable for a local business of your choice.

3 Bring to class as many samples of letterheads as you are able to obtain (try to get at least five). Be prepared to discuss the appropriateness of each.

4 Using a separate sheet of paper for each, set up a letter in each of the following letter styles:

    a Indented style   **d** Hanging-indented
    b Full-blocked   **e** Blocked
    c NOMA Simplified

Use the inside address and company name and signature given below. Select an appropriate salutation and complimentary closing. In place of the body of the letter, use lines to represent the copy; as:

_____

_____.

_____

_____.

Inside Address	*Company Name and Signature*
Mr. William B. Rogers	Marvelon Rug Company
1732 Keats Road	James A. Burkett
Washington 8, D. C.	Vice-President

5 Visit two different firms in your community. Find out what letter style each uses and why. If possible, obtain a sample of the letterhead, envelopes, and second-sheet paper each uses. These will be used to prepare a bulletin board display.

Vocabulary and Spelling Refreshers

1 **Words Often Confused.** Attendance, attendants; intolerable, intolerant.

2 **Choose Your Word.** Which of the words that follow each of these sentences is nearest in meaning to the italicized word in the sentence?

   a Louise's remark *insinuated* that the guest had invited herself to the luncheon. (1) denied, (2) hinted, (3) claimed, (4) questioned.

   b My aunt *deprecates* the loss of the little niceties of life. (1) undervalues, (2) appreciates, (3) regretfully disapproves, (4) misses.

   c My grandfather *ceded* some of his land for the new college campus. (1) assigned, (2) sold, (3) purchased, (4) mortgaged.

   d Because of Mr. Clark's many *commitments* for December, he regrets that he will be unable to address your group on the 15th. (1) trips, (2) financial burdens, (3) commissions, (4) promises to do various things.

Letters That Ask and Transmit / 353

e We are weary of those *perennial* jokes about mothers-in-law. (1) stupid, (2) far-fetched, (3) unceasing, (4) tasteless.

3 **Which Is Right?** Which spelling in the following groups is correct?

a vegitable, vegatabel, vegetable
b relavant, relevant, revelent
c occasionally, ocassionaly, ocasionally
d chaufeur, shoffeur, chauffeur
e Philipino, Filipino, Fillippino

Communication in Action: *Learn to Like It*

Give a one-minute talk on the following statement by King George V of England. Use dramatic examples if you can.

"The secret of finding happiness is not to do what you like to do, but to learn to like what you have to do."

Section 2 Everyday Business Letters

UNIT 42

Letters That Ask and Transmit

Everyday Business Letters

How many times have you seen a TV giveaway advertisement and made a mental note to send for the item being offered. Or you may often run across advertisements in magazines that invite you either to clip a coupon or to write a short letter or postal card asking for a booklet or a sample. Perhaps you frequently write R.S.V.P. letters (letters that say you will or will not accept) in response to invitations to attend important functions.

In every business many such letters must be written—letters in which the writer may make a simple request, send for something, confirm an appointment, acknowledge receipt of something, or express thanks for a favor. Because for you—and for the businessman—these letters are very common rather than special, this type of correspondence is best classified as *everyday*. Writing everyday letters does not require a great deal of literary talent—they are usually quite simple to write—yet this does not mean that everyday letters are not important.

As a beginner in business, you will write many everyday letters. In fact, most of the letters you write are likely to fall in the *everyday* category. Some will be written on your own initiative, and others will be suggested by your employer. You should not look upon everyday letters as routine, however. No letter is actually routine, if the word *routine* suggests that the letter does not warrant your best writing effort. Regardless of a letter's purpose or length, every letter requires careful planning and thoughtful writing in order to do the job intended.

Everyday letters may be divided into three groups—*transmitting* letters, *asking* letters, and *answering* letters.

Characteristics of Asking Letters

In writing a letter that makes a request, you must ask yourself this all-important question: What kind of letter would *I* like to receive if I were being asked for something? You would probably want the writer to be as *brief* as possible—to avoid wasting your time trying to determine what he wants. On the other hand, you would want the writer to give you *complete* information so that you won't need to write him for more details. And you would probably expect the writer to be *courteous* and *tactful*—no "do-it-or-else" demands.

While these characteristics are applicable to any kind of business letter, they are especially important in asking letters—particularly when you want a favorable response to a request that will benefit you.

Asking Letters Should Be Brief. Simple, everyday asking letters should be brief—not cluttered with unnecessary detail. Too many details waste the reader's time and confuse him as to what the writer wants. Consider the following letter:

Gentlemen:
Last Monday when I was shopping with my best friend, Myrtle Frobosch—she is really not my best friend, although I like her very

much—we saw some of the cutest blue kitchen curtains in your store. You know, the ones that have a panoramic picture effect across the top border—Monterrey, Mexico, I think, and the most cunning tie-backs. Myrtle preferred the peach ones and I liked the red ones. But then our kitchens are not the same color. Besides, I never did like peach. It has no distinction — no splash, you know.

What I really want to know is, may I exchange the red curtains I bought for the blue ones? The price is $8.75, and they are called Fiber Mist.

Sincerely yours,

Ridiculous? Of course. This letter is an adaptation of one that appeared on the joke page of a national magazine some years ago. The letter serves to illustrate the pitfall into which many writers fall: overstating the situation. Some people are inclined to ramble in a simple letter. You have already seen that the entire first paragraph in this letter could have been omitted—with much better results!

Look at the following letter. Note that this letter says what needs to be said—no more, no less—then stops.

> Gentlemen:
>
> I should like to subscribe to Life Magazine. A money order for $13.50, the special two-year subscription rate, is enclosed.
>
> Please send the magazine to me at my home: Miss Patricia Ann Hammert, 814 Kensington Street, Duluth 7, Minnesota.
>
> Very truly yours,

Asking Letters Should Be Complete. In striving for brevity, the writer should not overlook the fact that he must give complete information. Business firms often receive letters that contain no address (and frequently the writers of such letters are the most vocal about the poor correspondence habits of the firm to which they have written!). Besides the address, other important information may be lacking, too. Suppose you were the reservation clerk of the hotel that received the following letter written by a beginning stenographer asking for a hotel reservation for her boss. Could you make the necessary reservation?

> Gentlemen:
>
> Please reserve a room in your hotel for May 15.

While this letter certainly passes the brevity test, it is lacking in sufficient information. What questions need to be answered before an intelligent reply can be given by the hotel? Of course, the hotel needs to know the name of the person who is to occupy the room. If there are other persons in the party, their names should be given, too. Does the guest want a single room or a double room? What time will he arrive? (Rooms are usually not held after 6 p.m. unless the person making the reservation asks that it be held "for late arrival.") The hotel will also want to know how long the guest plans to stay. Other information that might be given—although it is not always essential—is the guest's preference for a room location, the price he expects to pay, and any special services he may expect—if any of these things are especially important to him.

Here is the letter a superior secretary would have written:

Gentlemen:

   Please reserve a single room for Mr. Harold Mansett, treasurer of our Company, for the evening of May 15.

   Mr. Mansett will be arriving about 7:30 p.m., so please hold the reservation for late arrival. Mr. Mansett prefers a room facing Lake Michigan.

   Kindly confirm this reservation.

                                   Very truly yours,

If Mr. Mansett has other preferences that his secretary knows about, she will, of course, make them known to the hotel.

Asking Letters Should Be Tactful and Courteous. Pleasant words like "thank you," "please," "grateful," and "appreciate" will do more to make the reader want to go out of his way to help you than will a brusque demand. Here are some typical *beginnings* for effective asking letters:

May I please . . . .
I should be grateful if you will . . . .
I should appreciate having . . . .
Will you please . . . .
Please send me . . . .

Following are typical *endings* for effective asking letters:

I am certain we can count on your co-operation.
I shall appreciate this help.
I should welcome your suggestions.
We shall be grateful for this special service.

When Should Reasons Be Given? When stating a reason will help the reader to give you better service, then your letter should state the reason for your request. For instance:

> Dear Mr. Parker:
>
> Last week you gave a set of records, "Typing to Music," to a group attending your press conference on new discoveries in typewriting self-instruction. Unfortunately, I was not able to be at that conference; but I would very much like to have a set of the records. Several of our employees are brushing up on their typewriting, and I have an idea that records such as these would be very beneficial to them. At least, I should like to listen to the records and prepare a descriptive write-up for our personnel bulletin.
>
> I shall be grateful, Mr. Parker, if you can arrange to send me these records. Incidentally, I understand the press conference was most successful; and I regret that I had to miss it.
>
> Cordially yours,

If the request is obvious, and the reader is *expected* to grant it without question, there is no need to explain the reasons. For example:

> Gentlemen:
>
> Please send me the free reprint, "New Dimensions in Stereo Sound," that you offered on last night's Frank Morrison TV program.
>
> Thank you.
>
> Very truly yours,

Typical Asking Letters

Examples of various types of asking letters are illustrated on the following pages. Here are specific suggestions for writing letters of this type:

1. When asking for something, you should write to a particular individual, if possible, rather than to a company. If you do not know the name of the person, you can help to speed the handling of your request by indicating the department you think will handle the matter. For example, if your letter concerns employment, you would address the Personnel Department; if it concerns an order, you would address the Sales Department; if it concerns advertising or customer relations, you would probably address the Public Relations Department or the Advertising Department.

Above all, be sure you have spelled all names correctly and have written them exactly as the addressee prefers to have them written.

2. Be sure that *you* are clear in your own mind as to what you want to know. You are then much more likely to make your request clear to the reader.

3. "Thank you" is always in good taste, but you should not thank someone in advance, with "Thank you in advance" or, worse still, "Thanking you in advance."

4. Do not make unnecessary work for the reader by asking for information that you could have obtained from reference books or other sources available to you.

5. If the reply is to be a special favor, a stamped, self-addressed envelope should be enclosed.

Here are some examples of typical asking letters. Notice how these letters carry out the suggestions made for writing such letters.

For Information

```
Gentlemen:

     Would you please give me the name of your dealer
in the Bridgeport area? We are interested in getting
estimates on water-softening equipment and supplies for
our Fairfield plant.

     We shall appreciate having this information as
soon as possible.
                              Very truly yours,
```

For Literature or a Free Service

```
Gentlemen:

     Please send me a copy of "Beauty Magic for Modern
Homemakers" advertised in yesterday's Herald Examiner.
I am also interested in a booklet you published several
months ago, which I recently saw at a friend's home--
"Make Your Own Rug." Do you have a copy to send me?

     I have learned a great deal about home decoration
from your various publications; and I, as well as my
friends, appreciate this wonderful service.

                              Sincerely yours,
```

Often a postal card will serve as well as a letter in making routine inquiries; in fact, many companies prefer them. For instance:

```
Gentlemen:

     Please send me "Filing Secrets," the booklet
advertised in this month's Modern Methods magazine.

     Thank you.
                              Sincerely yours,
```

Ordering a Product or a Service. Most business firms of medium and large size use a purchase order form when ordering goods. Such a form centralizes in the hands of one department the responsibility for ordering merchandise and helps to eliminate the possibility of any Tom, Dick, or Harry's ordering goods on his own initiative. Too, a purchase order form is quicker to prepare than a letter.

Orders may also be placed on an order blank supplied by the company from which goods are being bought. A number of small companies use these order forms.

A third way of ordering merchandise, used widely in small companies, is by means of letters and postal cards.

In preparing order letters, accuracy is extremely important. Figures and items must be checked and rechecked. To make an order letter easier to read and to check, the smart stenographer places each order item on a separate line. For instance:

```
Gentlemen:

     Please send us hand stamps as follows:

Quantity                    Item
    2          No. 613 B (PAID)
    4          No. 721 X (Company name to be:
                 ARNESON NOVELTIES, INC.)
    1          No. 41 (Name: HORACE T. ARMENTIER)
    1          No. 41 (Name: J. FRIEDA CUFFNEY)

     Our check for $28.80 is enclosed. May we have
these stamps by September 18. We have an urgent need
for them at that time.

               Very truly yours,
```

Requesting Appointments. In business, customary practice is to make appointments by telephone or letter when you wish to call on an executive at his office. Of course, if the appointment is local, the use of the telephone is quicker and less expensive. Out-of-town appointments are often made by letter.

```
Dear Mr. Jackson:

     I am planning to spend the day in Fort Wayne on
April 14 and should like very much to talk with you or
one of your associates while I am there. We are setting
up a wage-incentive program in our organization, and I
have been told that you have a very effective plan at
Hoffman.

     Would you find 10 a.m. on the 14th a convenient
time to see me? An hour of your time should be suffi-
cient and would mean a great deal to me.

               Cordially yours,
```

Asking Special Favors. Still another type of asking letter that often must be written is one requesting a special favor. Such a letter is usually a little more difficult to write than those already discussed, for here you are asking a person to do something he may not have expected to do. In business, customers are expected to write for catalogues or to make appointments. Sometimes, however, a businessman receives a request that is a little out of the ordinary.

Of course, these letters must contain the same characteristics as any other asking letters. However, they must have an added "something"—an appeal that will make the reader want to grant this special favor. In the letter below, can you find this special "something"?

> Dear Mr. Gardner:
>
> The Neosho Chapter of the NSA is having its annual Boss-Secretary Night on Thursday, November 18. We should like very much to have you as our guest speaker.
>
> Our members and their bosses (we expect about 80 people in all) have expressed a particular interest in hearing a lively talk on "Better Letters." We are especially interested in having our bosses hear something about what the secretary can do to help her employer with his communications problems. Our program calls for a forty-minute presentation from the speaker; but you may take a little more or a little less time, as you wish. Probably you know that this night is the highlight of our year's meetings and, while it has a serious purpose, is usually on the "lighter" side.
>
> Several of us enjoyed your very interesting article in the August issue of Your Girl Friday magazine. In fact, you can build your speech along the very same lines, if you wish.
>
> I hope you can accept this invitation, Mr. Gardner. If you can, I will write you again giving you all the details—time, place, and complete program plans.
>
> Cordially yours,

Transmitting Letters

A check, a money order, or an important business paper sent by mail should always be accompanied by a letter. A letter helps to identify what is being sent so that the recipient knows exactly what you *intended* to send. The letter also provides a valuable record for future reference. When remittances or business papers are accompanied by a letter, the carbon copy answers the question: "I wonder whether I sent that salary survey to Johnson as I promised?" or "How many copies of the Mayberry agreement did I send to Lawford and Hines?"

New York Life Insurance Company

51 MADISON AVENUE, NEW YORK 10, N. Y.

POLICY

52 063 566

MATURITY DATE

8/6/59

FACE AMOUNT OF POLICY

$1,000

CURRENT DIVIDEND

$6.43

TERMINATION DIVIDEND

$7.50

DIVIDEND DEPOSITS

none

AMOUNT OF CHECK

$1,013.93

POLICY

1958 DIVIDEND

We are pleased to enclose our check for the amount indicated at left. Your policy matured on the date shown and the check represents the face value of the policy plus accredited dividends.

If you have any questions about this, let us know, won't you? It will be a pleasure to be of service to you.

HOMETOWN GENERAL OFFICE

Courtesy New York Life Insurance Company

Printed forms like this one make it possible for a business to process great numbers of letters a day. Individual details are easily inserted on the typewriter and, because they are grouped, are available to the reader at a glance.

Transmitting letters should:

1. Identify *what* is being sent and *how many* (if money, the *amount*)
2. Specify any action necessary on the part of the recipient
3. If transmitting money, identify the purpose for which the money is to be used—to apply on account, in payment of a

certain invoice number, for services rendered, or for purchases
made

Note the following example.

Dear Mr. Rencroft:

    Enclosed are the original and one copy of the con-
tract for your manuscript, "A Boy's Story of the War
Between the States." Please sign both copies, return
the original to me, and retain the carbon.

    The review of your manuscript by Bosley Carruthers
was extremely complimentary. As you know, our target
date for publication is October 15. I'll be in touch
with you when editing begins.

                    Sincerely yours,

Learning Exercises

1 In a magazine or a newspaper, find an advertisement offering a
free pamphlet or booklet that you might like to have. Clip the advertisement. Then write a letter requesting the booklet or pamphlet
and attach the advertisement to your letter. After your letter has
been returned to you by your teacher, you may actually send for the
booklet or pamphlet.

2 Write a letter to Mr. William Gregory, personnel manager for
the Tyler Manufacturing Company, 1328 Robin Street, Canton 11,
Ohio, requesting an appointment to discuss job opportunities in his
firm.

3 Write a letter to a hotel in a place you would like to visit this
summer, making the necessary reservations for all members of your
family.

4 Assume that you work for Mr. Kenneth Fremont, a lawyer who
has a small office in a rural community, and that you need to order
some supplies from your nearest stationer, the Wadley Stationery
Company, 14 Hamilton Street, Fort Anne, Iowa. One of the salesmen, William Andrews, usually handles your order. You need the
following items: 12 boxes of paper clips, 2 bottles of permanent blue
ink, 6 reams of white bond paper, 6 black typewriter ribbons, and
1 ream of onionskin paper. Write the order letter.

Vocabulary and Spelling Refreshers

1 **Words Often Confused.** Elicit, illicit; key, quay.

2 **Are These Statements Truthful?**

a A possessive is never written without an apostrophe.
b Two singular nouns connected by *and* used as the subject of a sentence require a plural verb.
c Synonyms are words that have exactly the same meaning.
d The prefixes *counter* and *contra* impart the meaning of "against" to a word.
e The same expression may be written sometimes as two words and sometimes as a hyphenated word.

3 **When "e's" Are Needed.** In which of the following words should an *e* appear in the blank space?

a sens__ble   **c** judg__ment   **e** griev__ance
b notic__able   **d** courag__ous   **f** liv__liness

Communication in Action: *Eager Beaver*

You have been on your job for three weeks. Every morning you are at your desk a few minutes before starting time, and you return promptly from lunch. The others in your office usually do not settle down at their desks until 15 minutes past the hour. Your popularity is suffering, and you've heard yourself referred to as the "eager beaver." Today you were embarrassed when your supervisor said to the entire staff, "I wish all of you were as conscientious as [you] about starting to work on time." What should you do? Discuss.

UNIT 43

Letters That Answer — Acknowledgments

Suppose at Christmas an aunt sends you a check for $20, for which you are very grateful. You can use the money! You would be ungracious, wouldn't you, if you did not write her a letter of thanks? In fact, you probably would not let many days elapse before getting the letter in the mail—while the thought was fresh in your mind.

A customary business practice—and always very good business—is to acknowledge by letter any money or business papers received, favors granted, appointments made, and agreements reached orally. The first reason for writing letters of acknowledgment is that writing such letters is the courteous thing to do. A letter from you acknowledging receipt of something or confirming something tells the recipient that he need not worry—you have received safely what he sent.

A second, and equally important, reason for writing acknowledgment letters is to avoid misunderstandings or mistakes. If you have received an order and will make shipment as soon as possible, the customer will want to know. If he does not hear from you, he may assume that you did not receive the order; or he may wonder what you are doing about it if you did. A written acknowledgment assures him that you have the merchandise in the quantity he requests and that you are going to fill his order quickly.

A third reason for writing acknowledgment letters is to provide a record. Records are the memory of business. You would not want to trust your own memory as to the date on which you promised delivery of an order; the carbon copy of your acknowledgment, therefore, provides the information.

Acknowledging the Receipt of Money

In every instance, the receipt of money should be acknowledged. Remember these special rules when writing letters acknowledging the receipt of money:

1. Express thanks for the money, even though payment may be long overdue.

2. Be sure to mention the amount that is received. This letter provides a valuable record for the future. Rather than just saying, "Thank you for your check," say, "Thank you for your check for $88.95."

3. When appropriate, mention how the money is to be used—to apply on account, to be used as full payment for merchandise or services, or whatever the purpose of payment.

4. If you can think of something pleasant to say to the sender, doing so is always in good taste. "We appreciate your prompt payment," or "Doing business with you is always a pleasure," or "I hope you will enjoy your new Visi-View floor lamp."

Following are typical examples of letters acknowledging the receipt of money.

To Apply on Account

Dear Mr. Roundtree:

Thank you for your check for $16.75. This amount has been applied to your account, leaving a balance of $33.50.

We appreciate your promptness in making your payments, Mr. Roundtree; and we are always pleased to serve you.

Sincerely yours,

For Merchandise

Dear Miss Krasna:

I appreciate your being so prompt in sending the money order for $10 in payment of the 20 copies of "Adventures in Sound" that we sent you recently.

I hope that you and your fellow members of the Listeners Club are deriving much enjoyment from these materials. We have already mailed over 15,000 copies of the booklet.

Cordially yours,

Acknowledging Business Papers

Important business papers—such as contracts, securities (stocks and bonds), notes, insurance policies, bids, and the like—should always be acknowledged promptly, since they are often just as important as money. In writing such letters, be specific as to just what was received and the number. If any action is required on the part of the recipient, this should be made clear in your letter. Here is an example:

Dear Mr. Horn:

I received today two copies of the signed contracts for servicing our office machines for the coming year. Thank you.

As indicated by our agreement, we shall expect service to begin on September 1. I hope this will be the beginning of a mutually profitable association.

Cordially yours,

Acknowledging Orders

Orders for merchandise should always be acknowledged. Form letters or postal cards may be used for this purpose in larger companies; however, individually written letters are much more effective. Customers especially appreciate the "extra touch" of a personal letter.

Hotel Riviera

Chicago 19, Illinois

June 10, 19--

Your request for a single room with shower for April 13 and 14 is acknowledged. Your rate will be as close to $12 per day as possible. All reservations are held until 6 p.m. unless otherwise requested.

Thank you.

Louis Guaglia

Manager

Many hotels use printed form letters or cards like this one to acknowledge reservations.

When a customer places an order, he is interested primarily in one thing: when will he get the merchandise? This information should be supplied early in the letter. A formula for writing acknowledgments of orders usually includes the following:

1. A "thank you" for the business received
2. A statement concerning the time and method of delivery
3. Any special instructions
4. An offer to be of further service

Notice how this formula is put to work in the following letter:

Dear Mr. Cartright:

Thank you

Thank you for your order for a Power House Outboard Motor. The motor is being shipped today by prepaid freight.

When shipped and how

Special instructions

Would you do us--and yourself--a favor? Just as soon as your Power House "37 Plus" arrives, please fill out the card attached to the motor and mail it back to us. Receipt of this card will tell us that the motor arrived in good condition and will also serve as a record of our special two-year guarantee.

Offer to be of further help

I hope you have many happy hours of motor boating. Let us know how we can help you further. Incidentally, Neptune Marina, in Norfolk, carries a complete line of parts and accessories for your Power House "37 Plus."

Sincerely,

Carl Forslund, inc. *QUAINT AMERICAN®
  ✱ REGISTERED TRADE MARK

122 E. FULTON ST.
Grand Rapids 2, Michigan
June 23, 19--
Wednesday morning

At last, a cool day

Good Morning, Mr. Zimner:

   We are indeed pleased to receive your
order. Enclosed is your acknowledgment,
C-24710. Will you please keep this handy so
that you may refer to your order number in
case of need.

   Thanks very much for shopping with us,
Mr. Zimner. We hope you'll call on us again.

Sincerely,

Carl Forslund

CARL FORSLUND

CF:pb

Courtesy Carl Forslund, Inc.

Some companies prefer to acknowledge orders individually. Note
the informality of the date line in this letter.

Confirming Appointments, Orders, and Agreements

Orders and agreements made orally (in person or by telephone)
or by telegraph should be confirmed by letter. Appointments made
by telephone, at meetings, or over the luncheon table are usually
confirmed in writing. If the persons making an appointment by telephone are at their desks, a note on the desk calendar is usually a
sufficient reminder. Otherwise, the safest policy is to follow up with
a letter. By providing a written record of appointments, agreements,
and orders, letters perform a most valuable function in business.

Confirming an Appointment

Dear Bob:

   I was glad to see you at Rotary last Tuesday, and I enjoyed chatting with you about some of the problems of handling volume correspondence.

   You promised to tell me more about how you have improved correspondence procedures in your offices and suggested that we get together for lunch on the 16th. Unless I hear from you, I shall assume that our appointment is still "on." I'll plan to arrive at your office about 12:15.

                              Sincerely,

Confirming a Telephoned Order

Dear Mr. Hughes:

   Thank you for telephoning us your order this morning. We are shipping by book post today the following:

       250 copies of "Better English," by Corwin
       100 copies of "Reading Faster," by Walsh and
           Kirkley
       175 copies of "Your Speech Shows," by Morey

   We appreciate your placing this order with us and hope these books will be fast sellers for you. Our invoice will follow in a few days.

                              Yours very truly,

Confirming a Telegram

Dear Mr. Hackett:

   This morning I wired you as follows:

   CAN SUPPLY 100 VISI-GIDE LOOSE-LEAF BINDERS IN
   WESTERN SADDLE LEATHER BY OCTOBER 16 AT $3.70 EACH.

   We shall be happy to have your order, Mr. Hackett. Would you please let us know by October 1 whether you wish us to ship these binders. Our stock is low, and the demand is heavy right now.

   We have this same binder in imitation morocco in either blue or black. The price of the morocco binders is $3 each.

                              Cordially yours,

Learning Exercises

1 The Walters Manufacturing Company follows the policy of acknowledging every order and every payment it receives from customers. On the other hand, the Reliable Desk Company does not believe in acknowledging the receipt of orders or payments because this procedure adds to the cost of doing business. Which company has the better policy? Why?

2 Rewrite this poor letter that was written to acknowledge an order from a hardware store for 100 waste cans, 25 hammers, and 75 boxes of ½-inch screws.

> Dear Sirs:
>
> Thanks for your recent order. We're glad to have your business.
>
> We will send your order just as soon as we can.
>
> Begging to remain,
>
> Yours Truly,

3 Assume that the Raymond Book Company must send you $10 for some supplies ordered from your firm.

> **a** Should they send cash? How should they send the money? Why?
>
> **b** Should they send a letter to accompany the payment? Why, or why not?
>
> **c** Write an appropriate letter of acknowledgment to the Raymond Book Company, 110 Hudson Place, Chicago 52, Illinois.

4 Following the formula suggested for writing acknowledgments of orders, write a letter to the Wells Manufacturing Company in reply to their order of May 15 for 20 Rite Time clocks.

5 Assume you are employed by the Gay Vacationer Hotel at Myrtle Beach, South Carolina, and receive a request for a double room with bath for Mr. and Mrs. William Jeffers for the week of July 6. On a form like that illustrated on page 366, fill in the information necessary to acknowledge the reservation.

Vocabulary and Spelling Refreshers

1 **Words Often Confused.** Fiscal, physical; holy, holey, wholly, holly.

2 Accented Syllables. In the following words, which syllable should receive the primary accent?

a dis-charge´   d pos´-i-tive-ly
b ap´-pli-ca-ble   e su-per´-flu-ous
c ex´-qui-site   f ac-cli´-mate

3 Making Contractions. If you wished to contract the following words and phrases, what forms would you use?

a national   d I will   g does not
b we are   e they have   h it is
c I shall   f continued   i department

Communication in Action: *Responding to Gossip*

Today in the lunchroom an office gossip made several uncomplimentary remarks about your supervisor—her poor taste in clothes, her general appearance, and her bad disposition. Six other employees at your table heard the remarks, and everyone looked at you as if he expected a retort. What would you say, if anything?

UNIT 44

Letters That Answer—Responses

Pick up a copy of any popular magazine or newspaper, and you will see pages and pages of advertising. Some advertisements gently nudge you; some are persuasively convincing; some try to shock or startle you. All hope to do one thing: build interest in the advertiser's product or service. Your favorite radio or TV program is probably paid for by advertisers who hope to convince you that you will benefit from choosing their products. Advertising is all around us. Every business aims to develop friendly interest and attitudes on the part of the buying public, because businessmen know that these are the things of which customers are made.

Everyone employed in business is expected to do his part in making friends—the retail salesperson, the deliveryman, the switchboard operator, the receptionist, and the letter writer. One of the main purposes of advertising is to get readers and listeners so interested that they make a trip to their dealer for a closer look at the product or write a letter asking for more information. The businessman, therefore, welcomes customer inquiries about products or services as opportunities to make friends—to sell. What a waste of the advertiser's money if, on this "last mile" between casual interest and customer action, someone failed to do his share in getting the desired results!

Form Letters of Response

Letters of response are among the most important—and are probably the most numerous—of those written in business. They are written in response to coupons that have been clipped from advertisements or containers; in response to return cards that accompany sales letters; in response to orders; or in response to requests for information or favors.

Suppose you work for a company that recently began to distribute a new sports car—the Porpoise. Advertisements have appeared in national magazines, in newspapers, and on nationwide radio and TV. The company is delighted, of course, when letters start coming in, because these letters are proof that the company's ads are attracting interest that can eventually turn into sales. Such questions as the following arrive:

> What is the name of a dealer near Midville? What models are available? What is the cost of a convertible? How many miles a gallon can I expect from this car? How long will it take to get delivery? What colors are available? Are parts easy to get? Where can I get more information?

If such inquiries are large in number, the company will probably develop a form letter (either printed or typed on an automatic typewriter) that may be sent to all those who write. In addition, in order to save money as well as to present the product in the most favorable light, the company will probably prepare special booklets in which photographs, descriptive information, and sales advantages are included. Often, a printed letter is the first page of such a booklet. In any event, some type of letter of response is needed; merely to mail a booklet would not be wise. And the more personal the letter can be made to look, the more successful it will be.

Here, for example, is a form letter sent in response to coupons, cards, and general inquiries about the Porpoise Sports Car:

Dear Miss Pope:

Naturally, we are delighted that you are interested in the Porpoise. Thank you for giving us a chance to tell you more about this fine new sports car that has just received Sports Car National's "Best Newcomer of the Year" Award.

The enclosed booklet, "Continental Contemporary," was prepared especially for you and others like you whose taste runs to the bold, the daring, the unusual—the discriminating. Only in the Porpoise does the true sports car lover find all his dreams come true!

May I suggest that you visit your dealer _____ to test drive the Porpoise "Flamenco" or the Porpoise "Matador." Only when you get behind the wheel of the Porpoise can you fully appreciate the sensational advantages of this little masterpiece. You will be thrilled with its daring lines, its sauciness, its verve.

Of course, you are always welcome to write us for any additional information you may need.

Cordially yours,

Note that space is provided on the first line of the third paragraph for the appropriate dealer's name. In addition to form letters, fill-in cards are often used to answer inquiries.

Individual Response Letters

Many inquiries, of course, cannot be answered by a form letter or a postal card. And even if they could, some companies consider inquiries important enough to deserve individually written replies. Note the following inquiry and response:

Gentlemen:

Please send me a copy of "Connecticut Kitchens," advertised in Restful Living magazine. I am interested in remodeling my kitchen in Western Pine.

While I am at it, I am also thinking of having my kitchen floor recovered. Do you have any suggestions for colors that would blend with pine?

Sincerely yours,

Dear Mrs. Larkin:

We are delighted to send you a copy of "Connecticut Kitchens" as advertised in Restful Living magazine.

Western Pine is a versatile and highly practical paneling for your kitchen, Mrs. Larkin. It will blend beautifully with just about any color or decorating scheme you choose. A striking example of color harmony is illustrated on page 9 of the enclosed booklet. The floor is in Brownstone Red, a new color that is very popular with decorators. The paneling is finished in Puritan Pine "Minwax." Several other possibilities are shown on pages 3, 4, 7, and 12.

May I suggest that you visit your Western Pine dealer in Williamsport to ask him to help you plan your kitchen. Many Connecticut Kitchen dealers offer a free decorating service to customers.

Thank you for writing.

Sincerely yours,

Rules for Writing Letters of Response

You have already seen that letters of response are essentially sales letters, and the rules for writing them are the same as those for other good will letters. There are, however, four rules that are worth special mention here.

Be Prompt. There is nothing that says so well, "We are interested in you" as a prompt reply to an inquiry. Some companies insist that all mail be acknowledged within forty-eight hours after it is received; others set twenty-four hours as the maximum length of time before a reply is sent. Even if a reply cannot be given to a customer's inquiry, the inquiry at least should be acknowledged and the writer told when he will have his answer. For example:

Dear Mrs. Quigley:

I appreciate very much your letter asking about the proper way to care for leather-topped furniture.

Because we have had so many similar requests from lovers of Paxon's leather-topped originals, we have prepared a special booklet giving complete instructions. It is called "Leather Magic," and we expect delivery of this booklet from the printer within ten days.

You may be sure, Mrs. Quigley, that a copy of "Leather Magic" will be sent to you just as soon as possible. In the meantime, I think you will be interested in Roger Wilton's newest creation--"Wide Open Spaces," the outdoor furniture of the year. It is being featured at Bampton's, in Berkeley, this month.

Sincerely yours,

Some letters must be referred to another person or to a branch office in another city. If the reply is likely to be delayed beyond forty-eight hours, the person who originally received the letter should acknowledge it, telling the customer how the request is being handled. For example:

```
Dear Mr. Phillips:

     Your request for information about delivery on the
new Electric Eye Hair Dryer has been referred to our
Atlanta district office. You see, Mr. Phillips, each
district office is supplied with a quota of this fast-
moving dryer. In some areas, dealers are well supplied;
in others, sales have run much higher than expected and
stocks are temporarily low.

     Mr. Mark Griffith, manager of our Atlanta office,
will write you within a few days telling you exactly
what the situation is in that area. In any event, I am
sure that you will not have to wait long for delivery
once your order is placed. Our factory is now operating
at full capacity. We are certain that you will find the
Electric Eye Hair Dryer worth waiting for!

                              Cordially yours,
```

After sending this letter to Mr. Phillips, the writer will attach a blind carbon copy of it to Mr. Phillips' original letter (or a photocopy) and send them to Mr. Griffith, the manager of the office in Atlanta. This will help Mr. Griffith attend to Mr. Phillips' request more quickly.

Be Helpful. Montgomery Ward and Company, in a special bulletin to its letter writers, once wrote, "When you are writing a letter to a Ward customer, remember—you are talking to your boss." For this reason, you should provide the customer with as much help as you think he will need. As you have seen, providing special printed information is one way to be helpful. Other special helps might include price lists, catalogues, samples, and the like. Most important of all, however, is a willingness on the part of the writer to "reach out" and find ways to be helpful. The little extras on the correspondent's part often mean the turning of a simple inquiry into a sale. Note the following:

```
Dear Mr. MacKenzie:

     I am sorry that we cannot help you. We do not
manufacture aluminum doors and storm windows. We make
only aluminum paneling for building construction.

                              Yours truly,
```

This letter isn't very helpful, is it? The thoughtful letter writer might have handled the situation in this manner:

> Dear Mr. MacKenzie:
>
> Thank you for writing to National Aluminum about aluminum doors and combination windows.
>
> No doubt, Mr. MacKenzie, you have confused us with another firm of a similar name. We manufacture only aluminum paneling for building construction. The organization to which your letter should be addressed is: National Home Aluminum Specialties, Inc., 7472 Jackson Boulevard, Memphis 18, Tennessee.
>
> Sincerely yours,
>
> P. S. You might be interested in the enclosed folder that describes our products.

Be Complete. When writing a letter of response, you should be certain that you have answered the inquirer's questions as fully as possible. If your company provides printed information that is sent to those who write, make sure it answers all the questions asked. Often, the customer will have a special problem not covered in the printed information. In this case, the letter might be written as follows:

> Dear Miss Holbrook:
>
> We are delighted to know that you are interested in the new Lektrawax Polisher. Most of the questions you raise are answered completely in the illustrated booklet enclosed. I hope you will read it carefully, noting the various models and the special features of each.
>
> As to your question about a trade-in allowance for your old polisher, may I suggest that you discuss this matter with your dealer in Des Moines--Younker's Department Store. Policies on trade-ins vary from store to store.
>
> Thank you for writing.
>
> Cordially yours,

In some cases where a form letter is used, a P. S. with the reply to the correspondent's special question may be individually typed at the bottom of the letter. For example:

> P. S. Because of the already low price of the Watkins office clock, we are unable to offer any special discounts for quantity purchases.

Be Courteous and Friendly. It costs nothing in money or time to be courteous and friendly when writing letters of response. Observe how the following letter is friendly, courteous, and sales-slanted:

Dear Miss Greene:

We are so pleased that you thought of Lowry's Town House for the annual "Secretary—Boss Night" of the Westbrook Chapter of the National Secretaries Association.

We have two excellent private dining rooms—the Plantation Room and the Garden Court. Each is decorated in a distinctive motif, and each is perfectly suited to a group such as yours. Many organizations hold their monthly and annual banquets in these delightful rooms. Each banquet room seats 100 to 125 persons and is equipped with a loudspeaker system, a piano, and a movie projector and screen. The Plantation Room also has a raised dais where the speaker's table may be placed. Both rooms are still available for May 10.

The decor of both the Plantation Room and the Garden Court assures you of delightful dining in an absolutely private atmosphere. Each is air-conditioned and sound-conditioned. As you know, Lowry's Town House has an excellent reputation for the finest meals and service. I am enclosing our banquet menu, featuring full-course dinners ranging from $3.50 to $5.

I should be happy to show you these two lovely dining rooms, Miss Greene, when it is convenient for you to visit Lowry's Town House. Would it be possible for you to have lunch here with me one day next week? Just telephone me at GRayson 7-2491.

May I urge you to make your reservations early. We do not know just how long these facilities will be available for the May 10 date, and we would like to have you with us.

Cordially yours,

The writing of answering letters may be a daily routine in many offices; but such letters should not be handled in a routine, mechanical fashion. They are very important because each person who writes to the firm is already interested in the product or service sold by the company. Firms spend thousands of advertising dollars each year just to create customer interest. So when interest is evidenced by an inquirer, be sure to capitalize on it by answering with a polished, sales-promoting letter.

Learning Exercises

1 Rewrite this poor letter written in answer to an inquiry.

Dear Dr. Brown,

Your letter of the 10th inst. received. Thanks for your interest in our pianoes.

We do not no what size you want, the type (upwrite, babygrand, spinnet) or the kind of wood. Please let us no.

When we recieve this info. we will send you full particulars. Trusting to here from you real soon, we are

Very Truly Yours

2 You are secretary of a fraternity or sorority. You receive an inquiry from a person interested in becoming a member, requesting information about how to join, how often the group meets, where it meets, what activities it has, and what the dues are. Write a letter to this person, giving all the information requested.

3 The Acme Insurance Company writes to the president of Atlantic College for a list of graduates so that the Company may solicit them for insurance. The policy of the College is not to release lists of graduates. Write an appropriate letter that denies the request but retains the good will of the correspondent.

4 Bring to class a letter you or a member of your family has received in response to an inquiry. Criticize it in relation to the qualities of a good reply letter as discussed in this unit.

5 Write an appropriate letter that could be sent to accompany a booklet, "How to Get the Most from Your Poli Movie Camera."

Vocabulary and Spelling Refreshers

1 **Words Often Confused.** Raise, raze, rays; costume, custom.

2 **Which Preposition?** Indicate the prepositions that should be used in the blank spaces in these sentences.

a My sister has a prejudice _____ mystery stories.
b *Dread* is synonymous _____ *fear.*
c The game was so exciting that I became completely oblivious _____ time.
d I am not at all satisfied _____ the results of the investigation.
e The supervisor does not approve _____ the behavior of the new typist.
f His property is adjacent _____ my father's.

3 Add an "e" at the End of —

A word meaning:	To result in a word meaning:
a Pertaining to or characteristic of mankind	Kind, merciful, tender
b Sung by a choir or chorus	A simple tune sung in unison
c Ethical	A courageous state of mind
d Melodious, harmonious	A social entertainment featuring music
e Characteristic of cities	Smoothly polite

Communication in Action: *Positive and Friendly*

Positive statements are more likely to win friends than negative ones. Rewrite the statements below to make them more friendly.

1. Really, Mrs. Jones, you can't blame us if you didn't follow the printed instructions included with each mower.

2. I'm sorry, but we can't make an adjustment unless you return the merchandise in a reasonable length of time.

UNIT 45

The Secretary's Responsibility for Correspondence

One of the most important responsibilities of the secretary and of other assistants to executives is handling correspondence. The busy executive depends on his secretary to receive, open, and sort incoming mail and to handle all the necessary details to get letters written and in the mail. Many secretaries spend over half their time working with correspondence. The ability to handle correspondence routines effectively is one of the qualities that distinguishes the private secretary from the stenographer.

This unit, however, is not intended just for those who expect to be secretaries. Other office workers—bookkeepers, clerks, stenographers, and typists—also have the responsibility for handling mail and, in some cases, for writing letters for their employers. Therefore, this material is valuable for all students aspiring to office jobs.

Routine for Incoming Correspondence

Most employers expect their secretaries to open and sort incoming mail. In smaller offices, the secretary may receive and distribute the mail for the entire organization. In a large company that has a central mailing room, letters are sorted by departments; and the receptionist or another employee within the department re-sorts and distributes mail—unopened—to the appropriate persons. The secretary's step-by-step procedure for handling incoming mail for her employer is as follows:

1. Letters marked "Personal" are separated from the rest of the mail. These personal letters should be delivered unopened.

2. Other letters are opened, preferably with a letter opener to avoid damage to the contents.

3. The envelope is examined carefully to make sure that any enclosures mentioned in the letter are included. If an enclosure is missing, this fact should be noted in the margin of the letter and initialed.

4. The letter should be checked to see that it contains the return address of the sender; if not, the envelope should be attached to the letter.

5. To be sure the envelope is empty before it is thrown away, it should be held to the light and carefully examined.

6. All incoming mail should be date-stamped. Note the date stamp on the letter on page 381. In many offices, the time element is so important that the hour, as well as the date, is stamped on incoming mail. An electric clock-dating machine is used in many large firms.

Reading the Mail. The secretary can often save time for her boss by reading the mail carefully before delivering it to him. Some employers prefer that the secretary underline the important points in each letter so that he may read it more quickly; also, these underlined passages serve as signals to him when he is dictating a reply. The secretary may also make marginal notations concerning action that has been taken. You will find examples of underlining and marginal notations on page 381. The secretary should also verify figures, dates, and computations in incoming mail. If previous letters or other documents will help the employer to understand what the letter is about, the secretary should attach them to the incoming letter.

An employer who has a large volume of correspondence may instruct his secretary to digest the important letters for quick reading. Such a digest (shown below) is especially helpful when the boss is away and a large volume of correspondence awaits him upon his return.

```
              DIGEST OF IMPORTANT MAIL

                   May 6-10, 19--

      The following items need your attention. All mail
    has been acknowledged. The item checked is urgent.

        May

         6   Mr. Gordon Fuller    Wants an appointment with
                                  you when you return.
         7   Memo from Credit     Want your recommendation
             Dept.                on several customers
                                  whose accounts are
                                  delinquent.
       ✓10   Mr. Leon Graves,     Very upset about not hav-
             Essex Mfg.           ing received his order.
```

Delivering Mail to the Employer. The mail should be placed on the employer's desk in order of importance. For example:

1. Telegrams (on top)
2. Mail marked "Personal" or of a personal nature
3. Regular first-class mail
4. Circulars and advertisements
5. Magazines and newspapers

If there is much traffic in the boss's office, place the letters in a manila folder so that they will not be seen by others. If there is a great volume of mail, the secretary may also separate the different types in different manila folders.

"To Write or Not to Write—"

Some executives appreciate having the routine mail answered by the secretary; others prefer to dictate every letter. The new office worker will soon learn his employer's preferences. If the employer has entrusted letter-writing responsibilities to you, he may indicate his wishes right on the incoming mail; or he may prefer that you tell him which letters you can answer. An executive secretary may write

Machine Foundry Company   SPring 5-6000

500 MADISON AVENUE
AKRON 10, OHIO

January 11, 19--

Mr. George Ames
Atlas Manufacturers
Cleveland 15, Ohio

Dear Mr. Ames:

 Thank you for your prompt attention to <u>our order</u> No. 16438 for ten lathes.

After uncrating the lathes, we found that the <u>set-up instructions were not included</u>. Would you be good enough to <u>send</u> us <u>ten copies</u> of set-up instructions for <u>X13-14-86</u> lathes. In addition, we should very much like to have your service supervisor <u>check our set-ups</u> when he is next in our vicinity. <u>When is he scheduled to be in this area?</u>

We know that we can count on your usual good service to handle these matters for us.

Very truly yours,

Howard Lawrence

HOWARD LAWRENCE

HL:TM

A letter that has been date-stamped, underlined, and annotated.

a rough-draft reply to routine correspondence, attaching it to the incoming letter before the employer has an opportunity to read it. Or she may simply make the notation "I will answer" on the incoming letter or tell her boss how she proposes to answer, thus: "I'll tell him you will be away on the 18th" or "Will send."

Even if the boss dictates all his correspondence, he may expect the secretary to "edit" his letters—that is, smooth out the writing style and correct the errors in grammar, punctuation, and computations. "This is about what I want to say—you 'fix it up' " is a direction often given to the secretary. But not all executives feel this way about correspondence. Some want every word, every comma, every paragraph to appear just as they dictated it—wrong though they may be. The best advice for the new secretary is to transcribe the boss's dictation just the way he gave it. If she discovers errors, she might tactfully say, "Mr. Jamison, don't you think it would be better if we itemized those directions in 1-2-3 order? They might be easier to follow." Gradually, the executive will trust his secretary to use her best judgment in "polishing up" his dictation—that is, if she can back up her suggestions with effective performance.

If the employer is in the office, he will probably prefer that letters composed by the secretary be written for his signature. This poses the question: "Should I write the letter as I believe it should be written, or do I write it the way I think he wants it?" As long as the secretary is writing *for her employer*, she must write the letter as she thinks *he* would write it. She should study the carbon copies of previous letters so that she can match his style as closely as possible.

Sometimes the employer will ask the secretary to sign his letters for him, in which case it is customary for her to place her initials immediately below the signature. Some employers, however, would rather the secretary "fake" his signature—especially when writing to people whom he does not know personally. Whichever procedure is followed is a matter of individual preference and often depends on how much the employer trusts his secretary and on how well she can match his signature.

Here is an example of a letter written by the secretary for her employer.

Dear Mr. Atkins:

Mr. Watson has asked me to acknowledge, with gratitude, the copy of "Fifty Years of Shipbuilding—the Story of Perkin-Bullmer." He was very pleased to have it.

I am sure you know that Mr. Watson has been very busy with the reorganization of the Danbury Ridge plant. During this month, he has been out of the office more than he has been in. I know he will want to write you just as soon as he has a "breather."

The book is beautifully illustrated and looks very interesting. I know Mr. Watson will enjoy reading it.

Very truly yours,

Linda Raglan

Linda Raglan
Secretary to Mr. Watson

Types of Letters Written for the Employer

The types of letters written most often by the secretary include: letters making reservations, asking letters, letters referring matters to others, thank-you and acknowledgment letters, letters about appointments, transmittal letters, and follow-up letters. You have been introduced to several of these already. Some are so important to the secretary that they will receive additional emphasis in this unit.

Making Reservations. In making hotel and travel reservations, either the employer's signature or the secretary's may be used. Refer to Unit 42 for additional information on writing letters making reservations.

For the Employer's Signature

Gentlemen:

  Please reserve a single room for me for July 8, 9, and 10. I shall be arriving about four o'clock on the 8th and will leave the morning of the 11th.

  I should like an outside room, with shower, at a rate not exceeding $10.

         Very truly yours,

Asking Letters. Asking letters may be written for the secretary's signature or for the employer's, depending on his preference. The message is only slightly different. For example:

For the Employer's Signature

Gentlemen:

  Last week I was on American Flight 614 from Chicago to St. Louis. During a conversation with me, the stewardess mentioned a kit of materials containing luggage stickers, maps, and a set of "Junior Pilot" wings that American gives to passengers with youngsters. When I deplaned, I forgot to pick up the kit. I think my nephew would enjoy having these souvenirs, since he is very much interested in planes.

  If you can possibly send me a kit, I would be very grateful--and you would make a five-year-old boy very happy!

         Sincerely yours,

For the Secretary's Signature

Gentlemen:

  Last week, Mr. Millard E. Watson was on American Flight 614 from Chicago to St. Louis. He meant to take

with him one of the kits containing luggage stickers,
maps, and a set of "Junior Pilot" wings when he deplaned but did not remember to do so.

Can you possibly send Mr. Watson one of these
kits? He very much wants to present it to his five-
year-old nephew, who is extremely interested in planes.
Both Mr. Watson and his nephew would be very grateful,
I am sure.

Very truly yours,

Letters Referring Matters to Others. The executive may not be able
to give personal attention to letters sent to him that are really
meant for someone else. In that case, the secretary nearly always
writes an acknowledgment letter for her own signature and attends
to any necessary follow-through with the other person. Here is an
example:

Dear Mrs. Blanford:

Thank you for writing about your article describing your recent sailing trip to Puerto Rico. It sounds
very interesting.

Our publication, Fleet Owner, is a magazine circulated to owners of fleets of trucks and buses for
commercial hauling and transportation. We do not feature articles of consumer interest and, of course, our
magazine is limited to land transportation.

There are several consumer magazines that feature
articles such as the one you describe. Two of the most
popular are The Yachtsman, 44 East 20th Street, and
Ahoy!, 688 Lexington Avenue, both in New York City.

Very truly yours,

Follow-Up Letters. The secretary is expected to follow up on correspondence for her employer. Enclosures mentioned in an incoming
letter may not have been included, the secretary's request for an
appointment for her boss may have gone unanswered, promised
materials may not have arrived, expected action may not have taken
place, and so on. Such letters are usually written by the secretary for
her own signature. Here are some examples:

Gentlemen:

In your letter of May 14, you mentioned that you
were sending us the deed to the Harper estate. However,
the deed was not included in the envelope.

Just as soon as we receive this deed, we shall be
able to complete the final arrangements for the transfer of title.

Very truly yours,

Dear Mr. Judson:

Will you be able to see Mr. Pickens when he is in
Wichita next week? He hoped to hear from you before he
left on a ten-day trip this morning. Since he did not,
he has asked me to inquire and let him have the information before he leaves Fort Wayne on Tuesday.

I expect to be in touch with Mr. Pickens by
telephone later this week. Could you wire me collect
telling me whether you can see him when he is in
Wichita?

Cordially yours,

While-the-Boss-Is-Away Letters

Whether the secretary writes letters for her employer or not, when
he is out of the office she is expected to acknowledge important
letters and explain any delays caused by his absence. While-the-
boss-is-away letters are usually brief, courteous, and noncommittal.
By *noncommittal* is meant that the secretary should be careful not
to reveal private company matters in her acknowledgments. Often,
this means not saying where the boss is or what business he is on.
She must also be careful not to express opinions that may be in
disagreement with those of her employer. For example, if she works
for a publisher and receives a magazine article in her boss's absence,
she would *not* say:

Thank you for sending us the article, "Ceramic
Magic." It is extremely good, and I know Miss Talbert
will want to publish it in the next issue of Busy Hands
magazine.

If her boss feels differently about the article, this letter will put
her (and him) in an embarrassing position. The noncommittal, but
courteous, letter the secretary might write is as follows:

Dear Mrs. Wolpert:

Thank you for your article, "Ceramic Magic,"
which you wish to have considered for publication in
an early issue of Busy Hands.

The editor, Miss Ida Talbert, is out of the office
on a short business trip. When she returns, you may be
sure that she will write you her reactions.

Sincerely yours,

Note that the secretary has said that Miss Talbert "is out of the
office on a short business trip." It is usually best not to reveal more
than this. Such information as "Miss Talbert is in Miami on vacation"
or "Miss Talbert is in Akron this week investigating a new printing

plant" would not be appropriate. The safest phrase, when in doubt, is: "Miss Talbert is out of the office this week."

Here is another example of tact and discretion used in writing a noncommittal letter for the employer:

> Dear Mr. Erskine:
>
>   While Mr. Stimson is out of the office, I want to acknowledge receipt of your bid on the Fullerton shopping area project and the report that accompanied it.
>
>   Shortly after Mr. Stimson returns (he is due back on August 12), I know he will get in touch with you.
>
>   Yours very truly,

When the employer is away and the correspondence cannot wait for his return, letters are often referred to another individual in the company. Before referring letters to another executive, the secretary must be sure that she has his permission, as well as that of her boss, to do so. Only urgent or highly important letters will usually deserve this action.

> Dear Mr. McGinnis:
>
>   Thank you for your letter of April 17 to Mr. Kent.
>
>   Mr. Kent will be out of the office for about two weeks, so I am referring your letter to our Sales Manager, Mr. T. J. Loring. You will be hearing from Mr. Loring just as soon as he has an opportunity to study your proposal.
>
>   Cordially yours,

Learning Exercises

1 The boss leaves the following handwritten letter for you to type. Make the necessary corrections and prepare a perfect typed copy.

Bill Jones, Mgr.
Essex Tire Corp.
St. Louis, 8, Mo.

Dear Bill;
*   Rec'd your letter and was glad to here from you, however, I'm sorry I can't see you next week. I'll be out of town on business the first part of the week the latter part I start my vacation.*

I'd like to talk over the matter of the increased Tire orders so perhaps you and ~~we~~ can get together over the luncheon table when I return. I'll ~~write~~ phone you when I get back and arrange an apointment.

Yours truly

2 Assume that your boss, Richard King, sales manager of King Furniture Co., is on a three-week vacation in Hawaii and that you receive the following letter from a very good customer on July 8. Your boss is not due back from his vacation until July 25. How would you handle the situation?

Dear Mr. King:

The fifteen bookcases we ordered arrived today. However, only one of these bookcases has glass doors. Our order No. 1653, dated June 2, definitely specified glass doors for all fifteen of the bookcases.

Since we need these bookcases for our sale beginning July 23, we are wondering what you can do about this situation. We are already overstocked with bookcases without doors, so we cannot use the additional ones that were sent to us by mistake.

We hope we will hear from you immediately regarding the action you are taking.

Very truly yours,

As Mr. King's secretary, write whatever letters you think necessary to take care of this problem.

3 Mr. King has been invited to be a guest at a luncheon meeting of the Civitan Club on July 14. Write the president, Mr. Wilson, explaining that Mr. King cannot attend; he will be in Chicago on business at that time.

4 In each of the following situations, indicate whether you think a secretary would be able to compose the letter or whether the boss should write it.

 a Your boss would like a sample copy of *The Executive's Monthly Magazine.*
 b A customer would like to have an extension of time to settle his account.

c A customer is having trouble with a machine purchased from your firm.

d Your boss would like to make a reservation for a single room at the Sheridan Hotel in Cleveland, Ohio, for May 5, 6, and 7.

e Your boss is sending a check for $10 to cover a year's subscription to *The Executive's Monthly Magazine*.

5 Write a letter for each of the above situations that you indicated the secretary should be able to handle.

Vocabulary and Spelling Refreshers

1 **Words Often Confused.** Extent, extant, extinct; collision, collusion.

2 **Are These Statements True?**

a A period always follows an abbreviation.

b Indirectly quoted remarks are not enclosed in quotation marks.

c *Come and* is considered illiterate for *come to.*

d In dividing words, you should never separate two-letter beginning syllables from the rest of the word.

e Nouns ending in *s* are always plural and require a plural form of verb.

3 **Those "shun" Endings.** To each of the following add the termination pronounced "shun."

a illustra_____   **c** electri_____   **e** coer_____

b provi_____   **d** repeti_____   **f** aver_____

Communication in Action: *I, Me, and My*

Personal conceit is often revealed by the overuse of personal pronouns such as *I, me,* and *my.* Eliminate as many references to self as you can in the following sentence: "I think my department would improve if I could arrange for three of my people to rearrange my furniture I have in my office."

Section 3   Letters for Problem Situations

UNIT   46

Psychology Applied to Problem Situations

Businessmen are faced with problem situations every day. Because of distances involved, many of these problems must be solved by letters. In some instances, a letter may completely solve the problem; at other times a letter may only help to alleviate it. And frequently a letter must say, "No, we cannot do anything to help you." Such a letter must make the recipient feel that the "No" is justifiable. The writer of business letters must be able to handle all types of problem situations tactfully, following his company's policies and at the same time making the customer feel satisfied with whatever action is taken.

Selling Your Point of View

This is an old rhyme often quoted by sales managers to teach new salesmen the basic art of selling:

"To sell John Smith what John Smith buys
You must see John Smith through John Smith's eyes."

What does this rhyme mean? Broadly, it means that, if you hope to sell a product to a customer, you must first put yourself in your customer's shoes. Try to look at things the way the customer looks at them. You wouldn't think of trying to sell Mr. Smith a hat by emphasizing its long-wearing qualities when he is interested only in how he will look in it. To sell Mr. Smith a hat, you must try to imagine how he thinks and why he thinks as he does.

Each business letter written for a problem situation requires all the skill in human relations and all the persuasive reasoning the writer can muster. Each requires the writer to imagine how he would react to the reply if he were in the other fellow's place. Anyone can tell a customer "where to get off." However, being able to express a point of view in such a way that the reader accepts it and is *still your friend* is a high art. Those are the three magic words: *still your friend.* As you write each letter in which you must break some unpleasant news or make an apology, ask yourself this question: Will he still be our friend after he reads this? Of course, it is sometimes impossible to keep friends when you have to tell them "No," regardless of how hard you try. But you must *assume* that you can.

Guides to Writing Letters for Problem Situations

Experience has shown that, by using the following suggestions for writing letters for problem situations, the writer has a better chance of having his point of view accepted.

Give Reasons. If a person knows *why* a request has been refused, he still may be disappointed; but he is not so resentful. Suppose you asked your father to let you use the car on Monday night; and he said simply, but perhaps explosively, "no!" How would you feel? You probably would not mutter and grumble in his presence, but you would as soon as you were out of range of his hearing.

Suppose, however, that he had said, "I'm sorry, but your mother and I need the car to visit your Aunt Sally, who is in the hospital in Ardway." What a difference this explanation makes—simply because now you know why you cannot use the car.

In business, resentment destroys good will. Every refusal, then, should be accompanied by a logical, convincing reason. This reason, of course, is usually the true reason, not an invented one. Consider the following illustrations of logical reasons for not granting requests:

> . . . Neither would it be fair to you if we made an exception in allowing another customer a discount to which he was not entitled.
> . . . so it would not be ethical to reveal information that we have pledged our distributors to keep confidential.
> . . . and, therefore, because so many of our employees were out ill during the epidemic, we are about ten days behind in filling our orders.
> . . . We are certain that you will see that you will save 3 per cent on each purchase if you continue buying on a cash basis rather than charging your purchases.
> . . . so it is only because we have so many articles on the same subject that we must return your manuscript to you.
> . . . Since we know that our customers would not want to buy merchandise that has already been used, we cannot accept returns on any phonograph records.

AMARILLO • BEAUMONT • CORPUS CHRISTI • DALLAS • EL PASO • FORT WORTH • HOUSTON • MIDLAND • WACO • WICHITA FALLS

Southwestern DRUG Corporation
FULL-LINE FULL-SERVICE WHOLESALE DRUGGISTS

P. O. BOX 6099
DALLAS 22, TEXAS

My five-year-old daughter

asked me this morning, "Daddy, who are we mad at today?"

First I told her it was "whom," and then I gave her a long list of names ... yours was included. But I explained to her that at this point we were only "play mad." You see, Kathy wants to go to California this year and visit Disneyland. I've been hearing about it since January. Well, her old man is unable to take his vacation now. He can't until Southwestern Drug's Christmas Trade Catalogue is "put to bed." And some of our good friends have not sent their catalogue page inserts to us.

Our deadline was July 8. Then we had a final deadline of July 15. For our "kissing cousin type" friends we shall have an absolutely final deadline of July 22. But that's it!

By July 22 we must receive your 3,500 inserts — measuring 8 1/2 x 11, trimmed — if we are to include them in the catalogue.

We both lose sales if your sheets don't arrive on time. Let's both of us try to prevent that.

Now, Kathy doesn't appreciate your problems and my problems. She just wants to go to Disneyland ... and in a hurry.

Drop me a note — today — and let me know when your sheets will arrive, please.

Best regards,

Fred E. Farr
Fred E. Farr, Director
Advertising and Sales Promotion

*distribution
with
"Sell-thru"*

Courtesy Southwestern Drug Corporation and The Dartnell Corporation

Chatty and original, this letter catches attention and gets quick results.

Know Company Policy. Company policy reflects the company's attitude toward its customers, its employees, and the public at large—in short, its policies are its rules for doing business. Major policies are sometimes put in writing in employee manuals—policies regarding credit, refunds, contributions to charitable organizations, discounts, purchasing procedures, personnel relations, and so on. Other policies are merely understood. When there is an established company policy, of course you must follow it. If your firm does not allow discounts after ten days, there is not very much you can do except refuse to allow such discounts when customers ask for them. Remember these five rules concerning interpreting company policy:

1. Be sure you have all the facts before you start to write.

2. Regardless of the answer you must give, always be courteous.

3. Never lose your temper, especially in writing.

4. Give reasons for your actions as tactfully as possible.

5. In the absence of established rules, do the thing that you honestly believe is best for your company.

Have the Right Attitude. It has been said that anyone who has the right attitude can compose a good letter, even though he may not be a good writer, and that, if a good writer has a sour attitude, it is impossible for him to write an effective letter. There is much truth in this statement.

What is the "right" attitude? It is looking at situations fairly. It is displaying genuine interest in what you are doing. And most important of all, it is *caring* about the results of your actions. To reflect the right attitude toward those to whom you write letters, you must believe firmly in your company and its policies; you must have faith in the ability and judgment of those who supervise you; you must know thoroughly and believe in your company's product or service; and you must want the company to succeed. If you have a "let-George-do-it" or a "why-should-I-worry?" attitude, you can hardly expect to handle correspondence for problem situations effectively. An indifferent attitude does not reflect genuine interest; it reflects selfish interest.

Avoid Negative Attitudes. Never write with a chip on your shoulder. To do so is to display a negative attitude for your company that may cost *them* money and *you* your job! Suppose you work for a mail order house and a customer writes requesting that she be allowed to return for credit a pile coat she bought recently. The coat is an inexpensive one—$68.95—and the customer writes complaining about its "matty fur" and "cheap look." The customer should know that she can't expect real fur at so low a price. A good fur coat costs hundreds, even thousands, of dollars. Besides, your catalogue description says that this is an economical coat made of a furlike fabric that will wear well if not steamed. Your company policy is not to accept wearing apparel for refund unless the garment is actually defective in workmanship. What will be your attitude as you start to write your reply? Will you be annoyed—and, what's worse, show it? If your attitude is one of anger or impatience, you are likely to say something like this:

```
Dear Mrs. Antonine:

    You claim that the pile coat you purchased from us
is of poor quality and does not measure up to your ex-
pectations. What do you expect from a $68.95 coat? I
```

refuse to believe that anyone could be so unreasonable
as to think he can buy a mink coat at such a ridicu-
lously low price. Besides, if you don't take care of
your coat, no wonder the fur has begun to mat! Surely,
you don't expect. . . .

There is no point in going on. The customer who received this
letter would become extremely annoyed after reading the very first
sentence. When she read the second sentence, she would be down-
right insulted. From then on, no matter what you say, you are not
going to "get through" to her; you have lost her attention and her
interest. Even though the customer is wrong and has no basis for
expecting an adjustment, the writer has not even made allowance
for the possibility that the customer simply doesn't know any better.
Arguing with a customer or insulting him hinders rather than helps;
it merely magnifies in the customer's mind the complaint he already
has against the company. In fact, the letter gives support to the
customer's belief that the company is not a good one to deal with!
He is lost forever as a customer of this company.

Now let's look at a reply that reflects the right attitude. The purpose of this letter is the same—the customer is wrong and the basic
policy will not change—but the letter goes about saying so in an
entirely different manner.

Dear Mrs. Antonine:

Thank you for writing us about the coat you purchased recently. We like our customers to be satisfied
with their purchases.

The "Storm Queen" is one of the finest deep-pile
coats that can be found anywhere at the low price of
$68.95. Of course, it is not fur; a fur coat would cost
at least several hundred dollars. The "Storm Queen"
was designed especially to combine the luxury of a
furlike fabric resembling mink with chic styling and
finished workmanship. While the "Storm Queen" is cut
from surprisingly good-quality fabric for an inexpensive garment, it was not intended to compare with
expensive furs. You will find a full description of the
coat on page 1184 of our Fall and Winter Catalogue. You
will also note in this description that our policy does
not permit us to accept the garment for credit.

Perhaps you have found that you would prefer a
fur coat after all, Mrs. Antonine. If this is the case,
I should like to call your attention to the fine fur
creations described on pages 1186 to 1192. These coats
are highly recommended, and I know you would be very
pleased with one of them.

Sincerely yours,

In order to accentuate the positive in writing letters for problem situations, take particular care to avoid negative words. Some of the negative words you should avoid are:

error	neglected	unfavorable
failure	poor	regret
displeasure	trouble	unsatisfactory
dissatisfied	unfortunately	

Learning Exercises

1 In each of the following situations, indicate in a written statement how you would say "No" and still retain the friendship of the person making the request.

  a Jim wants to borrow Bill's history textbook overnight, but Bill wants to use it tonight.

  b Jack already owes Tom 75 cents, and he asks to borrow another 25 cents from Tom.

  c Mary Jane is invited to a dance by Art; but she would rather go with Ed, who has also invited her.

  d Ken works in Pat's Record Shop on Saturdays. A customer wants to return a record because it is scratched. There is a conspicuous sign on the store wall saying: "Records may not be exchanged or returned. Examine them carefully before making your purchase."

2 In the following letter, indicate the negative words and attitudes that should be avoided.

Dear Mrs. Thompson:

    We were sorry to get your letter of complaint about the error in sending you the wrong set of dishes. Our order clerk failed to read the order ticket properly and made the mistake of thinking "Maxton" was "Marston."

    We will rectify this mistake if you let us know when it will be convenient for us to pick up the wrong set of dishes.

    Please accept our regrets. We hope we have not incurred your displeasure.

        Very truly yours,

3 Rewrite the letter in Exercise 2 as you think it should be written.

Vocabulary and Spelling Refreshers

1 **Words Often Confused.** Confidently, confidentially; lesser, lessor, lessee.

2 **Do They Make You Wince?** Some of these sentences contain crudities of expression. Spot them and indicate correct substitutions.

  a I'm bringing this mail down to Mr. West.
  b He inherited considerable from his aunt.
  c I can't hardly wait for tomorrow.
  d There lay the purse just where I had dropped it.
  e She hadn't ought to have done it.

3 **"Ei" or "Ie"?** Should *ei* or *ie* appear in the blank spaces in these sentences?

  a The w—rd case was very dec—ving because it w—ghed nearly 50 pounds, yet was only a little over a foot in h—ght.
  b Th—r large f—ld y—lds a var—ty of crops.
  c In old front—r towns on the prair—, n—ghbors often banded together for protection against f—rce animals.

Communication in Action: *A Shoplifter*

Merchandise has been disappearing from your counter, and the store detective tells you that there has been a flurry of shoplifting lately. Then today it happens. You can scarcely believe what you see—an attractive young woman stuffing into a shopping bag the blouse you have been showing her. You had just turned your back to wait on another customer. What would you say to the shoplifter? (Obviously you must delay her long enough to get the store detective.)

UNIT 47

Claim and Adjustment Letters

No matter how efficient a business tries to be, mistakes will happen. The customer may receive the wrong merchandise, invoices or statements that contain errors, slow service, or even discourteous treatment at the hands of employees. A letter in which a complaint is expressed, in which the customer indicates that he feels he has a claim against the company, is called a *claim letter*. The company for which you work will doubtless receive some claim letters; in turn, the company will have occasion to write claim letters to those from whom it buys. To promote the company's, and your own, best interests, you need to be familiar with claim situations and with the principles of writing effective claim letters.

The Nature of Claims

Customer claims generally deal with one of the following:

Merchandise—Orders incorrectly filled; unsatisfactory quality of merchandise; goods damaged or delayed in shipment

Amounts of Money—Errors in statements and invoices; misunderstandings regarding price or terms of payment

Service—Delays in filling orders or requests for service; improper treatment by employees; failure to follow up

The person writing a claim letter is interested in one thing: satisfaction. If the merchandise is faulty, he wants it replaced at no cost or inconvenience to him. If the service is poor, he wants an apology and assurance that service will improve; he may even want some compensation for the inconvenience caused him. If an error has been made, he wants it corrected. In order to get satisfaction, the claimant must present his case carefully and thoughtfully to the person he feels is at fault.

Suppose you ordered a lamp from a mail order house, specifying a light-green shade. When the lamp is delivered, you are disappointed to find that a pink shade was sent—and a pink shade simply will not do. You become quite upset and a little angry, asking yourself, "How could they make such a stupid mistake?"

How would you begin your letter? In the first place, you should not write the letter while you are angry. Cool off first. You can do a much more convincing job when you are calm and can see the situation in a reasonable light. The mistake was not intentional; mistakes never are. If your letter were written in anger, it might begin like this:

```
     It was certainly careless on somebody's part to
send me a pink lamp shade when I asked for a green one.
Don't your order clerks know how to read? I simply do
not understand . . . .
```

Such a letter would do more harm than good. After you had had time to think, you would be sorry you had written it. And you would surely get much more willing co-operation from the seller if you were courteous. You can imagine how much sympathy you would get from the order clerks with your insulting remarks! A letter like the following will accomplish your purpose and do it much more successfully:

> When I unpacked the new milk-glass lamp I received from you today, I was disappointed to find that you sent me a pink lamp shade instead of the green one specified in my order.
>
> Would you please send me immediately the green shade requested (Catalogue No. 21G1044) and tell me what to do with the pink one.
>
> I should appreciate your taking care of this matter as quickly as possible. I am expecting guests on April 10, and I should like to have the new lamp shade before that time.

Principles of Writing Claim Letters. The following basic principles should be used in writing all claim letters:

1. Explain carefully and tactfully what is wrong.

2. Include any details necessary to identify your claim—dates, catalogue numbers, styles, order numbers, and the like.

3. Indicate the loss or inconvenience you have suffered (if any), but don't exaggerate.

4. Explain, in general, what you believe the company should do about your claim; but don't be unreasonable in your request.

5. Avoid negative accusations or threats, such as "I demand," "I must insist," "you will have to," "unless you," "why can't you," etc.

Here is an example of a claim letter that follows these rules:

> Dear Mr. Valder:
>
> This morning I received your statement covering my purchases from March 16 to April 12. I note that I was not given credit for the 12 "Lycoming Beauty" rose bushes that I returned on March 1.
>
> I assume that there was no question about these rose bushes—they appeared to be dead, a fact that did not come to light at the time I accepted them from the driver. I gave them to your truck driver when he was here on March 1, and he left me a receipt for them. There has never been any difficulty in the past when I returned unsatisfactory merchandise in this manner.
>
> I am sending you my check for $317.20. You will note that I have deducted the amount of the 12 rose bushes that were returned—$24.60. If you need any further explanation, I know you will write me.

```
            The azaleas are real beauties this year, and I
       shall have to get a new supply when your driver makes
       his next trip to Lawrence. They are going very fast.
                         Very truly yours,
```

Remember, in writing claim letters you are likely to get better service, more consideration, and more satisfaction if you explain the situation calmly and in a reasonable manner. Do not jump to conclusions. Assume that the company to whom you are writing will accept your side of the story—not that they will be on the defensive. Usually, they will be on the defensive only if you are unreasonable.

Adjustment Letters

In writing adjustment letters, you are on the other side of the fence. Your customer has the claim and he writes *you*. He may be dissatisfied with your merchandise, your service, or your general efficiency. A good company welcomes customer comments because they afford an opportunity to remedy faults that may exist. It is your job to see that the customer receives fair treatment—fair to him, of course, but also fair to your company. Since adjustment letters sell satisfaction, they are really sales letters.

Most firms have established broad policies for making adjustments. Some are very generous and practice the motto, "The customer is always right." Others are not so eager to please the customer, especially if he is in the wrong. Even in the most generous organizations, there will be numerous occasions when claims cannot be granted. And regardless of the fact that established policies exist for most adjustment situations, there will always be exceptions. For example, it is not inconceivable that an old customer who has patronized a firm faithfully over the years will receive a little more consideration than a new customer who is merely shopping around for the best buy. Many factors enter into the decision as to whether or not an adjustment will be granted. Often there is simply no policy to cover an adjustment situation, and the letter writer must weigh all the evidence and do what he thinks is fairest to his customer and to his employer.

Principles of Writing Adjustment Letters. The writer of adjustment letters must, under all circumstances, use patience, tact, and diplomacy in his replies. The following four principles should always be observed in writing adjustment letters:

1. Answer promptly.
2. Show the customer that you understand his problem.

3. Tell the customer exactly what you are going to do about the problem.

4. Avoid negative words and accusations.

Reply Promptly. The longer a customer waits for a reply to his claim, the angrier he gets and the harder it is to soothe his ruffled feelings. Show the customer that he is important enough to warrant your immediate attention to his problems. For instance:

```
     "Right after I finished reading your letter of
June 10, I looked into the matter of . . . ."
     "We lost no time tracing the discrepancy in the
invoice you wrote about . . . ."
     "Good news! The lawn mowers arrived this morning,
and they are already on their way to you."
     "To make sure that there would be no slip-up this
time, I personally saw to it that your order . . . ."
     "Your letter arrived this morning, and we have
already started a tracer on your shipment."
```

Show Understanding. Do you know the word *empathy?* It means looking at a problem from the other fellow's point of view—seeing it as he does. Those who have claims to make want first of all to have someone understand why they feel as they do. Your letter will be more effective if it expresses empathy. For example:

```
     "We know how you feel about . . . ."
     "You are entirely right about . . . ."
     "Indeed, we can understand that . . . ."
     "Your point is well taken, and . . . ."
     "We ourselves have been in the same situation,
and . . . ."
     "Surely you have a right to feel that . . . ."
```

Be Exact. Tell the customer exactly what you are going to do about his claim. If you are in a position to grant it, say so immediately and describe how you are going about it. For instance:

```
     Our check for $16.04, which is a refund on Invoice
No. A 1428, will be sent to you this week . . . .
     Within a day or two you will have your new green
lamp shade to replace the pink one you received . . . .
     You have been given full credit for the eight dead
batteries, amounting to $73.15. While these batteries
were carefully inspected when they left our warehouse,
they . . . .
     We are pleased to replace the plastic hose on your
Royal Vacuum Cleaner with a new "Tite-Nit" hose made
```

of nylon. Several of our customers reported the same
difficulty with the plastic hose and . . . .

You are entirely right. The discount to which you
were entitled was not shown on your February statement. You may be sure, however, that . . . .

Even if you are not able to grant the claim, you should be exact
in telling the customer why; as:

We wish we could offer you an adjustment on this
clothing, but our inspection shows that the suit has
been worn several times and is soiled. You can understand, of course, that . . . .

Time slips by so fast that we can understand how
it happened that your May 8 check contained a discount
deduction of $12.70--although the 10-day discount
period had expired. Would you like to send us a check
for $12.70, or shall we add this amount to your next
statement?

Nothing would please us better than to accept your
"Jolly Jack" guitar for refund, but we are bound by
the terms of the guarantee that you received with your
instrument. If you check, you will find that the
guarantee mentions . . . .

Avoid Negatives. Negative words tend to put an unhappy claimant
in an even more irritable frame of mind. On the other hand, positive,
pleasant words help to take the edge off his irritation. In fact, you
should try to conclude your letter with a positive statement that will
build good will. In the following examples, notice the difference in
tone in the positive statements as compared with the negative ones.

Positive: Thank you for your helpful letter of June 3.
Negative: We have received your complaint of June 3.

Positive: We are so glad that you called our attention
to the late arrival of your order No. 4286.
Negative: We are sorry to hear of the unfortunate delay
in the delivery of your order No. 4286.

Positive: Thank you for the friendly suggestion made
in your letter of July 8.
Negative: Your July 8 criticism has been received.

Positive: We will check even more carefully than usual
all your future orders.
Negative: Please accept our apologies for sending you
unsatisfactory goods.

Positive: Our driver brought your parcel back to the
store because the house number was omitted
from the address.
Negative: Because of your failure to give us your house
number, our driver had to bring back the
parcel, thus delaying delivery for three days.

Classes of Adjustments. The writer of adjustment letters is faced with four different types of problems:

1. When the company for whom he works (the seller) is at fault
2. When the person making the claim is at fault
3. When the responsibility is divided between the seller and the customer
4. When a third party, such as the transportation company, is at fault

When the Seller Is at Fault. If you are the seller of goods or services and you are entirely at fault in an adjustment situation, you will usually, of course, grant the claim. And you should do so willingly. Just as you have greater respect for the person who readily admits his mistakes, the customer respects the company that cheerfully fulfills its responsibilities without quibbling about it. When you must grant a claim because it is your fault, follow an outline such as this:

1. Tell the customer the good news immediately—preferably in the first paragraph.

2. Explain how the mistake happened (if you have an explanation). Don't be afraid of embarrassment—it is folly to try to save face when you are unquestionably wrong.

3. Express appreciation to the customer for his understanding and assure him that you will do your best to see that he receives better treatment in the future.

Dear Mr. Lathan:

On Friday of this week, we will send you by parcel post, special handling, 200 "Cougar" pennants to replace those that were printed in white instead of yellow. There will be, of course, no charge for these.

I have tried to find out what caused the confusion, but I have no explanation—or excuse. The only possible reason I can offer is that two members of our production department were out ill last week, and we had to use inexperienced help for two or three days.

Please excuse us this time, Mr. Lathan. We can take a little solace from this situation: we have started a new training program for all those who are likely to be called into emergency service in the production department. We expect that this precaution will help us to give you better service.

You may dispose of the 200 pennants that you received. It is not necessary to return them to us. Thank you for giving us an opportunity to be of service to you.

Very truly yours,

When the Customer Is at Fault. In many instances, the customer's
request for an adjustment is not justifiable and his claim must be
refused. Of course, this fact must be established conclusively before
a letter is attempted. You cannot automatically *assume* that the
customer is wrong; therefore, all the facts should be obtained and
weighed carefully. "Make sure you are right, and then go ahead"
is good advice in writing letters of this type. Even though you know
you are right and the customer is wrong, however, this type of letter
is still one of the most difficult to write. Somehow you must convey
to the customer the idea that you are following the only course open
to you and that, as a reasonable person, he will agree with you.

Suppose a customer writes that he wishes to return for credit
several items of merchandise he purchased several months ago.
The reason he gives for his return is that the merchandise he received was not that which he specified in his order. Of course, you
are skeptical immediately. Why did he wait so long before reporting
the error to you? After looking up the order, you find that he did
receive the merchandise he asked for; he even paid the bill. You
conclude that he is merely trying to unload some stock that he can't
sell. In this particular case, you cannot accept the merchandise for
credit.

In writing the reply to this claim, follow an outline something like
this:

1. Thank the customer for writing you, restating the adjustment
he believes should be made.

2. Explain why it is not possible to grant the adjustment.

3. Offer helpful advice, if possible.

4. Assume that the customer accepts your position as fair, and
close the letter on a friendly note.

The letter might read:

Dear Mr. Krause:

Thank you for writing us about the "King Comfort"
hassocks that you wish to return for credit. Immediately after receiving your letter, I rechecked your
order of May 11. I found that your original order
specified 12 "King Comfort" hassocks in flamingo and 12
"King Comfort" hassocks in beige. The bill of lading
matches your order in every respect. In fact, you have
already paid the invoice for this shipment.

Under the circumstances, we cannot accept these
hassocks for credit. This particular line was discontinued by the manufacturer in July, and we are now
featuring "Royal Rest" hassocks. Several of our dealers, however, reported considerable success in moving
the "King Comfort" line. Premier Furniture, in Oceola,

found that one of the biggest sales features is that
the hassocks can be used with both indoor and outdoor
furniture. The plastic cover included with each hassock
makes this a really all-purpose item. Have you tried
running an ad on these hassocks in connection with your
summer furniture clearance sales? I think you will
find doing so profitable.

Several new items of furniture for fall have arrived. Particularly exciting is the new line of Radwick
Maple originals for every room in the house. Look over
the enclosed folder describing some of these authentic
period pieces. I think you will want to send us your
order; people everywhere are already talking about
Radwick. This line promises to be among the best sellers we have had in years.

Sincerely yours,

As explained previously, you will sometimes grant adjustments
even though the customer is clearly at fault. The risk of turning
down a good customer may be too great or the amount of the adjustment may be so small that refusing to make the adjustment
would be poor business. In such a case, you should take full advantage of the opportunity to "give in" gracefully and to build good
will. For example:

Dear Mr. Braun:

We'll be glad to make an adjustment on the invoice
you wrote us about in your letter of March 6. Would
you please return the invoice to us?

When we advertised the reprints of the article
"You Can't Automate People!," we mentioned that in
quantities of 1,000 the reprints could be purchased for
40 cents each; in less than 1,000 lots, the price is
50 cents each. In each case, these are actual costs to
us. However, I can see now that this was not entirely
clear in our advertisement; and I am happy to give you
the 40-cent price on the 100 you ordered. As soon as we
receive your invoice, we shall issue a new one in the
amount of $40.

Thank you for writing us. I hope you will be able
to make effective use of these reprints. The demand for
them has been exceedingly heavy.

Cordially yours,

When the Fault Is Divided. Occasionally, the seller and the customer share the responsibility for error. For example, the customer
may have misunderstood your policy because it was not stated
clearly or because the salesman calling on him gave him the wrong

impression. Of course, you should cheerfully acknowledge your error; at the same time, you may try to convince the customer that he shares some of the responsibility too.

> Dear Mrs. Baker:
>
>   I am pleased to write you about the high-fidelity Angel recording (Mendelssohn's "Elijah" by the Huddersfield Choral Society) that you returned recently.
>
>   Upon examination of the records, our inspectors found that Sides 1 and 2 were apparently played with a blunt needle. May I suggest that you examine the needle of your phonograph before playing any records. A record is only as good as the needle playing it.
>
>   I am sending you a replacement for the first record; the other two have been checked by our inspectors and are in excellent condition.
>
>   I am also enclosing a booklet describing the various needles recommended by Angel—available at any authorized Angel record dealer.
>
>   Very sincerely yours,

In the foregoing example, the customer may have been entirely to blame; but just where the responsibility lies is not clear. At any rate, note that the seller gives the customer the benefit of the doubt—in a gracious manner—but suggests that similar occurrences in the future will be the fault of the customer.

When a Third Party Is at Fault. Quite often the roots of a claim lie neither in the customer's nor in the seller's actions but in the carrier's. Since the carrier assumes responsibility for safe delivery of any shipment accepted, the customer's claim is usually against him rather than against the seller, who has a receipt showing that the merchandise was in good condition at the time it was released to the carrier. When a shipment arrives in a damaged condition or is "short," the company to whom the claim is made may do one of two things:

1. Take the responsibility for the adjustment, and make a claim against the carrier.

2. Suggest that the customer enter a claim with the carrier, since the matter is really between the buyer and the carrier.

Following is an example of a letter from a supplier to a dealer who received a badly damaged television set:

> Dear Mr. Lamar:
>
>   We are sending you today by Maywood Shippers a LaForge Crestwood television set to replace the one

damaged in shipment. I know you have a customer waiting for this set, and I wanted you to have it as soon as possible.

We are entering our claim against the Ohio Western Railroad for the set you received. Will you please leave this set in a convenient place until the inspectors from Ohio Western call on you.

Cordially yours,

Learning Exercises

1 The following letter of complaint was received by the Ace Radio-Television Company.

Gentlemen:

I recently purchased a Claridge High-Fidelity Phonograph from you. When it arrived, it was badly scratched. The tone is horrible and the playing arm squeaks. In addition, your repairman is not able to do anything with it. I just think it is cheap merchandise, which is probably all you carry. I should have known better than to buy anything from your "junk" shop.

Very truly yours,

a Criticize this letter, pointing out all its faults.
b Write the letter you think should be written in reply if the customer had a legitimate claim.

2 Suppose you had purchased a washing machine from the Albemarle Appliance Store and, after you used it four or five times, the washing machine broke down and required adjustment. You were billed $7.50 for the adjustment and felt that the charge was not justifiable since this was a new washer. You wrote to the store, and this is the letter you received in reply.

Dear Mr. Sinclair:

We are sorry that we cannot cancel the $7.50 charge for adjusting your Rex Washing Machine.

We have to pay our repairmen high salaries, and we must account for every call they make. Since the adjustment necessary was probably due to your overloading your washer, we feel that it was your fault, not ours. Therefore, why should we suffer the loss?

Yours very truly,

a How would you feel if you received this letter?

b What is wrong with the tone of the letter?

c Indicate several possible ways this claim might have been adjusted.

d Rewrite the letter so that it has the kind of tone you would like it to have.

3 A mirror you purchased from a factory in another city arrives with a large crack through the center of it. The mirror was well crated and marked "Glass—Handle with care."

a Write the letter making your claim.

b Compose the adjustment letter you would write if you were employed by the shipper, who found that the Ohio Railroad was at fault in transporting the mirror.

Vocabulary and Spelling Refreshers

1 **Words Often Confused.** Disposition, deposition; disprove, disapprove.

2 **Number, Please!** Substitute the correct forms for any incorrect styles of numbers in these sentences.

a The price range for this type of ranch house is $20,000–35,000.

b Please deliver my order to my home, 1,350 Broad Street, this city.

c In just five years this neighborhood has deteriorated tremendously.

d 450 catalogues were mailed yesterday.

e At three-fifteen the thermometer registered ninety-five degrees.

3 **Single or Double "l"?** Should one or two *l*'s be used in the blank spaces in these words?

a acce__erate

b appa__

c bu__etin

d inte__igent

e misce__aneous

f mo__asses

g Phi__ippines

h vani__a

Communication in Action: *Write as You Talk*

Saying something aloud before writing it helps to give naturalness to your expression. Rewrite the following paragraph as you would *say* it. See how much your writing can be improved.

"In accordance with your request of July 6, a check was made in your favor and mailed on that date. Failure to respond earlier was an oversight on the part of the accounting department. Measures have subsequently been taken to avoid such an occurrence in the future."

UNIT 48

Credit and Collection Letters

Hundreds of thousands of Americans enjoy many things today that they probably would not have if it were not for credit privileges. Perhaps the house you live in, the family automobile, your television set, and much of your clothing were purchased on credit. A conservative estimate reveals that more than 75 per cent of all business in the United States is transacted on credit. The housewife buys merchandise on credit from the retail store; the retail store purchased its stock on credit from a wholesaler; the wholesaler, from the factory; and the factory purchased its raw materials from various suppliers—also on credit. The chain is almost endless. And the use of credit continues to grow. Many Americans travel, dine, and obtain hotel accommodations on a credit basis merely by producing a convenient credit card.

Even though millions of dollars' worth of business is done on credit each year, the losses from bad debts are surprisingly small. Most businessmen estimate that, of their total charge accounts, less than 1 per cent will be uncollectible. One reason for this comparatively small ratio of loss is that credit privileges are not granted in a hit-or-miss fashion. Before businessmen grant credit, they make reasonably sure that they will be paid for the goods they sell; each prospective charge-account customer is investigated carefully before credit is extended to him. Another reason for the small ratio of loss is, of course, that most people are fundamentally honest.

Credit Letters

A person wishing to establish credit will usually go to the store for an interview with a member of the credit department or write or telephone for a credit application form. Such an application is illustrated below.

Courtesy Carl Forslund, Inc.

A credit application form for an individual.

When the store receives the applicant's credit application, the credit manager immediately begins to investigate the references that have been supplied. In some cases, he will merely ask for a credit investigation by the local Retail Credit Bureau of which he is a member. Or, he may write or call the stores that have been listed by the applicant as places where he has previously bought on credit. Usually, these reference letters are form letters, such as:

Gentlemen:

Mr. Gordon Rodgers, of 1010 Franklin Street, Hampton, has requested credit privileges from us and has given your firm as a reference.

We should very much appreciate your answering the following questions about____Mr. Rodgers____:

1. How long has he had an account with you? _____

2. Was there a maximum amount allowed? _____ If so, how much? _____

3. Did he make payments according to your terms? _____

4. Does the applicant still owe you? _____ If so, how much? _____

5. Do you consider him:

_____ An excellent credit risk
_____ An average credit risk
_____ A poor credit risk

A self-addressed, stamped envelope is enclosed.

Very truly yours,

Letters Granting Credit. If the decision regarding an applicant's request for credit is favorable, the letter writer faces one of his most pleasant writing tasks—that of telling the customer the welcome news. The following outline may be used as a guide in writing letters granting credit:

1. Welcome the customer, expressing your wish for a pleasant association.

2. Describe special privileges to which he is entitled.

3. Explain the terms of payment.

4. Encourage him to use his new charge account and offer any special assistance.

Dear Mrs. Larkin:

We take great pleasure in opening a charge account at Capwell's in your name. I feel sure that this will be the beginning of a long and mutually pleasant association.

As a charge customer, you will enjoy many privileges at Capwell's. For instance, our charge customers receive advance notices of special sales, so that they may take advantage of wonderful bargains before they are offered to the public at large. Charge customers, too, are entitled to free gift wrapping on any purchase of $1.50 or more. Your account plate is good at our Terrace Restaurant, at our Calorie-Watcher's Bar, and in our Book Rental Department. Use your plate for anything and everything!

On the first of each month, you will receive an itemized statement of your purchases made through the

25th day of the preceding month; purchases made after
the 25th appear on the following month's bill. Remittances are expected by the 10th.

I hope you will make regular use of your charge
account. Remember, everyone at Capwell's is dedicated
to the slogan that is taken from the first three
letters of our name--CAP: "Capwell's Always Pleases."
Let us know if we ever fail to measure up to it.

Sincerely yours,

Many stores notify acceptance of applications for credit by a
printed announcement card.

Letter Refusing Credit. If the credit manager determines from the
information he has gathered that a credit applicant is a poor risk,
he will have to write a letter turning down the request. No letter is
more difficult to write. Regardless of what is said, the writer is, in
effect, telling the customer that he does not warrant the store's faith.
Of course, a letter refusing credit must be very tactful. Remember,
you want the customer to continue buying from you on a cash basis.

Some credit men believe that you should not come right out and
tell the applicant that he is being refused credit. They feel that such
an uncomplimentary statement violates the trust and confidence of
those who supplied information about the applicant. Therefore, they
hide behind generalities, hoping the applicant will come to the store
in person to discuss the matter. Such a noncommittal letter follows:

Dear Mr. Peterson:

Your desire to open a charge account at Young's is
a real compliment.

On the basis of the information we have received
regarding your credit standing, we feel that we cannot
give you a definite decision at this time. There are
several matters that should be discussed in person with
you before we can make a definite commitment.

I shall be glad to talk with you about credit
privileges when you can visit us.

Very truly yours,

Other credit men believe that it is not ethical to use this subter-
fuge—that the writer should, in the applicant's own interests, set
forth the exact reason for the refusal. For example:

Dear Mr. Peterson:

You have paid us a compliment by requesting credit
privileges at Young's.

As in the case of all those who apply for credit, Mr. Peterson, we made a careful investigation of your capital resources and your ability to handle additional credit. I believe you will agree that purchasing on installment a new car, two large appliances, and a piano--while making payments on a new home--is stretching your present income a little too much. I know you will understand why you should not endanger your credit reputation by taking on additional credit obligations.

Please continue to allow Young's to serve you on a cash basis until such time as you are able to reduce your present obligations. When the circumstances are more favorable, you may be sure that we shall welcome the opportunity of considering your application again.

Cordially yours,

Letters Stimulating Credit Business. Business firms welcome the opportunity to grant credit—to the right people, those who will use it wisely. In fact, because they know that credit customers are bigger buyers and generally more loyal customers, stores often put on special campaigns to encourage credit customers to make more frequent or larger purchases. These letters are combined good-will-sales letters in that they stimulate both interest and sales for the firm.

Retail stores often will invite steady cash customers to open charge accounts on the theory that they will like the convenience of shopping in this manner and will, of course, be encouraged to make more frequent purchases. Here is a letter encouraging a cash customer to avail herself of a charge account:

Dear Mrs. Perkins:

You are cordially invited to open a charge account at Benson and Black.

Hundreds of our customers enjoy the convenience of a charge account. They are able to shop without having to carry large sums of money; and they often, too, enjoy the convenience of shopping more easily by mail or by telephone. Merchandise that you really need now can be purchased now, and you will not have to defer the pleasure of using it.

Benson and Black "pampers" its charge customers in many ways, and you will be delighted with the personal attention you will receive. Why not come in and let us show you how easy it is to open an account--and use it immediately?

Sincerely yours,

Collection Letters

Most of the people who have been granted credit pay their bills faithfully and on time. Some people, however, need to be reminded when their accounts are past due. The person who writes collection letters must assume that every customer is fundamentally honest and fair and that he intends to pay his bills. This attitude is necessary to maintain the basic principle of credit—mutual faith. Therefore, the experienced credit man practices the philosophy that "the customer *is* trustworthy until he is proved otherwise."

Gentle Reminders. Most stores send out statements each month to those who have charge accounts. These statements serve as reminders to pay. At the same time, they furnish the customer with a record of his purchases.

At one time, charge customers looked upon the statement as a "dun"—and that is what it was called. Today, however, we expect to receive a statement of our account each month; and we welcome it.

A statement of account is all that most people need to prod them into paying. No additional reminders are necessary. But sometimes statements are mislaid or forgotten. If the store does not receive payment within a specified number of days after the statement is sent (the number of days allowed between reminders will depend on the store's experience with the customer; quick-paying customers are usually given more time between reminders), they may simply send a second statement, marked *Second Statement,* and hope this will be sufficient. To this second statement the store may attach a special sticker or affix a stamp, as illustrated here.

Courtesy Ever Ready Label Corporation

Stickers like these are often affixed to a second statement of account.

The second reminder may be a form letter or a card reminder such as illustrated here.

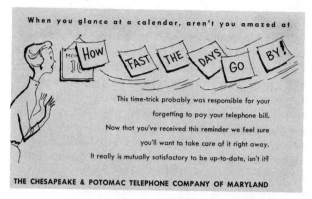

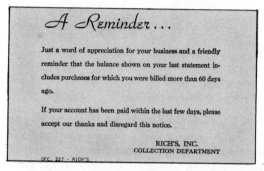

You will notice that these reminders are very impersonal and very gentle. There is a good reason for this. At this stage of collection, the credit manager doesn't want the customer to feel that he is being singled out. The customer's attitude may be, "Why is he picking on me? I'm only a few days late." In this instance, a personalized message is not so effective as a printed notice or a form letter.

More Persuasive Letters. If the various notices just discussed do not bring results, additional reminders will, of course, be necessary. The procedure to be followed from this point depends greatly on the customer. If his credit record is good, the store may continue to remind him with gentle hints. If there is some past history of tardiness in paying, the next reminder may be more forceful. If the store, because of past experience with the customer, suspects that he will be difficult to collect from, stiffer reminders may be written earlier. There is no standard pattern for all customers or for all businesses; many factors determine the frequency and the type of letters sent to collect past-due accounts.

Following is a typical pattern in a collection system:

	Number of Days After Regular Billing
1. Second statement	30
2. Stronger request	45
3. Urgent request	60
4. Threat of legal action	75
5. Letter from attorney or agency	90–100

To illustrate a collection situation, let us assume that Mrs. Marvin Jones has a charge account with Dell's Department Store. Dell's records show that Mrs. Jones, whose husband is a building contractor, has had an account for about a year. She has made frequent purchases since that time and has always paid her bills; but each month two or three reminders have been necessary before the account was paid.

During June, Mrs. Jones purchased a rattan chaise longue and a redwood dining set for outdoor use. The amount of her purchase was $87.88. A statement was sent on July 1, followed by a routine form letter on July 31 (like the one illustrated on page 417), with no results. What type of letter should now be sent to Mrs. Jones? This will depend on the kind of person the store thinks Mrs. Jones is. Obviously, a more personal message than has been sent heretofore is now required, so that Mrs. Jones will know that the appeal is being made directly to her. But, if the store considers her merely careless or forgetful rather than deliberately slow, they will be careful not to offend her—she is still a profitable customer.

Dear Mrs. Jones:

Haven't you overlooked something? According to our records, you received a statement of your account in

early July. On July 31 we sent you a reminder that your
balance of $87.88 had not been paid.

    I know that this matter is merely an oversight and
that you will mail us your check right away. Better
still, why not come to the store in person to take care
of the account? While you are here, stop in to see
the new shipment of barbecue grills we have just received. In gleaming aluminum, these grills are as
handsome as they are practical.

Cordially yours,

Notice that this letter gently chides the customer for her oversight. Note, too, that she is indirectly complimented by the implication that there is no cause for worry on your part—you know she
will pay. The letter ends with a sales message, because at this stage
you wish merely to plant an idea, not to offend the customer by
overdoing your plea.

If this letter does not get results (and in most cases it will), you
will have to use a different approach. Again, the time elapsed between the letter just illustrated and the next one will depend upon
the customer and the store. In most cases, the time between letters
grows progressively shorter. If there is a problem in receiving payment, the store does not wish to drag the matter out; the customer
may get the impression that it really isn't important.

Appeals. There are several appeals the store may use in writing the
next letter if the "it-was-merely-an-oversight" letter does not get
results. The one most often used for the next step is the appeal to
fair play: "We have kept our part of the bargain—won't you keep
yours?" The following letter illustrates this appeal:

Dear Mrs. Jones:

    Suppose a good friend of yours wanted to borrow
your new outdoor redwood dining set for a lawn party
she was giving. Because you like her and wish her party
to be a success, you gladly consent—even offer to
help her move the furniture to her house for the occasion. Of course, it is understood that the furniture
will be returned promptly after the party.

    How would you feel if your friend kept the furni-
ture and said nothing about returning it? She even
ignored a couple of reminders from you that it should
be returned. My guess is, Mrs. Jones, that you would be
somewhat bewildered—and a little annoyed.

    We find ourselves in a similar position regarding
your account. We gave you credit privileges because we
felt you would not abuse these privileges. Yet, you

have not paid for your June purchases; and you have not
responded to the three notices we have sent you. We are
naturally curious to know why. We sold you a chaise
longue and a redwood dining set in good faith, and we
have tried to see that you were pleased in every way.
But we believe you also have a responsibility to show
us that our faith in you was justified.

      Won't you send us your check (the amount is
$87.88) right now--this minute, while it is fresh in
your mind? If you can't pay the entire amount, why not
come in and discuss payment with us. Perhaps we can
arrange a plan whereby part of the amount due may be
paid now and the balance later.

                      Sincerely yours,

Notice the strong appeal to the sense of fair play. Also notice the
store's willingness to make suitable arrangements for partial payment. If this appeal does not bring the desired results, the credit
manager has some cause to be worried about the intentions of the
customer. His next letter will be much stronger. Some stores would
make the next letter an ultimatum: "Either pay us now or we will
turn your account over to our collection agency." (A collection
agency is an organization whose business is to collect delinquent
accounts for other businesses. The agency makes its income by retaining a percentage of the money it collects on each account.) Indeed, some stores would not have waited this long before sending a
threatening letter. If the customer is to be given one more chance
before he is sent a "pay-or-else" letter, this letter should be an appeal
to his pride. For example:

Dear Mrs. Jones:

      If we received an inquiry concerning your credit,
we would like to say: "Of course, Mrs. Jones is an excellent charge customer--she always pays her account
and, what's more, it is paid on time." If we received
such an inquiry today, however, unfortunately we would
not be able to be so positive. You have been a good
Dell customer, and we value your friendship. For some
unexplainable reason, however, you have given us reason
to doubt your intentions concerning settlement of
your account. Frankly, we cannot imagine what is wrong.

      Please help us to help you. Your credit reputation
is a valuable asset, and we do not want to see it
damaged. Your credit reputation is in danger, however,
unless you send us your check immediately. The amount
is $87.88.

                    Very truly yours,

Miller & Rhoads

INCORPORATED *The* SHOPPING CENTER

RICHMOND, VIRGINIA

CUSTOMERS ACCOUNTS DEPARTMENT

March 17, 19--

Mrs. Robert Reeves
One Circle Drive
Richmond, Virginia

Dear Mrs. Reeves:

We've looked everywhere . . .

but, as yet have been unable to locate your payment in
the amount of $37.83   made   February 3
However, if you will please send us your cancelled check
or receipt, we shall be glad to check further. Enclosed
is a self-addressed, stamped envelope for your convenience.

Please accept our apologies for this inconvenience and you
may be assured your reply will receive our immediate
attention.

                    Sincerely,

                    E J Brachin

                    Customers Accounts Department

ETB/ic

Courtesy Miller & Rhoads Inc.

An impersonal form letter used to remind the customer that his account is still outstanding. Note the typewritten inserts.

If the foregoing letter does not elicit immediate payment, the credit man has no alternative but to assume that the customer does not intend to pay. Usually, however, he will give the customer one last chance before placing the matter in the hands of a collection agency or in the hands of the store's attorney, who will bring suit against the customer. The letter of ultimatum may read as follows:

Dear Mrs. Jones:

    Will you please mark the date of September 15 on
your calendar. This is an important date to you, be—

cause, unless your account is paid by that time (the amount is $87.88), we shall be forced to place your account in the hands of a collection agency. I am sure you realize that this is a drastic step, and it is taken only when we have reason to believe that a customer does not intend to pay his account.

    Of course, such a step will damage your credit reputation; and we wish it were not necessary for us to take it. There is only one way you can stop us: send us your check immediately, or at least let us know your intentions. This is the last notice you will receive from us.

Very truly yours,

Collection-Letter Series. As you have seen, collection letters are often written in a series. There may be as many as six letters in a series, beginning with the first reminder and ending with the final ultimatum. Many large department stores and mail order houses have developed several series of collection letters—as many as five or six different series. Each series may be independent of the other, or letters in one series may be interchangeable with one or more in the others. For example, letter 3 in Series A may be substituted for letter 4 in Series B and so on. Collection-letter series are usually duplicated form letters; the typist merely fills in the name and address. Some firms, however, prefer to give their collection letters a more personal touch (these command more attention) by having them typed on an automatic typewriter. Each letter in a series is given a code number, and a careful record is kept of those that have been sent to the customer.

Acknowledging Payment. When a customer responds to a collection letter by making full payment of his account, some stores write him a special thank-you letter. For example:

Dear Mr. Lubeck:

    I was pleased to have your check for $116.20. It has been credited to your account, which is now completely clear.

    All of us at Roth's appreciate your co-operation, Mr. Lubeck. We hope you will continue to let us serve you in every way we can.

Sincerely yours,

Sometimes a customer sends only a portion of the amount due. This payment should be acknowledged by letter. At the same time, the customer should be asked very tactfully when the balance may be expected. Since the partial payment indicates a willingness to

The Esterbrook Pen Company

DELAWARE AVENUE AND COOPER STREET, CAMDEN 1, NEW JERSEY, U.S.A.
TELEPHONE: WOODLAWN 3-3460 · CABLE ADDRESS: ESTERBROOK, CAMDEN

Gentlemen:

If you keep "fiddling around" with payment of our past-due balance . . .

. . . it will take more than a fire extinguisher to put out the conflagration blistering your credit background.

Playboy Nero didn't "care" - but I'm sure your business reputation is important to you.

So, who wants to call out the "legal smoke eaters."

Re:

B. E. Van Dyke
Credit Manager

AMERICA'S OLDEST PEN MAKER

Courtesy The Esterbrook Pen Company and The Dartnell Corporation

A letter in a collection series. The address and the amount would be individually inserted on the typewriter.

pay, drastic steps should not be necessary to recover the remainder due.

Dear Mr. Carter:

Thank you for your check for $100 to apply on your invoice of July 11 for $156.25.

We have credited your account for $100, leaving a balance of $56.25. We know you will take care of the remaining balance as quickly as possible, and we shall appreciate your letting us know when we may expect your check.

Cordially yours,

Sometimes a recipient of a collection letter admits frankly that he cannot pay. Of course, the credit manager is not greatly concerned about retaining such a customer; but he is very much interested in getting the money due. Writing an angry response to such an admission will have no results. Bringing suit will be costly and unpleasant. The only alternative is either to grant a delay and request small weekly or monthly payments or to have the customer sign a note for the amount due. Sometimes both are demanded. The following is an example of such a letter:

> Dear Mr. Carter:
>
>   Thank you for writing us so frankly about your inability to pay your account of $150. I appreciate your being so frank with us.
>
>   I know you are sincere in wanting to meet your obligations, and I want to be just as sincere in helping you to do so. We can arrange for you to make monthly payments of $50 until your account is settled in full. If you will sign the enclosed 90-day promissory note, we will set up your account in three monthly payments.
>
>   Cordially yours,

Learning Exercises

1 As a wholesaler of electric appliances, you receive a request from a retailer to open an account. Investigation of the retailer's business activities, particularly his credit experience, reveals that he would make a poor credit risk. He has many outstanding debts and is a slow payer. Write a letter to him turning down his request but attempting to retain him as a cash customer.

2 The Carolina Manufacturing Company has sent you two orders accompanied by checks. You have made some discreet inquiries and have learned that the firm is a good credit risk. You would like to add the firm to your accounts receivable list. Write a letter inviting the firm to open an account with you.

3 You write letters for a department store. Mrs. Thomas F. Lawson has been a very good customer, but for the last three months she has purchased very little. Write a letter designed to build up her account.

✓ **4** Assume that you are the credit manager for the Wilding Book Company. Prepare a series of four collection letters that may be used for delinquent accounts. Leave blank the amounts and dates in the body of the letter.

5 George T. Dumont has given your name as a credit reference. He has always paid you, but he never pays on time. Although you have kept him on your books, you consider him "slow pay." Write the reply to the request for reference.

6 Mr. Walter Campbell, one of your customers, sends you a check for $200 on a long overdue account for $350. Write Mr. Campbell thanking him for the check and inquiring tactfully when you may expect the balance.

7 One of your new customers, Mr. Clark Bronson, writes that he cannot pay the $150 he owes you. Prepare a letter to Mr. Bronson.

Vocabulary and Spelling Refreshers

1 **Words Often Confused.** Conscious, conscience; cereal, serial.

2 **Short for What?** For what words or phrases do the following frequently used abbreviations stand?

a approx.	**d** contd.	**g** r.p.m.
b ctge.	**e** ex lib.	**h** vs.
c Conn.	**f** Messrs.	

3 **How Do You Spell Them?** The following "words" appear as they are pronounced. How are they spelled?

a lăm	**d** ku	**g** kē
b trŏf	**e** thō	**h** i
c gōst	**f** nōn	

Communication in Action: *Punctuation Discussion*

"When I have the slightest doubt about the need for a comma or a semicolon, I always put it in," says Freda Moore, a secretary. "But my boss says that overpunctuating is worse than no punctuation at all. In fact, he thinks that just the opposite rule should apply: 'Don't punctuate unless failure to do so will cause the reader to misinterpret what you say.'" Discuss these points of view. Is either of them entirely correct? If not, formulate a rule of your own.

UNIT 49

Letters for Other Problem Situations

You already have learned that some letters are easier to write than others. Letters that comply with requests, for example, are not too difficult to write because they tell the reader what he wants to hear. They say, "Yes, we are pleased to do as you request." Sometimes, however, you cannot comply with a request, because:

1. The information you need is incomplete
2. The request made is unreasonable
3. Circumstances prevent you from granting the request

Incomplete Inquiries

Suppose you receive an inquiry that is not clear or complete. Any attempt on your part to answer such a letter fully will probably fail to satisfy the customer. What you must do is write asking him for the information you need. Such a situation must be handled courteously and tactfully, without giving the correspondent the impression that he was negligent or careless. Suppose, for example, that you work for a photographer who receives this letter from a customer:

Dear Sir:

I would like to have some photographs made of myself. I am unable to get into town and have no telephone. Therefore, would you please send me your prices?

Very truly yours,

In order to supply the correct information, you must know more about the customer's needs. Here is a tactful, helpful, and courteous response:

Dear Mrs. Allan:

Thank you for calling on us for your photographic needs. I know that we can please you with our superior work—and at modest prices.

In order to give you the price information you need, please supply the answers to the following questions and return this letter to us in the envelope enclosed. No postage is required.

1. What size photograph would you like?
   Passport or identification
   (2 1/2 x 2 1/2)   _____
   Miniature (3 1/4 x 4 1/2)   _____
   Standard size:
      3 x 6 inches   _____
      4 x 5 inches   _____
      5 x 7 inches   _____
      8 x 10 inches   _____

2. How many copies do you plan to order?   _____

3. Please check one of the following:
   Black and white____ Brownette____ Color____

Just as soon as we receive this information from you, we shall be happy to send you complete prices.

We hope you will give us an opportunity to serve you very soon. Please let us know when you would find it convenient to make an appointment to have your photographs made.

Sincerely yours,

Note that the writer makes it easy for Mrs. Allan to send the necessary information. And in no way is an implication made that Mrs. Allan was at fault in not supplying all the details in her letter of inquiry.

Unreasonable Requests

Businesses sometimes receive unreasonable requests for information or service. Note the following:

Gentlemen:
   I am interested in buying one of your Electro Percolators. A friend told me he could get me one wholesale.

In order to know whether I'm get-
ting a good price or not, I would appreciate
having the wholesale price of the Electro
Percolator.

Very truly yours,

This request is not a reasonable one, since wholesale prices are confidential between manufacturer and dealer. Nevertheless, you should not tell the correspondent that his request is unreasonable, even though it is. You must attempt to retain his interest in your product. Look at this tactful reply that tries to sell the customer on buying through regular channels:

> Dear Mr. Herbert:
>
> Your interest in buying an Electro Percolator pleases us very much. You have selected the finest coffee maker available anywhere at any price.
>
> The suggested retail price of the Electro is $29.95; and once you have seen the Percolator, you will agree that it is well worth every cent. This low price allows only a modest profit for the manufacturer and the dealer.
>
> I wish I could tell you the wholesale price of the Electro Percolator; but standard business ethics, Mr. Herbert, require us to keep this information confidential between the manufacturer and the dealer. I know you will understand the reasons behind this policy.
>
> Four stores in Salt Lake City carry Electro appliances—Goodson's, Star Appliances, Utah Hardware, and Friedman–Jones Department Store. All these dealers are featuring Electro products this month. I hope you will let one of them show you his complete line. When you buy from an authorized dealer, you are sure of getting service on the product.
>
> You will be absolutely delighted with the Electro Percolator. Once you have tried it, you will know why discriminating coffee lovers say, "I didn't know coffee could taste so good!"
>
> Sincerely yours,

Delays in Filling Orders

When the customer has been "sold" on your firm to the extent that he places an order, he has a right to expect fast, courteous service. Unfortunately, delays do happen; and the letter writer has little control over them. He does what he can to satisfy the customer and hopes that the customer will understand. For example, here is a letter acknowledging an order from a new customer. The writer wants very much to give the customer good news—but he is unable to do so.

Dear Mr. Hathaway:

We were naturally very pleased to have your first order for Tempo Sports Shirts. You are most thoughtful to comment on our ad in Men's Wear magazine. Apparently, a good many others saw the ad, too, because we have been "swamped" with orders for the Tempo line.

I am sending you today two dozen each of small, medium, and large sizes in assorted colors. The remaining four dozen of each will be shipped out on Monday of next week. I am embarrassed, Mr. Hathaway, that you should be inconvenienced on your very first order; but I know you will understand when I tell you that we were not prepared for this rush of business. You may be sure that we have ordered our factory to gear up for "round-the-clock" production in order that we may keep all our dealers supplied.

I think you will find it just as hard to keep Tempo Sports Shirts in stock—they are so very popular! Why not place your order now for a new supply? We promise our usual prompt service on your next order.

Sincerely yours,

In writing letters of this type, observe these rules:

1. Always tell the customer first what you *can* do, then what you *can't* do. (We are sending some shirts now; the rest will have to be sent later.)

2. Keep the tone positive. Even though you must apologize for the delay, don't overdo it. Assume that the customer understands. (This rush of business naturally caught us unprepared.)

3. Re-establish the customer's confidence in your firm by encouraging him to place additional orders. (Place your next order now. We will give it our *usual prompt* service.)

Refusals of Orders

The primary purpose of any business, of course, is to sell goods or services for a profit. Usually, nothing makes a business happier than to receive an order. Under some circumstances, however, orders must be refused. The most common instance is that of a consumer who tries to purchase directly from a wholesaler. The wholesaler must refer him to a retail store. This letter is not so much a refusal as an explanation and a referral. In writing it, the correspondent should follow three steps:

1. Thank the customer for his order.
2. Tell the customer why his order cannot be accepted.
3. Tell the customer where he can obtain the merchandise and encourage him to buy while his interest is high.

Following is a typical letter refusing an order. The letter was sent by a national manufacturer to a customer who ordered directly from him.

Dear Mrs. Warren:

Thank you for your order for a Worksaver Steam Iron. We are delighted that you chose this fine product. Worksaver does, indeed, live up to its motto, "Takes the dread out of ironing."

Since we distribute our products through local dealers only, I cannot serve you directly, Mrs. Warren. I am pleased, however, to refer you to the Lincoln Appliance Center at 115 West Main Street in River Grove. The Lincoln people will be delighted to show you their complete line of steam irons and many other fine Worksaver appliances.

I am returning your check for $15.95 and hope that you will make a trip to Lincoln Appliance Center right away for your new Worksaver. You will find that it is one of the wisest appliance investments you have ever made.

Sincerely yours,

Invitation Refusals

A business organization and its employees receive numerous invitations to participate in exhibits, to speak before groups, or to take part in various kinds of community activities. Most businessmen feel that it is wise to participate in these affairs—they help to build good will for the business. However, not all such invitations can be accepted because of time or financial limitations. In writing a letter refusing an invitation, you should include these three important points:

1. Express appreciation for the invitation.
2. Give a logical reason for having to refuse.
3. Keep open the possibility of accepting a similar invitation in the future (if desirable).

Note the following example of a letter refusing an invitation to speak:

Dear Mr. Miller:

I was pleased and flattered to have your invitation to speak at the October meeting of the Retired Men's Club of the Paxton YMCA.

Unfortunately, Mr. Miller, I shall not be able to accept your invitation because I shall be out of town during the last two weeks in October. This is an important business trip for my company, and I am afraid it is impossible for me to postpone it. I am genuinely sorry that I cannot be with you.

I shall be delighted to appear before your group at some later date. If you wish me to do so, I hope you will let me know at least a month in advance. Incidentally, the subject of "How to Make Your Retirement Income Go Further" suits me just fine.

Cordially yours,

Information Refusals

Businesses sometimes receive requests for information that must be refused. The request may be unreasonable, or the information sought may be confidential. For example, a physician or a hospital cannot divulge medical information about a patient; a bank will not give information regarding its depositors except to those authorized by the depositor to receive such information. Letters refusing to give information are usually brief and to the point. Study the following examples:

Dear Mr. Wargo:

I am sorry that I cannot comply with your request for information about Miss Sally Moreno. Personal data concerning our employees is considered highly confidential information, and only our personnel department has access to it.

Very truly yours,

Dear Mr. Frosch:

I appreciate your letter in which you ask for information concerning markup rates on drug products sold in our store. Markup rates vary considerably, Mr. Frosch, and it is impossible for me to give you a figure that would apply to all drug products. Putting together detailed information would require more time than we can afford just now.

I should like to refer you to Service Bulletin #16, "Markups in the Drug Industry," issued by the State Bureau of Commerce and Industry in Austin. This 25-cent booklet contains markup rates for the drug industry as a whole, and I am sure it will be helpful to you.

Cordially yours,

***Fairfield's* • THE MAGAZINE OF TODAY •**

1111 Madison Avenue • New York 3, New York

August 3, 19—

Mr. Kenneth Barton
38 Albion Street
Corwin, New York

Dear Mr. Barton:

Thank you for giving me an opportunity to read your manuscript, "Safari to Shangri-La." I have shared the manuscript with several assistants on the editorial staff, and they all found it immensely enjoyable.

Unfortunately, Mr. Barton, we find that our readers can "take" only two or three adventure stories each year; and our files are bulging with at least a dozen good adventure articles awaiting publication. While yours is good enough to add to the others, I do not think it fair to you to keep your manuscript when we have no idea if and when we can use it. Therefore, I am returning the manuscript with the hope that you can sell it elsewhere.

Your writing style is delightful. Have you ever done anything in the area of whimsical family humor—articles on commuting, gardening, entertaining, and so on? We can't seem to get enough manuscripts on these topics, and I think you have the talent for doing some good writing. Why not try your hand at one of these topics and let me see it?

Cordially yours,

Roger Hawer

Roger Hawer
Editor

RH:msj

When rejecting a manuscript that has been submitted for publication, the letter writer must be especially tactful and diplomatic.

Refusing Unearned Discounts

Occasionally, a customer may figure the discount on his bill incorrectly; or he may take advantage of a discount when he is not entitled to it. The business may do one of three things:

1. Return his remittance and request a check for the correct amount.

2. Accept the remittance and ask for an additional remittance to make up the difference.

3. Accept the remittance and add the difference to the customer's next bill.

In any event, a letter must be written to the customer. Under no circumstances should the situation be ignored. In fairness to other customers who abide by the rules, the business cannot afford to make exceptions. In writing the customer, point out the error tactfully and appeal to his sense of fair play—doing both without offending him. Study this example:

Dear Mr. Wheaton:

Thank you for your check for $2,450 in payment of your March invoice. We appreciate the many opportunities you have given us to serve you.

We notice that, in the past, you have always paid your invoices within the discount period in order to take advantage of the saving. As you know, we can afford to give this discount because prompt payment enables us to make a similar saving on our purchases.

When a customer does not make payment within the discount period, we do not make any saving either. In this instance, you have waited seventeen days before making payment. Of course, this is seven days beyond the maximum allowed.

Because you are a good customer and because this is the first time you have gone beyond the discount period, we should like to allow the discount. However, if we did so, we should be unfair to our customers who pay within the ten-day period. They would lose confidence in us, and so would you.

Therefore, Mr. Wheaton, we know that you will send us with your next remittance the $50 remaining in your account.

Very sincerely yours,

Learning Exercises

1 Assume that you are employed by the World-Wide Travel Agency and receive this inquiry from William Tucker, 114 Floyd Avenue, Rochester 2, Minnesota.

```
Gentlemen:

     Please send me information about vacations, in-
cluding prices, etc. Thank you.

                    Very truly yours,
```

a Criticize Mr. Tucker's letter, telling why you think it is a good or a poor letter.

b What information should you have from Mr. Tucker in order to be of the greatest help to him? Make a list of everything you should know.

c Write to Mr. Tucker requesting the information you need.

d What aids would you use in answering Mr. Tucker after he supplied the necessary details?

2 The following letter was sent in reply to a request for information about the wholesale price of Koolray summer rugs. It is against company policy to reveal wholesale prices other than to authorized dealers. What is wrong with this letter? Rewrite it as you think it should have been written.

```
Dear Sir:

     We are sorry that we cannot tell the wholesale
price of Koolray summer rugs. Wholesale prices are
the personal business of our firm and our authorized
dealers only. Frankly, we are surprised at your
request.
                    Yours truly,
```

3 Your firm receives an order for 50 Delta porch gliders from a furniture store that has not previously done business with you. You welcome the business, but unfortunately you are out of stock on the gliders. It will take about ten days to fill this order. How would you handle the situation? Write the kind of letter you would like to receive if you were the company placing the order.

4 The Mi-Ty Explosives Company receives a request to conduct a school group through its plant to see how explosives are made. Because of the danger involved, however, the company prohibits visitors from entering the plant. Write a letter turning down the request but retaining the good will of the correspondent.

5 Criticize the following letter. Then rewrite it as you think the letter should be written.

Sir:

     We can't accept your order for one of our Gaxton mixers. Only The Wilson Dept. Store in your city is authorized to handle the sale of Gaxton products. We are, therefore, returning your check for $39.95.

                 Yours, truly,

6 The Brentwood Ladies' Aid Society requests a donation from your firm for their Building Fund Drive. This is one of hundreds of similar requests received by your firm. You are asked to compose a letter that your employer might send refusing the donation in such a way that none of the members, many of whom are good customers, will be offended.

Vocabulary and Spelling Refreshers

1 **Words Often Confused.** Appraise, apprise; pretend, portend.

2 **Those Capitals.** Correct the capitalization in these sentences.

  a We fear that mayor horton will not be able to attend.
  b I have just bought mother a gift for mother's day.
  c They waited several hours before the Prime Minister's house.
  d I am looking forward to studying Chemistry.
  e Hudson bay, in Canada, is 850 miles long.

3 **Plaguing Plurals.** What are the plurals of these words?

  a witness   **c** 1950   **e** lb.
  b century   **d** foot   **f** assets

Communication in Action: *Telephone Conversation*

Criticize the following telephone conversation. Then rewrite it as it should have been handled.

  Person Answering: Hello.
  Caller: Who is this?
  Person Answering: Who do you want?
  Caller: I was trying to get the advertising department.
  Person Answering: This is the advertising department.
  Caller: Is Ralph Pearson there?
  Person Answering: Yes.
  Caller: May I speak to him please?

UNIT   50

Writing Effective Sales Letters

Every business letter you write is a sales letter; for every letter attempts to sell merchandise, service, an idea, or simply good will. When a letter requests a free pamphlet, your reply accompanying the pamphlet is designed to sell good will. When you write a collection letter, you are trying to sell the customer the idea of paying his account. Even a letter applying for a job is a sales letter—the writer is selling his services.

Most frequently, however, you think of a sales letter in connection with selling merchandise or service. "Experience the thrill of stepping from your bath and wrapping yourself in a luxuriously fluffy, absorbent Marcan towel!" or "Your car is in safe, reliable hands when you bring it to Ronnie's Garage for service!" are typical of the sales statements you are accustomed to hearing or reading. As you study this unit, which will emphasize the writing of letters selling merchandise or service, you should keep in mind that the very same principles apply to writing letters selling ideas or good will.

Steps in Planning

A sales letter is effective if it achieves its purpose—whether that purpose is to get a prospect to come to the store for a friendly visit or to get him to place an order by return mail. In any event, the effective sales letter requires careful planning. This planning involves the following steps:

1. Determine the aim of your letter. What do you want the reader to do?

2. Determine the kind of individual to whom you are writing—your market. Are all your readers businessmen, or do they represent all types of professions and occupations?

3. Select the appeals that are adaptable to your market. Why would people want to buy your product—what will it do for them?

4. Organize the facts according to a logical, effective, and easy-to-follow plan.

5. Use language and mechanical features suited to both your product and your audience.

Determine Your Letter Aim. Why write the sales letter? A sales letter may be written to accomplish any one of five purposes—to get the customer to buy now, to develop an interest in your product that will induce him to buy later, to keep the name of your organization in the customer's mind, to get the customer to visit your place of business, or to get the customer to try your product or ask questions about it. You must determine which of these purposes you would like your sales letter to accomplish—and build your letter around this one purpose. If your aim is to get the customer to buy now, your letter will build up to the point of getting the reader to take immediate action. If the aim of your letter is to get the customer to visit your place of business, then the letter should be directed towards this end. For example, the Hick's Clothing Center, to get new customers to visit the store, offered a free gift (most of the gifts were small items like a handkerchief, a pair of socks, or a necktie) to everyone who would pay them a visit. Here is the letter the Hick's people wrote:

Dear Friend:

We have a gift for you! At the bottom of this letter is a number—your gift number. Everybody with a numbered letter receives a gift from us—without obligation! Nothing to write and no purchase required. How do you get this gift?

In our store window we have posted a list of numbers, and each number is followed by a handsome gift—a man's suit, a raincoat, a complete lady's ensemble, to mention but a few. Just compare your letter number with those posted in our store window. Then present your letter to me, and I will give you your gift. Come in any time between now and Friday, April 14.

While you are at our store, you will want to get acquainted with the "Wonderful Difference" in buying clothing in our big, beautiful, exciting house of values. You have never seen such a large selection of men's, women's, and children's clothing! Everything from the tip of your toes (shoes) to the top of your head (hats).

Come in for your free gift on or before April 14.
It will be a pleasure to meet you personally and to
present your free gift to you.

                              Cordially yours,

                              HICK'S CLOTHING CENTER

Your gift number is:
14896   Bill Rogers, Manager

In the following letter, the aim is to get the reader to make further inquiry about the service offered.

Dear Mr. Thompson:

Congratulations on your appointment to the position of Office Manager for the Rego Oil Company in Los
Angeles, announced in last night's Evening Bulletin.

Like most people, you probably dread the chore
that accompanies moving from one locality to another.
First, the hours of wrapping and packing; and then, additional hours of unpacking and unwrapping. Well, put
your mind at ease—Wide World Moving Company is at your
service to help make moving painless and pleasant.

Just tell us your moving date. And 24 hours before
that date, our corps of courteous, efficient packers
will come to your home with all the necessary equipment
and supplies. They will carefully wrap and pack every
item—from your most delicate china to your grand
piano. And everything will be properly packed to avoid
any damage. Though we are insured for any loss or
damage, our packers and movers do their job so well
that our claims are phenomenally small.

Moving day is here! Our movers arrive promptly at
the designated hour and carefully and quickly load all
your belongings into our moving vans. You don't have
a care or a worry. And when the van reaches its destination with your belongings, again our crew takes over
to help you with your unpacking.

Wide World really makes moving a pleasure. So
telephone us at PAcific 2-3686 and ask our representative to call on you to discuss our low rates and to
determine your packing needs.

                              Very sincerely yours,

Each of these preceding letters had one specific goal, and the letter was built around that goal. A letter that tries to accomplish too many things at the same time usually winds up accomplishing nothing.

Determine Your Market. To whom is the sales letter being sent? to a mass audience—*all* the people in a particular area, regardless

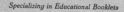

Specializing in Educational Booklets

THE ECONOMICS PRESS, INC. • P. O. BOX 460 • MONTCLAIR, NEW JERSEY • Tel. Pilgrim 6-3364

My Blessing, Not My Doom

The enclosed booklet, we suspect, will still be around long after the writer is dead and buried.

It's an amazing message. It tells people to work better and harder--yet they still like it. We've never published a booklet which brought so many letters of praise from plain, ordinary people--or from company presidents either.

You can read "My Blessing, Not My Doom" today, then read it again six months from now with equal pleasure. More than 4,000 companies have distributed copies to their employees. One actually distributed it twice--30,000 copies each time.

You've never read it? Just open the booklet and try the first two pages.

If you want copies of this message for your employees, they are always available. We reprint periodically to keep it in stock. Just send us your order on the enclosed card--your copies will be shipped immediately.

Sincerely,

John L. Beckley

John L. Beckley
Publisher

Courtesy The Economics Press, Inc.

An effective sales letter. Can you tell why?

of occupation, income, educational background? or to a selected audience whose tastes and interests might be very similar? The kind of reader the sales letter will have should determine, to a large extent, the kind of letter that is written. If you are selling air conditioners, you must first determine to whom the sales letter is to be written—to consumers who want the comfort and convenience of the air conditioner, to retailers who want to make a profit in reselling the air conditioners, or to industrial users who may be more concerned

with the economies to be effected by using your particular brand of
air conditioner. The same sales letter could not be used very effectively for all three groups, even though the product is the same.

The following letters were sent from the same furniture store.
Letter 1 was sent to all customers who previously had made purchases at the store. Letter 2, however, was sent only to businessmen
in the community.

Letter 1

Dear Friend:

   Put a red circle around May 2 on your calendar! On
May 2 our spectacular May Furniture Sale begins--and
you will want to be at our store when the doors open
at 9 a.m.

   Every piece of furniture--lamps, rugs, and bed-
ding, too!--will be reduced in price from 10 to 60 per
cent. Just to give you a few examples of the savings in
store for you--a beautiful 4-piece mahogany bedroom
suite that originally sold for $475 is marked down to a
low $295! Mattresses and box springs that sold for
$59.95 each will be sold at $47.95 each. And every item
you purchase during this week-long sale will represent
a substantial saving to you.

   You won't want to miss this sensational sale--so
be here bright and early on May 2. Remember, our Home-
Furnishing Account calls for only 10 per cent down,
with the remainder budgeted over 36 months.

                              Cordially yours,

Letter 2

Dear Mr. Finch:

   Have you taken a good look around your office
lately? Is your furniture drab and shabby looking? Does
your office give your firm the appearance of success
and prosperity--or does it make your clients think
"this man must not be doing very well"?

   Now is a very good time for you to visit our
Office Furniture Department. Every item is reduced 10
per cent through the month of July. Our decorator is a
specialist in office layout and furnishings. He can
help you select appropriate matching furniture, rugs,
and draperies--and his advice is free for the asking.
You will be under no obligation to make your purchases
from us, but you can't beat our low prices and large
selection anywhere else in Redwood City.

   Call DRexel 9-8756 and ask for Mr. Draper. He will
be happy to make an appointment to visit your office
and help you with your redecorating problems.

You can't afford to miss this once-a-year sale of office furniture and furnishings. So to take advantage of expert free advice and substantial savings--call or come in to see us today.

Sincerely yours,

Select Appropriate Appeals. When the writer of sales letters has determined the market he wishes to reach, he must then determine the appeals his product will have for the reader. Although the air conditioner discussed on page 435 will do the same thing for every-

---

D'Orlay

MAKER OF THE WORLD'S FINEST PERFUMES

35 FIFTH AVENUE

NEW YORK 5, NEW YORK

April 17, 19--

Dear Miss Carlton:

Who wouldn't love <u>you</u>!

No man could help being attracted to you when you are veiled in a flower-fresh fragrance. Our newest fragrance in D'ORLAY perfumes is "Intoxication," which has a scent all its own. It clings lovingly to you and makes you feel as fresh as sunlight. Never before have you felt so entirely feminine and beautiful.

Just sniff the stationery you now hold in your hands and see how exciting its scent is. This is our <u>new</u> "Intoxication"!

After you have used the sample of "Intoxication" that is attached to this letter, we are sure that you will wish us to RUSH your bottle of this exquisite perfume to you at once.

Just sign the enclosed card and return it to us in our reply envelope, which requires no postage. We know that you will enjoy this new "heaven in a bottle."

Sincerely yours,

Jean D'Orlay

Jean C. D'Orlay
President

JCD:jm

A sales letter written in an informal, personal style to appeal to a feminine audience.

one who uses it, different people will be moved to buy it for different reasons. The home consumer probably is primarily concerned with comfort and relaxation; the office or industrial user, with increased efficiency of employees. Some appeals, however, are effective for every kind of audience. Most people like to save money, so the thrift of operation of the air conditioner may appeal to both the home consumer and the office or industrial user.

A sales letter for air conditioners sent to home consumers might read:

Dear Mr. Carmichael:

Do you remember the prolonged heat and humidity of last summer? For five nights in a row the temperature did not go below 76 degrees.

Before long, another summer will be with us, bringing with it many uncomfortable days--and nights. But this year, you don't have to let the hot weather get you down!

The new Rexaire Air Conditioner has just arrived. You can now look at its beautiful design and try its superb cooling power. The 2-ton model will comfortably cool the average 5-room home, providing 24 hours of relaxing comfort and restful sleep. In addition, you breathe pure air, free of the dust and pollen to which so many of us are allergic. Its quiet operation and low-voltage consumption make the Rexaire a pleasure to own.

Why sacrifice all this for the few cents a day it costs to own and operate the Rexaire? Come in today-- you'll want to see and try Rexaire, the ultimate in modern air conditioning.

Cordially yours,

Notice that several appeals are used in this letter—pleasure, comfort, health, and thrift. From these appeals, buying points must be developed. For example:

Appeal	Buying Point Developed
Pleasure	Helps you to relax and enjoy your home
Comfort	Helps you get a restful night's sleep
Health	Purifies air; helps people with allergies
Thrift	Low initial cost and cost of operation

A letter attempting to sell air conditioners for office use might read:

Dear Mr. Buckley:

How would you like to increase the efficiency of your office workers by 10 per cent this summer? Tests

in over one hundred business offices using the Rexaire
Conditioner have proved that worker efficiency increased 10 per cent after the Rexaire was installed.

    Increased worker efficiency means greater profits
for your organization--thus the Rexaire pays for itself
in just a few short years. Your initial cost for installing the Rexaire is the lowest it has been in the
last ten years--and, if you would like to spread this
cost, you have 36 months in which to pay. In addition,
improvements in the new model make your operating costs
low. A 1-ton unit consumes only 25 cents' worth of
electricity each working day. Isn't that a small sum to
pay for the comfort and increased working efficiency
of your employees?

    Won't you call us today and ask us to send our
engineer to determine the air-conditioning needs of
your office? Each day's delay in installing Rexaire
costs you money.

                    Very sincerely yours,

Notice that the emphasis in this letter is different from the emphasis in the letter sent to home users. Here the emphasis is upon
increased worker efficiency, low initial cost, and low operating cost.
Since the primary purpose of a business is to make a profit, both
increasing worker efficiency and keeping costs low contribute to this
profit motive. The buying points developed from these appeals are:

Appeal	Buying Point Developed
Thrift	Low outlay cost
Thrift	Low operating cost
Profit	Increased worker efficiency

The sales correspondent has a choice of many different appeals.
Which he uses depends upon the aim of his letter, the nature of his
product, and the kind of market he is trying to reach. People usually
spend their money for these reasons:

For comfort (air conditioner)

To make money (stocks)

To save money (storm win-
dows)

To save time (pressure cooker)

To imitate others (buckskin
shoes)

√To be different (exclusive hat)

For health (toothpaste)

For enjoyment (television set)

For cleanliness (soap)

To avoid effort (power lawn
mower)

To attract the opposite sex (perfume)

To escape physical pain (corn
and callus remedy)

To gratify curiosity (a new
household gadget)

To protect family (life insurance)

To be in style (a fur coat)

To avoid trouble (casualty insurance)

To take advantage of opportunities (investment property)

For praise (jewelry)	To protect reputation (charitable contribution)
To be popular (an automobile)	To satisfy appetite (candy)
To safeguard possessions (fire insurance)	For beautiful possessions (a colored telephone)

An Effective Letter Plan

You are now ready to begin composing your sales letter. You must, therefore, gather all the facts about your product and the various appeals that may be used and organize them according to an effective plan. This plan calls for four steps, the ABCD's of sales letters:

1. Attracting attention
2. Building interest and desire
3. Convincing the reader
4. Directing favorable action

Let's take a look at what is involved in each of these steps.

Attracting Attention. A sales letter can attract the reader's attention even before it has been removed from the envelope. The envelope may be colorful—instead of the traditional white. It may contain a picture or a phrase, such as illustrated here.

A catchy slogan on the flap or on the face of an envelope is often used to stimulate interest in the contents.

One company that sells Holland tulip bulbs has its sales letters sent from Holland, using a Dutch postage stamp and postmark.

When the letter has been removed from the envelope, it can continue to attract attention through these devices:

1. Tinted stationery

2. An unusual letterhead

3. A colored typewriter ribbon

4. An unusual letter style, such as the hanging-indented or inverted-paragraph style discussed in Unit 41

5. *An unusual style of type, such as the script type illustrated in this sentence*

6. Typing the entire letter in capital letters or certain words or sentences all in capitals

7. Underscoring key words or phrases

8. Using italicized words for emphasis

9. Using dashes or exclamation points for emphasis—such as: "Call us today—tomorrow may be too late!"

All these devices are aimed at attracting attention. However, you would not "gimmick" the letter to the extent that these eyecatchers get in the way of the message.

The opening paragraph of the letter—the very first sentence—may excite curiosity or start a train of thought or attract attention in some way that will make the reader continue reading the letter. These opening sentences may be either questions or statements, but they should be original and concise. Questions should not be phrased so that they could be answered by a mere "Yes" or "No." Statements should contain a startling, new, interesting, or different fact. Here are some examples of opening sentences that have proved effective.

Pertinent questions:

How would you like to be the best-dressed woman in town?

Want to save 4 cents on each gallon of fuel oil you buy for your home?

How much is your family worth to you?

If you lost your job today, how would you pay your bills?

Startling or significant statements:

They said it couldn't be done, but we did it!

Electric typewriters increase production 10 per cent!

You can't afford to be without one!

Three out of four families use hospital service at least once each year.

The device selected to attract attention should be determined primarily by one or more of these factors:

1. The kind of firm sending the letter (Is it a conservative bank or a store selling gardening supplies?)

2. The nature of the product (Is it religious books or contemporary fiction?)

3. The kind of audience to receive the letter (Are they doctors or bricklayers?)

Building Interest and Desire. When you have succeeded in getting the reader's attention, you must hold that attention. The best way to do it is to build interest—by vividly describing your product so that the reader can actually "see" it. With colorful, descriptive words like those listed below, you can make the reader visualize himself using your product and getting satisfaction from it. To stimulate the reader to buy your product, you must use appeals that will stir his emotions.

To sell floor wax:	It's a bright shine. A tough shine. An easy-to-wipe-up shine.
To sell canned frozen oyster stew:	Savory oyster stew with plump, pampered oysters.
To sell laundry soap flakes:	Softness—you can feel it in the <u>flakes</u> . . . feel it in the <u>clothes</u>!
To convince readers to send for a catalogue from a plant nursery:	Lifelike illustrations you can almost smell and touch!
To sell oranges:	Big, plump wedges . . .
To sell hardwood paneling:	The soft beauty and warmth of fine hardwoods.
To sell porcelain bathroom fixtures:	The porcelain finish is glass-smooth.
To sell small cars:	The man who is fed up with bigger, thirstier cars switches to _____.
To sell air travel:	For travel elegance, fly with us!
To sell electric typewriters:	A pleasure to type; a pleasure to sign; a joy to read.
To sell golf balls:	The sweet click at the tee is the music of the finest ball in golf.
To sell soft drinks in cans:	And cans chill so fast, keep the flavor fresh and full of zip.
To sell a station wagon:	From a frisky, sturdy little work horse to the jauntiest little sedan of them all!
To sell a soft drink:	You'll really welcome the cold crisp taste that so deeply

	satisfies . . . the cheerful lift that's bright and lively.
To sell a deodorant:	New roll-on deodorant with staying power.
To sell an air deodorant:	Makes air smell flower-fresh.
To sell mustard:	A mustard that is shy, retiring, is no mustard at all; a great mustard should manage to be a delightful contradiction of emphatically hot and delicately mild.
To sell fruit punch:	The circus-red color, the candy-and-ice-cream taste.
To sell shampoo:	Hair so satin-bright, satin-smooth, too!

Suppose you are selling high-fidelity phonographs. You have attracted the reader's attention by asking, "How would you like to bring the concert hall into your living room?" You hope that the reader is interested—or at least curious enough—to find out how this can be done. So you must vividly describe to him your product in use, appealing to his desire for pleasure. You continue your letter:

> You have just come home after a tiring day at the office. You relax in the comfort of your favorite easy chair. But you must ease your mind, too, of the many tensions of the day. You flip the switch on your Magnasound High-Fidelity Phonograph and suddenly the room is filled with the soft tones of your favorite music. You are carried away to the concert hall—every note, every tone is as clear as though the orchestra were performing in your living room. Soon both your mind and your body are completely at ease, and the cares and tensions of the day are forgotten.

Convincing the Reader. If you have done your work well to this point, the reader is already partially convinced. At least, you have developed his interest to a strong degree. If he really wants to buy, he can find reasons for doing so. Nevertheless, you must still convince the reader that it will be definitely to his advantage to own the product. In fact, you must be able to convince him that he really cannot afford NOT to buy it. Therefore, you are ready now to bring out other features of the product that will appeal to him. You have attempted to sell the reader on the beautiful performance he can expect from the Magnasound and the effect that performance will have on his pleasure and relaxation. Now, what other features might appeal to him? He certainly would like to have a piece of furniture that will enhance the beauty of his living room and win praise from others, so you tell the reader:

> Your guests, too, will appreciate the pleasure of concert-hall fidelity when you invite them to your home for an evening of listening pleasure. They will admire the beautiful woods of your Magnasound--whether you select a mahogany, pine, or walnut cabinet. Both inside and out, you will own the finest piece of phonograph equipment produced at a reasonable price.

Now the reader may think, "Well, this Magnasound is going to cost more than I can afford." You must convince him that this is not so. Therefore, your letter might continue:

> For only 10 cents a day, you cannot afford to be without the many pleasures the Magnasound will bring you. Your present phonograph can serve as a down payment, and you have two months until your first low payment will begin.

Directing Favorable Action. You have now reached the point where, if each of the preceding steps has accomplished its purpose, you must move the reader to act. Some action-getting suggestions that you might use are:

1. Enclosing a return envelope or postal card
2. Suggesting partial payments, spread over a period of time
3. Suggesting that the reader "act now before it is too late"
4. Offering special inducements for prompt action ("This special low price is in effect only until May 1.")

The letter you wrote to sell the Magnasound High-Fidelity Phonograph, therefore, might conclude as follows:

> If you act before May 15, you can take advantage of our special $150 trade-in allowance instead of the usual $100. In addition, you may select $10 worth of any records we have in stock. Won't you come in today and listen to the Magnasound?

A Sales Letter Illustrated. The following is an example of an outstanding sales letter, showing each of the steps in the ABCD's of sales letter writing.

> Dear Mr. Chapman:

Attracting attention	How would you like to turn your lawnmowing chores into a pleasant activity? The Madras Riding Mower can do just that--and here's how:

BETTY'S no miracle worker

but she *can't* make a mistake!

REPLY CARD

Mr. Raymond T. Keane
Trans-Mix Manufacturing Co., Inc.
320 West Monroe Street
Philadelphia 6, Pennsylvania

Betty is smart, attractive -- and superefficient.

But she's still a GIRL as you can plainly see. Mistakes in transferring numbers and typing did occur, before her wise Boss switched
to OZAMATIC Order-Invoicing.

Now, Betty no longer has to rewrite ordering and shipping information,
her errors are eliminated -- and she now does her by herself all the
work that formerly took the time of seven!

If you want to learn how to transform your GIRLS (and men, too) into
errorproof, more efficient clerical workers, just mail the card you'll
find in the window above.

You'll promptly receive a free copy of "OZAMATIC Order-Invoicing" --
the idea-packed booklet that points the way to greatly simplified
order filling and shipping, speedier billing and back-order handling.

It shows how rewriting, typing, and rechecking are eliminated -- and
how you can do away with costly billing machines.

You'll find that this booklet may suggest ways to effect important payroll savings or to use the time of your clerical staff to better advantage.

Get all the facts about the fast, easy, labor-saving OZAMATIC copy-
ing method -- which can be beneficial to your business -- and your
profits.

Simply drop the above reply card in your outgoing mail. No stamp, addressing or signature is needed. And there's no obligation, of course.

Sincerely,

J. A. Travis

James A. Travis
Manager - Marketing

OZALID
DIRECT COPY SYSTEMS

A DIVISION OF GENERAL ANILINE & FILM CORP. • JOHNSON CITY, N. Y.

Courtesy Ozalid

In how many different ways does this sales letter appeal to the reader?

The Madras Ri ding Mower has many features few other re el mowers have:

1. You can sit in a comfortably pad-
ded seat while you mow your lawn.

2. The Madras has an automatic
starter that requires only a flip of a
switch.

**Building interest
and desire**

3. The Madras has a 5-gallon capacity
fuel tank--no stopping to fill the tank
during mowing.

4. It has such an easy steering wheel
that even a woman can steer the Madras
with little effort.

5. The Madras bags clippings and
leaves so that no raking is necessary.

**Convincing the
reader**

Nowhere can you get such value as you
get with Madras. Take your choice of the
19-inch at $99.95, the 20-inch at $119.50,
or the wide-cut 22-inch at $149.50. Your
dealer will give you a generous trade-in
on your present mower and can arrange low
monthly payments on the balance. So why
deny yourself the pleasure of the easy-
operating Madras?

**Directing favor-
able action**

Visit your dealer today to see the
many models he has available. If you will
present this letter when you purchase a
Madras during the month of May, your
dealer will give you without charge a 5-
gallon gasoline can with a handy pouring
spout--a $6.95 value, if you act now!

Yours for a pleasant summer,

Follow-Up Sales Letters

Frequently, more than one sales letter will be sent to a prospective
customer to convince him to buy. In selling higher priced items, for
instance, more than one letter may be necessary to do the job. If no
action results from the first letter sent, one or more additional letters
may follow. These follow-up letters often comprise what is called a
sales campaign or a "wear-out" series. Sometimes as many as eight
letters will be sent, depending upon the product, its cost, and the
nature of the market. Each letter in the series is spaced about ten
days apart. And an attempt is made to vary the appeal in each letter,
with the hope that one of the appeals, or the way it is presented, will
ultimately convince the reader to take action. Preferably, the letters
will be short and will each concentrate on one principal sales feature.

If possible, the opening paragraph of each letter should be so constructed that the additional letter seems a natural development. Suppose that, in the first letter attempting to sell the Magnasound Phonograph, you enclosed a postal card for the prospective customer to let you know that he would like to have a five-day home trial. Since the postal card was not returned, the second letter in the series might begin:

```
        We note that you have not yet taken advantage of
our 5-day no-obligation trial of the wonderful Magna-
sound. Perhaps you feel that you will be obligated to
buy. May we assure you that this will not be the case.
At the end of five days, just telephone us to pick
up the Magnasound. No questions will be asked; no sales
pressure will be exerted. If the trial use of the
Magnasound does not convince you, we don't want you to
keep it.
```

Another letter in the series might appeal to the economical side of the reader by stating:

```
        After March 1, all phonographs will increase 10
per cent in price. If you act now, you will save
yourself $8.95, a saving that will enable you to buy
two of your favorite record albums
```

Learning Exercises

1 For each buying reason given on page 439, name at least one other product or service that may be bought.

2 Write an opening sentence that might be used in a sales letter for each of the products or services listed on page 439.

3 Assume that your class is going to put on a play in the school auditorium to raise money to send the football team to another city for a championship game. Write a letter that could be sent to each member of the PTA urging him to attend the play.

4 Write a sales letter that would be sent to *each* student in the school urging him to buy a yearbook. Write another sales letter that would be sent only to graduating seniors.

5 Rewrite Sales Letter 2, this time appealing to a mass audience.

Vocabulary and Spelling Refreshers

1 **Words Often Confused.** Detract, distract; carton, cartoon.

2 **A or An?** Should *a* or *an* precede these words?

a hour	**c** umpire	**e** history
b woman	**d** owner	**f** European

3 **Catch the Misspellings.** Which of the following commonly used words are misspelled?

a receive	**c** occasion	**e** untill
b beleive	**d** occurence	**f** seperate

Communication in Action: *Obtaining Information*

As assistant manager of a hotel, you are responsible for authorizing all checks cashed for guests. The cashier has sent Mr. Pickens to you. He wishes to cash a personal check for $50. What questions will you ask Mr. Pickens before you approve his check for payment? With another student, enact the scene as you think it might happen. Remember, you must get the information you need, yet retain the good will of the guest.

UNIT 51

Public Relations Letters

There is no doubt that effectively written sales letters help to stimulate business—if they didn't, they would not be so widely used. However, the letter that tries to convince the reader to buy is not the only kind of letter that helps to make sales. In addition to the kind of sales letter discussed in the previous unit, the alert businessman uses letters to build public relations—and good public relations ultimately create sales. The term *public relations* is a difficult one to define. In essence, it means that the customer feels that the firm is more interested in satisfied customers than it is in just making a sale. A business that has conveyed this feeling to its customers does not have to worry about sales. Public relations letters, then, are letters written to show the firm's concern for the customer.

Characteristics of Public Relations Letters

Although public relations letters have as an underlying motive the increasing of sales, they do not "push" a product or service. Instead, they are subtle means of building good will. The writer hopes to impress the firm name and its product or service on the reader so that, when the need arises for this product or service in the future, the customer will think of the writer's firm.

Public relations letters (sometimes called sales promotion letters), then, are a special type of sales letter that sells indirectly. In fact, the chief difference between public relations and sales letters is that public relations letters *seem* to be selling nothing at all. Instead, they are written with an eye to the future; that is, with the thought that, if you treat your customer well today, perhaps he will buy from you sometime in the future.

Public relations letters are generally written to accomplish one of the following purposes:

1. To express appreciation to customers for their business ("Thank you for your business during the past year.")

2. To capitalize on some special occasion—a holiday or a birthday, for example ("We should like to wish you and your family a joyous holiday season.")

3. To offer to be of service to the customer ("We have opened a branch bank in your neighborhood, and you will find that doing your banking with us will be even more convenient.")

Expressing Appreciation. You may not feel that you are accomplishing much when you write to a customer thanking him for his business. However, a courteous "thank you" serves as a gesture of good will and paves the way for future business with the customer. Don't you like to feel appreciated? When someone thanks you for something you have done, don't you feel an inner glow of satisfaction? So it is when a firm to whom you have given your business takes the time to thank you for your patronage; you certainly feel more kindly toward that firm. The next time you need their product or service, you will be more likely to think of dealing with this firm than with any other.

How do you think the recipient of the following letter might react to it?

Dear Mrs. Briggs:

As another year draws to a close, we can't help feeling very grateful for having customers like you.

We want you to know how much we appreciate the business you have given us during the past year. We hope that you have derived much satisfaction from your purchases.

Please remember that we are here to be of service to you. We hope that during the coming year we may continue to serve you.

                    Cordially,

Such a letter as this will not sell a specific item, but it will certainly cement good relations. Notice that the letter is written in a friendly style and does not "push" the reader in any way.

Capitalizing on Special Occasions. A holiday, the beginning of a new season, a birthday or an anniversary, the arrival of new merchandise, a new type of product, a new service, or some other special event—any of these may prompt the writing of a letter to your customers. Of course, in letters of this type, you do not attempt to sell a specific item. However, by making the customer aware of the new service or product—or calling his attention to some special event—you may be indirectly stimulating his desire to buy. In these letters you are attempting to give the customer the impression of doing him a favor rather than trying to make a sale.

For example, in the following letter you are reminding customers with fur coats that it is time to put their coats in storage to protect them from moth damage.

Dear Mrs. Fitzroy:

Spring is here—so can summer be far behind?

With the approach of warm weather, you should start thinking about the proper care of your furs. You can't afford to forget about them now that the cold weather is over—Mr. Moth would like nothing better, for he is always hungry and furs offer him a delicious meal.

Do you know that we have the largest and most up-to-date fur storage facilities in Centerville? When you store your furs with us, they are certain of receiving de luxe care. Look at what this care includes:

1. Our driver will pick up your furs at your home and bring them to us in our specially treated storage truck. Your furs are protected even while in transit!

JEFFREY'S DEPARTMENT STORE

210 EASTLINE AVENUE
GLENBROOK, INDIANA

May 17, 19--

Dear Customer:

You've
Earned

10¢	Is it worth 10 cents a line to you to read this
20¢	letter?
30¢	We'll gladly pay you that amount--but only if
40¢	you read the entire letter.
50¢	Now, we reason this way: You really are a valued
60¢	customer. But lately you haven't been in even
70¢	to say, "Howdy." We would like you to come back;
80¢	we would like to see you often; we would like
90¢	you to reopen your account. We think that it is
$1.00	better for us to have a long-time customer like
$1.10	you on our books than a new customer whom we
$1.20	don't know. And since it would cost us at least
$1.30	$2.50 to open a <u>new</u> account, we would rather pass
$1.40	this amount to you.
$1.50	So we say, "Here is a $2.50 'check' on the house."
$1.60	Come in and select anything you wish, to the value
$1.70	of $25 or more, from our extensive stock of nation-
$1.80	ally advertised clothing and shoes for the entire
$1.90	family. Invest in that household appliance--pop-
$2.00	up toaster, steam iron--you have been dreaming
$2.10	about. Or do your gift shopping early for such
$2.20	items as diamonds, watches, radios.
$2.30	The enclosed "check," worth $2.50, is your down
$2.40	payment.
$2.50	Why not come in tomorrow.

Cordially yours,

Bill Jeffrey

Bill Jeffrey

BJ:csl

This letter does not attempt to sell a specific item but rather to interest the reader in visiting the store.

2. When the furs arrive at their summer home, the pockets and sleeve cuffs will be carefully brushed to remove any possible source of moth damage.

3. Your furs will then be expertly cleaned and refreshed——made to look like new!

4. Sealed in a plastic jacket, your furs will be placed in our cold——b-r-r——storage vaults to rest until you need them again.

5. Next fall, when the air starts getting nippy again, telephone us——and, the following day, your furs will be brought back home again.

Worry-free protection of your furs is yours when you use Garner's Fur Storage Service. Don't let Mr. Moth dine on your furs.

Very sincerely yours,

Opportunities for building good will are numerous for the alert businessman. For example, if a personal or business acquaintance of the businessman wins an honor or is elected to office in an organization, the businessman might send a note of congratulations, such as the following:

Dear Mr. Ashley:

I read with a great deal of pleasure, in last evening's Times-Herald, of your election to the office of president of Rotary.

I should like to offer my sincere congratulations upon your receiving this honor and to extend best wishes for a most successful term of office.

Sincerely,

A very simple note, but don't you think Mr. Ashley would appreciate such thoughtfulness? Similarly, good wishes might be extended to a new business establishment or to a business that has moved into new quarters. Any special events, such as these, offer an ideal opportunity for building good relations with your customers.

Offering to Be of Service. Another important function of the public relations letter is that of offering to be of service to the customer. Whereas the sales letter says, "Buy," this letter says, "Let us be of service to you."

The following letter was written by a department store to let customers know about a new type of charge account for home furnishings. Again, no particular item is being sold—instead, the impression is being given that here is something new the store is

An expression of appreciation—like this note to a customer whose account is in good order—helps build good will for the company.

THANK YOU

Maybe it's just human nature
but generally there is correspondence
between a customer and a company
only when there is a problem. This is an exception.
You are a good customer with a highly
satisfactory payment record and, as such,
are one of the most prized assets of our business.
We want to express our appreciation
for this fine record and for your patronage.
We hope that our policy of supplying you
with top products and friendly service
will continue to please you.

M O B I L   O I L   C O M P A N Y
9-34-011

Courtesy Mobil Oil Company

doing for the convenience of its customers—and it is doing them a favor by telling them about it.

Dear Mrs. Jay:

Martin and Richards has added a new service to make it more convenient for you to buy home furnishings on a deferred-payment plan. May we tell you about this new plan?

Whenever you buy home furnishings totaling $50 or more, tell the salesman to open a Home-Furnishings account for you. This will automatically spread your payments over a 12-month period, with each month's payment added to your regular monthly charge account. For example, suppose you purchase new living-room furniture totaling $150. You pay nothing down; but, each month, when you receive your regular monthly statement, you

will find a charge for $12.95 to apply on your home-
furnishings payment, plus a very small carrying charge
Isn't this an easy way to handle your home-furnishings
charges? No separate payments or payment books to worry
about. All your payments are included on your regular
monthly statement.

The next time you need any home furnishings cost-
ing $50 or more, remember to say, "Please open a Home-
Furnishings account for me."

Sincerely yours,

When a new family moves into the community, some progressive
businesses send a welcome to the new resident and offer their
services to him. If the service is not a costly one, an invitation to
try the service with no charge or at a reduced cost is not an uncom-
mon gesture. For example, here is a letter written by a dry-cleaning
establishment to new residents who move into the community it
serves:

Welcome to the Roger family . . . .

We are delighted to have you as residents of
Hazelwood and hope that you enjoy living and working
here as much as we do.

We hope that you will give us an opportunity to
show you the excellent dry-cleaning, pressing, and
shirt-laundering service we make available to Hazelwood
residents—and at low cost, too! Our courteous
drivers will pick up and deliver your clothing and
shirts, or you may prefer to bring them to either our
Market Street or our Randolph Avenue stores. Both have
convenient drive-in windows, so that you don't even
need to get out of your car—and you save 10 per cent
by using our cash-and-carry service.

We are enclosing an introductory card that en-
titles you to a 50 per cent discount on your first
order—no matter how large or how small. Won't you come
in to see us and let us give you a personal welcome to
Hazelwood.

Sincerely yours,

Learning Exercises

1 List as many circumstances as you can under which public relations letters might be written.

2 Assume that you are employed by the Washington Life Insurance Company and that you wish to enlarge your field of operations.

You therefore plan to write letters to the parents of each new baby whose birth is announced in the local newspaper. Write an appropriate letter of congratulations that will indirectly sell your insurance.

3 One of your customers, Mr. William Gaines, has just been elected to serve on the City Council. Write him an appropriate letter that will help develop good public relations.

4 You are employed to handle the correspondence for a local dairy. What is your best source of new customers? Write an indirect sales letter that would be appropriate to send to this source of new customers.

5 As manager of the Townsend Automobile Service Company, you wish to call attention to your new "Quick-Wash" automobile washing service. Write an appropriate letter to your customers announcing this service.

Vocabulary and Spelling Refreshers

1 **Words Often Confused.** Annul, annual; emigrant, immigrant.

2 **Oh, Those Pronouns!** Select from the pronouns within the parentheses the one that is correct in each sentence.

  a I will make my explanations to no one but (he, him).
  b Is Jack as tall as (he, him)?
  c If only the winner could have been (we, us)!
  d There is no doubt as to (who, whom) is to blame.
  e (We, Us) boys have signed up for active service.

3 **Respell These Names.** Using standard spellings, respell these clever names that manufacturers have devised for their products.

  a Ry-Krisp Crackers   d My-T-Fine Pudding Mix
  b Spic and Span Cleanser   e Pepomint Lifesavers
  c Cut-Rite Waxed Paper   f Sunkist Oranges

Communication in Action: *Planned Absence*

Today at the office you learn that you cannot come to work tomorrow. You have a very good reason. Which of the following would you use in dealing with your supervisor: (*a*) Telephone him to-morrow? (*b*) Tell him today? (*c*) Just forget it on the theory that he will not find out? (*d*) Ask your co-workers to tell him in the morning? (*e*) Some other way? Discuss.

UNIT 52

Using Writing Skills to Get a Job

The most important letter you may ever write is a letter applying for a position. This letter may be the first test of how well you have mastered the letter-writing principles presented in this book. If effective, an application letter may succeed in opening doors leading to a bright future in business for you. The letter alone will rarely get you a job, but it may lead to a personal interview and so set you on your way. Many business firms get hundreds of applications, and they cannot possibly follow up on each. Therefore, the letter of application is often used as a basis on which to select the applicants who seem best fitted and from whom a final choice will be made.

Of course, many people obtain employment without writing a letter of application—and that may be the case with you, too, in your first job. However, the letter of application is only one way in which you will use your writing skill—and, sooner or later in your business life, you will be faced with the task of writing some type of letter concerning employment.

Presenting Your Qualifications

The application letter is a sales letter—a letter that attempts to sell your personal services to an employer. The principles of writing sales letters, therefore, concern application letters, too. One of the most important of these principles is that the writer should have a thorough knowledge of the product he is selling. In an application letter, the product is *you*. So before you make application for a position, whether by letter or by some other means, you should first take an inventory of what you have to sell.

The Data Sheet. The best way to present your qualifications to a prospective employer is through a data sheet. A data sheet is a summary of your qualifications that may be sent with a letter of application; may be sent by itself; or may be presented by you to the interviewer. It should be pleasing in appearance and look well balanced and uncrowded. The headings should be made to stand out by underlining them, typing them in all capital letters, or isolating them so that they are distinct from the rest of the copy. Notice how they are handled in the effective data sheet illustrated on page 458.

A data sheet is a personal record that highlights your good points. Since the data sheet is a personal thing, it should reflect your personality and should not be merely a copy of another person's data sheet. In fact, the emphasis on your data sheet may change with each position for which you apply. In each case, you would emphasize your qualifications for the particular job you are seeking. For example, if you apply for a position requiring a high degree of skill in taking dictation, your shorthand training—with transcribing and typewriting speeds and grades—should be emphasized. On the other hand, if the position calls for skill in working with numbers, you should emphasize instead your arithmetic and bookkeeping training.

Experience. The previous experience you may have had can be an important factor in determining whether you are qualified for a position. Therefore, no successful experience should be omitted. If you have not had a full-time position, then be sure to specify any part-time experience you may have had that has contributed to your training. Even if the experience you have had is not closely related to the type of position for which you are applying, it may indicate to your prospective employer that you can get along with people, that you are dependable and resourceful, and that you possess other desirable characteristics of successful workers. Therefore, be sure to mention even such experience as temporary or part-time Christmas, Saturday, or afterschool work; volunteer work for a teacher, relative, church, or community agency. And, if you were in the armed forces, state your classification and highest rank.

Be sure to include these facts about your experience:
1. Name and address of employer.

Personal Record

of

John C. Cusher
65 Dunwood Road
Weston, Missouri

Telephone: 3902

PERSONAL DETAILS	Age: 19 Birthdate: April 5, 1942 Birthplace: Weston, Missouri Height: 5'9" Weight: 165 lbs. Health: Excellent Special interests: Sports, ham radio
EDUCATION	Graduate of Weston High School, 1960 Major Subjects: Bookkeeping, Typewriting, and General Business Extracurricular Activities: Basketball, Ham Radio Club Now studying Accounting at Elora Business Institute evenings
EXPERIENCE July, 1960, to present	Assistant bookkeeper at Traders National Bank, Weston. Duties: posting, checking, and auditing.
January, 1958, to July, 1960	Stock clerk at Brigg's Department Store, Weston, on Saturdays and evenings.
Summers, 1957 and 1956	Farm work.
REFERENCES	Mr. Joseph Lennon Accounting Department Elora Business Institute Weston, Missouri Telephone: 3300 Mr. Judson Grief Accounting Department Traders National Bank Weston, Missouri Telephone: 3510 Mrs. Sylvia Kapra Personnel Department Brigg's Department Store Weston, Missouri Telephone: 3811

A detailed data sheet gives the prospective employer a complete picture of the applicant. Such a data sheet is usually sent with a short covering letter.

2. Type of work you performed. It is best not to give just a title but to include a brief description of the work.

3. Dates of employment.

4. Highest salary received.

Employers frequently prefer that you start your employment listing with your latest employment and work back to your first employment. A prospective employer is usually interested in what you have done most recently. In listing experience by dates, leave no gaps unaccounted for; or the prospective employer may wonder why you have omitted certain dates.

References. Common courtesy requires that you obtain permission before using a person's name for reference. The letter requesting such permission is discussed in Unit 53. Ordinarily, only three or four names need be listed; but others should be available to attest to your experience, education, and character. If possible, select your references according to the job for which you are applying. And let the reference know what kind of position you are applying for so that he will be guided in his reply. If you are applying for a position as bookkeeper, for example, a reference from someone in that field of business would be more appropriate than one from your family doctor. When you ask someone to write a letter of recommendation, enclose a stamped envelope addressed to the prospective employer.

The following information should be given about each reference:

1. Full name, correctly spelled
2. Title—such as *Mr., Mrs., Dr.*
3. Name of business and address
4. Title of his position
5. Telephone number

Filling Out Employment Applications

Most business firms like to have a standardized record for each employee. You will probably be asked to fill out an official application form either before or after you have been hired. Frequently, the personnel interviewer uses the application form as he interviews you. Since he is familiar with this form, he can quickly select from it items about which he may question you. Too, the application form provides a great deal of information about the applicant other than the answers to the questions asked—information regarding the legibility of his penmanship, his accuracy and carefulness, his neatness, and his ability to follow written directions.

EMPLOYMENT APPLICATION

L & B INC.

Date *July 18, 1961*

Name (Last Name First) *Colborne, Julia Ellen* Age *19* Born: Mo. *8* Day *2* Year *42*

Address *7 Maple Place, Adelphi 3, Md.* Telephone *HA. 1-7040* Soc. Sec. No. *312-85-1261*

How long have you lived at this address? *19 years* Citizen? *U.S.A.*

Male _____ Female *✓* Weight *116* Height *5'4"* Any serious illness? *None*

Single *✓* Married _____ Other _____ No. Children _____ Ages _____

Other Dependents _____ Explain _____

What kind of work are you applying for? *Secretarial or Stenographic*

What special qualifications do you have? *Shorthand: 120 w.p.m.; Typewriting: 70 w.p.m.; Bookkeeping*

What office machines can you operate? *Duplicating, calculating, voice writing*

Who referred you to us? *My aunt, Mrs. James Boulton*

Do you have any relatives working for this Company? *Mrs. Boulton*

MILITARY SERVICE RECORD

Have you served in the U. S. Armed Forces? *No* From _____ To _____

Branch of Service _____ Duties _____

Rank or rating at time of enlistment _____ Rating at time of discharge _____

Type of discharge _____ Any disability? _____

EDUCATION

SCHOOL	DATE FROM	DATE TO	NAME OF SCHOOL	CITY	COURSE	DID YOU GRADUATE
GRAMMAR	9/47	6/55	Heights School	Adelphi	—	Yes
HIGH	9/55	6/59	Adelphi High School	Adelphi	Academic	Yes
COLLEGE	9/59	6/60	University of Maryland	College Park	Economics	No
OTHER	7/60	7/61	Loris Business School	Washington, D.C.	Commercial	Yes

EXPERIENCE (ENTER LAST JOB FIRST)

NAME AND ADDRESS OF COMPANY	DATE FROM	DATE TO	LIST YOUR DUTIES	STARTING SALARY	FINAL SALARY	REASON FOR LEAVING
Goudy Realtors 88-120 Mayflower St Adelphi 1, Md.	7/60	7/61	General clerical, including payroll	$47	$50	Desire secretarial job
Fremont Bakery 55 West Street Adelphi 1, Md.	summers 1957-1959		Salesclerk	$40	$40	Return to school

REFERENCES (NOT RELATIVES)

NAME	ADDRESS	OCCUPATION
Richard Meyer	151 Queens Rd., Hyattsville	Pharmacist
Mrs. Elmo James	Youth Council, Adelphi	Director of Youth Council
Miss Ruth Comfort	U. of Maryland, College Park	Instructor in English

A job applicant may be asked to complete a printed application form. Notice the various categories into which such a form may be divided.

Here are some suggestions to follow in filling out application forms:

1. Bring with you:

a. A filled fountain pen. Most pens provided for public use are not dependable. And a scratchy or ink-blotched application form will reflect on your neatness.

b. Two copies of your data sheet, one for the interviewer and one to use in filling out details on the application blank.

c. Your Social Security card, if you have previously worked.

2. Avoid asking unnecessary questions. Become familiar with the type of questions usually asked on an application form.

3. Write legibly. Your handwriting does not need to be fancy, but it must be legible. You should take particular care that any figures you write are clear. If the interviewer has difficulty reading your writing, you will start your interview with one strike against you—if you get as far as an interview!

4. Be accurate and careful. Recheck all the information you have included. Have you given your year of birth where it is asked for, and not this year's date? Is your telephone number correct? Be careful to avoid any readily discernible evidences of carelessness.

5. Don't leave any blanks. If the information asked for does not apply to you, draw a line through that space or mark it, "Does not apply." Otherwise, the interviewer may think you were careless and did not see some of the items.

6. Follow directions exactly. An applicant who cannot follow directions that he has before him and may read several times certainly will not be able to follow the many oral instructions given on the job once and not repeated. If the directions say to print, then do so. If the directions call for last name first, don't put your first name first. If you are asked to start your employment record with your last job, then don't list your jobs in chronological order.

Learning Exercises

1 Make a list of all the sources of positions in your community.

2 Prepare a personal data sheet outlining your qualifications for a position. Describe the abilities and skills you expect to have when you are ready to apply for a job.

3 Obtain, from two local business concerns, applications for a position with those firms. Fill them out just as you would if you were going to apply. Be prepared to discuss these application forms in class.

Vocabulary and Spelling Refreshers

1 **Words Often Confused.** Born, borne; coarse, course.

2 **Wanted: Adjectives.** What are the adjective forms of these verbs?

a permit	**c** benefit	**e** indulge
b admire	**d** extend	**f** transfer

3 **"Ant" or "ent"?** Should *ant* or *ent* be added to the following to form the correctly spelled words?

a defend__	**c** superintend__	**e** depend__
b persist__	**d** excell__	**f** descend__

Communication in Action: *Placing a Printing Order*

As chairman of the program committee, you are to have tickets printed for the annual employee dance. Use your own ideas about time, place, and cost. For the ticket, prepare a dummy copy that will give the printer an idea of what you want. Then, make a list of the things you will want to find out before the job is actually assigned to a printer.

UNIT 53

Writing Employment Letters

As a business worker, you probably will have occasion to write one or more of the following types of employment letters:

1. A letter of application. This letter may be written in response to a newspaper advertisement; at the suggestion of a relative, friend, teacher, or business acquaintance; or at your own instigation, even though you do not know of a specific job opening in the business to which you write.

2. Letters requesting references or permission to use someone's name as a reference.

3. An interview follow-up letter to thank the employer for granting you the interview and to re-emphasize some of your qualifications that particularly fit you for the job.

4. A letter accepting a position.

5. A letter refusing a position.

6. A thank-you letter to each person who helped you in your job-seeking campaign.

7. A letter resigning from a position.

The Letter of Application

No letter you write will be more important to you than a letter of application. In most cases, the prospective employer has no basis other than your letter to judge your qualifications. A successful application letter can give a prospective employer a favorable impression of you that may earn you the privilege of a personal interview. You should, therefore, take great care in planning and writing an application letter.

Appearance. The appearance of the application letter gives the reader a clue to the appearance and work habits of the writer. A sloppy letter suggests that the writer may not be careful about his own appearance or about his work habits—and this is not the kind of impression you want your letter to make.

The writer of an application letter should put his best foot forward. He wants the prospective employer to be favorably impressed and to grant him an interview. The physical appearance of the letter can do much to help create this favorable impression. Follow these instructions, therefore, in preparing your letter:

1. Use a good grade of 8½-by-11 bond paper. Be certain that it is clean and free from smudges and finger marks both before and after you use it.

2. Typewrite your letter of application, unless you have been specifically requested to submit an application in your own handwriting or unless it is impossible to use a typewriter. If you write your letter by hand, be certain to use your most legible handwriting. Here is a brief summary of some suggestions to follow when typewriting or when writing your letter by hand:

When typewriting	When writing by hand
a. Make no strikeovers.	*a.* Avoid ink smudges.
b. Make very neat erasures.	*b.* Keep your lines of writing straight.
c. Use a black ribbon that is neither too worn nor too smudgy.	*c.* Write slowly and carefully so that each word is readable.

3. If possible, address yourself to an individual in the organization.
4. Be sure to give your full name, address, and telephone number.
5. Don't forget to sign the letter.

Organizing the Letter. Since every application letter should be accompanied by a data sheet that gives your qualifications in detail, the letter of application need not be long and detailed. Instead, it should serve to introduce your data sheet. If, for some reason, a data sheet is not included, the letter may be longer and present more details about your qualifications.

The principal elements of an application letter include:

1. A statement expressing interest in a particular position.

2. A statement indicating that a detailed data sheet is enclosed and pointing out some of your special qualifications for this particular position. You also may indicate why you wish to be employed by this particular organization.

3. A statement telling where and how you can be reached to make arrangements for a personal interview.

These three elements need not follow any special plan but should be varied to fit the particular situation.

Beginning the Letter. An application letter may begin in any one of several ways. A challenging question makes an effective beginning, provided the writer's qualifications can meet the challenge made. Some illustrations of this type of opening are:

> Does your organization need a work expediter—someone who can really make the wheels of progress move?
>
> Can your typists produce 40 letters every day—letters that you would be proud to sign? I can—and I can prove this ability.
>
> Is there a place in your organization for a young man who is conscientious and eager to learn, even though inexperienced?
>
> Can you use a secretary who can relieve you of many of your daily routines? I'm your girl Friday.

Another good beginning for an application letter is a summary statement of your qualifications. This beginning gives the reader an immediate indication of your ability and training—and, if they seem to reflect what he is looking for, he will read further. Here are some examples:

> My ten years of successful accounting experience should qualify me for the position of chief accountant with your firm.

>   Two years at Moore's Business School have provided
> me with the training in clerical work that should
> qualify me for the position of general clerk adver-
> tised in The Evening Register on May 18.
>   My service record, added to my four years of
> business training at Keene College, should be of in-
> terest to an organization that wants a well-trained,
> willing worker.

When you have been told about a vacancy by another person—an employee of the organization or a friend of the person to whom you are writing or a teacher or guidance counselor—it is often effective to use that person's name (with his permission) in your opening paragraph. For example:

>   Mr. James Alden, your office manager, has told me
> that you need a secretary. I have had four years of
> experience as a private secretary and believe I have
> the qualifications you require.
>   Miss Irene Lawrence, who is employed in your ad-
> vertising department, indicated that you are looking
> for an advertising manager. Would my twelve years of
> experience as a copy writer and layout specialist be of
> interest to you?
>   My guidance counselor, Mrs. J. N. Blunt, has
> talked with me about the excellent opportunities for
> bookkeepers in your firm. I should like to be con-
> sidered for one of these positions.

Developing the Body of the Letter. In the body of the letter, you should offer support for the statements made in the opening paragraph. Emphasize the highlights of your educational background and business experience, making reference to the enclosed data sheet. You may also indicate why you would like to be employed by the firm to which you are applying. Following this suggested plan, the body of your application letter might sound like this:

>   I can take dictation at 120 words a minute, op-
> erate a switchboard, answer routine letters, and type
> accurately and rapidly. I have also had training in
> modern filing procedures. For the past two years, I
> have had an opportunity to become familiar with these
> business activities in the offices of Bryant and Lane,
> Incorporated.
>
>   As the enclosed data sheet indicates, my training
> and experience have equipped me, I believe, to fill
> the position of general office worker with your firm.
> Since I have always been interested in the advertising
> field, I am particularly eager to be employed by an
> outstanding advertising organization like yours.

Concluding the Letter. A good conclusion tells the reader what you wish him to do. In a letter of application, you would like the reader to grant a personal interview. Therefore, ask for an interview and make your request easy to grant. Here are some suggested ways to accomplish this:

> May I have an appointment for a personal interview? You may telephone me at LIberty 2-4878.
> I need only twenty minutes to convince you that I am the man you need to fill your vacancy. May I have an interview at your convenience? Just jot down a convenient day and hour on the enclosed self-addressed postal card.

If the prospective employer is located some distance away, the applicant may write:

> I am planning to be in Westerville on June 9 and 10. May I see you on either of those days?

Sample Letters of Application. The following letter of application for a position as stenographer was written by a high school student with limited business experience.

Letter 1

> 8207 Shelley Lane
> Denver 4, Colorado
> May 16, 19—
>
> Mr. George S. Dickerson
> Personnel Director
> Atlas Manufacturing Company
> 2014 Market Street
> Denver 10, Colorado
>
> Dear Mr. Dickerson:
>
> Mr. Lawrence, who is in charge of placement at Larkin High School, has told me that there is an opening in your organization for a competent stenographer. If I may have a few minutes of your time, I should like to tell you why I think I can satisfactorily fill that opening.
>
> You will notice on the enclosed data sheet that I have had two years of shorthand dictation and transcription training at Larkin High School and have achieved a high standard of speed in both shorthand and typewriting. During this period of training, I worked part time in the principal's office, where I took dictation, typed, handled the switchboard, filed, and performed the duties of a receptionist. Last summer, I worked full time as a vacation replacement stenographer at the Denver First National Bank. You will find

additional details on the enclosed data sheet, as well as the names of references who can speak for my training and my experience. I enjoyed my work as a stenographer and am confident that I can adequately fill your vacancy.

I can be ready to start work on June 19.

You may reach me at MOuntain 3-8906 any day after 3:30 p.m. I hope that I may have the privilege of a personal interview at your convenience.

Sincerely yours,

Letter 2 was written by a young man applying for a bookkeeping position.

Letter 2

4314 Sunset Road
Middletown, Illinois
June 2, 19—

Box 176
Middletown Herald
Middletown, Illinois

Gentlemen:

Two years of high school bookkeeping, followed by a year of accounting in the evening school program at Middletown Business School, have given me a thorough preparation in all phases of bookkeeping work.

I am presently employed as an accounts receivable clerk, but I should like to find a position where I can make wider use of my bookkeeping training and where I shall have an opportunity to get into a more advanced phase of accounting. I plan to continue my accounting training through an evening school program.

The enclosed data sheet provides all the details of my education and experience and suggests a number of people from whom you may obtain references regarding my character and ability.

May I have a personal interview? I may be reached by telephone at REgent 4-6967, Ext. 413, from 9 a.m. to 5 p.m. or at DExter 5-8734 after 6 p.m.

Sincerely yours,

Requesting References

Almost every prospective employer likes to have references regarding the character, training, experience, and work habits of job applicants. You may need to supply only the name, title, and address of references, leaving to the interested prospective employer the task of obtaining the references he desires. Under some circumstances, you may request that the person speaking on your behalf write a letter of reference directly to the prospective employer. In most cases, a letter of reference that you carry with you is not too effective.

Before using a person's name as a reference, you should request his permission to do so. This permission may be obtained in person, by telephone, or by a letter such as the following:

Dear Mrs. Hudson:

I am applying for a position as file clerk with several firms in this city.

Since I was a student in your Office Practice class, where I had excellent filing instruction, I should like permission to use your name as a reference.

I am enclosing a self-addressed postal card for your reply.

Sincerely yours,

If you are writing to request that a reference be sent directly to a prospective employer, you may say:

Dear Mr. Martin:

I am applying for a clerical position with the Bank of Danville.

Since I have worked on a part-time basis for you at the Second National Bank, I should appreciate your sending a reference for me to Mr. W. L. Watkins, Personnel Director at the Bank of Danville. I am enclosing an addressed, stamped envelope for your convenience.

Sincerely yours,

Follow-Up Letters

The Interview Follow-Up. If your application letter has succeeded in obtaining a personal interview for you, the next letter you should write will follow the personal interview. This letter may serve one or more of the following purposes:

1. To thank the interviewer for the time and courtesy extended to you

2. To let the interviewer know you are still interested in the position

3. To remind the interviewer of the special qualifications you have for this position

4. To return the application form that the interviewer may have given you to take home to complete

5. To provide any additional data requested by the interviewer that you may not have had available at the time of the interview

Here is a letter that accomplishes all five purposes:

> Dear Mr. Mason:
>
> Thank you for talking with me yesterday about the vacancy in your bookkeeping department. You gave me a very good insight into what would be expected of anyone who fills this position.
>
> I am very much interested in the job you have available and feel that my experience with the Lyons Automobile Company during the past two years will prove a definite asset in fulfilling my duties.
>
> I am returning the completed application form and am also enclosing the photograph you requested. A transcript of my school grades is being sent to you by the principal of the high school I attended.
>
> I hope that you will consider my application favorably and that you will let me know if I may provide you with any additional information. Thank you again for your courtesy.
>
> > Sincerely yours,

The Letter of Acceptance. If you are notified by mail that you are being offered the position for which you applied, you should write a letter of acceptance. This letter:

1. Acknowledges the offer
2. Notifies your employer-to-be of your acceptance
3. Reassures the employer that he has chosen the right person
4. Informs the employer when you can report for work

The letter of acceptance may read:

> Dear Mr. Wilton:
>
> I was delighted to receive your letter of June 19 offering me the position of clerk-typist with the Phoenix Bank.
>
> I am most happy to accept this position and will make every effort to be the kind of worker that is an asset to the business.
>
> Since our graduation activities will be over on Friday, June 26, I can report for work on Monday, June 29.
>
> I am looking forward to my association with you and the others at the Phoenix Bank.
>
> > Sincerely yours,

The Letter of Refusal. Perhaps you have been offered a position for which you made application, but you have also received another offer that you feel is better. You should return the courtesy extended to you by writing a tactful, friendly letter of refusal. This letter may read:

Dear Mr. Wilton:

Thank you for offering me the position of clerk-typist with the Phoenix Bank.

I am sorry that I cannot accept your kind offer, but I have had another position offered to me that I feel will provide greater opportunities for advancement.

Please accept my sincere appreciation for the many kindnesses you have extended to me.

Very sincerely yours,

Thank-You Letters. The persons who have written reference letters for you undoubtedly helped you obtain a position. You should be courteous enough to let them know that you have accepted the position. You might write:

Dear Miss Axelrod:

Thank you so much for writing a reference for me to Mr. William Landrum.

I am sure you will be pleased to learn that I have accepted a position as Mr. Landrum's secretary and will begin work next Monday.

I hope some day to be able to repay you for your kindness.

Very cordially yours,

The Letter of Resignation

Occasionally, you may need to write a letter resigning from a position. Regardless of your reason for resigning, your letter should be friendly in tone and tactful. Some day you may want this employer to give you a reference, and you want him to remember you favorably. The following letter is a good example of a letter of resignation.

June 15, 19—

Dear Mr. Norvell:

I wish to resign from my present position effective June 30, in order to accept a position with the Mackin Insurance Company.

I have enjoyed my work at the Industrial Life Insurance Company; but in my new position, I shall have more opportunity to use my stenographic training. In addition, I shall have more opportunities for advancement.

I wish to thank you for the many kindnesses that have made my work here for the past two years such a pleasant and worthwhile experience.

Sincerely yours,

Learning Exercises

1 The following advertisements appeared in yesterday's edition of your local newspaper. Write a letter of application answering one of these advertisements.

> BOOKKEEPER for Springville National Bank. High school graduate, male or female. Apply to Mr. D. C. McComb.

> TYPIST, General Insurance Company. Male or female; must be accurate and fast. Apply to Personnel Director.

> CLERK for Rockport County Tax Office. Some typing, filing, and ability to work with numbers. Apply to Supervisor of Personnel, James Davis.

2 Write a letter to one of your business teachers requesting permission to use his or her name as a reference.

3 You have had a personal interview for one of the jobs in Exercise 1. Write a follow-up letter to the person who interviewed you.

4 You receive a letter notifying you that you have been selected to fill the vacancy for which you applied. Write a letter accepting the position.

5 Suppose you preferred to accept another position; write a letter refusing the position offered to you in Exercise 4.

6 Write a letter to the business teacher who wrote a letter of reference for you, notifying the teacher that you have accepted a position.

7 You have been employed as a general office worker for the past eighteen months in the small business owned by Mr. Donald Luce. You have been offered a position with a larger firm, with opportunity for advancement. Under what circumstances would you give written rather than oral notice to Mr. Luce? Why? Write an appropriate letter resigning from your position.

Vocabulary and Spelling Refreshers

1 **Words Often Confused.** Decent, descent, dissent; imitate, intimate.

2 **Choose the Correct Word.** In each of these sentences select from the words within parentheses the one that conveys the meaning correctly.

- **a** Under a city (ordnance, ordinance) Christmas trees in public places may not be lighted.
- **b** The speaker's veiled (illusion, allusion, delusion) to "the enemies within" was understood by all.
- **c** The (areas, arrears, arias) of the two plots are nearly the same.
- **d** I have promised to make a (canvas, canvass) for new members for our Glee Club.
- **e** Why is Texas called the "(Loan, Lone) Star State"?

3 **One Letter Short.** Only one letter is missing from each of the following. Spell the correctly completed words.

a acordance	**c** recurence	**e** promisory
b anser	**d** inteligent	**f** conscientous

Communication in Action: *Innocent Bystander*

You are a salesperson in the floor-covering section of a large store. Your telephone rings, and it is a customer asking about rug-cleaning fluid. This item is not carried in your department but in the house-wares section. When you tell the caller that you will transfer him, he says, "This makes the third time I have been given the run-around—everyone transfers me to someone else. Don't you people know what you're doing down there?" What would you say?

Section 5   Other Business Communications

UNIT   54

Social-Business Correspondence

Why Social-Business Correspondence?

Many people feel that business is impersonal and that one's business life should be kept separate from one's personal or social life. To do so would be nearly im-possible. In fact, success in business depends to a great extent upon the depth of good feeling that exists be-tween a business and its customers, vendors, associates, and even competitors. You should not, therefore, con-fine your friendly relations to face-to-face encounters. Letters, too, may serve as friendly ambassadors of good will.

Some of the people with whom you do business be-come personal friends; a great many of them become known to you on more than a strictly formal business basis. The business executive receives invitations from his business associates outside the company to attend social functions; often he is granted special favors or receives gifts. From time to time, a business person whom he knows receives a promotion or a special honor. Or a business acquaintance may be struck by a personal tragedy—serious illness, an operation, or a death in the family. These situations call for letters to be written and provide opportunities for building friendly relations.

Of course, the purpose of social-business letters is not sales promotion. They are just as appropriate as letters to your weekend host or to personal friends who have been especially thoughtful. The businessman who takes the time to write social-business letters will be remembered, and such letters will reflect personal credit on him. They will undoubtedly build good will for his company, even though this is not the underlying purpose of social-business letters.

You already know that all special favors should be acknowledged by a personal letter. If a friend invites you to spend a weekend, you will write a thank-you note upon returning home. When someone presents you with a gift for your birthday, Christmas, graduation, or some other special occasion, you always write a letter of appreciation. Likewise, acts of kindness while you are hospitalized or during periods of personal grief should always be acknowledged by letter. If someone helps you obtain a job, gets hard-to-obtain concert or theater tickets, or goes out of his way to be thoughtful, a letter of appreciation should be written. In business, the same courtesies should be shown.

Kinds of Social-Business Letters

Many executives who every day write effective business letters dealing with business matters find it difficult to compose social-business letters. As a junior correspondent, you may be asked to write some of these social-business letters. Here is an excellent opportunity to reveal your abilities.

Letters Expressing Thanks. A businessman who receives a gift or is granted a special favor should acknowledge the gift or favor and express his appreciation. The following are examples of thank-you letters frequently written by business executives and employees. Each letter illustrates a different style that may be used in writing social letters for personal or business use.

For a Gift

```
                                        3304 Bradley Lane
                                        Rochester 4, New York
                                        December 29, 19—

Mr. Ralph Jensen
Dexter Publishing Company
Racine 4, Wisconsin

Dear Mr. Jensen:

        I was delighted to receive the Old-World maps you
so thoughtfully sent to me. They are going to be framed
for my office, and they will look mighty handsome
with our new mahogany paneling.
```

Thank you very much. Perhaps the next time you visit us, you can see to what good use I am putting your most thoughtful gift.

Sincerely yours,

For Special Favors

RONALD ASTOR

1215 Glendale Avenue   San Diego, California

June 25, 19--

Dear Mr. Randolph:

I appreciate more than I can say your thoughtfulness in getting tickets for Mrs. Astor and me to "Lady Beautiful." We enjoyed this musical show enormously--and the seats were just about perfect.

Thank you for helping to make our visit to New York a memorable one.

Cordially yours,

44 Ronson Boulevard
St. Louis 16, Missouri
December 26, 19—

Dear Helen,

Mrs. Fitzroy called last week, asking me to show her my complete line of cosmetics. She mentioned that you had recommended me to her.

I feel sure that this opportunity to display my wares to Mrs. Fitzroy represents an enormous potential in sales. It is up to me now to come through — you have certainly done your part and more.

Thank you, Helen! I'll telephone you next week to let you know if I succeed. Perhaps we can arrange to have dinner together.

Sincerely,

Letters of Congratulation. The following are examples of letters of congratulation. These letters are usually written by the person who is to sign them, especially when the writer is a personal friend of the individual whom he is congratulating.

Sincerely,

To an Employee. Whenever a businessman takes the time to recognize a milestone in the career of one of his employees, his thoughtfulness is certain to be rewarded in terms of a more productive employee. How do you think Marcia would react to this letter from her employer?

Dear Marcia,

In the ten years you have been with Drysdale's you have seen our company grow from a small local factory to a nationwide organization. Responsible for this remarkable growth are highly productive and faithful employees like you. It is a pleasure for me to write this letter of congratulation on your tenth anniversary, for it gives me an opportunity to thank you for your contribution to our success.

As head of our filing department, you have set up a highly flexible and effective system for handling the increasing volume of records. I am sure you have heard the often-repeated statement around the office, "If you don't know, ask Marcia." This is indeed a tribute to your efficiency.

I look forward to working with you in the years ahead. When I think of the slogan, "Drysdale's is people," I can't help calling to mind a picture of Marcia Haskins and all those like her who help to make our organization the congenial, effective group it is today.

Sincerely yours,

Letters of Condolence. Letters of condolence are among the most difficult to write. Such letters should be brief and dignified. Obviously, the writer should not be maudlin or recall too vividly the grief recently suffered. Such letters are nearly always written by the person signing them—rarely by a secretary or an assistant. Some businessmen prefer to send a sympathy card rather than a letter, feeling that cards can convey much more effectively the delicate words of consolation. Following is an example of a letter of condolence:

```
Dear Mark,

     I was saddened to learn of the death of your
mother last week. Please accept my sincere sympathy.

     When my mother passed away two years ago, a friend
sent me a copy of the enclosed poem by Thaddeus
Milburn. I have received much consolation from the
poetic words, and I thought they might help to comfort
you as they did me.

     My thoughts are with you and your family in your
hour of grief.
                              Sincerely yours,
```

To give the letter a more personal touch, it should be written by hand rather than on the typewriter. However, except in the case of a close, personal friend, a typewritten message is acceptable. When the typewriter is used, the inside address is usually placed at the foot of the letter (see page 336).

Formal Invitations and Replies. Occasionally, business people receive formal invitations—to an open house, a special party to honor a distinguished person, a special anniversary, or a formal social gathering. Such invitations are usually engraved or printed and are

---

The Literary Club

requests the pleasure of your company

at a tea

in honor of

John Whitleaf

on Saturday, May the sixth

at four o'clock

Suite 13 of the Howard Building

Please reply

> *Mr. and Mrs. George Randolph*
> *request the pleasure of the company of*
> *Mr. and Mrs. Lawrence Wentlow*
> *at dinner*
> *on Monday, the fourth of April*
> *at eight o'clock*
> *8106 Keats Road*
> *R.S.V.P.*

written in the third person. Note the printed invitation on page 477 and the handwritten one here.

Handwritten invitations are written on plain white note paper. In some instances, invitations are typewritten; but this practice is not recommended.

Replies to formal invitations are often requested, as indicated in the illustrations by *Please reply* or *R. S. V. P.* (an abbreviation of the French *Répondez, s'il vous plaît,* which means "Please answer"). If the invitation is written in the third person, the reply is also written in the third person and follows the wording and arrangement of the invitation. The following illustrate a formal acceptance and a formal refusal of invitations.

Acceptance

> *Mr. William Gregory*
> *accepts with pleasure*
> *the kind invitation of*
> *The Literary Club*
> *to attend a Tea on*
> *Saturday, May the sixth*
> *at four o'clock*
> *Suite 13 of the Howard Building*

Refusal

Mr. and Mrs. Lawrence Wentlow
regret that a previous engagement
prevents their accepting
the kind invitation to dinner
at the home of
Mr. and Mrs. George Randolph
on Monday, the fourth of April

The Master Letter Writer

To be classified as an expert business correspondent, you must be able to write letters that do not deal directly with business transactions. There is a social side to business that calls for the writing of social-business letters, letters that would be written by a person of good breeding in a similar situation in private life. Because these letters are admittedly difficult to write, the junior correspondent who can compose them will be a well-rounded, proficient writer of business letters.

Learning Exercises

1 Assume that a salesman who calls frequently at your firm sends you a gift at Christmas (you may decide what the gift is) in appreciation of your courtesy to him. Write him a thank-you letter.

2 A friend of yours recommended to Mr. Henry Lowell that he consider placing all his printing work with your firm. Write an appropriate letter of appreciation to this friend.

3 You read in last night's local newspaper that a business acquaintance received a promotion. Write a letter of congratulations.

4 One of your employees was named "Junior Executive of the Year" by the local Junior Chamber of Commerce. Write him a letter that shows how proud your firm is to have the type of employee he represents.

5 One of your employees receives a 25-year pin for loyalty to the firm. Write him a letter in honor of this event.

✓6 The father of a good business friend of yours died this week. Write your friend a letter of condolence.

7 Prepare a formal invitation to attend an open house in honor of the new offices your firm has opened. This invitation is to be printed and sent to all the firm's customers.

8 You have received two formal invitations for dinner on the same evening. You must accept one and refuse the other. Write the appropriate acceptance and refusal.

Vocabulary and Spelling Refreshers

1 **Words Often Confused.** Liable, libel; ingenious, ingenuous.

2 **Pick the Synonym.** Which of the three words following each of these phrases is closest in meaning to the italicized word in the phrase?

    a *Visionary* plans. Successful, tried, fanciful.
    b *Perceptible* change. Great, appreciable, invisible.
    c A *pretentious* wardrobe. Showy, unnecessary, well-selected.
    d An *unbiased* opinion. Unfair, impartial, inconsistent.
    e An *inimitable* style of writing. Tiresome, commonplace, matchless.

3 **Wanted: Apostrophes!** Where are apostrophes needed in the following sentences?

    a If youll play the violin, Ill sing a solo.
    b Theyre all wearing their galoshes. Where are yours?
    c Its time for the baby to have its nap.
    d We require a two weeks notice on all orders.
    e Whose brief case is this?

Communication in Action: *Listening*

Your instructor will read a short article. Listen carefully, trying to absorb every important detail. Be prepared to give an accurate oral summary of the article.

UNIT 55

Writing Memorandums

The memorandum is a form of business letter and should be written with as much care as a letter. The main difference between a memorandum and a letter is that the memorandum is written to a person in one's own company, while a letter is written to someone outside the company. Memorandums are used to communicate with other employees regardless of where the employees may be located—whether in the same building or in a branch office hundreds of miles away.

Because the interoffice memorandum form was designed to save time, the formality of an inside address, salutation, and complimentary closing is dispensed with. In other respects, however, office memorandums and letters have a great deal in common, as you will see from the following discussion.

The Tone of Memorandums

In some companies, where business relationships are quite formal and the executives are not on a first-name basis, memorandums are likely to be written in the third person, thus:

```
It is believed that . ..      (instead of "I believe")
It will be seen that . . .    (instead of "You can
readily see that")
It is recommended that . . .  (instead of "I recom-
mend")
The requested report has been completed . . .
(instead of "I have completed the report you asked for")
```

In most companies, however, memorandums are written in first person just as are business letters. There is no hard-and-fast rule about tone in memorandums. The manner in which they are written will depend upon the preferences of the management in the company by which you are employed. Those who maintain that inter-office correspondence should be formal believe that information will be more accurately presented and more objectively read if "I" and "we" are kept out of the message. They believe that, in a memo written in first person, it is easy to confuse fact with opinion. However, the trend is decidedly away from the stiff, formal writing style that characterized business letters and memorandums several years ago.

The tone of the report is influenced also by the position held by the writer in relation to that held by the person to whom he is writing. Obviously, a person writing to the company president is less likely to be casual and breezy than if he were writing to an equal in rank. However, the personality of the individual receiving the memorandum is what actually determines its tone. The president may like informality, for example, whereas a minor executive might insist on complete objectivity and an impersonal writing style.

Writing the Memorandum

There are usually three main parts to a memorandum:
1. The heading
2. The subject
3. The message

The Heading. The heading of a memorandum may be printed and appear as follows:

The Dryson Hardware Company · *Memorandum*

DATE

TO   FROM

SUBJECT

Sometimes a simpler form is used that merely says:

MEMO from the desk of _____

If the writer uses a great many memorandums, his name may be printed in the space provided for it.

In the TO and FROM section, the title of each of the persons is often included, particularly when the memorandum is being sent to a person whose office is in another city.

```
TO: Mr. Gordon Kessler, Office Manager
FROM: Ralph Sisson, Treasurer
```

The Subject. The subject, a brief statement telling what the memorandum is about, helps the reader to prepare himself for the contents. For example, the subject may read:

```
SUBJECT: Proposed Budget for Capital Outlay for 19--
```

The Message. The message is usually in three parts. The first part tells the reader why the memorandum is written. This may include telling the reader what you are going to do and how. The second part conveys the information—the details—telling the reader what you said you were going to tell him, in the manner you indicated. Finally, the memorandum gives suggestions for future action or requests guidance on future action. Note how these parts stand out in the memorandum illustrated below.

BULMER INC.   *memorandum*

April 27, 19--

Note that a title precedes addressee's name, but not writer's	TO: Mr. Vernon O. Harris, Advertising Manager FROM: Milton David
Keep subject brief, but be specific	SUBJECT: Advertising Space in Office Equipment Magazines in 19--
Why the memorandum is being written	The analysis of advertising space in the four leading trade magazines you asked for in your memorandum of January 16 has now been completed.
Information the report is to convey	Twelve issues (January through December, 19--) of each of the four leading trade magazines in the office equipment field were analyzed. The pages of advertising for each magazine for the entire year were then totaled and averaged.

These averages are as follows:

Office Equipment World	--	32
Today's Office	--	29
Modern Office Equipment	--	26
Office Facts	--	19

Suggested future action

I am attaching the monthly figures from which these averages were obtained. In preparing the report, I also classified the types of advertising—furniture, machines, stationery and forms, and miscellaneous. If these figures would be of interest to you, please let me know. It will take only a short time to put them in tabulated form.

M. D.

When Are Memorandums Written?

Many business firms advise their employees to put in writing all important information that crosses their desks. Written records help to fix responsibility. If you are sending important papers or documents to another person, for example, it is best to transmit them by memorandum so that, if they become lost, there will be no question as to whether or not they were actually sent.

TO: Mr. Leland Warren   DATE: June 4, 19—

FROM: Sarah Freeman

SUBJECT: Safeway Meat Comparison Test

Attached is the Safeway Meat Comparison Test report that you asked to see.

Would you please return the report to me when you have finished with it. Incidentally, Mr. Walston has asked that this report not be circulated outside the company.

S. F.

The following is an example of a request correctly written in the form of a memorandum.

DATE: May 2, 19—

TO: Mr. Charles L. Coleman, Office Manager

FROM: Patricia Ann Thompson

SUBJECT: Request for Extended Vacation

As you know, I plan to attend my sister's wedding in Memphis in June; and I am taking my two weeks' vacation allowance for the occasion.

After the wedding, I plan to drive my mother to Biloxi, Mississippi, to visit her sister, who is hospitalized. If permissible, I should like to extend my vacation two extra days for the purpose of making this trip. My vacation, therefore, would begin on Monday, June 8; and I would return on Wednesday, June 24, instead of Monday, the 22d. Naturally, I should expect to forefeit my salary for these two extra days.

May I have your decision on this request sometime this week so that I may let my family know my plans?

P. A. T.

Displaying Detailed Matter

A memorandum containing a great many details will be easier to read if each point is numbered in 1-2-3 order, each number starting a new paragraph. Enumerations also help the reader to refer by number to specific points when he is replying.

When the memorandum contains statistical matter, the writer should display this material in tabulated form for easier reading. Note the following example.

OFFICE MEMORANDUM **ITEM** INCORPORATED

TO	Mr. Blackwell, Sales Manager	FROM	R. J. Keene, Advertising Manager
LOCATION	Room 604, 3d Floor	LOCATION	Room 312, 8th Floor
SUBJECT	Monthly Advertising Report	DATE	April 3, 19--

Following is the monthly summary of the advertising expenditures for March:

1. Magazine Advertising

	Space	Cost
Modern Business	$\frac{1}{2}$ page	$375.00
Office Supervision	1 page	200.00
Today's Manager	$\frac{1}{4}$ page	90.00
Equipment Dealer	$\frac{1}{4}$ page	35.00
Total Magazine Advertising		$700.00

2. Circular Advertising

	Quantity	Unit	Cost
Circular B (Mfg. List)	3,000	.113	$ 340.00
Circular X (Office Mgr. List)	2,800	.099	278.00
NBI Letter (General List)	6,000	.079	472.00
Total Circular Advertising			$1,090.00

Total spent during March	$1,790.00
(February:	$1,782.00)

Of special interest is the new printing rate on the NBI Letter. Although the rates for Circular B and Circular X have increased slightly over last month, we were able to lower the unit rate on the NBI Letter from .098 to .079 because of the new size and format.

Mr. Kingston, of Premier Printing, is now getting new cost estimates on Circulars B and X based on our revised design of these pieces. We are hopeful that we can bring our total costs down to $1,600 and still have more effective circulars.

R. J. Keene

Learning Exercises

1 Write a brief memorandum announcing a meeting of one of the clubs to which you belong.

2 Write a request to your supervisor asking that your vacation be changed from the two weeks beginning July 5 to the two weeks beginning July 12. Point out that during the week of July 5 you have some personal business that prevents your going away at that time.

3 Send a memorandum to your teacher, summarizing a meeting or class discussion in which you recently participated.

4 Your office manager would like to set up a standard form for printed memos. Draw up a sample memorandum form and send it to him, together with a memorandum indicating the standards you followed.

5 The football coach asks for a memorandum summarizing the equipment and uniform needs for next season. Prepare a detailed memorandum.

Vocabulary and Spelling Refreshers

1 **Words Often Confused.** Passed, past; charted, chartered.

2 **Matching Definitions to Words.** Match each simple definition in column A to the word in column B to which it applies.

A	B
a To sparkle	1 adjacent
b Quiet	2 liberate
c Situated near	3 peculiar
d To serve as a witness	4 glisten
e To set free	5 tranquil
	6 deceive
	7 polite
	8 testify

3 **What's the Superlative?** What are the superlative forms of the following adjectives and adverbs?

a early	**c** empty	**e** many
b economical	**d** good	**f** thin

Communication in Action: *Formality in the Office*

Office custom differs as to the use of first names. Some companies insist that all employees use the title *Miss, Mrs.,* or *Mr.* when referring or talking to another employee. In other companies, there is no rule. Discuss how a new employee should address his co-workers and his superiors when he starts to work.

5-20-66

UNIT 56

Writing Business Reports

Not too many years ago, most businesess were so small that the owner could, and frequently did, keep in close personal touch with everything that went on in his firm. When the president or manager of the company wanted information, he would merely go to the person who could supply it and ask a question such as: "Jim, how's that new production plan working?" Information acquired this way could be remembered, for there were relatively few matters to remember and there was more time to study each thoroughly. Business did not move at such a rapid pace as it does today.

Today, in most businesses, the owner or manager cannot possibly keep in touch personally with all the operations in the firm he heads. Even the various department heads haven't sufficient time to supervise personally all the activities under their direction. Many businesses are so large and complex that a firm may be scattered throughout a particular section of the country or throughout all the United States—in fact, much business activity is now on a world-wide basis. When a businessman needs information of any kind, he must get it through written communications—business reports.

What Is a Business Report?

Essentially, a report is a presentation of facts. The report may be periodic—that is, submitted at regular intervals—such as a monthly report from the advertising manager telling the sales manager how much money was spent on advertising or a weekly report on absenteeism submitted by each department manager to the general manager. Or the report may be yearly, such as a report on production in each department as compared with production in the preceding year.

There are many types of reports, serving many purposes. Some reports are analytical; some are reports of experiments; some give the results of surveys and investigations; some reports tell the owners the progress being made in the business. Reports may go from employees to management; or they may be made to stockholders, supervisors, employees, or customers.

The memorandum form discussed in Unit 55, page 481, may be used for most reports written in business, even reports as long as five or six pages. Often, however, longer reports are more formal and a memorandum or *letter of transmittal* may accompany the report. A letter of transmittal serves several purposes in a formal report:

1. Tells why the report is being made
2. Gives the purpose and scope of the report
3. Acknowledges sources of information and help

Some types of businesses use the longer, more formal report very frequently. An engineering firm, for example, requires greatly detailed reports on huge construction jobs; in fact, several reports may be required on each phase of the job. A company specializing in market analysis (product testing, plant location, advertising media, and the like) has need for many formal reports—actually, the report is the end product of their business. Chemical, petroleum, drug, and similar manufacturing enterprises require formal reports from research and laboratory personnel who are conducting experiments on new products.

Preparing a Formal Report

The pattern of the formal report varies with the type of business for which it is prepared. Many companies adopt their own standard pattern for reports and even develop special paper on which the reports are written. Regardless of form, most longer reports will contain the following basic parts:

1. Introduction
2. Summary
3. Body
4. Conclusions and recommendations

Introduction. The introduction includes a background statement as to why the report was written, what its purpose is, how the data were gathered, what the report does *not* include (delimitations), and what materials and equipment were used. Such a background statement is necessary in every report. By knowing the "why" of a report, the reader is better able to evaluate the findings and the conclusions.

Suppose you have been asked to survey the office equipment in the company by which you are employed. The company management has had numerous complaints from office workers in recent months that the equipment these people must operate is antiquated and inadequate. Management has had conflicting reports from various supervisors and has decided to employ a specialist—that's you—to give them an unbiased report on the true situation. This is how you might introduce your report:

```
          SURVEY OF OFFICE EQUIPMENT AT MELSON'S, INC.

Purpose. This report has been prepared at the request
of J. K. Ronzoni, manager of office services for
Melson's, Inc. The purpose of the report is to deter-
mine whether the existing office equipment in the com-
pany is adequate to serve growing needs. By "equipment"
is meant such office machines as typewriters, adding
machines, calculators, duplicating machines, book-
keeping machines, and similar mechanical equipment.
This report does not include a survey of office furni-
ture, such as desks, tables, chairs, and similar items.

How the Report Was Prepared. In gathering the data for
this report, all department heads were interviewed, as
well as every employee who operates an office machine
as his primary responsibility. These employees include
typists, stenographers, bookkeepers, secretaries,
mimeograph operators, computing-machine operators, and
general office clerks. One full day was spent in each
department observing the various operators at work. In
each case, the machine was thoroughly examined in terms
of the job it is intended to do.
```

Summary. The next part of the formal report is the summary. The summary is a brief presentation of the findings, and it is placed early in the report so that a busy executive will not need to read the entire report to get the gist of it. The summary may be only a paragraph in length or it may be several pages, depending upon the amount of material that has been gathered. Following is a partial summary of the report on the survey of office machines:

Summary. This investigation reveals that a large number of the office machines now used at Melson's, Inc., are in need of replacement. The following tables summarize the equipment picture at this time:

TABLE 1

TYPEWRITERS

Model	Total Machines	Year of Manufacture			Condition		
		Pre-1950	1950-55	1956-60	Good	Fair	Poor
Royal	18	7	7	4	9	3	6
IBM Electric	6	3	3		1	3	2
Underwood	11	7	3	1	4	3	4
Remington	8	6	2		1	4	3
Smith-Corona	4		1	3	3	1	

Of course, there would be charts for each of the items of equipment surveyed. You can see how quickly a busy manager can get an idea of the condition of the equipment from such tables.

Body. The body of the report is concerned with the presentation of the pertinent facts that have been gathered. These facts must be carefully assembled and clearly presented. And the report writer must be sure of the accuracy of the data included. If he needs to check ten times before he is certain that the figures and statements are correct, then he checks ten times. There is no excuse for careless assumptions or errors in a written report; those who read the report depend entirely upon the writer's honesty and accuracy.

Conclusions and Recommendations. Up to this point, a report tells why it was written and what the facts are. Perhaps this is all that is required, and a statement of the writer's conclusions is not necessary. In some cases, however, if no conclusions are given, the report may have an "up-in-the-air" effect. If the report writer has been asked to include his conclusions and recommendations in the report, this may mean, of course, that the executive who asked for the report has faith in the writer's judgment. The writer's conclusions tell the executive what the facts gathered mean to the writer and what he thinks should be done about the matter reported on. If conclusions and recommendations are not asked for, the writer must use his best judgment. The subject matter of the report may not require a conclusion—the report may be a fact-finding one that leaves no room for a personal observation. The nature of the report and the wishes of the man who requested the report will determine whether or not a statement of conclusions is necessary. In any event, conclusions can be drawn only from the data in the report—not from observations that have not been proved by the actual findings included in the body of the report. In the case of the office machines survey, a statement of conclusions and recommendations might begin as follows:

> Conclusions and Recommendations. On the basis of this investigation, the facts reveal that our office equipment is generally old and is inadequate for our purposes. If the company is to expand its customer services as planned, more and newer equipment will be needed to do the job. Office personnel are often slowed down by mechanical failures of the equipment they are operating. These operators, for the most part, are skillful, hard-working people; but they cannot be expected to do their best with their present equipment.
>
> The following steps are recommended:
>
> 1. That a plan be considered whereby each office machine is replaced on a periodic basis; for example, every five years
>
> 2. That the company study the possibility of a service contract with a reputable office machines company to keep all machines in efficient operating condition
>
> 3. That a system be installed whereby machine failures are reported more promptly to the supervisor

There might be a dozen or more such recommendations.

Tone of the Formal Report

Most formal reports are written in the third person. The readers of these reports are interested mainly in the facts that have been gathered. If personal pronouns, such as *I*, *you*, and *they* are used, the report may lose some of its objectivity—personalities do sway opinions. As mentioned before, however, there are no basic rules that will apply to all companies.

The good report writer prefers the understatement to the overstatement. For example, in presenting his conclusions and recommendations, he would *not* say:

> Obviously, the facts point out clearly that we should reorganize the sales promotion department.

Instead, he would say:

> On the basis of the findings, consideration of a
> reorganization of the sales promotion department would
> seem desirable.

The good report writer would *not* say:

> In my opinion, supervisors are not giving adequate
> time to the training of workers in their departments.

Instead, he would say:

> Some of the workers appear to lack adequate train-
> ing, and the supervisors may find the setting up of
> special classes for them very worthwhile.

The writer of formal reports must look upon himself as an objective reporter who has no "ax to grind." The closer he sticks to the facts and the more objectively he reports them, the more valuable his report will be to those who must make the final decisions.

Mechanics of Report Writing

Expert typing and setting up of a report will increase the forcefulness of the communication by helping the reader to read rapidly and to absorb quickly the main points.

The long, formal report usually consists of the following parts:

1. Cover
2. Title page
3. Letter of transmittal
4. Table of contents
5. Introduction or preface
6. Summary
7. Body of the report
8. Conclusions and recommendations
9. Supplementary material or appendix

Also included may be a bibliography; special supplementary material such as folders, photographs or drawings, charts, maps, etc.; and, in rare instances, an index.

Reports should be typed on plain white bond paper, 8½ by 11 inches. All reports should be double spaced, and each page after the first should be numbered. A left margin of approximately an inch and a half should be allowed for binding. Top, bottom, and side margins should be an inch.

Most longer, formal reports require a title page. The following illustrates the title page that might be prepared for the office machines survey report:

SURVEY OF OFFICE EQUIPMENT NEEDS
AT MELSON'S, INC.

March 12, 19—

Prepared for: J. K. Ronzoni

Prepared by: Wilson Shepherd

Headings. The report writer should be generous in the use of headings throughout the report. In typing headings, the following points should be observed:

1. Headings of equal value should be typed alike throughout the report.

2. Headings that indicate principal divisions are usually centered and capitalized. They may also be spaced out and underscored.

3. Subordinate, or secondary, headings may be written flush with the left margin or indented. They may also be written outside the margin or centered within the body of the report. Whatever style is adopted should be followed consistently throughout the report.

4. More space should be allowed above a separate-line head than below it.

5. Unless the heading is in the form of a question, no punctuation should be used after separate-line heads. A run-in paragraph heading, however, requires a period.

The following illustration shows how headings may be arranged in a report that contains a number of subdivisions:

T I T L E

M A I N   H E A D I N G

FIRST ORDER SUBHEAD

SECOND ORDER SUBHEAD

T h i r d   O r d e r   S u b h e a d

F o u r t h   O r d e r   S u b h e a d

Fifth Order Subhead.

Sixth Order Subhead.

Binding. When the report is completed, it may be bound at the side with staples (usually three vertical staples close to the left edge) or fastened at the top with a paper clip. Some reports are placed inside a special folder made for the purpose; others are bound by special backing paper of a heavy stock.

Learning Exercises

1 Assume that you have been asked by your office manager to prepare a report on the improvement of the office forms used by your firm. He wants to know what forms are being used, how they are used, who uses them, what forms might be simplified or discontinued, what standard forms are available from firms specializing in the preparation of office forms, what has been the experience of other firms with office forms, and any other information that would be helpful in improving your office forms.

   a Prepare an outline of this proposed report, even though you are not going to gather the information.
   b Describe the procedures you would use in gathering the information and preparing the report.
   c List the sources of information you would use.

2 Your supervisor (your instructor) has asked you to investigate the method of handling coffee breaks in five firms in your area. Interview five employees of different firms and prepare a report of your findings.

3 Type an attractive title page for the report you prepared in Exercise 1.

4 Your instructor would like a report on the work experience of students in this class. Prepare this report, using a chart to summarize the findings.

Vocabulary and Spelling Refreshers

1 **Words Often Confused.** Suit, suite, sweet; rout, route, root.

2 **Wanted for Murder!** Each of these sentences "murders the King's English" in some way. Correct the gross errors.

a Everyone was there except my brother and I.
b Him and me goes fishing every Sunday.
c May I have the lend of your fountain pen?
d I had ought to be going.
e May I have this here piece of cake?

3 **How Is "sh" Spelled?** In each of these words, the sound of *sh* occurs at the point indicated by the blank spaces. Spell the words.

a finan__al   c defi__ent   e man__on
b ses__on   d pa__ence   f na__on

Communication in Action: *A Delivery Error*

You place an order by telephone to a local stationery store for ten columnar pads for use in the accounting department. Two weeks later the deliveryman brings in ten *cartons,* each *carton* containing ten columnar pads. Of course, it is a mistake; but you know the driver is not to blame—his delivery ticket shows ten *cartons.* How would you handle this problem?

UNIT   57

Telegrams, Minutes, and News Releases

In addition to letters, memorandums, and business reports, there are three other types of written communica-

tions that business employees may have occasion to prepare. These are telegrams, minutes of meetings, and news releases. The extent to which each is used often depends upon the type of business and the nature of the business activity.

Communicating by Telegraph

The fastest method of sending a written communication is by wire. When the businessman wishes a message to arrive in the shortest possible time and wishes to have a written record of it, he usually telegraphs. For long distances, a wire is cheaper than a telephone call. Also, a wire often can reach a person who cannot be reached by telephone. Perhaps the two most important advantages of wire communications are the speed of delivery and the written record they provide.

Another advantage of the telegram is that it attracts attention. People look upon telegrams as urgent and demanding of immediate action. For this reason, telegrams are often used in sales promotion, where their speed and "for-the-record" advantages are not important. They are also sometimes used to collect delinquent accounts—wires often get action where letters and telephone calls do not.

There is only one domestic telegraph company—Western Union. Telegraph messages may be filed (placed) at any one of their hundreds of offices throughout the United States, or they may be placed by telephoning a telegraph office. They may be sent prepaid or collect. Delivery may be made by messenger or by telephone. Messages transmitted to a home are usually relayed by telephone; to a business office, by messenger. If you receive a telegraph message by telephone, you may request the telegraph company to mail you a copy of the telegram.

Full-Rate Telegram. The full-rate telegram is the fastest of all the wire communications, for it is transmitted immediately after being received in the telegraph office and is usually delivered to the addressee within a few minutes. The cost of a telegram—and all other wire communications—is based on the distance it is to be sent and on the number of words it contains. The minimum charge for a full-rate telegram is based upon 15 words. Therefore, you can send 15 words as cheaply as you can send five or ten. Additional words beyond 15 are charged for by the word.

Day Letter. The day letter is a relatively economical method of sending longer telegraph messages. The minimum charge is for 50 words; additional words are charged for in groups of five. The day letter is cheaper than a full-rate telegram because its delivery may not be quite so fast (day letters are sent when there is a lull in transmitting

Courtesy The Western Union Telegraph Company

A correctly prepared full-rate domestic telegram.

full-rate telegrams). Usually, however, a day letter will be delivered within an hour or two after being filed.

Night Letter. The night letter is the cheapest of the three types of telegraphic messages. It may be filed at any time up to 2 a.m., for delivery the following morning. Thus, under most circumstances, it is not so fast as the full-rate telegram or the day letter. The minimum charge is for 50 words; additional words are charged for in groups of five.

Composing the Message. Because telegraph messages are charged for according to the number of words they contain, they should be kept brief. The able composer of wires, therefore, has the ability to pack into the fewest possible words a clear and complete message (as shown above). Intent as he is on keeping the number of words to a minimum, however, he knows that sacrificing clearness and completeness to conciseness is false economy. If he needs the sixteenth word in a full-rate telegram in order to be sure that the message will be understood, he will use that sixteenth word.

Suppose you wish to wire for a hotel reservation. You could compose the following message:

> Would appreciate your reserving for me a single room with bath, medium priced, for the night of Wednesday, August 17. Will arrive before 9 p.m. Please confirm this reservation.

This full-rate message contains 29 words, a total of 14 words more than the 15 on which the minimum charge is based. The extra words are not needed, and they represent money thrown away. Here is the revised wire, containing 15 words:

> Reserve single room, bath, medium priced, for August 17. Will arrive before 9 p.m. Confirm.

Look at the following rather chatty rush-delivery telegram:

> Ship immediately green topper, size 16, on our order No. 48263. Customer leaving for Florida Monday and wants to take topper with her.

Twenty-three words were used to say what could have been said in eight words, like this:

> Rush green topper, size 16, on order 48263.

Since you have seven words left to use, you might emphasize the urgency of the request by adding, "Must have topper by the seventeenth."

Telegrams are often of assistance in collecting bad debts. The "Hurry, hurry!" air that surrounds a wire sometimes gets results that are not achieved by letters. Here is a telegram that is a "last-ditch" effort to collect from a customer who has ignored all collection letters:

> Unless your account is paid in full by September 15, our attorney will start legal action. (16 words)

Sixteen words are used in this telegram, but the wording could have been held to 15 by writing "Is fully paid" instead of "Is paid in full."

Very often only a slight revision is necessary to fit the message into the minimum-rate number of words. In the following telegram, the code word "Antel" could be substituted for "Please reply."

> Have you shipped order numbers 174296, 164598, and 167776? Check shipment. Please reply. (16 words)

You could also have a total of 15 words by omitting "and" in the series of order numbers.

Minutes of Meetings

In the typical business, many committees operate within the company. Each department may have several committees that meet periodically—usually once a week, every two weeks, or monthly. If you are working in the sales department, for example, there may be committees on advertising, sales conferences, commissions, forms control, and so on. The purpose of committees is to discuss various problems and to make recommendations to management.

The written record of the proceedings of a meeting is called the *minutes* of the meeting. Since most meetings in business are informal (that is, do not follow the rules of parliamentary procedures), the minutes are also informal. The minutes usually include the date, time, and place of the meeting; the name of the presiding officer; a list of those present as well as those absent; and the time of adjournment. Discussions should be summarized.

Usually the minutes are signed by the person who took them and sometimes by the presiding officer as well. Minutes are usually duplicated, and copies are sent to each person present at the meeting and to other designated officials. Following is an illustration of minutes of a meeting of the Employee Recreation Committee of the Lovejoy Corporation.

MINUTES OF THE MEETING

of the

E M P L O Y E E   R E C R E A T I O N   C O M M I T T E E

Lovejoy Corporation

2 p.m.

April 14, 19——

Presiding: Vincent L. Hamm, Chairman

Present: Anne David
           John Eulan
           Oscar Fields
           Lars Lindstrom
           LaSalle Meredith
           George Prescott

Absent: Phil Andrews
           Mary Hallock

This meeting was devoted primarily to the question of whether or not Lovejoy Corporation should encourage company-sponsored summer recreational activities for employees.

Mr. Fields stated that he believes most people are too busy during the summer months to participate in company recreational activities. Many belong to local softball leagues, skin-diving clubs, sailing groups, etc. Others would rather be with their families. He believes we should abandon the recreation program for the summer.

Miss David said that the Girls Club will probably prefer to remain active through the summer. They have several activities already planned—sightseeing tours, beach parties, and boat trips.

Mr. Eulan mentioned that the library has received several new films on European travel, and arrangements could be made to show these in the building during the summer months. He recommended that a special bulletin be prepared on these films and suggested a title like "Armchair Travels." Many of the employees are of Italian and Irish descent, and color films about these countries are of special interest.

Mr. Lindstrom recommended that a questionnaire be prepared and issued to each employee to find out whether an organized program of recreation is desirable this summer.

Mr. Hamm endorsed Mr. Lindstrom's idea and appointed Messrs. Andrews, Lindstrom, and Meredith and Miss Hallock as a committee to draw up the questionnaire. After the questionnaire is approved, it will be turned over to the Personnel Department for mimeographing and distribution.

The meeting was adjourned at 3:45 p.m.

(Signed) *Anne David*

Anne David, Secretary

Minutes of Formal Meetings. Minutes of meetings that follow parliamentary procedures more closely are somewhat different in form from informal minutes as illustrated on page 499. Note the use of topical headings for easy reference. Note, too, that the recorder has briefly summarized the speaker's remarks.

THE SOONER STATE CLUB OF CHICAGO
MINUTES OF MEETING, JULY 27, 19—

TIME AND PLACE — The regular monthly meeting of the Sooner State Club of Chicago was called to order by the president, Jordon Thomas, on Friday, July 27, 19—, at 2 p.m., in the Pioneer Room of the Bismarck Hotel.

MINUTES — The minutes of the last meeting were read and approved.

TREASURER'S REPORT — The following report was given by Clif Downs, the Treasurer.

Balance on hand, July 1, 19—	$1,676.40
Collected during the year (July 1, 19— to June 30, 19—)	3,042.12
Total	$4,718.52
Paid out during the year	3,004.19
Balance on hand, July 1, 19—	$1,714.33

COMMITTEE
REPORTS

The report of the <u>Nominating Committee</u> was given by the Chairman, Paul Rykers. A slate of nominees for next year is to be presented at the next meeting.

The report of the <u>Half-a-Century Celebration</u> was given by the Chairman, Verna Millstone. Three area banquets are being held on August 21—Gary, Winnetka, and Aurora. Arrangements are being handled by local chairmen.

OLD BUSINESS

The question of whether dues of the organization should be increased was brought up for further discussion. It was moved, seconded, and passed, THAT DUES FOR THE CURRENT YEAR REMAIN THE SAME AS LAST YEAR AND THAT A SPECIAL ASSESSMENT BE PERMITTED IF ADDITIONAL FUNDS ARE REQUIRED.

NEW BUSINESS

After a discussion about the possibility of designing a gold "Sooner" pin for the members, a committee consisting of Paula Myers, Chairman, Fred Weir, Ed Maestro, and Clyde Morris was appointed to report at the next meeting.

PROGRAM

Meredith Cave introduced Mr. Alexander Hayhurst, whose topic was, "What's New in the Sooner State." Mr. Hayhurst said in part:

"The Sooner State is experiencing rapid economic growth. Many new industries have moved there—including chemical, manufacturing, and government enterprises. New sources of water supply—hundreds of man-made lakes have been built—make it an attractive place from both a recreational and an industrial standpoint. There is still a large supply of labor, too. Transportation is improving rapidly each year—several new highways are now under construction."

Mr. Hayhurst urged all members of the club to boost the Sooner State wherever possible.

The meeting adjourned at 4:45 p.m.

Respectfully submitted,

C. A. Miller

C. A. Miller, Secretary

Resolutions. Resolutions to express sympathy, appreciation, congratulations, and the like are often passed at formal meetings. The form of resolutions follows a rather definite pattern, as illustrated here.

Notice that the paragraphs giving the reasons for the resolution are introduced by the word *WHEREAS* (followed by a comma) and that the paragraphs stating the action to be taken are introduced by the word *RESOLVED* (also followed by a comma).

```
              IN  MEMORIAM

             Resolution Adopted by
The Board of Directors of the Plainfield Sales Company
  On the death of Morris Erlich, a member of the Board

    WHEREAS, our beloved colleague passed away on
March 6, 19--; and

    WHEREAS, Mr. Erlich had served the company long
and faithfully, being one of its most sympathetic and
hardest working members; and

    WHEREAS, his wise counsel and unselfish services
will be missed not only by the members of the Board and
the officials of the organization but also by the com-
munity at large: Therefore, be it

    RESOLVED, That we, his fellow Board members, take
this means of expressing our deep appreciation for his
untiring and unselfish service to the Plainfield Sales
Company and to the community; and, be it

    RESOLVED, further, That we extend our sincerest
sympathies to his widow, Mrs. Sara Erlich; to his son,
Steve Erlich, Maplewood, New Jersey; and to his
brother, Mr. L. G. Erlich, Dallas, Texas; and, be it

    RESOLVED, further, That a copy of these resolu-
tions be spread upon the minutes of the Plainfield
Sales Company; that a copy be sent to the members of
the immediate family, as referred to above; and that a
copy be supplied to the press of the city.

    Adopted, unanimously, by the Board of Directors of
the Plainfield Sales Company, this ninth day of March,
19--.
                      (Signed) David Munhall
                               Chairman of the Board

                      (Signed) P. E. Mayberry
                               Secretary
```

News Releases

All businesses are eager to get as much publicity as possible in newspapers and magazines, on radio or television—wherever there is a reading or listening audience. Larger businesses—even colleges—employ publicity directors whose job is to attract public attention to the organization. The old saying attributed to a movie star, "I don't care what you say about me as long as you spell my name correctly," indicates how valuable publicity is to some people. Most businesses, however, want only stories that show them in a favorable light, for public confidence is at stake.

The physical form in which the planned news or publicity is given to news outlets is called a *news release.* Any subject that the businessman thinks may be of public interest or may bring his name before the public may be the basis for a news release. It may be an announcement of the promotion of a major executive or of a new product or service, a retirement, a death, an honor for an employee, the election of employees to civic posts, company anniversary celebrations, and the like. News releases are usually written, or at least approved, by one executive in an organization. In larger firms, a department of public relations or of publicity handles such releases. In smaller firms, releases may be written by various executives. To prevent inaccurate or conflicting information from leaking out, however, these releases are usually channeled through one executive.

The purpose of the news release is to get into print. Newspaper and magazine editors receive hundreds of news releases every day from all types of businesses and individuals. The editor appraises these releases by one basic rule: Is this item of current, specific interest to the readers of my magazine or newspaper?

Form of the News Release. The style in which releases are written is highly important. Since an editor cannot use them all, everything else being equal, he will usually print those that require the least amount of additional checking and editing. Therefore, a release should give complete information and follow as closely as possible the newspaper style of writing.

News releases may be typed, mimeographed, or printed. Carbon copies should never be sent to an editor. Releases should be kept as brief as possible—rarely more than a page and a half. The shorter and more interesting the news release, the better its chance of getting into print.

Companies that issue a great many news releases have special forms on which to write them. Reporting a story on a special news release form is much more effective than writing a letter. Editors like to be able to read quickly; they cannot waste time going through the formalities of a letter. Like a letterhead, a news release form usually contains the name, address, and telephone number of the company. This information, however, may be placed at the bottom of the form. In addition, the name of the person who issued the release and who is authorized to give additional information is included.

Note the following about the news release illustrated:

1. The news release is double spaced. This is a "must" for all news releases.

2. The side margins are generous, and plenty of space is left at both top and bottom.

3. At the beginning of the story, a brief headline is given so that the editor may learn quickly what the release is about. For example, "New Plastic Skin-Diving Equipment Announced" or "New Vice-President Appointed" or "Printing Press Handles Sheets 110 Inches Wide." (The editor will nearly always write his own headline, and the writer of the news release should not be disappointed if his is not used.)

4. Note the term at the top of the form, "For Immediate Release." This means that the story may be printed immediately upon receipt. Sometimes the firm likes to issue a news release several days in advance of the time it is to be used, in which case it will be marked, "To be released on July 1" or "Not To Be Released Before July 1."

5. At the end of the release, the following symbol appears: —xxx—. The three *x's* stand for "30," the telegrapher's signal of former days signifying "the end."

If the news release is long, subheads inserted between paragraphs of news text will help break the monotony of type.

If there is more to come than the first page, the word *more* is added in parentheses at the end of the first page: (more).

Writing the News Release. Whether your story heads for the wastebasket or the composing room will depend mostly upon the words you use in your first paragraph. The first paragraph should summarize the basic idea of the story. It should stand by itself if need be, giving the *who, what, why, when,* and *where,* as stories appearing in newspapers generally do. For example:

```
     Appointment of Gregg W. Kahn as general sales
manager of the Verona Plastics Company, Mulvane,
Pennsylvania, has been announced by Gilbert A. Olgar,
president.
```

NEWS *from* **artco** **FOR RELEASE**
MANUFACTURING COMPANY
138 FRANKLIN AVENUE
SPRINGFIELD, OHIO
LAWRENCE 9-9100

UPON RECEIPT

Gerald F. Fresno

NEW DISPOSABLE ASH TRAY ANNOUNCED

An ash tray that is economical enough to dispose of after use will be on the market by July 1, it was announced by Artco Manufacturing Company, Springfield, Ohio. The product is made of papier-mâché and is especially treated with a thin asbestos coating. Fire from cigarette, cigar, and pipe ashes will not burn it.

Made to sell for under a nickel, this new ash tray is the housewife's answer to the drudgery of cleaning ash trays after each use. This new product--under the brand name of Ashkleen--is collapsible, permitting the housewife to fold it so that the cigarette butts are "canned"--no mess while disposing. It comes in a variety of designs and colors, to suit any decor.

A special feature of the Ashkleen is that cigarettes do not have to be snubbed out--they may be placed in the bottom of the tray, where they will extinguish themselves. A cleverly constructed vacuum chamber does the trick.

Ashkleen is packaged in lots of a dozen. They may be bought after July 1 in leading department and variety stores.

-XXX-

A news release prepared on special letterhead.

This release will probably be revised by the editor of the newspaper or magazine as follows:

Gregg W. Kahn has been named general sales manager of Verona Plastics Company, Mulvane, Pennsylvania.

Don't write:

Gilbert A. Olgar, president of Verona Plastics Company, Mulvane, Pennsylvania, has announced the appointment of Gregg W. Kahn as general sales manager.

The news angle to the story is Gregg W. Kahn's appointment. Olgar adds nothing to the story. Put the accent on Kahn, where it belongs. After the lead paragraph is written, move on to the secondary, or background, facts. For example:

> He succeeds R. Robert Lewis, who retired October 1.

Additional background worth noting may then be given. For instance:

> The new sales manager joined the firm in 1936 as a salesman. In 1945, he was made district manager and in 1950 was appointed assistant sales manager.

If the editor has to "kill" part of the release because of space limitations, he will "kill" it from the bottom up. Therefore, the most important information should come first.

Here is an example of a well-written news release:

FROM: F. G. Renkin, Jr.
          Fisher Drug Company
          Philadelphia, Pennsylvania

RELEASE: IMMEDIATE

BLACK NAMED ADVERTISING MANAGER AT FISHER

Appointment of Shelton T. Black as advertising manager of the

Fisher Drug Company, Philadelphia, has been announced by

Douglas Sherman, president.

He succeeds Donald H. Chevalier, who retired October 1 after

thirty years.

The new advertising manager joined the firm in 1936 as a steno-

grapher in the chemical division. In 1940, he was made executive

assistant to the sales manager; and in 1950, he was appointed

assistant advertising manager.

Mr. Black lives in Swarthmore, a suburb of Philadelphia. He

has three children. During World War II, he served with the U. S.

Navy as aide to the Commander of the Third Fleet in the South

Pacific.

In commenting on his new post, Mr. Black paid tribute to the fine work done by his predecessor. "Our basic advertising policy remains unchanged," said Mr. Black. "We shall continue to search for new media and new methods, of course; but for the time being we will concentrate our efforts in trade magazines and newspapers."

Learning Exercises

1 Your employer wishes to send the following message from your office (Buffalo, New York) to the San Francisco branch as quickly as possible. It is 4:30 p.m. when he gives you the message he wishes typed and delivered to the telegraph office. What class of message would you recommend? Why? How many words are in the message? Can you save the firm some money by reducing the number of words? If so, reword the message.

> WE HAVE NOT RECEIVED THE ORDER FOR 50 PAIRS OF LA VOGUE SHOES. WE NEED THEM NOT LATER THAN MARCH 5. PLEASE CHECK INTO THIS AND ANSWER BY TELEGRAM.

2 Type the revised telegram from Exercise 1 on a Western Union form.

3 You are going to reserve a room with bath for your employer, Ralph Dixon, at the Park-Sheraton Hotel in Detroit for April 5 and 6. He does not plan to arrive until late on April 5. Mr. Dixon would like a medium-priced outside room. He would like a confirmation. Prepare a full-rate telegram, using as few words as possible.

4 Write up minutes for a class session or a meeting, using the informal form discussed in this unit.

5 Prepare a formal set of minutes for an actual meeting you attended. If you have not attended such a meeting, you may make up the necessary information.

6 Prepare a news release for one of your school activities—a sports event or a special meeting of one of the clubs to which you may belong.

7 Your employer is being promoted from assistant office manager to office manager. Prepare a news release, making up the necessary names and background information.

Vocabulary and Spelling Refreshers

1 **Words Often Confused.** Wave, waive; bearing, baring, barring.

2 **One Word for Several.** Select a single word that may be substituted for each of the following phrases.

a during the time that   d in connection with
b in this day and age   e at the present time
c reach a decision   f in order that

3 **Forming Present Participles.** What are the present participial (*ing*-ending) forms of the following?

a   vary   c compel   e equal
b   accumulate   d benefit   f delay

Communication in Action: *Clichés*

Clichés are phrases that have been used over and over again so many times that they are worn out. Because they are worn out, they make writing and speaking dull and uninteresting. Rewrite the following clichés, using fresh, new words:

1. We traveled *far and wide;* in fact, we *circled the globe* many times.

2. It is a situation that I *view with alarm,* yet I am *helpless to interfere.*

3. The child is *as playful as a kitten* and *sleeps like a log;* when he awakes, he is full of *boundless energy.*

4. She was scared; she was as *white as a sheet* and her *hair stood on end.*

SPEAKING
FOR
BUSINESS

UNIT 58

The Art of Conversation

You will do a great deal of writing for business, but more often you will speak for business. And, both in oral and written communication, you must build good will and develop effective human relations. Speech—the speech carried on by people talking together—is one of the main avenues to friendly relationships. You can observe speech at work everywhere you look, for you carry on conversations all during your waking hours. For instance, the small talk that goes on in school before and after classes is conversation. When your instructor tells you about assignments to be done, there is a give-and-take of oral communication that is conversation, the same kind of conversation that takes place when your supervisor on the job instructs you about work to be done. When you meet a person for the first time, conversation is the means by which the acquaintance is made. You converse when on the telephone, when being interviewed for a job, when receiving office callers. In fact, conversation punctuates all your activities—and it will always do so—both in your business and in your social life.

The Good Conversationalist

The ability to carry on a fruitful conversation is an art; and, as you know, any highly developed art is the result of *knowledge and practice.* This unit deals with the characteristics of a good conversationalist and will give you the knowledge you need to develop the art. The practice, however, is up to you. Begin by learning that the good conversationalist:

1. Is a good listener
2. Is genuinely interested in people
3. Knows conversational topics of general interest
4. Uses only his share of conversation time
5. Knows when and how to end a conversation

Is a Good Listener. A good listener pays attention—and shows interest—whenever anyone speaks to him. How can you develop this reaction so that it is second nature to you? Every time someone addresses you, tune out everything else in your mind and tune in exclusively on the speaker. Look at him and make a conscious effort to follow the thoughts behind his words. By every expression of face and body, show that you are interested in what he is saying. He will respond to your attention by giving more of himself in conversation and by seeking your company in the future.

Now consider the person who does not know how to listen. He may have the habit of gazing off into space; he may play with his hands or with an eraser, crack his knuckles, or doodle on paper. When he is tired, his facial expression and slumped body show his boredom. He displays to the world his lack of courtesy and causes other people to avoid him. But once a person realizes that poor listening habits will betray him to his friends and associates, he will work to replace any negative mannerisms with attitudes of respect and courtesy that will reflect his genuine interest in people.

Is Genuinely Interested in People. If you want others to listen to what you have to say, you must first show genuine interest in them. What is the secret of being really interested? Sincere interest is a reflection of genuine respect for people, of appreciation of associates and friends—not for their beliefs or for their position in life, but for what they are. A lack of respect for an individual or for a group is a negative attitude that will show up in any conversational give-and-take. Everyone, therefore, must train himself to take a positive approach towards people with whom he converses, for only then will his conversation reflect a true interest in each person and in what each person says to him.

The following suggestions will help you develop and increase your interest in other people:

1. Look for the positive side of each person and for the positive side of the ideas he expresses. A person's best point, for example, may be a pleasant smile. Look for that smile. If something is said that might be interpreted either favorably or unfavorably, take it as favorable. When you are on the lookout for the good side of people and for the constructive aspects of ideas, you'll usually find them; and you won't have time to dwell on anything negative.

2. Encourage the other person by voicing a compliment whenever such praise is called for. Everyone, including you, appreciates sincere acknowledgment of his good qualities. One important result of being alert to pay compliments when deserved is that you develop within

yourself the respect and admiration you need to display genuine interest in a conversation.

3. Be attuned to the overtures of people who seek conversation with you. In an introduction, for example, you may be asked direct questions about school, your job, or your hobbies. Don't be a bore by giving your life's history. Recognize the questions as conversation overtures. Welcome them, and reciprocate with inquiries of your own that will lead to an exchange of information and show your interest in the other person.

4. Remember to use names in a conversation. A person's name is sweet music to him. When you are first introduced, be sure that you hear the name correctly. If you aren't sure, ask the person to repeat it. You might say, "I didn't understand your name" or "How do you pronounce your name?" or "How do you spell your name?" Then pronounce the name yourself, to fix it in your mind. And be sure to use it at appropriate intervals—and in saying good-by.

Knows What Topics of Conversation to Use. People are generally interested in each other. But sometimes a person may have difficulty starting or holding a conversation, particularly with strangers, because he doesn't know what to talk about. Awkward or embarrassing silences can be avoided if you have some knowledge of subjects of general interest, subjects to avoid, and subjects and techniques that help to get a conversation started.

Current events, people in the news, the world around you—these are topics that appeal to most people. Amusing anecdotes—in their proper place—are also helpful in a conversation, for laughter often brings people together. A new play, a new car, the different way in which one company is now marketing its product will give the conversation something to grow on. Of course, to be able to contribute, you must first be informed yourself—well read and up to date on current topics of interest. Thus, the fuel for conversation comes from reading, observing, and listening. In addition, however, you need to know what topics to avoid in conversation.

The rule to remember about topics to avoid is: Avoid any topic that may hurt a person's feelings or dampen the interest of your listeners. Personal criticism or a statement that reflects negatively on another person, present or absent, can be detrimental to good feelings. Controversial subjects—politics, religion, race, people's strong beliefs—all are dangerous ground. Personal aches and pains and distressing problems with which you are faced are boring or disturbing to others. They will serve only to bore your listeners. Do you see how well the rule helps you judge topics of conversation in terms of the feelings and interests of others?

Conversations don't just happen—someone starts them. Armed as you now are with a knowledge of desirable and undesirable topics, you can have confidence in your ability to start and to carry on interesting conversations that will help you grow and develop. Someone must accept the responsibility of getting the conversation off to a good start—and it might as well be you. You will reap the rewards of a satisfying discussion if you know how to select and introduce interesting topics.

What topics you might select depends to some extent on the person with whom you are talking—his age, sex, background, and interests. If you have just met, you might try one, then another, general topic. From his reactions, you begin to learn something about him and can guide the conversation accordingly.

Shares Conversation Time. Good sportsmanship is as essential in a conversation as it is on the baseball field. You can't be at bat all the time. The rules of the conversation game require that every player have his turn at talking—and at listening. Of course, the person who breaks the rules of conversational fair play reveals his lack of polish. The silent individual who won't accept his responsibility to contribute is basically selfish. The person who monopolizes the conversation may do so because he has too high an opinion of himself; or he may ramble because he is nervous. To avoid taking more than your fair share of conversation time, you must develop conversational sensitivity.

A sensitive conversationalist recognizes the point at which he may begin to lose the interest of the other parties in the conversational exchange—by the tone in which answers are given or by the distant look in the listeners' eyes. These are cues to the sensitive person to give the other fellow a chance to talk or to steer the conversation to a new topic. Because the sensitive conversationalist is aware of and genuinely interested in others, he does and says the right thing at the right time—even when it comes to ending a conversation.

Knows How to End. Many people find themselves groping for ways to end a conversation. They may have to reach to avoid seeming abrupt or giving the impression that they are bored or tired of the conversation. You, however, as a polished conversationalist, will not be guilty of these faults. You can learn to conclude a conversation naturally by your tone of voice and by your choice of words. Using a gentle tone of finality, for instance, you might say, "It has been good to talk with you. I hope we can meet again soon." Or you might give a logical reason for withdrawing, as for instance, "Could we continue this interesting talk a little later? I must . . . ." You may have an appointment; you may have work waiting for you—right this minute; you may be expecting a call. Whatever the reason and however interesting the conversation, there comes a time when it must end. And a sensitive conversationalist recognizes the exact ending point and knows how to close a conversation in a polished, friendly manner.

Learning Exercises

1 Everyone has some praiseworthy qualities. Think of the people in your class, and then make a list of one complimentary remark you might make about each. Check your list. Could any of the compliments be mistaken for flattery? What is the difference? Discuss.

2 Suppose you have been introduced to a person whose name you did not understand. List as many techniques as you can for getting his correct name, remembering it, and using it in conversation. Demonstrate one of your techniques with another class member.

3 Make a list of questions you could use to begin a conversation that will lead to an exchange of information. Demonstrate with another class member how you would use these questions.

4 List four general topics, each of which you could use in conversing with one of the following people: (*a*) a child of six; (*b*) a member of the football team; (*c*) one of your parents; (*d*) a bank president.

Vocabulary and Spelling Refreshers

1 **Words Often Confused.** Threw, through, thorough; device, devise.

2 **Spot the Intruder.** Each of the following lines contains four words. Three of the words are synonymous. The fourth is an antonym. Spot these intruders.

    a Flexible, pliable, easily bent, inelastic
    b Exhaustive, superficial, complete, thorough
    c Counterfeit, genuine, real, true

d Reputable, honorable, estimable, base

e Alleviate, augment, allay, lighten

3

Does It End in "ar," "er," or "or"? Complete the following by adding *ar*, *er*, or *or*—whichever is correct

a cig___   c simil___   e partn___

b ledg___   d aviat___   f col___

Communication in Action: *Listening for Facts*

Listen to the story of Pierre Boudreaux and Clementine LeBouef, which your instructor will read. Be ready to prove from what you hear that, for every dollar spent for printing and duplicating a business form, it costs $20 for clerical and administrative work. Take notes as you listen.

UNIT 59

Meeting the Public — in Person and by Telephone

Responsibility for Public Contacts in Business

Hundreds of salespeople and retail, wholesale, and manufacturing agents talk with countless callers daily, both in person and by telephone. By untold thousands, business people in offices also meet and talk with the public—to receive reservations at travel agencies, airlines, railroads, and theaters; to receive or pay money at collection windows in department stores, banks, and utilities; to receive orders for services or repairs; to receive complaints and make adjustments; to give information at garages, office machines companies, and other service organizations; and to render personal services in medical centers, doctors' offices, and other professional establishments. Millions of people earn their living primarily through meeting the public in person or by telephone.

In a business office, almost everyone meets the public at one time or another. The receptionist or switchboard operator usually makes the initial contact, transferring a call or referring a caller to the appropriate person or office. In smaller offices, a clerk-typist, file clerk, bookkeeper, or stenographer may be asked to help callers, in addition to performing his other duties. And just about everyone in an office has a telephone at his elbow for use in his job. Anyone planning to enter business, therefore, can expect to be responsible for some aspect of meeting the public and should be prepared to discharge this responsibility to the best of his ability.

To be a good business host, then, you need to augment the training you already have by giving careful attention to the basic rules for meeting callers. You need to learn, also, how these rules may be applied to meeting a caller in person and to meeting the public by telephone.

Basic Rules for Meeting the Public

The rules for meeting the public—in person or by telephone—have as their foundation courtesy, consideration, and friendly warmth. These are the same qualities that make a visitor at your home feel welcome, comfortable, and at ease. Applied specifically to business callers, the rules are:

1. *Give Prompt Attention to All Callers.* Recognize a caller's presence immediately. If he is calling by telephone, answer his call promptly, before the second ring if possible. Have you ever waited and waited for a telephone call to be answered? Have you ever had to stand and wait for someone to attend to you in a store, feeling completely ignored? If so, you know that, as you waited, you became increasingly uncomfortable, even angry. You hung up the telephone receiver, or you turned on your heel and walked out of the store. In a well-run business, this could not happen. Salespersons, for example, are trained to recognize a caller immediately. If a clerk is busy with one customer, he will glance and nod at a waiting customer or say pleasantly, "I'll be with you in a moment." Then the caller knows that he is not being overlooked. You, as you meet the public, must follow the same procedure and give prompt attention to all callers.

2. *Greet Callers Pleasantly.* The tone of voice you use to greet people should be cheerful and friendly. Even an irate caller will feel better when he hears your pleasant, "Good morning, Mr. Jabson. How nice of you to call." Of course, if you don't mean it, it is best not to say it; your tone of voice and your facial expressions will show your caller that you are not sincere.

A. Devaney, Inc.

Courtesy, tact, and a smiling voice make you a good will representative of your company when you meet the public in person or by telephone.

Vary your greeting. Treat each visitor as though he were in some way special—he is! And try to make the greeting fit the occasion. For example, an automobile salesman approaching a customer who is behind the wheel of a new demonstrator might say, "It's a comfortable feeling to sit behind the wheel of a new car, isn't it?" One of the following greetings may fit other situations: "Good morning." "What may I show you?" "Whom do you wish to see?" "How may I help you?" "What a pleasant surprise!" "We were expecting you." "How nice of you to call." "How are you today?" Just adding the name of the person, if you know it, will make the greeting extra special for the caller. Often, too, the same words may be varied by a change in emphasis or in the way they are said. You must make it a point to greet all callers with a pleasant tone of voice and a friendly word, varying the form of greeting as seems appropriate.

3. ***Treat All Callers as Honored Guests.*** Be friendly and courteous to everyone. Never let a caller's voice or appearance influence what you say to him. Some very important people do not dress expensively; and not everyone has had the advantage of voice training you have had. It would be unwise to assume that a modestly attired person or a person with a thick accent is not worthy of your consideration. Every caller deserves the same courteous and considerate treatment.

You must be prepared to have some irritable or even discourteous callers. Treat these people with an understanding smile and gloss over their discourtesies. You represent the firm, and these people are your guests. If you must make some response, express sympathy: "I'm sorry you feel that way." Your own graciousness will often mollify the caller's anger and might even make him friendly again toward you and your company.

4. ***Obtain Needed Information.*** Before you can refer a caller to someone else, you must find out his name and the reason for his call. You can then relay this information to the boss, who will determine whether he or someone else will handle the call.

Because people sometimes resent being asked about their business, it takes a polished business host to elicit the needed information without endangering pleasant relations. To a telephone caller, you might say, "May I tell Mr. Johnson who is calling, please?" When greeting a caller in person, you might point a pen over a pad and say pleasantly, "Your name is . . . ?" And, as you write the name on the pad, you will probably repeat, "Oh, yes, Mr. Jeffrey L. Adams." Next, you would ask, "And you would like to see Mr. Evans about . . . ?" and also write his answer on your pad. Filling in a leading question is a natural thing to do, so your caller usually will freely and willingly supply the information you need.

5. ***Save the Caller's Time.*** Let a caller know if he has to wait. On the telephone, if the wait is to be longer than two or three minutes, it is usually better to take the number and call back. You can say, "I'll have to get the information from the files, Mr. Poston. It will take about five minutes to do so. May I have your number and call you back?"

Let a caller know how long he must wait, even if it is a relatively short time. You might say, "I'm sorry, but Mr. Jenson will not be available for at least another hour. Would you like to make an appointment for later?" Or, "Mr. Jenson is in a meeting but should be free in about five minutes." The caller will appreciate your consideration.

6. ***Be Discreet.*** Protect your employer in what you say—and don't say. If your boss is late in arriving at the office, for example, don't say, "Mr. Duncan has not come in yet this morning." The tactful thing to say is, "Mr. Duncan is out of the office just now. I expect him in a few minutes." Make certain that your remarks reflect favorably on your employer.

Protect your employer's business, also. Certain business information is confidential, and you must keep it so. Imagine what a visitor would think of your company (and you) if you were indiscreet enough to say, "Business is so poor that Mr. Duncan had to let fifty workers go last week." A prospective customer would not be favorably impressed! So be discreet in what you say.

7. ***Keep Within Your Authority.*** Know the limits of your authority and don't exceed them. If you think your company will replace a defective part, for example, but it is not your responsibility to make adjustments, don't say, "Certainly we'll replace this for you. Just take it to the service department." You, and your company, will be embarrassed if for some reason the service department is unable to make the adjustment. Keep within your authority by saying, "Why don't you talk with Mr. Johnson in the service department." Be sure to know the names of the people in your company who can make various kinds of decisions. You can then help callers by referring them to the appropriate person, and you will be keeping within your authority.

8. ***Say "No" Gracefully.*** Some decisions that you must convey to a caller will be unfavorable to him. Be pleasant but firm. Your knowledge of how to say "No" in a letter will help you. Review Unit 49 so that, when you must refuse a caller, you can do so without losing his good will.

9. ***Show a Genuine Desire to Serve.*** The good host usually extends his guests an extra courtesy or adds a thoughtful touch to make the visit memorable. In business, too, the good host will be on the lookout for the little extra that makes the difference. One business host, for example, helped an out-of-town caller who was concerned about his plane reservation. "While you're talking with Mr. Smith," she said, "I'll call the airline to reconfirm your reservation." As a result, the caller was able to give his full attention to the business at hand; and a new customer was made.

With these basic rules in mind, you are ready to receive the public—in person and by telephone. But there are certain differences in the way you would greet telephone callers and in-person visitors.

Special Applications to Telephone Callers

Telephone techniques differ somewhat from techniques for greeting callers in person, for two very good reasons: (1) the nature of voice-to-voice conversation, and (2) the technical equipment used.

Voice-to-Voice. A telephone caller is unable to see the other person's facial expressions or surroundings. He is dependent entirely upon the voice at the other end of the line. In voice-to-voice meetings, therefore, you must make the following specific applications of the rules for greeting callers:

1. Identify yourself immediately. The caller cannot see you. He needs to know whether or not he has the right number, company, or person. A switchboard operator usually identifies only the firm's name: "Joplin and Lewis"; "Bannister's Wholesale"; or "This is Abigail and Blakeman Furniture Company." In answering an office or departmental telephone, identify both the office and yourself. You might say: "Dr. Ritter's office, Miss Gallagher speaking"; "Personnel, Mrs. Jamieson"; or "Good morning. This is the sales department, George Nance speaking." "Accounting, Kennedy" is technically correct, but the abruptness of the identification might confuse some people; and the purpose of this identification is to indicate who you are. Whatever greeting you may use, remember that on the telephone you must identify yourself at once.

2. Keep the person at the other end of the line informed. The telephone caller can't see what is happening. You must tell him. If you must leave the line to get some information, excuse yourself, saying, "I can find that information in just a few minutes, if you wish to hold the line." Of course, all delays must be explained; and best business practice requires that you report to the caller every minute. You can make an appropriate remark like, "We're still trying to locate Mr. Poston," or "I'm sorry, Mr. Poston is still talking on the other line. Do you wish to wait, or shall I have him call you?"

You must also let your caller know verbally that you are following what he says. He can't see the nod of your head or your facial expression to know that you are still with him. You can show that you are listening attentively by a simple verbal response such as "Uhhuh," "M-m-m," or even "Yes."

3. Make sure that you are ready to take down any data the caller may give you. Have pencil, paper, and message forms ready for use near the telephone. Then you won't delay the caller with, "Will you wait while I get a pencil?" Be sure, too, to verify the message. After taking the message illustrated on page 521, you would verify the information by saying: "You would like Mr. Poston to call

```
To: Mr. Poston
─────────────────────────────────
        HERE'S A MESSAGE FOR YOU
  Mr. Maxim
─────────────────────────────────
  OF    ──────
─────────────────────────────────
  PHONE NO. To 7-5321  EXT. ──
  ☐ IS WAITING          ☑ TELEPHONED
      TO SEE YOU        ☐ RETURNED YOUR CALL
  ☐ CAME TO SEE YOU     ☑ PLEASE PHONE
  ☐ WANTS TO SEE YOU    ☐ WILL CALL AGAIN

  ─────────────────────────────
  ─────────────────────────────
  ─────────────────────────────
  ─────────────────────────────

  TAKEN BY              DATE         TIME
          cvl          3/31/--      4:35
```

A telephone message form.

you, Mr. Maxim. Let's see, you spell your name M-A-X-I-M? And your number is TOledo 7-5321? Thank you. Good-by."

Technical Equipment. The telephone is a sensitive electronic tool. Knowing how to use it correctly will enable you to greet telephone callers courteously and efficiently. Follow these suggestions:

1. Hold your lips from a half to one inch from the mouthpiece. Don't let the mouthpiece slip down under your chin, and don't cut off your voice by holding your hand over the mouthpiece.

2. Adjust your voice to the equipment. Remember, you don't have to shout over the telephone. Use your natural voice. But enunciate clearly so that you will be understood.

3. Transfer calls efficiently and expeditiously. To transfer a call from the outside to another extension within the company, say to the caller, "If you will hold on for just a moment, I'll have your call transferred." With that, depress the telephone plunger to the count of *1-2-pause* several times until the operator returns to the line. Then say, "Will you please transfer this call to Mr. Alison on extension 2317."

4. Avoid irritating mechanical noises. If you must leave the line, place the receiver on a book or magazine. The noise made when the receiver is dropped on a desk or bumped is magnified over the wire and will not be appreciated by the caller. At the completion of a call, place the receiver gently in the cradle for the same reason. Of

course, the courteous telephone host will allow the caller to replace the receiver before he does.

Do you see now how to apply the basic rules for communication in person to communication on the telephone? You will have little difficulty if you remember that telephone calls are voice-to-voice contacts and require the use of special techniques.

Learning Exercises

1 Your office manager asks you to write an S.O.P. (standard operating procedure) of one page or less for all office workers who receive telephone calls. Cover especially the following points of procedure:

    a Supplies and materials to be available at each telephone
    b Promptness in answering calls
    c Proper identification
    d Practice in handling delays
    e Personal calls during business hours

2 Suppose you are a salesman who calls on customers in person and also by telephone. Make a list of the different techniques that you would use in selling your product by telephone and then in person.

3 Mr. Elkton has left word that he is not to be disturbed. Yet a caller insists, "But I must see Mr. Elkton. I'm leaving town and won't be back for six months." What would you say? Select one of the following; then defend your answer in a paragraph. Discuss in class.

    a "I'm sorry, Mr. Elkton isn't seeing anyone today."
    b "Mr. Elkton is going to be in conference all afternoon, but let me talk with his secretary again."
    c "Mr. Elkton can't be disturbed."
    d "Why didn't you say so? I'll see whether he can work you in."

4 Select one of the following situations to enact before the class. How would you give the unfavorable decision to the caller?

    a The contract to build an addition on your plan was awarded to a competitor of the caller at a saving of $10,000.

b A caller wishes to charge some merchandise, but he has exceeded his credit limit and has not paid a recent overdue invoice.

c Your employer does not wish to see a caller. "He's nothing but a time waster," your employer has said.

Vocabulary and Spelling Refreshers

1 **Words Often Confused.** Co-operation, corporation; eligible, illegible.

2 **Nouns from Verbs.** Give the nouns that may be formed from these verbs.

a clothe	**c** expend	**e** annoy
b devote	**d** expand	**f** unite

3 **Does It End in "ary," "ery," or "ory"?** Complete the following by adding *ary, ery,* or *ory*—whichever is correct.

a diction____	**c** necess____	**e** direct____
b embroid____	**d** hist____	**f** sal____

Communication in Action: *Ethical Behavior*

Use the small-group technique to discuss the following situation for five minutes. In reporting back to the entire group, formulate a principle of ethics that you believe should govern such behavior.

Situation: Tom "borrowed" $2 from the office petty cash fund. He put it back the same day, so no one knew about it.

UNIT 60

Working with Groups

Group Work in Social and Business Life

Who isn't at some time called upon to participate in or to lead a group? It may be a small club, a religious group, an extracurricular or special interest club in school, a civic club or service group, an adult educational or recreational group, or a political or fraternal group. Most people belong to and participate in one or more groups.

In business, too, management increasingly depends upon groups for planning and for decisions to help solve problems. Many business groups and committees are organized to make use of the talents and ideas of all employees. Often the work of every person in the group—leaders as well as members—will be assessed to help determine who should be promoted. Why? Management can observe how well a person works in a group and how effectively he talks with others—an important basis for advancement. Therefore, it is wise for every person planning to enter business to know how to participate in group work both as an active member and as a leader.

The Group Member

For every leader in a group there are usually many more working members. You, therefore, will probably serve more often as a member than as a leader. Knowing and practicing the following principles will help you be a valuable and contributing group member.

1. *Respect the Opinions of All Other Group Members.* It is easy to respect the opinions of people whom you like and whose ideas agree with yours. A good group member, however, respects the opinions of all others. He is courteous to everyone; and, because he is open minded, he is attentive to each member of the group.

You already know the rules of common courtesy and consideration that a group member should practice: listening with courteous attention and responding with pertinent comments. The test of an effective group member, however, is whether he listens attentively and responds courteously even to those whom he may dislike or with whom he may disagree. Discourteous behavior—fidgeting, gazing into space, or trying to strike up an unrelated private conversation—marks the group member as a poor risk for promotion. The courteous person, on the other hand, is considerate of everyone at all times. He may have strong convictions, but he does not close his mind to a different point of view. He knows that, by considering the ideas and beliefs of others, he will grow and learn; he will gain a new respect for the thinking of others; and he will become a more effective person.

2. *Use Only Your Share of Talking Time.* Every member has a contribution to make to a group. Some people, however, because they have an exaggerated opinion of the value of their ideas, attempt to

monopolize a meeting. The good group member knows that everyone has an equal right and responsibility to express himself; and, by limiting his own talking, he makes sure that he does not rob others of their fair share of talking time.

3. *Help to Harmonize Differences of Opinion.* Because he is able to see the points of value in each opposing view, the good group member often helps to harmonize differences. He not only recognizes merit but also encourages compromise when different factions take conflicting positions. He might say, for example, "There is value in your proposal, and I can see how it would work under certain circumstances. Yet, there is merit in the other plan, too. Shall we take the best from each?" By emphasizing areas of agreement, the good group member is able to harmonize differences of opinion.

4. *Help to Keep the Discussion Pertinent.* It's easy in a group for some members to let their talking wander from the discussion at hand. The good group member keeps his own remarks pertinent to the subject and also helps channel the ideas of others to the topic at hand. He may do it by identifying the goal or purpose of the group: "As I understand it, our purpose is to . . ." Or, when the discussion begins to wander, he may ask, "Let's see now, what is it we hope to accomplish in this meeting?" He may help to summarize progress made or point out stumbling blocks to meeting the goal. To keep the discussion pertinent, the good member acts as a conscience to let the group know whether or not it is getting the job done.

Attitudes to Avoid. Knowing the positive principles that constitute good group membership is very important; but as important is an understanding of the attitudes and practices that prevent efficient, effective group work. Having such an understanding will help you avoid the pitfalls of group membership and make you better able to harmonize differences of opinion and to keep a discussion on the main track. The following types of people hinder the smooth progress of a group:

1. *Selfish-Interest Pleader.* "I don't care what the rest of you think, what I want to see is this . . . ," says the selfish-interest pleader. He has decided what *he* wants. Everything he says and does is intended to help him get his way despite the good ideas of others.

2. *The Blocker.* The blocker is opposed to every new idea. "That isn't the way to do it. Here's what we've been doing for years. . . ." or "That's an idiotic idea. It won't work." Whatever the idea is, the blocker is against it. He often displays a negative, stubborn resist-

ance. He opposes in a disagreeable manner and frequently without reason.

3. *The Aggressor.* The aggressor is usually unaware of the feelings of others. He may try to build his own importance by deflating the ego of others: "That's a silly thing to do. If I were doing it, here is how I'd go about it." (But, alas, such a person usually avoids doing much!) He may attack the group, its purposes, or the importance of the topic. He usually attempts to assert his superiority by trying to manipulate the group. As the name implies, the aggressor wants to dominate.

4. *The Sympathy Seeker.* The sympathy seeker may accept responsibility to do something for the group, but then he doesn't carry it through: "I thought Joe was supposed to do that," or "I was just so busy that I couldn't get that done." Alibis, confessions of shortcomings, and exaggeration of personal problems are all used to gain the sympathy of the group. Such a person would like the group to compliment him for his weaknesses!

5. *The Disinterested Bystander.* The disinterested bystander may make a display of his lack of involvement. Through playboy tactics, he may attempt to disrupt. Or he may patronize the group with a frozen smile that permits him to escape mentally from the boring proceedings.

Success as a Group Member. Study your role in a group. Make sure that you practice the principles that contribute to group success. And eliminate all actions that might prevent you from being a good group member. Remember, it is from among the good group members that a leader is usually selected.

The Group Leader

A person who consistently blocks group action will not need to know how to lead a group. He won't be given the opportunity. You, however, who know and practice the positive principles that help a group function, will soon be selected for a leadership post—an honor, but also a serious obligation. Before you take on the responsibility as chairman for a group, therefore, make sure that you know your duties and accept them willingly and without reservation. Then you will be in a position to perform your duties completely and with dispatch as you plan a meeting and conduct it.

Planning a Meeting. As chairman of a group, you will usually plan all meetings—whether programs or business meetings. If the group does not have a constitution or bylaws to define your responsibilities, you can usually assume that you are responsible for all aspects of planning—place and time, publicity, pattern of the program, and speakers and other participants.

The Program. The first step is to write a plan for the program. The plan you prepare should answer the following questions: (1) What is the purpose of the meeting? (2) What theme or topic is to be considered? (3) Where and when will the meeting be held? Should reservations for a room or hall be made now? (4) Who will attend? (5) How many will attend? (6) What publicity will be needed? (7) How much money is available for speakers, arrangements, decorations, etc.? (8) What people or subcommittees should be appointed to make arrangements, sell tickets, publicize, act as hosts, etc.? (9) What form or pattern should the program take—speaker or symposium of speakers? demonstration? panel discussion? mock television or radio program? panel, with audience questions and answers? debate? small group discussions—brainstorming? other?

Delegating Authority. At this point in planning, you may feel overwhelmed by the size of the job ahead of you. Don't be, however; for an important characteristic of the leader is his ability to delegate authority. Specific tasks are assigned to other people to do, and usually in writing. Delegate as many details as you can, but be sure to follow up on each assignment. Carbons of letters of committee appointments or of letters written to the speakers can be used as a tickler file. To avoid any last minute slip-up, send out reminders to all committees and speakers at least two weeks before the meeting. If you have carefully planned and effectively delegated responsibility, you can go before the group with a feeling of confidence that the meeting you conduct will be a memorable one.

The Agenda. In an agenda for a business meeting, the discussion items should be listed in the order of expected controversy. For instance, the first item will be the one most likely to meet with almost total agreement. Next will come the item on which the leader expects less agreement, and so on. A sound psychological principle is behind this practice. If a group starts by agreeing, the members will be in a congenial and positive frame of mind that will carry over to succeeding discussion topics. An untrained leader may start his meeting with the "big question," the topic likely to provoke the widest difference of opinion, and then wonder why nothing was accomplished at the meeting.

Conducting a Meeting. You, the chairman, set the tone for the meeting as you follow the agenda or program. If you are stiff and formal, the other people on the program are likely to be stiff and formal, too. If you are natural and informal (but in good taste, of course), the others on your program will probably be natural and informal, too. Most audiences today prefer a chairman who conducts an informal kind of meeting, whether or not parliamentary procedure is used.

Parliamentary Procedure. The bylaws of most clubs state that business will be conducted according to Robert's *Rules of Order.* Robert's *Rules* are to parliamentary procedure what Emily Post is to etiquette; and, as chairman, you will need to know some of the basic principles of Robert's *Rules* and how to apply them. For example, you should know how to call a meeting to order and how to determine whether or not a quorum is present; how to make and follow an agenda; how to recognize members who wish to make a motion; what an appropriate motion is and how it is seconded, amended, and voted upon; and how to adjourn a meeting. Most organizations will appoint a parliamentarian to help the group leader, but the chairman who possesses a working knowledge of the rules is that much ahead.

Introducing a Speaker. An introduction should be short and simple and should include: (1) some gracious remark that will make the speaker feel warmly welcome; (2) a statement of the speaker's topic; (3) a brief summary of the speaker's background or special interests; and (4) presentation of the speaker by name. The announcement of the name of the speaker is usually made last, so that it serves as a signal for the speaker to leave his chair and begin his talk.

Responding to a Speech. The chairman, of course, wishes the meeting to end on a high note. After an effective talk, he needs to say very little. Even after a speech that has not been so good as expected, the chairman shouldn't say too much. One or two comments about the importance of the talk or a short anecdote to leave the audience in good spirits is all that is needed. You would thank the speaker, express appreciation to those who helped plan the meeting, and adjourn.

Learning Exercises

1 Which of the following statements were made by people who practice principles of good membership? Do any of the statements represent an attitude that is likely to hinder group progress?

    a "What you are saying, then, is that we should hold the meeting in January."

b "I don't know about the rest of you, but I'm tired."

c "When I was in the J. C.'s, we didn't do it like that."

d "I wonder, as I listen to your arguments, just how your plan will help us pay our club's debts and keep us from going deeper into the red."

2 (*a*) Write a plan for an important program for a group to which you belong. Include a speaker. Use the questions on page 527 as your guide. (*b*) Write the introduction you will use to present the speaker.

3 Write a letter to the person you have selected to be the speaker, requesting him to address your group.

4 Write a letter appointing a chairman for one of the following committees: (*a*) decorations, (*b*) host, (*c*) arrangements, (*d*) publicity.

Vocabulary and Spelling Refreshers

1 **Words Often Confused.** Censor, censure; read, reed, red.

2 **The Correct Modifier.** From the modifiers enclosed in parentheses, select the correct form for each sentence.

a Of the two file cabinets, I prefer the (tallest, taller).

b Our late start has hurt our chances (some, somewhat).

c I do not like (that, those) kind of plays.

d Tom is (sure, surely) qualified for that job.

e I am (real, really) pleased to know he passed.

3 **To Hyphenate or Not?** Choose the item that answers each of the following questions correctly.

a Which one of the following compound nouns *should* be hyphenated: half dollar, vice president, real estate?

b Which one of the following compound nouns should *not* be hyphenated: per-cent, trade-mark, son-in-law, cure-all?

c Which one of the following expressions should *not* contain hyphens: an up-to-date chart, New-York theaters, large-sized coats, six-year cycle?

d Which one of these words containing prefixes should *not* be hyphenated: ex-chairman, co-operate, re-enter, re-invest?

Communication in Action: *Writing a Telegram*

Purchase Order No. 2578-S was mailed by your company to Klaff and Kline on February 5. The order (for office chairs) was marked *Urgent*. Confirmation was received from Klaff and Kline on February 10 and delivery promised by March 1. It is now March 5 and the chairs have not arrived. Compose a telegram to Klaff and Kline to find out "why" and "when."

UNIT 61

Giving a Talk

Almost every person finds himself, at some time, in the position of talking to an audience. His contribution may be short, such as introducing a speaker as mentioned in Unit 60. He may be a member of a panel, talking about one phase of the subject under discussion. He might be giving a five- or ten-minute talk, or he may be asked to give the main speech at a meeting.

Whatever the length of the talk, everyone who is invited to speak should feel complimented by the invitation. If you, for instance, are asked to give a talk, someone must believe that you have ideas, suggestions, or experience that would be of value to others. But perhaps you do not feel confident that you will be able to communicate them to others. You realize that a really effective talk is the result of more than just knowing your subject. The good speaker not only knows what he is talking about but also knows how to prepare and deliver his speech. He has learned the techniques of preparing and giving a talk, the techniques that you will learn in this unit.

Preparing the Talk

A good talk involves careful preparation. The speaker-to-be must be ready to cover his subject thoroughly and must work hard to organize the talk before giving it. You, then, when preparing a talk, must:

1. ***Determine Your Purpose and Topic.*** First of all, you must know
the purpose of your talk. Are you going to inform, explain, convince,
entertain, or combine two or several of these? Only when you know
why you are going to talk will you be able to select the subject of the
talk. Ask yourself these questions: Why was I asked to speak to this
audience? What is the occasion and reason for this meeting? How
long am I expected to talk? What does the group expect to gain from
listening to me? What do I hope the audience will find valuable in
listening to me? Am I personally in harmony with the interests and
background of this group? How can I capture the audience's interest? The answers to these questions will guide you in selecting
a topic that will be timely and interesting.

2. ***Consider Your Audience.*** Who is your audience? What is their
age, sex, experience, educational and social background, economic
status, and interests? A talk presented before one group may have
little appeal for another. For example, a discussion of the electronic
computer that would be exciting to office workers might cause a
group of plumbers and pipe fitters to go to sleep. Failure to know and
to consider the audience might seriously impair the effectiveness of
the talk.

3. ***Limit Your Subject.*** Don't select a four-hour subject for a ten-
minute speech. It is usually better to make two or three specific
points in a talk—and do it well—than to ramble about on too broad
a topic. The secretary who talked about "Office Automation" would
have presented a more interesting talk had she limited her topic to
"How the Electronic Computer Affects My Job." Limit your subject
so that you can emphasize two or three specific points in the time
allotted to you.

4. ***Collect and Organize Your Materials.*** Collect much more information about your subject than you will use. Use 3-by-5 cards to jot
down ideas as they occur. Use your own personal experiences; talk
with people around you; read newspapers, magazines, books. Take
copious notes from as many sources as you can. As you organize the
material you have collected, you will be able to select the most important ideas to include in your outline.

5. ***Prepare Your Outline.*** A good outline is a "must" in preparing a
talk. Refresh your knowledge of outlining by reviewing Unit 27. Your
card notes, arranged and rearranged according to major ideas and in
order of importance, are the raw materials for organizing the outline. Note, in the following sample, that only important ideas are
included.

YOUR JOB OPPORTUNITIES IN BUSINESS

I. Introduction
  A. Response to the chairman and a few remarks and pleas-
     antries about the audience and occasion
  B. Importance of the topic to the audience
  C. Preview of the major points to be discussed
     1. Put your best foot forward to get the job
     2. Learn and advance in the job
     3. Satisfactions I receive from my job
II. Put your best foot forward to get the job
  A. Job seekers who fail
  B. The average job hunter
  C. The superior job hunter who does put his best foot forward
III. Learn and advance in the job
  A. *Etc.*
  B. *Etc.*
IV. Satisfactions I receive from my job
  A. *Etc.*
V. Concluding remarks

6. *Arouse and Hold Interest.* The success of your outline, and later
of your talk, will depend on how well you are able to arouse and hold
the interest of your audience. Make sure that you have variety and
spice in your talk. Insert an amusing anecdote here and there. Emphasize new ideas. You can hold interest by using personal experiences and examples and by appealing to your audience's desire for
happiness. Your talk should have a certain element of suspense as the
plot unfolds. Complicated ideas, such as figures or statistics, should
be omitted, simplified, or supplemented by charts and graphs. As you
prepare your talk, consider carefully how you will arouse and hold
the interest of the group.

7. *Talk, Don't Read or Recite.* How should you prepare your talk?
Should you write your speech word for word? use only your outline?
use notes on 3-by-5 cards? plan to talk without notes? These methods
are all used by speakers to prepare their talks. Some people prefer
not to speak from a written manuscript. They feel that their talk
would sound stilted and read, instead of natural and informal. Whatever method you select, be sure that your talk will sound natural, not
like a speech-class recitation.

A written talk will be of value as you practice your presentation.
It will enable you to fix each idea in your memory and to time your
delivery. Having memorized the *what* and *how* of your talk, you can
then use brief notes when you deliver it.

8. ***Practice, Practice, Practice.*** As you practice, try to anticipate the conditions of the actual talk. Imagine your audience in front of you. Stand erect and look at the audience. Talk loud enough for the person in the farthest corner of the auditorium to hear you. Make slow and deliberate movements. Use hand gestures sparingly, and then only as they seem natural to you. And, if a mirror is available, practice your talk in front of it. The person you see there should be your severest critic, as he tells you about your facial expressions and your platform appearance. Perhaps you can enlist the help of family and friends too, to listen and offer suggestions. Don't be satisfied with your practice until the talk flows along from idea to idea without the aid of a written text.

Delivering the Talk

Now that your talk is ready, how well are you going to deliver it? The following pointers will help you to present eloquently the thoughts and ideas that you have so carefully prepared.

Platform Manners and Bearing. Face the fact that you will be nervous as you wait for your introduction. The careful preparation of your talk will lessen, but not overcome entirely, your natural nervousness. If you find yourself afflicted with a case of stage fright, take a good, deep breath before you open your mouth. This will relax your vocal cords, and your first words will not squeak out. Then console yourself with the thought that you must be a very intelligent person. The speakers who are not at all nervous are those who give talks very frequently or who do not know enough to be frightened. A little nervous anticipation is good for you. It will key you up and give your delivery an added sparkle.

Tips to Talkers. Study carefully the following tips. They represent the principles of giving a good talk; and if you know them and use them, your audiences will say, "What a fine speaker!"

1. ***Check Your Volume.*** You know how disgruntled, disinterested, and bored listeners are if they can't hear what a speaker says. Don't let this happen to your audience. If possible, before the meeting check your volume in the hall or room where you are to speak. Have someone stand in the back of the room to tell you when he can hear you perfectly. If you cannot make this test, or if there is any question about being heard, ask at the beginning of your talk whether everyone can hear you and adjust your volume accordingly.

2. *Keep Your Chin Up.* The good speaker keeps his head up for the purpose of directing his voice out to the audience. You, then, will be careful to keep your chin up so that your words will reach your listeners, instead of dribbling down your shirt front.

3. *Use a Conversational Tone.* Remember that you are talking to an audience, not giving an oration. Your voice should reflect the warm, easy, conversational tone that you would use if you were talking to a group of your very good friends. Also remember that you will destroy any warmth created by your tone if you allow a critical, scolding, or sarcastic note to creep in.

4. *Look at Your Audience.* An audience responds favorably to a speaker who seems to be talking directly to each person in the audience. One way of making your listeners feel that you are talking to each one individually is to look directly at the assembled people. Look at those in the middle section, then at those to the right, and then to the left. As you look, you may see nothing but a blur, a mass of faces. Let your eyes rest on different sections of the blur, and the audience will feel that you are giving a person-to-person talk. And, with experience, you will begin to see the faces and expressions of individual listeners.

5. *Conceal Your Nervousness.* Do your knees shake when you are nervous? Then, when you give a talk, arrange to stand behind a lectern. When nervous, do you shift from one hip to the other? Conceal this telltale sign of nervousness by training yourself always to stand with your weight evenly distributed on both feet. Do your hands feel as big as hams and do you twist those hands when you are nervous? If so, you would be wise to keep your hands out of sight, probably clasped behind your back. Whenever possible, avoid holding a paper, for nervousness will cause the paper to rattle like leaves in a hurricane. Your talk, you see, will be easy and comfortable if the audience thinks that *you* are easy and comfortable.

6. *Break Yourself of Objectionable Mannerisms.* Do you know whether or not you have objectionable mannerisms? When you talk, do you toy with objects? clear your throat or wet your lips frequently? punctuate everything with "uh" or "anda"? overuse slang expressions? You may not know that you have any such mannerisms, so ask some of your friends to watch and listen and report on any that they may observe. A speaker who has even one annoying habit cannot give a successful talk, for mannerisms distract the audience and obstruct the thoughts you are trying to convey.

7. *Use Only the Time Allotted.* If your assignment is to talk for five minutes, don't talk for six minutes. A program involving different speakers is usually timed to the last minute; anyone who does not keep to his time limit forces other speakers to shorten their talks. Not only is the long-winded talker thought inconsiderate, but he is also marked as egotistical. He evidently thinks that what he has to say is so important that the other speakers can be disregarded. To avoid going over the time limit, you might ask the chairman of the meeting to give you warning when you have only one minute of your allotment left.

8. *Observe How the Audience Accepts What You Are Saying.* You can, and should, train yourself to watch the audience and to be sensitive to its changing moods. If, as you talk, you see a blankness on the faces before you, this is the signal that your listeners need perking up. You might then tell one of the amusing stories you keep on reserve. Remember, however, that jokes are like dynamite in that they are effective only if used intelligently. Any story or anecdote that might offend members of a particular race, creed, or political party would blow your speech sky high.

If your audience seems tired, if the hour is late, or if the previous talks have been overlong, you have two choices open to you: accept the situation as a challenge and give such an interesting and sparkling performance that everyone will be jolted out of his lethargy, or have pity and cut your talk to the bare essentials. You might decide that it is better to omit most of your speech than to give it before a weary audience.

9. *Watch Your Last Few Words.* A beginning talker frequently betrays his inexperience by lowering his voice as he says the last few words or by dashing off his ending in a hurried rattle. Of course a beginner is happy to see the end in sight and is eager to get the ordeal over. What a pity, though, to spoil the effect of a fine talk with a poor finish! Remember to keep your pitch up and to observe good timing to the very end.

Learning Exercises

1 The following major topics were selected from preliminary notes for a talk on "Your Job as a Secretary." Rearrange them in order of their greatest to least importance to an audience of seniors in high school. Be prepared to justify your selection of the three most important and the three least important topics.

Preparation for a secretarial position; what I failed to learn in school; how I applied for my job; the job interview; my letter of application; employment tests and how I took them; my first day at work; the number of stenographers and secretaries in my company; how I learned my job; my supervisor and co-workers; planning for and obtaining my promotion to secretary; job benefits in salary, vacation, retirement, sick leave, etc.; what I do in my job; the little things that please my boss; my most embarrassing mistake; office customs of behavior and dress; how I prepare an itinerary and make reservations for a trip; handling callers in person and on the telephone; how I handle incoming correspondence; methods I use to take dictation and transcribe; filing; problems that puzzle me about my job.

2 List on the left side of your paper the three most important topics you selected in Learning Exercise 1. On the right, list the sources of information you would use to prepare further for your talk.

3 Select one of the following job classifications about which you think your class would like information. Collect, organize, and make an outline for a five-minute talk. Prepare your talk and give it to the class.

Bookkeeper or accountant
Public accountant and auditor
Administrative assistant to the company president
Secretary or stenographer
Receptionist or messenger
Calculating-machine operator
Retail salesclerk
Automobile (or other specialty) salesman
Key-punch operator
Payroll clerk

Vocabulary and Spelling Refreshers

1 **Words Often Confused.** Overdo, overdue; sole, soul.

2 **Time on Your Hands.** Should *sometime, some time,* or *sometimes* appear in the following blank spaces?

 a I have not been to the movies for _____.
 b The furniture should be delivered _____ tomorrow.
 c The bus passed the corner _____ ago.
 d _____ the sun shines during a shower.
 e Mr. Dennison will give _____ to the report tomorrow.
 f An inexpensive purchase is _____ false economy.

3 **Abbreviation Problems.** Which of the following sentences contain incorrect uses or incorrect forms of abbreviations? Give the correct substitutions.

    a Enclosed is your policy no. 84756, showing change of beneficiary.

    b The Dr. will be here in a half hour.

    c Mr. Jas. Graham, Jr., is in the reception room.

    d Please have some flowers sent to Miss. Young.

    e Our agent sails for S. America on Mon.

    f My aunt has been invited to speak to the D. A. R..

Communication in Action: *Say It Better*

Rewrite the following letter. Simplify the content and keep it friendly.

"We were forced to discontinue some time ago Wearwell tires as a stock item in our inventory and are therefore unable to fill your kind order for four of them. In consequence of this, therefore, we regretfully return your check made in our favor for $113.35 and request that you write us again."

UNIT 62

The Employment Interview — Communication at Work

Communication and the Employment Interview

Of all oral communication, none is more important to the business person than the employment interview; for his very living depends on its success. The employment interview is also one of the best examples of communication in action, because it is in the interview that the job applicant is able to show that he possesses the communication skills required in a business job.

Make no mistake, however: employment officials seek to determine the quality of all communication skills—

reading, writing, listening, and speaking. Why? Because office jobs require effective communication skills. Businessmen hire only people who will meet the standards of communication for the job.

Preparing for the Interview

An employment interviewer judges a job applicant on how well he knows his own qualifications, how well he knows the job, and how effectively he is able to relate the two. Careful planning and preparation are required, as discussed in the following paragraphs. Study these suggestions thoroughly, for the way you apply this knowledge in preparation for the employment interview will determine whether or not you stand out from among all the applicants.

1. *Know Your Qualifications.* Before the interview, be sure you have collected and reviewed the needed information about your personal qualifications. If you wrote a letter of application (as discussed in Unit 53), refresh your memory about what you said. If you prepared a data sheet (Unit 52), memorize the facts you included. Have a transcript of school credits at hand and review the subjects you have taken. Have available, too, a list of class activities you have participated in, clubs and organizations you belong to, honors you have won, and hobbies and sports you are interested in. Know your school average and your attendance and tardiness record. How embarrassing to be asked about your personal qualifications and not be able to remember exactly!

On his desk, the interviewer may have written information such as the application letter or form, the data sheet, school records, statements from previous employers, or letters of reference. In all probability, he will ask you about these records, to expand or clarify them. And the interviewer will note how accurately your knowledge of your qualifications tallies with the written records he has before him. Prepare yourself, therefore, by collecting and reviewing all data on your qualifications. And have the information at the tip of your tongue so that you can answer questions readily and accurately.

2. *Know the Job.* Many employers advertise for experienced applicants to fill a position. They believe that an experienced person is more likely to know the job—what is expected and how specifically to perform. But the requirement of experience is not the handicap it may at first seem to an inexperienced applicant. An inexperienced applicant may sometimes compensate for his lack of experience by learning all he can about the specific job for which he is applying. He is then prepared to show the interviewer that he makes up for

his lack of experience by having a realistic understanding of what the job involves and what is expected of him.

To learn about a job, you can talk with employees in that particular field. Before you leave school, you may invite a recent graduate who is now working in the company of your choice to speak to the class. If you have an opportunity to do so, take a field trip through the offices or plant. Read about the products manufactured or about the services or goods sold. Through friends, you may even be able to learn something about the people who own or operate the company and about the particular person who will interview you. The more you know about the job, the company, and the people you will meet, the better equipped you will be to relate your abilities to the specific job.

3. *Relate Your Qualifications to the Job.* Well-intentioned, well-qualified applicants have been known to enter a personnel office with a general statement such as, "I want to apply for a job." This shows a lack of wisdom and an immaturity not wanted in business. The person as much as says that he has not considered what job he wishes to apply for, what qualifications he has for the job, or how his qualifications are related to the needs of the specific job. This applicant usually does not get past the receptionist. To avoid such a disappointment, you must prepare for the employment interview by considering how your abilities fit you for the job for which you are applying.

Conducting Yourself in the Interview

Having prepared carefully for the interview, you radiate self-confidence and poise as you enter the employment office. At the interview, however, you will also be judged on decorum; that is, on the propriety of your dress and conduct as well as what you say.

Appearance. Meticulous care in grooming and in the selection of clothing, as discussed in Unit 11, is of major importance to you as an applicant. The clothing you wear to the interview should be neat, clean, comfortable, and, of course, appropriate. Business people dress conservatively and unobtrusively. As the interviewer talks with you, he will notice such details as nails, teeth, make-up, and hair. A full eight hours of sleep the night before will contribute to your fresh, alert appearance—the appearance that marks the good office employee. On the other hand, any detail of appearance and dress that attracts unfavorable attention will count against you. The trained interviewer knows that there is a direct relation between personal habits and work habits—slovenly appearance, slovenly work; neat appearance and proper dress and grooming, neat work. Make your appearance speak favorably for you at the interview.

Manner and Manners. Good manners are often taken for granted; but any lapse or omission is noticed immediately. One interviewer makes it a practice to drop something on the floor just to see whether the applicant will pick it up. So mind your manners; and practice the following five tips on common courtesy and etiquette.

1. Be on time or a few minutes early for an appointment. Not only is it rude to be tardy, but lack of punctuality may make the interviewer wonder whether you as an employee would be late often. The interviewer might also conclude that obtaining a position with his firm is unimportant to you, since you are late. Rushing to arrive on time will leave you breathless, however; so start early enough to allow for unforeseen delays.

2. Meet the unexpected with poise, tact, and good humor. If the interviewer is not ready to see you, take a seat and occupy yourself while you're waiting. Imagine the childish impression a person makes who says, "But Mr. White told me that he would see me at ten o'clock."

3. Follow the lead of the interviewer. Remember, you are his guest. Shake hands if he offers to do so, and grasp his hand firmly. A limp handshake indicates weakness. Wait for an invitation before seating yourself. It is the host's privilege to seat you where and when he wishes. You are being a good guest if you follow the interviewer's lead.

4. Practice all principles you learned in Unit 58 about conversation. The tact and graciousness you exhibit in any conversation are of particular importance in the interview. Listen earnestly and eagerly. Don't interrupt, even if the interviewer is long-winded and you think of something you wish to tell him right away. Follow his conversation leads and show him that you understand the implications of what he says. Don't bore him with long, overly detailed answers; but do give him more than a meek "Yes" or "No" in answer to his questions. Of course you would not contradict him or imply that you think he is wrong; this is rude under any circumstances. Because you know the topics to avoid in conversation, you will not make remarks that offend. By following the principles of good conversation, you will demonstrate your good breeding in the interview.

5. Show appreciation for the time the interviewer has given you and for his interest. At the close of the interview, remember to thank the interviewer, just as you would thank your host when leaving his home. Don't let the excitement and tension of the interview make

you forget this courtesy. Failing to show appreciation is a breach of manners, and it spoils an otherwise effective interview.

What You Say. The speech principles you have already studied will aid you in demonstrating the effectiveness of your oral communications. Have you worked to improve your voice? How is your grammar? diction? vocabulary and pronunciation? Do you still say "yeah" when you mean "yes"? If you have worked hard and applied all you have learned, you can forget how your voice and speech sound; they will do you credit. You can concentrate on what you say.

Did you know that what you say reflects your attitudes and so tells what kind of person you are? During the interview, for example, you may betray that you are overly interested in salary, your lunch hour, vacation, sick leave, or short working hours. You may reveal that you are more interested in loafing than in working—and interviewers have a responsibility to employ people who want to work!

Understanding the intent of the interviewer's questions will help you answer more intelligently. Here are some typical interview questions, with the reasons behind them and also suggestions as to what you might say in reply.

1. *Why have you selected this kind of work?* The interviewer wishes to know how interested you are in the work and what your goals are. An answer like "Oh, I just need a job" shows lack of purpose. Isn't the following a better answer? "I've wanted to be a secretary ever since I started school. That was my reason for studying stenography. I believe I'll like this type of job, too." This person knows what she wants from a job; she has interest; and she has a purpose.

2. *If you had your choice of job and company, what would you most like to be doing and where?* Watch your answer to this question! The interviewer is trying to gauge just how satisfied you will be working in this job and in this company. The best answer, if you can truthfully say so, is: "Mr. Shaw, the job I want is the one for which I am now applying. The company? Yours. Five years from now, I hope to have proved myself and to have been promoted to greater responsibility."

3. *What are your hobbies?* The interviewer is not interested in swapping information about his stamp collection. He wants to find out whether you have broad interests, for a person who has few outside interests is likely to become listless about himself and about his job. Be ready to list briefly your major interests in hobbies and sports.

4. *In what extracurricular activities have you participated? To what clubs do you belong? What offices have you held? What honors*

have you received? These and similar questions are asked to determine the scope of your interest in people—whether you were able to work with people and whether you have leadership qualities. These are the characteristics of a well-rounded, well-adjusted individual. In preparing for the interview, review your extracurricular activities so that you can give the facts without hesitation.

5. *Would you be willing to work overtime if necessary?* Employers like to see a willingness, even an eagerness, to perform well in a job. Overtime may be required seldom; but, if it is, employers want to have people who will accept this responsibility. You would be entering a job with the wrong attitude if you were not willing to work overtime when necessary. So your answer to this question should be that you are willing to work overtime.

Learning Exercises

1 Make a list of your personal and educational qualifications to fill one of the following positions: secretary, clerk-typist, bookkeeper, calculator operator, receptionist, retail salesclerk. From the standpoint of an interviewer, make a similar list of qualifications you now lack for the job.

2 Make a list of your leisure-time pursuits. Include all extracurricular activities, clubs, offices held, and honors won that you might mention in the employment interview.

3 Make a check list of grooming and dress that you could use as a reminder before going to the employment office for an interview.

4 As personnel manager for the largest industry in your community, you have an opening for a general clerical worker. Make a list of questions you might ask an applicant and explain what each answer would tell you about the potential employee. In class, enact the interview, using your questions.

Vocabulary and Spelling Refreshers

1 **Words Often Confused.** Breath, breathe, breadth; indignant, indigent, indigenous.

2 Prefix and Suffix

a Does the prefix *re* in *reorganize, re-enter, reunion, re-establish* impart to the words the meaning of: beyond, again, under, after?

b Does the prefix *mis* in *misinformed, misrule, misrepresent, misapply* impart to the word the meaning of: wrongly, throughout, partly, before?

c Does the suffix *ician* in *electrician, musician, technician* impart to the words the meaning of: a specialist in, service of, the quality of, state of?

d Does the suffix *ist* in *journalist, organist, humorist, specialist* impart to the words the meaning of: the study of, the act of, the science of, one who?

3 Contractions. Replace the italicized words with correctly formed contractions.

a We regret that we *cannot* grant this request.

b *Let us* take a firm stand on this question.

c *I have* no idea *who is* coming.

d Miss Wood, you *need not* retype this table.

e That statement just *does not* make sense.

f *It is* a long road that has no turning.

Communication in Action: *Shake Hands or Not?*

Does a man ever shake hands with a woman when they are introduced? When is it appropriate? Does a woman ever rise when being introduced? If so, under what circumstances? When does a man rise upon being introduced? Enact the various situations suggested by these questions.

REFERENCE
SECTION

Forms of Address for Official Correspondence

Government Officials — Federal, State, and Municipal

The President

The President
  The White House
    Washington 25, D. C.
Sir: *or*
Mr. President: *or*
My dear Mr. President:

The Vice-President

The President of the Senate
  United States Senate
    Washington 25, D. C.
Sir:
          or
The Honorable . . . .
  The Vice-President of the United
    States
    Washington 25, D. C.
My dear Mr. Vice-President: *or*
My dear Mr. . . . . :

Cabinet Member

The Secretary of . . . .
  Washington 25, D. C.
Dear Sir:
          or
The Honorable . . . .
  Secretary of . . . .
    Washington 25, D. C.
My dear Mr. Secretary: *or*
My dear Mr. . . . . :

Members of Congress

Senator:
The Honorable . . . .
  United States Senate
    Washington 25, D. C.
My dear Senator: *or*
My dear Senator . . . . :

Representative:
The Honorable . . . .
  House of Representatives
    Washington 25, D. C.

My dear Congressman (*or* Con-
  gresswoman): *or*
My dear Mr. (*or* Miss, Mrs.)
  . . . . :

Chief Justice of the United States

The Chief Justice of the United
  States
    Washington 13, D. C.
My dear Mr. Chief Justice:
          or
The Honorable . . . .
  Chief Justice of the United States
    Washington 13, D. C.
My dear Mr. Chief Justice:

Associate Justice of the Supreme Court of the United States

The Honorable . . . .
  Justice, Supreme Court of the
    United States
    Washington 13, D. C.
My dear Mr. Justice:
          or
Mr. Justice . . . .
  Supreme Court of the United
    States
    Washington 13, D. C.
My dear Mr. Justice:

Ambassador

From Foreign Countries to the
  United States:
His Excellency
  The Ambassador of . . . .
    Washington 25, D. C.
Sir:
*Of the United States in Foreign
  Countries:*
The Honorable . . . .
  The American Ambassador
    Foreign Capital, Foreign
      Country
Sir:

Governor

The Governor of the State of . . . . .
 State Capital, State
Dear Sir:

or

The Honorable . . . .
 Governor of the State of . . . . . .
 State Capital, State
Dear Sir: *or*
My dear Governor . . . . :

State Senator

Senator from . . . . (District) . . . .
 The State Senate
 State Capital and State
Dear Sir:

or

The Honorable . . . .
 The State Senate
 State Capital and State
Dear Sir: *or*
My dear Senator . . . . :

State Assemblyman, Representative, or Delegate

(According to official name of the
 lower house in the respective
 state)

Assemblyman (or Representative
 or Delegate) from . . . .
 District . . . .
 The State Assembly (or House of
 Representatives or House of
 Delegates)
 State Capital, State
Dear Sir:

or

Same as second form for State Senator, with appropriate changes.

Mayor

The Mayor of the City of . . . .
 City, State
Dear Sir:

or

The Honorable . . . .
 Mayor of the City of . . . .
 City, State
Dear Sir: *or*
My dear Mayor . . . . :

Roman Catholic Clergy

Cardinal

His Eminence (given name) Cardinal (surname)
 Street, City, State
Your Eminence:

Archbishop

The Most Reverend . . . .
 Archbishop of . . . .
 Address
Your Excellency:

Bishop

The Most Reverend . . . .
 Bishop of . . . .
 Address
Your Excellency:

Monsignor

The Right Reverend Monsignor . . .
 Address
My dear Monsignor:

Priest

The Reverend . . . .
   Address
Dear Father:

Mother Superior

The Reverend Mother Superior,
   with initials of order
Address
Reverend Mother:

Sister

Sister . . . ., with initials
   of order
Address
My dear Sister:

Protestant Clergy

Protestant Episcopal Bishop

The Right Reverend . . . .
   Bishop of . . . .
   Address
Dear Sir: *or*
My dear Bishop:

Protestant Episcopal Dean

The Very Reverend . . . .
   Dean of . . . .
      Address
My dear Dean:

Methodist Episcopal Bishop

Bishop . . . .
   Address
My dear Bishop . . . . :

Other Clergymen

The Reverend Mr. (or Dr., if en-
   titled to a degree) . . . .
   Address
My dear Mr. (or Doctor) . . . . :

Jewish Rabbi

Rabbi . . . .
   Address
My dear Rabbi:

Military and Naval Personnel

Addresses. The addresses of both officers and enlisted men of the armed forces should include: (1) full title of rank or rating (as *Major, Sergeant, Ensign*), (2) branch of the service (as *Signal Corps, Ordnance Department*), and (3) some such abbreviation as *U. S. A.* (*United States Army*), *U. S. C. G.* (*United States Coast Guard*), which may follow either the personal name or the branch of the service.

Major General . . . ., U. S. A.
   Commanding General, Third Corps Area
Commander . . . .
   Medical Corps, U. S. N. R.

Sergeant ...., U. S. A.
First Tank Corps

Salutations. The formal salutation *Dear Sir* may be used for all ranks or ratings. For personal salutations, the following rules govern:

1. For Army officers above the rank of lieutenant, the title is used, as follows:

> For generals, lieutenant generals, major generals, and brigadier generals: *My dear General* ....:
> For colonels and lieutenant colonels: *My dear Colonel* ....:
> For majors and captains: *My dear Major* ....: and *My dear Captain* ....:

2. For Army lieutenants, either first or second, and for all noncommissioned Army officers, the salutation is simply *My dear Mr.* ....:

3. For Navy officers of the rank of admiral (including vice-admiral and rear admiral) and of captain, the salutation is *My dear Admiral* ....: or *My dear Captain* ....:

4. For all Navy ranks from commander down, the salutation is *My dear Mr.* ....:

Principal Parts of Verbs

Present	*Past*	*Past Participle*
be	was	been
begin	began	begun
bid (to command)	bade	bidden
bid (to offer to pay)	bid	bid
bite	bit	bitten
blow	blew	blown
break	broke	broken
bring	brought	brought
burst	burst	burst
catch	caught	caught
choose	chose	chosen
come	came	come
do	did	done
draw	drew	drawn
drink	drank	drunk
drive	drove	driven
eat	ate	eaten
fall	fell	fallen
fight	fought	fought
flee	fled	fled
fly	flew	flown
forget	forgot	forgotten

Present	Past	Past Participle
freeze	froze	frozen
get	got	got
give	gave	given
go	went	gone
grow	grew	grown
hang (by the neck until dead)	hanged	hanged
hang	hung	hung
hide	hid	hidden
know	knew	known
lay	laid (*not* layed)	laid (*not* layed)
leave	left	left
lend	lent	lent
lie	lay	lain
pay	paid (*not* payed)	paid (*not* payed)
ride	rode	ridden
ring	rang	rung
rise	rose	risen
run	ran	run
see	saw	seen
set	set	set
shake	shook	shaken
sit	sat	sat
speak	spoke	spoken
steal	stole	stolen
strike	struck	struck
take	took	taken
tear	tore	torn
throw	threw	thrown
wear	wore	worn
write	wrote	written

Correct Use of Prepositions

abide *by* (a decision)
abide *with* (a person)

abound *in* or *with*

acquit *of*

adapted *to* (a thing)
adapted *for* (by nature)
adapted *from* (an author)

affinity *between*

agree *to* (a proposal)
agree *upon* (a course)
agree *with* (a person)

agreeable *to* (*with* is permissible)

angry *at* (things or conditions)
angry *with* (persons)

appropriate *for* (a person)
appropriate *to* (an occasion)

beneficial *to*

bestow *upon*

buy *from*

compliance *with*

comply *with*

confer *on* (give to)
confer *with* (talk to)

confide *in* (place confidence in)
confide *to* (entrust to)

conform *to* (in conformity *with* or *to*)

convenient *for* (a purpose)
convenient *to* (a person)

conversant *with*

correspond *to* or *with* (a thing)
correspond *with* (a person)

credit *for*

deal *in* (kind of business)
deal *with* (people)

depend or dependent *on* (but independent *of*)

derogatory *to*

disappointed *in* (what we have)

discrepancy *between* (two things)
discrepancy *in* (one thing)

dispense *with*

employ *for* (a purpose)
employed *at* (a stipulated salary)
employed *in, on,* or *upon* (a work or business)

enter *into* (agreements)
enter *upon* (duties)
enter *in* (a record)
enter *at* (a given point)

exception *to* (a statement)

familiarize *with*

foreign *to* (preferred to *from*)

identical *with*

inferior or superior *to*

in regard *to*
with regard *to*
as regards

need *of* or *for*

part *from* (a friend)
part *with* (a thing)

plan or planning *to* (infinitive *to,* not preposition *on*)

profit *by*

retroactive *to* (not *from*)

thirst *for* or *after* (knowledge)

vary *from*

wait *for* (me)
wait *on* (a sick person)

Abbreviations

Streets & Addresses

Avenue	Ave.	Road	Rd.
Boulevard	Blvd.	Square	Sq.
Building	Bldg.	Street	St.
Park	Pk.	Terrace	Terr.
Place	Pl.		

Days of the Week
Sun.	Thurs.
Mon.	Fri.
Tues.	Sat.
Wed.	

Months of the Year
Jan.	Sept.
Feb.	Oct.
Mar.	Nov.
Apr.	Dec.
Aug.	

Names of States

Alabama	Ala.	New Hampshire	N. H.
Arizona	Ariz.	New Jersey	N. J.
Arkansas	Ark.	New Mexico	N. Mex.
California	Calif.	New York	N. Y.
Colorado	Colo.	North Carolina	N. C.
Connecticut	Conn.	North Dakota	N. Dak.
Delaware	Del.	Oklahoma	Okla.
District of		Oregon	Oreg.
Columbia	D. C.	Pennsylvania	Pa.
Florida	Fla.	Rhode Island	R. I.
Georgia	Ga.	South Carolina	S. C.
Illinois	Ill.	South Dakota	S. Dak.
Indiana	Ind.	Tennessee	Tenn.
Kansas	Kans.	Texas	Tex.
Kentucky	Ky.	Vermont	Vt.
Louisiana	La.	Virginia	Va.
Maryland	Md.	Washington	Wash.
Massachusetts	Mass.	West Virginia	W. Va.
Michigan	Mich.	Wisconsin	Wis.
Minnesota	Minn.	Wyoming	Wyo.
Mississippi	Miss.		
Missouri	Mo.		

Territories and Dependencies
Canal Zone	C. Z.
Puerto Rico	P. R.
Virgin Islands	V. I.

(Montana — Mont., Nebraska — Nebr., Nevada — Nev.)

Overworked and Repetitious Words and Phrases

Overworked	Fresher, More Specific
Along the lines of	Like
Ascertain	Find out
Asset	Advantage, gain, possession, resource
At all times	Always
By means of	By

Overworked	*Fresher, More Specific*
Deal	Agreement, arrangement, transaction
Factor	Event, occurrence, part
Field	Branch, department, domain, point, question, range, realm, region, scene, scope, sphere, subject, theme
Fix	Adjust, arrange, attach, bind, mend, confirm, define, establish, limit, place, prepare, repair
Forwarded	Sent
Inasmuch as	Since
In the near future	Soon, **or state the exact time**
Line	Business, merchandise, goods, stock
Matter	Situation, question, subject, point
Nice	Pleasant, agreeable
Our Mr. Smith	Our representative, Mr. Smith
Previous to, prior to	Before
Proposition	Proposal, undertaking, offer, plan, affair, recommendation, idea
Reaction	Opinion, attitude, impression
Recent communication	Letter of (**give appropriate date**)
Run	Manage, direct, operate

Unnecessary Repetitions

At about
Up above
Accept *of*
Both alike
New beginner
Check *into*
Co-operate *together*
Connect *up*
Continue *on* or *to remain*
Converted *over*
Depreciate *in value*
During *the course of*
And etc.
Past experience
Final completion
Follows *after*
Free *gratis*
Same identical

Indorse *on the back*
Inside *of* (If referring to time, use *within*.)
Lose *out*
May *perhaps*
Complete monopoly
Near *to*
As otherwise
Outside *of*
Over *with*
Customary practice
Rarely *ever*
Refer *back*
Remember *of*
Repeat *again*
Seldom *ever*
Both *together*

INDEX

Speaking for Business